Keynes's *General Theory*, the Rate of
Economics

Keynes's *General Theory,* the Rate of Interest and 'Keynesian' Economics

Keynes Betrayed

Geoff Tily

palgrave
macmillan

First published 2007 by
PALGRAVE MACMILLAN
Houndmills, Basingstoke, Hampshire RG21 6XS and
175 Fifth Avenue, New York, N.Y. 10010
Companies and representatives throughout the world

PALGRAVE MACMILLAN is the global academic imprint of the Palgrave
Macmillan division of St. Martin's Press, LLC and of Palgrave Macmillan Ltd.
Macmillan® is a registered trademark in the United States, United Kingdom
and other countries. Palgrave is a registered trademark in the European
Union and other countries.

ISBN 978-0-230-27701-4   ISBN 978-0-230-80137-0 (eBook)
DOI 10.1057/9780230801370

A catalogue record for this book is available from the British Library.

Library of Congress Cataloging-in-Publication Data
Tily, Geoff, 1965–
    Keynes's General theory, the rate of interest and 'Keynesian'
economics: Keynes betrayed / Geoff Tily.
        p.   cm.
    Includes bibliographical references and index.
    Contents: History—Theory—Macroeconomics after Keynes.

    1. Keynesian economics.   2. Macroeconomics.   I. Keynes,
John Maynard, 1883–1946. The general theory of employment, interest
and money.   II. Title.
    HB99.7.T55 2007
    330.15'6—dc22   2006051026

10   9   8   7   6   5   4   3   2   1
16   15   14   13   12   11   10   09   08   07

Transferred to Digital Printing 2011.

To Jake and Hebe

Contents

List of Figures and Tables

Figures

Tables

List of Abbreviations

AER	*American Economic Review*
BIS	Bank for International Settlements
BoE	Bank of England
CMI	Capital market inflation
EEA	Exchange Equalisation Account
EJ	*Economic Journal*
ERM	Exchange Rate Mechanism
EWP	*Employment White Paper*
GDP	Gross Domestic Product
ILO	International Labour organisation
IMF	International Monetary Fund
LoN	League of Nations
LFT	Loanable funds theory
LPT	Liquidity-preference theory
LSE	London School of Economics
MEC	Marginal efficiency of capital
MPC	Marginal propensity to consume
NDE	National Debt Enquiry
NFYG	Next Five Years Group
OMO	Open-market operations
QJE	*Quarterly Journal of Economics*

Acknowledgements

This book would not exist were it not for Professor Victoria Chick, my PhD supervisor. It all started with my enrolment in the Economics MSc at University College London. The Methodology course that Vicky offered afforded me welcome relief from the mainstream approach of the rest of the course. She introduced me to Keynes's work. She put a massive effort into my subsequent work. She allowed my ideas to evolve naturally, with gentle direction, and then fostered rigour and clarity with incisive comments (and with a great deal of patience). I would also like to thank Stephanie Blankenburg, for her enthusiasm towards my emerging work and her immensely valuable comments and warnings, and Jorg Bibow, Robert Brazelton, Sheila Dow, Gordon Fletcher, Geoff Harcourt, Colin Rogers, Roy Rotheim, Thomas Rymes, Brendan Sheehan, John Smithin and Jan Toporowski for invaluable encouragement and advice. The responsibility for the end result is of course my own.

Outside academia I owe much to Ann Pettifor, for having faith in the work and helping to convince my wife that I wasn't mad; Helen Kersely, for patience and tolerance, notwithstanding her culpability for starting it all off by introducing me to *The Culture of Contentment* (and, returning to academia, to the late J. K. Galbraith for writing it); and present and past colleagues at the Office for National Statistics (ONS) for belief, support, comments and discussion.

Thanks too to Amanda Hamilton, Katie Button and Adam Carroll-Smith of Palgrave Macmillan, to Karen Francis at the ONS for helping to get things ready for them and to Geetha Narendranath for production.

I am very grateful to the following for permission to quote from copyright sources: Blackwell Publishing, Cambridge University Press, Edward Elgar Publishing Limited, The Econometric Society, Oxford University Press, Macmillan, St. Augustine's Press and Thompson Publishing Services. Finally thanks to King's College Cambridge for granting permission to quote from Richard Kahn's and Nicholas Kaldor's unpublished papers.

The author and publishers have made every attempt to contact copyright-holders. If any have inadvertently been overlooked, the publishers will be pleased to make the necessary arrangements at the first opportunity.

1
Introduction

We might play with the idea that the inability of the interest rate to fall has brought down empires. ... Thus, it is of overwhelming importance that the optimum interest rate be determined by institutions and banking practice. And the bad effect of saving must be recognised. All past teaching has (if my view here given is correct) been either irrelevant, or else positively injurious. We have not only failed to understand the economic order under which we live, but we have misunderstood it to the extent of adopting practices which operate most harshly to our detriment, so that we are tempted to cure ills arising out of our misunderstanding by resort to further destruction in the form of revolution.

(Martin Fallgatter's notes of Keynes's 1933 lectures, quoted in Skidelsky, 1992, p. 502)

1.1 Keynes's solution to the Economic Problem

In the first half of the twentieth century, John Maynard Keynes provided a theoretical explanation for the operation of a free-market economy. This theory and the associated practical conclusions are lost to society. The 'Keynesian' economics that is most closely associated with John Hicks, Alvin Hansen and Paul Samuelson has betrayed not only Keynes's economic theory but also his policy conclusions. Throughout his life, Keynes was primarily concerned with monetary policy. Ultimately, Keynes set out debt-management, monetary and international financial policies that would facilitate the setting of appropriate rates of interest across the spectrum of liquidity.

The General Theory of Employment, Interest and Money not only demonstrated the effectiveness of fiscal policy but was the theoretical culmination of a prolonged enquiry into the nature of a free-market monetary economy. The theory offered a sophisticated diagnosis of the cause of what Keynes saw as the 'Economic Problem' of high unemployment, the business cycle and the extreme inequity of income distribution. The diagnosis concluded that the Economic Problem was not the inevitable condition of a free-market economy, but a consequence of a specific failure of policy: a long-term rate of interest that was too high. Following the diagnosis of monetary cause, the theory prescribed a monetary solution. His liquidity preference theory of the long-term rate of interest had the fundamental conclusion that the authorities could bring the rate under their deliberate control.

> The Bank of England and the Treasury had a great success at the time of the conversion of the War Loan. But it is possible that they still underrate the extent of their powers. With the existing control over the exchanges which has revolutionised the technical position, and with the vast resources at the disposal of the authorities through the Bank of England, the Exchange Equalisation Fund, and other funds under the control of the Treasury, it lies within their power, by the exercise of the moderation, the gradualness, and the discreet handling of the market of which they have shown themselves to be masters, to make the long-term rate of interest what they choose within reason. (*CW* XXI, p. 395)

In its historical context, the *General Theory* demonstrated both the feasibility and the validity of the deliberate reduction of short- and long-term rates of interest that, under Keynes's influence, the authorities had been pursuing since the Great Depression began. Moreover, according to the *General Theory*, low interest rates were a *necessary* component of the solution to the Economic Problem. Cheap-money policy should be a *secular policy*, implemented continuously.

> Unquestionably in past experience dear money has accompanied recovery; and has also heralded a slump. If we play with dear money on the ground that it is 'healthy' or 'natural', then, I have no doubt, the inevitable slump will ensue. We must avoid it, therefore, as we would hell-fire.... A low enough long-term rate of interest cannot be achieved if we allow it to be believed that better terms will be obtainable from time to time by those who keep their resources liquid. The long-term rate of interest must be kept *continuously* as near as possible to what we believe to be the long-term optimum. (ibid., p. 389)

Whether cheap-money policy is sufficient for prosperity is a question for practical experience, not theory. But even then, all other policy interventions, not least fiscal policy, should be regarded as *supplementary* to this secular monetary programme:

> My proposals for the control of the business cycle are based on the control of *investment*. I have explained in detail that the most effective ways of controlling investment vary according to circumstances; and I have been foremost to point out that circumstances can arise, and have arisen recently, when neither control of the short-term rate of interest nor

even control of the long-term rate will be effective, with the result that direct stimulation of investment by government is the necessary means. (Keynes, 1933, p. 675)[1]

Even in the specific case of fiscal policy, Keynes's conclusions were still inadequately depicted by his 'Keynesian' interpreters, who were seemingly less concerned with the diagnosis and prevention of the Economic Problem than the implementation of their own preferred cure. Keynes obviously advocated the use of public works for an economy in depression, although his analysis of the financing of such policies, though brief, offered a degree of sophistication not present in the 'Keynesian' interpretation. Furthermore, Keynes envisaged a specific and ongoing use of fiscal policy, both taxation and expenditure, as support to monetary policy. He argued that cheap-money policy should be set alongside a policy of re-distributional taxation in order to increase the marginal propensity to consume (MPC). The normal extent of government expenditure should then be dictated by the ability of these policies to reduce unemployment in their own right.

1.2 Neo-classical and 'Keynesian' economics

Now, no doubt, Keynes and his most intimate colleagues began by creating an open-ended system very different from the mechanical excellence of the old determinate 'science'. But its development and application would have implied an historical and sociological approach to the unique sequences of economic development. This the profession was fiercely unwilling to undertake.

Instead a new theoretical edifice was erected which could be reconnected to the neo-classical theory of harmony and just shares in the distribution of income. . . .

The 'Keynesian' Revolution gained acceptance because ultimately it was, after its formalisation, deeply conservative in character. (Balogh, 1976, pp. 83–4)

'Keynesian' economics was never a reconciliation between the *General Theory* and classical economics, but an alternative theory opposed to both the theoretical scheme and practical conclusions of Keynes's work. Furthermore, the originator of this theory was not Hicks, but Keynes's two contemporaries: Ralph Hawtrey and Dennis Robertson. Keynes was familiar with this work and referred to it as 'neo-classical'.[2]

Early neo-classical positions had been set out in Hawtrey's *Good and Bad Trade* (1913) and *Currency and Credit* (1919), and Robertson's *A Study of Industrial Fluctuation* (1915) and *Banking Policy and the Price Level* (1926). The authors developed classical theory in the light of the new emphasis given to credit creation at this time. Between the publication of the *Treatise on Money* and the *General Theory*, Robertson went on to make a number of contributions towards what would become the first of the 'Keynesian' versions of neo-classical economics. Hicks and Nicholas Kaldor acknowledged, retrospectively, the importance of Robertson himself and of these specific contributions:

> I cannot help suspecting that what has happened to Mr. Kaldor is something which I recognise from my own experience when I was writing *Value and Capital*. The effect on Mr. Kaldor's mind, as well as on my own, of the *General Theory* has been profound; but we have each of us been led, sometimes consciously, sometimes unconsciously, through Keynes to Robertson. (Hicks, 1942a, p. 55)

> In the early 1930's, 'Keynesian' ideas were in the air, long before the publication of the *General Theory* gave them a systematic expression. Professor Robertson's paper in the December, 1934 issue of the *Economic Journal* ('Industrial Fluctuation and the Natural Rate of Interest') is illuminating, for it clearly marks the transition from the old to the new methods of thought. (Kaldor, 1951, cited in Young, 1987, p. 57)

The *General Theory* was one of *three* contemporaneous theories; it was rivalled by both classical and neo-classical theory.

The almost unanimous response of the classical economists to the publication of Keynes's book was of hostility. Across the world, most academic economists refused to accept either Keynes's theoretical reasoning or his practical conclusions. Lionel Robbins's 1932 assertion that 'economics is the science which studies human behaviour as a relationship between ends and scarce means which have alternative uses' reflected classical economists distancing themselves from the practical failings of economic theory with which Keynes was specifically concerned. This state of affairs was not lost on reviewers of the *General Theory*:

> There has been of late years a general trend among economists, led by what might be described as the London School, away from the real world of economic affairs. A certain scorn even that economists should concern themselves with 'realistic economics' breathes in the whole tone of the manifesto of this school, Professor Robbins's *Nature and Significance of Economic Science*. (A. L. Rowse, September 1936, re-printed in Backhouse, 1999, p. 108)

Instead the *General Theory* was first criticised in detail by comparison with the neo-classical theory. In the years following the publication of the *General Theory*, many prominent economists made contributions to this neo-classical theory and pursued this approach to the critique of the *General Theory*. The monetary aspect of the theory was, and still is, known as 'loanable funds'. The various theories of Alvin Hansen, Roy Harrod, Hicks, James Meade, Franco Modigliani and Paul Samuelson are all developments of this neo-classical approach. Hicks's 1937 'Mr. Keynes and the "Classics"; a Suggested Interpretation' is only the best known of these contributions.

The universally recognised paradigm shift to 'Keynesian' economics at the end of the War reflected the 'formal' endorsement of this model, now expressed in simultaneous equations, and the dismissal of the *General Theory*. On a theoretical level, 'Keynesian' economics resolved all of the theoretical disputes between Keynes and his detractors in favour of the detractors in a manner that denied that the disputes had ever existed.

Only post-Keynesian economists have regarded the pursuit of these differences as important. A succinct and invaluable summary is contained in Geoff Harcourt's entry for 'bastard Keynesianism' in the *New Palgrave*:

> The starting point of this analysis was the expression of what was argued to be the analytical core of the *General Theory* in terms of the IS/LM general-equilibrium framework, associated especially with Hicks.... The attempt to confine Keynes's contributions within a small general equilibrium model allowed the neoclassical synthesis to occur....
>
> This interpretation of Keynes's contributions was regarded by Joan Robinson in particular (but also by Kahn, Kalecki and Shackle amongst others; for a contemporary view, see Chick, 1983) as illegitimate – hence the name, bastard Keynesianism.... Keynes argued that, because of the uncertainty which of necessity must surround decisions about investment and holding money, and because producers in a monetary production economy of necessity must produce in anticipation of demand and of a money profit, and must make contracts in money terms, there are no necessary equilibrating forces which take the economy to full employment either at a point in time or over the cycle.
>
> Moreover, Keynes himself stressed both the likely instability of his core functions, especially the investment and liquidity preference functions, *and* the dependence of this instability on movements in the economy itself, so that positions were not independent of paths. The IS/LM apparatus was therefore peculiarly unsuited to capture this vision of the operation of the economy, and the neoclassical synthesis itself was a denial of the revolution both in vision and in method which Keynes had provided. (Harcourt, 1987, p. 204)

On a practical level, 'Keynesian' economics supported the re-positioning of the policy debate from the role of monetary policy to the role of fiscal policy – a re-positioning that has held fast to the present day. As a consequence, the profound theoretical contributions and practical conclusions of the *General Theory* have been lost and, outside post-Keynesian economics, are yet to be subject to detailed and impartial critique.

1.3 Outline of the work

The discussion is divided into three parts. The first part sets out a history of monetary economics, examines Keynes's contribution to that body of work and its practical application, and then traces the history of the rival 'Keynesian' theory and practice. In Chapter 2, a theory of interest is set out, based on a discussion of the nature of money and the institutional development of banking. This both serves as the necessary monetary foundation to the work as a whole and provides an insight into the identification of the profound social and economic consequences that Keynes saw as following from the control of interest.

The second part of the work examines Keynes's theory. The presentation of the theory differs from Keynes's own, for the aim is different. Keynes sought to present a substantial and detailed theoretical statement of his *General Theory* as rival, and therefore in contrast, to the classical economics. My aim is primarily to present the theory in a manner that justifies the implementation of a secular cheap-money policy. First, I seek to explain why and how cheap money *can* be set; and second, why cheap money *should* be set. This involves an order of presentation different from that in the *General Theory* and the incorporation of elements outside the *General Theory* that throw light on the argument of the *General Theory* itself:

- aspects of monetary theory from the *Treatise of Money*;
- the debate on saving and investment that took place after the publication of the *Treatise*; and
- the deliberations and Report of the National Debt Enquiry (NDE) on monetary and debt-management policy for post-war Britain.

With the aid of these sources, the theoretical justification for specific practical policies is fully explained. Finally, going beyond Keynes's writings but based on them, the theory of the trade cycle is developed to include considerations related to debt- and capital-market inflations (CMIs).

The third part of the work turns to the loss of Keynes's theory and policy. In Chapter 8, Keynes's response to the rival neo-classical theory is examined. In Chapter 9, the key papers and events that saw the seamless substitution of 'Keynesian' theory and practice for Keynes's theory and policy practice are traced. This includes discussion of the later role of the 'Keynesians' in preparing the ground for abandoning their theory to Friedman's re-assertion of classical economics. In Chapter 10, the contributions of those economists that variously supported Keynes, opposed the 'Keynesian' construct and developed post-Keynesian economics are examined. These prominent and respected scholars consistently rejected the 'Keynesian' imposter and associated policy manoeuvres. Finally, Chapter 11 turns to the social and economic consequences of the loss of Keynes's economics. This discussion is anticipated in the next section of this introduction.

The primary audience for the work are the post-Keynesian economists who have built a school of thought on the rejection of 'Keynesianism' alongside the re-assertion of fundamental principles of monetary economics. But I am equally concerned that the work be in large part accessible to economists more generally. I have therefore attempted to offer background where possible and to ensure that the argument is self-contained. But some prior knowledge of the broad economic debate of the post-Second World War era and the key protagonists is inevitably assumed.

In terms of positioning this book within the broad church that is post-'Keynesian' economics, I am primarily concerned with a re-statement of Keynes to emphasise his monetary policy conclusion. My expositional technique, particularly in the more detailed theoretical chapters, is to set out what I regard as the essential theoretical components drawn from Keynes's and post-Keynesian economics and then to present and, to a limited extent, develop these components within the context of the policy perspective. Attempts to go beyond Keynes's discussion are primarily with a view to clarify, with the exception of the discussion of the role of debt inflations in the business cycle. I therefore make no comment on the growth, long-period and distributional theories that emerged in particular from the Cambridge post-Keynesians after Keynes's death. While my re-interpretation fits into the tradition of post-Keynesianism concerned with monetary theory, even within this school there are substantial theoretical differences and material differences in policy emphasis that I look to draw out and, where possible, to reconcile.

I should stress that I make no claim for theoretical precedence, beyond the re-arrangement of these existing components. Much of the work draws on primary sources, and I have not in general sought to trace all those who have subsequently emphasised the same components and approaches. Indeed, the longer historical retrospective suggests that much of economic reasoning involves the restoration of truths known to certain of our predecessors. Precedent for some of the most important notions of monetary economics extends to at least the start of the eighteenth century.

1.4 The social and economic consequences of the loss of the *General Theory*

The *General Theory* was a theoretical work. But it was written with matters of the most profound practical importance to the world uppermost in the writer's mind. Ultimately the practical application of the *General Theory* concerned the management of money across the world and what Keynes later referred to as 'the future economic ordering of the world between nations'.[3]

As Keynes saw from very early on, the gold standard was a seriously defective mechanism for the management of monetary economies. Instead a system was required that on the one hand permitted sufficient international liquidity for trade purposes, and on the other permitted autonomy over domestic monetary and other economic policies. The analysis of the *General Theory* justified the exchange management and capital control policies that he had advocated and that had been implemented throughout the world in the 1930s following the failure of the gold standard after the First World War. These initiatives were then precursors of his proposal for an International Clearing Union that was the British Government's contribution to the Bretton Woods' deliberations.

In the broadest possible terms, the social and economic history of the post-Second-World-War era could be regarded as a consequence of a two-stage dismantling of these initiatives.

First, at Bretton Woods, Keynes's proposals were watered down. The Bretton Woods Agreement, which gave governance of international finance to the International Monetary Fund (IMF), saw the proposed currency management policies replaced with an excessively inelastic exchange system, not dissimilar to the gold standard, under which currency crises would be commonplace. However, the agreement had the virtue of preserving capital controls. These facilitated the continuation of low long-term interest rates across the world for close to a quarter of a century. And in turn cheap money fostered the strong growth in private investment that underpinned the unprecedented era of prosperity known to posterity as the 'golden age'.

The second stage was the dismantling of Bretton Woods in the early 1970s and the financial liberalisation effected over the 1970s and start of the 1980s. In the early 1980s, long-term rates of interest rose rapidly and have remained at a high level ever since. According to this interpretation of the *General Theory*, the lower but more volatile investment – what the International Labour Organisation (ILO) has described as 'pervasive worldwide employment problems' (ILO, 2003, 'overview') – and the stark polarisation of the world between rich and poor have as root cause these high rates of interest. Moreover, after 25 years of dear money the financial condition of the global economy is highly precarious, based as it is on a structure of indebtedness and asset inflation of a degree unknown since the Great Depression.

The IMF has gone from the master of a controlled exchange regime to first the enforcer and now to the victim of a financial 'liberalisation' that is totally beyond its control. The vast majority of economists fail utterly to comprehend the forces unleashed by financial liberalisation and how they have served to degrade economic and social relations across the 'world between nations'.

We must re-learn the fundamental importance of bringing these forces to heel through the global management of money. In order to do so we must reject an economics based ultimately on the neutrality of money and turn once again to the *General Theory of Employment, Interest and Money*.

1.5 A note on the *Collected Writings*

The claimed restoration and elaboration of Keynes's argument does not rely exclusively on the *General Theory* but draws on the full range of Keynes's writings, beginning with his first contribution to monetary theory in March 1909. The most important source for this task is obviously *The Collected Writings of John Maynard Keynes* (*CW*) under the main editorship of D. E. Moggridge.[4] While the source is absolutely invaluable, attention must be drawn to a number of limitations.

In the first place, *CW* is not a complete reproduction of all of Keynes's economic writing. While omissions are understandable given the sheer volume of Keynes's work and of his private correspondence, it is of concern that a number of the papers omitted are, in my view, significant. In most cases my attention has been drawn to the existence of unpublished material through their use in the works of other authors (sometimes Moggridge's own). Any use of these papers in published work emphasises their non-trivial nature (insofar as published work is not trivial). The extensiveness of the omissions might be judged by the number of citations in this book that are noted as not published in *CW*.

An area of particular concern is the period between the publication of the *Treatise* and the *General Theory*. While Volume XIII is dedicated to papers from this period, there is very little material relating to the substantive steps towards the *General Theory* and hence very little detailed discussion of the implications of these crucial theoretical developments. In particular, there is no material relating to the elaboration of the notion of multiple equilibrium, very little detail on the savings–investment relationship and, perhaps most critically of all, virtually nothing as Keynes developed the theory of liquidity preference.

Apart from the content, the presentation of Keynes's theory in the *CW* is also important. Keynes's early work on monetary theory is scattered throughout the series – his early monetary lectures are included as the last chapter of Volume XII; his first papers on the monetary affairs of India are presented as Chapter 1 of Volume XI; his reviews and associated early published material concerning monetary theory appear as Chapter 5 of the same volume; and his later papers on India (from 1913) are in Volume XV. The arrangement is such that the early monetary work bears very slight relation to the central elaboration of his theories in Volumes XIII, XIV and XXIX. Moreover, the more detailed presentation of the material between the *Treatise* and the *General Theory* is in accordance with the 'Keynesian' perspective. All of the material relating to the savings–investment relationship is presented in a chapter 'Arguing out the Treatise', with the implication that it is not relevant for the *General Theory*. The next chapter, 'Towards the General Theory', then leads on the work of the so-called 'Cambridge Circus' and their role in the 'discovery' of 'output adjustment'.

This state of affairs is a significant complicating factor in any discussion of the broader theoretical and contextual considerations of the *General Theory*.

Notes

1. The source of this quotation is not included in the *Collected Writings* – see the last section of this introduction.
2. Keynes's used 'neo-classical' and 'classical' in a unique way. He listed those that he regarded as classical economists on page 1 of the *General Theory*; a later description from private correspondence contrasts classical economists with neo-classical economists: 'I mean by the classical school, as I have repeatedly explained, not merely Ricardo and Mill, but Marshall and Pigou and Henderson and myself until quite recently, and in fact every teacher of the subject in this country with the exception of yourself and a few recent figures like Hayek, whom I should call "neo-classicals"' (letter to Hawtrey, 15 April 1936, *CW* XIV, p. 24). (In the *General Theory* he refers to the neo-classical 'school' on page 177.) Keynes does not specify the differences in theoretical approach. My interpretation is that the original neo-classical economists were those who accorded prominence to monetary aspects of economics, but tended to endorse classical conclusions on matters of monetary policy (though taking a more eclectic approach on other policy issues).
3. *Manchester Guardian* 15/10/43.
4. E. A. G. Robinson and Elizabeth Johnson co-edited some volumes.

Part I
History

2
Monetary Economics and Monetary Policy

2.1 Introduction

> This Act [Bank Act 1844] was compounded of one sound principle and one serious confusion. The sound principle consisted in the stress laid on the limitation of the quantity of the representative money as a means of ensuring the maintenance of the standard ['whatever that standard might be', p. 14]. The confusion lay in the futile attempt to ignore the existence of bank money and consequently the inter-relationships of money and bank credit, and to make representative money behave exactly as though it were commodity money. (*CW* V, p. 15)

The whole body of Keynes's economics arose from recognition that classical theory did not provide an adequate representation of economic activity because it neutralised the role of money in the economic system. Economies were not based on the commodity money assumed by classical economics, but on *bank money*. Keynes saw that the evolution from commodity money to bank money had profound implications for economic theory, economic activity and economic policy. All his theories and practical measures were underpinned by a progressively more sophisticated analysis and treatment of this changed nature of money. The *General Theory* was, and remains, the culmination of this process and the pinnacle of monetary analysis.

This chapter is mainly concerned with these monetary foundations to his economics. But the discussion seeks to present the material in general terms, rather than drawing only on Keynes's work. Joseph Schumpeter, in his *The History of Economic Analysis*, distinguished between real and monetary economics as follows:

> **Real Analysis** proceeds from the principle that all the essential phenomena of economic life are capable of being described in terms of goods and services, of decisions about them, and of relations between them. Money enters the picture only in the modest role of a technical

13

device that has been adopted in order to facilitate transactions. This device can no doubt get out of order, and if it does it will indeed produce phenomena that are specifically attributable to its *modus operandi*. But so long as it functions normally, it does not affect the economic process, which behaves in the same way as it would in a barter economy: this is essentially what the concept of Neutral Money implies. Thus, money has been called a 'garb' or 'veil' of the things that really matter, both to households or firms in their everyday practice and to the analyst who observes them. Not only *can* it be discarded whenever we are analyzing the fundamental features of the economic process but it *must* be discarded just as a veil must be drawn aside if we are to see the face behind it. . . .

Monetary analysis, in the first place, spells denial of the proposition that, with the exception of what may be called monetary disorders, the element of money is of secondary importance in the explanation of the economic process of reality. We need, in fact, only observe the course of events during and after the California gold discoveries to satisfy ourselves that these discoveries were responsible for a great deal more than a change in the significance of the unit in which values are expressed. Nor have we any difficulty in realizing – as did A. Smith – that the development of an efficient banking system may make a lot of difference to the development of a country's wealth. . . . We are thus led, step by step, to admit monetary elements into Real Analysis and to doubt that money can *ever* be 'neutral' in any meaningful sense. In the second place, then, Monetary Analysis introduces the element of money on the very ground floor of our analytic structure and abandons the idea that all essential features of economic life can be represented by a barter-economy model. . . . [I]t has to be recognised that essential features of the capitalist process may depend upon the 'veil' and that the 'face behind it' is incomplete without it. It should be stated once for all that as a matter of fact this is almost universally recognized by modern economists, at least in principle, and that, taken in this sense, Monetary Analysis has established itself.[1] (Schumpeter, 1954, pp. 277–8, my bold, by permission of Oxford University Press)

In turn, the discovery and application of monetary economics have an importance to prosperity that is staggering – an importance that Joan Robinson, writing in 1951, well understood:

The most important influences upon interest rates – which account for, say, the difference between 30% in a Chinese village and 3% in London – are social, legal, and institutional. Side by side with the industrial revolution went great technical progress in the provision of credit and the reduction of lender's risk and great changes in social habits favourable to lending; and in the broad sweep of history these considerations are more significant than any others. (Robinson, 1951, p. 92)

What I regard as this *fundamental relation* between the development of credit, primarily through banking, and the fall in the rate of interest has eluded almost the whole of the economics profession ever since. While many have drawn and continue to draw attention to the importance of money, most statements of monetary theory are more concerned with the *quantity* of money rather than the *rate of interest* on money. Even John Kenneth Galbraith, who has done much to educate the world in these matters, generally does not give front place to the role of the rate of interest. And even Keynes himself, having revealed the importance of the rate of interest, did not go back to re-establish the connection with the development of bank money.

The discussion in this chapter therefore returns to the first principles of monetary theory in order to demonstrate how this fundamental relation occurs. I shall put forward an interpretation of how, as Schumpeter puts it, 'money [enters] on the very ground floor of our analytical structure'. I start with the concept of the *nature* of money, only coming later to the specific concepts of credit and endogenous money, on which the post–keynesian literature is based. In returning to first principles, this review covers a lot of ground that will be familiar and basic to monetary economists. I do so not only because of my hope to reach a wider audience; but also because, while discussion of monetary matters has moved forward very rapidly, some of the fundamental principles have not been clearly set out.

After the basic exposition of monetary theory, the discussion moves to a wider view. In Section 2.3, the rich heritage of monetary theory that (again) even Keynes does not spell out is outlined. In Section 2.4, some stylised empirical work, based on Sidney Homer's (1963) history of interest rates, seeks to establish the connection between banking, interest and prosperity. Lastly, in Section 2.5, the implications of what ultimately amounts to a profound relation between economic reasoning and prosperity for Marx's class conflict are addressed.

2.2 The fundamental relation between money and interest

2.2.1 The description of money

Money has both a conceptual and a practical nature. In *conceptual* terms, it is the unit of account or *numeraire* that facilitates the indirect exchange of labour for goods. ('Human effort and human consumption are the ultimate matters from which alone economic transactions are capable of deriving any significance', *CW* V, p. 120.) The notion that the prices of goods and labour can be expressed in a common and distinct quantity is of profound importance to economic activity. The *practical* nature of money is then the substance(s) and/or mechanism(s) that is (are) used as the medium of exchange to facilitate that activity, and that can also be set aside for the same purposes in the future. Keynes clarified this distinction as between 'money of account' and 'money':

> Perhaps we may elucidate the distinction between money and money of account by saying that the money of account is the description or title and the money is the thing which answers to the description. Now if the same thing always answered to the same description, the distinction would have no practical interest. But if the thing can change, whilst the description remains the same, then the distinction can be highly significant. (*CW* V, p. 3)

The concept of money began to develop when the 'thing which answers to the description' of 'money' was a *commodity*, usually a precious metal. 'High significance' attaches most substantially to the evolution of the 'thing' from precious metals to *bank money*, defined by Keynes as follows:

> [Next is] the discovery that for many purposes the acknowledgements of debt are themselves a serviceable substitute for Money-Proper [commodity money] in the settlement of transactions. When acknowledgements of debt are used in this way, we may call them Bank-Money – not forgetting, however, that they are not Money-Proper. Bank-Money is simply an acknowledgment of a private debt, expressed in the money-of-account, which is used by passing from one hand to another, alternatively with Money-Proper, to settle a transaction. (*CW* V, pp. 5–6)

The recognition of bank money perhaps sometimes follows, or leads to, the great theoretical advance that recognises 'Money is not the Value *for* which Goods are exchanged, but the Value *by* which they are exchanged' – a proposition that Schumpeter (1954, p. 322) attributes to John Law.[2]

In a modern bank-money economy, the large majority of transactions by value do not involve *cash* (i.e. notes and coins) but are simply based on transfers between bank accounts. Modern bank money is *intangible*; the amounts held by agents at any point in time are figures stored in a computer, printed occasionally on a bank statement. Equally, there is no tangible quantity corresponding to the aggregate of bank money in an economy at any point in time (although it is measurable). Tangibility is not a necessary characteristic of money. Bank money is acceptable as money because agents are content that it facilitates the fundamental exchange of labour into commodity, that is it satisfies the conceptual role.

However, bank-money economies continue to retain a role for *cash*. While the vast majority of economic transactions by value can be carried out without cash, a large number by volume still require the passing of cash from agent to agent. Banks are therefore obliged to supply their customers with cash according to their demand (given any credit or overdraft limit), and therefore are required to hold stocks of cash. As is well known, the *cash ratio* reflects the ratio of cash that banks hold for operational and prudential purposes to total deposits.[3] The operational assessment of this ratio is a probabilistic exercise akin to the setting of an insurance premium. Furthermore, the cash ratio is not a constant but a variable that changes over time. (Historically, it has fallen.) The most important influences on this variable are the degree of confidence in the banking system and the state of financial innovation (with substantial inter-dependencies).[4]

While the actual amount of cash required for economic activity is small,[5] its provision is of critical importance to that activity. The central bank, as monopoly supplier of cash, can exploit this requirement to take control of economic activity as a whole. The literature is mainly concerned with the central bank's ability to *control* the creation of bank money through either price/interest or volume mechanisms. But emphasis on the control aspect has led to neglect of the fundamental property of a bank-money economy. *Through its provision of cash, the central bank is able to set whatever rate of interest it chooses.* This statement is the most important conclusion of monetary theory when applied to practical policy. The theoretical considerations that lead to this conclusion are developed first; and the practical techniques that apply this conclusion are then addressed.

2.2.2 The theoretical nature of interest

The first stage of the theoretical argument is that *there is no necessary limit to the volume of credit that can be created in a bank-money system.* The intangible nature of money means that the extension of credit is simply a 'book' transaction. A loan involves on one hand a debt and on the other a credit to exactly the same amount to the same individual. The book transaction then enables the recipient to spend the bank money in the way desired. (In an overdraft system, the credit is first; the debt is then generated by expenditure and the associated increase of deposits comes to the sellers.) The main additional consideration is the need on the part of the bank creating the credit/debt for additional cash to set against the increased deposits. Given that central banks can theoretically print and supply cash according to demand, cash is not a necessary constraint (although regulators may try to make it so through institutional arrangements). Furthermore, the actual tendency for all banks to increase credit in parallel (i.e. cyclically) will also tend to limit the cash requirements for individual banks as cash will be deposited in one bank as a result of credit creation in another bank.

The second stage of the argument is that if there is no necessary limit to the volume of credit/debt that can be created then it is essentially a free good. A rate of interest is a price, and prices are paid for scarce resources. Keynes's *Treatise on Money* makes this point explicitly: 'Why then, ... if the banks can create credit, should they refuse any reasonable request for it? And why should they charge a fee for what costs them little or nothing?' (*CW* VI, p. 194). While there is a small cost in administering the banking system, these are likely to be akin to fixed costs – fairly independent of the volume of credit created – particularly given increasing technology.

2.2.3 The practical control of interest

In practice, the design and operation of banking systems exploit the nature of money in order to set the rate of interest. In general terms, control is achieved through the central bank *discounting* assets owned by commercial banks in exchange for cash.

As a result of lending, commercial banks will require a certain amount of cash and deposits at the central bank ('cash' hereafter), which will also depend on their assessments of the appropriate cash ratio. The central bank issues this cash in exchange for certain specified assets known as *eligible* assets. The actual value of the assets that commercial bank used for these purposes is also commonly known as the *reserve*.[6] Banks, therefore, purchase these assets in the open market in order to 'discount' them against cash at the central bank. The rate of interest at which the central bank discounts these assets is known as the *discount rate* and is, in turn, the rate that underpins all lending in an economy. (The availability of eligible assets is therefore a potential constraint on credit creation, it is discussed in the context of specific policies at the end of this section.)

These technical procedures for supplying cash are crucial to the operation of the banking system and more specifically to the setting of the rate of interest. Actual practical arrangements to effect this control of interest rates have evolved over time and vary among different countries; but the underlying general principle is that the central bank can control the price of credit if it provides an endogenous supply of cash to commercial banks, which determine the volume of credit.[7]

While detail may differ, systems according to these general principles are the norm. Keynes noted in the *Treatise on Money*: '... it is characteristic of modern systems that the central bank is ready to buy for money at a stipulated rate of discount any quantity of securities of certain approved types' (*CW* VI, p. 189). Galbraith (1975, p. 110) discusses the US banking legislation of 1900: 'It allowed the national banks, the good banks of the Establishment, to issue notes up to a full 100 per cent of the value of government bonds deposited with the Treasury'. Sir John Clapham's (1944) official history of the Bank of England goes further back into history: '... the business of discounting was always a principal way by which the Bank put its notes into circulation. Discounters, a pamphleteer wrote in 1707, "seldom require money but rather chose their notes" ' (pp. 122–3). On the other hand, as will be discussed, a gold standard is in principle at least opposed to such techniques.

2.2.4 The spectrum of interest rates

The banking story is not, however, the whole story. The rate of interest the central bank charges for cash is the rate for short-term lending to member banks. Rates in a market economy then vary according to the duration of lending, and to risk and inflationary considerations. Most important for policy are the considerations governing rates for different durations from short to medium to long, or across the 'spectrum' of interest rates. Keynes, and several before him, found that a fuller control across the spectrum of interest rates could be achieved through management of the issue of government debt.

In my view the theoretical framework that Keynes supplied to understand this spectrum was his greatest contribution to monetary theory. In order to do so, he turned from the analysis of money as a means of exchange in the *Treatise* to the analysis of money as a store of value in the *General Theory*. The theory of liquidity preference justified and more fully revealed the requirements for a policy aimed at control across the *spectrum* of interest rates. The practical techniques developed are outlined first in Chapter 3, and the theory is explained in Chapter 7.

2.2.5 Alternative approaches to money control

Lastly, any banking system that does not conform to the principles of the preceding discussion is likely to surrender at least a degree of control over interest. Some such systems developed due to legitimate concerns about a need to control the volume of money created. There are two basic approaches: limiting the amount of cash in circulation and restricting the issue of eligible assets. In Keynes's time, the British authorities adopted specific variants of both techniques. The most prominent method of cash control was the gold standard. This standard of 'sound money' originated in Britain with Sir Isaac Newton's 1717 prescription that the pound sterling should be exchangeable for gold at a rate of £3 17s 10½d per ounce. Under a gold standard, the amount of gold in the Bank of England set a limit to cash issue and therefore, it was thought, to credit. The flaw of this line of reasoning was that if the cash ratio fell, then limiting cash issue in this way would still permit growth in the supply of credit. On the other hand, if the constraint was binding, then restricting the cash issue could harm the ability to set the rate of interest through the discount rate, with excess demand for cash choked off by a rise in the short-term interest rates at clearing banks.

In historical terms, however, the original introduction of gold was probably of more importance to confidence than to the actual day-to-day operation of the banking system. It is feasible that the rate of exchange was rarely binding, particularly as confidence in banking arrangements would have steadily increased. In much the same way, Keynes's *Tract on Monetary Reform* argued later that the arrangement restricting note issue at the time (1924) 'has never yet been actually operative; . . . it is probable that, if it were becoming operative, it would be relaxed' (*CW* IV, p. 145). The evidence of longer experience is that actual instances of binding note-issue restrictions have been rare and very short-lived.

More generally, the notion of convertibility into gold fails to recognise the nature of money as the medium between labour and commodity. Perhaps gold convertibility was necessary for the acceptance of paper currency, but once paper currency was established gold was no longer necessary. Furthermore, the price and supply of gold were subject to forces which had no relevance to wider economic processes; such forces could and did lead to inappropriate monetary action from the perspective of real economic processes.

The second method of controlling the supply of money was controlling the issue of eligible assets. The arrangements outlined in the previous section allow banks to expand credit to whatever extent they like, so long as they have sufficient eligible assets.[8] In theory, if there are insufficient eligible assets, credit creation should be curtailed. However, such a shortage will again have the side effect of thwarting the ability of the authorities to set the rate of interest. Under these circumstances, prices of eligible assets will be forced up, and hence interest rates forced down. Historically, the most concrete example of this type of policy was the 'funding complex', pursued in the first third of the twentieth century by the British Government, under which the authorities preferred to borrow on long-term rather than short-term instruments (discussed in Chapter 6). It is notable that under the present system the Bank of England discounts both gilts and bills, which implies an intention to avoid such an outcome.

Both methods may afford a degree of control, however imperfect, over the aggregate quantity of money. The consensus today, of course, is that control through the rate of interest is appropriate, that is the setting of price is regarded as superior to trying to set the volume. In order to do so, the volume of money created must be accepted.[9]

2.2.6 Implications of the control of interest

But these issues concerning control should not detract from the more fundamental properties of a bank-money system. The importance of the preceding discussion goes far beyond the commonly understood ability to use the short-term rate of interest for demand management or other policy purpose. A bank-money system permits a more fundamental control of interest as money ceases to be a scarce resource.

The development of banking means that an abundant supply of cheap credit will be available to industry. It can scarcely be doubted that such conditions will be conducive to production, investment and hence employment. As will be shown in Section 2.4, the evidence of experience is that interest rates fall sharply as banking develops, and prosperity follows. The three most profound examples are the banking systems that developed first in Italy, second in the Netherlands and third in Britain, alongside the Renaissance, the Reformation and the Enlightenment, respectively. With these systems in place, economic activity was no longer so straightforwardly bound up with the behaviour and interests of those holding wealth. And, as Karl Marx would identify, the industrial capitalist would become a force to be reckoned with. These considerations are touched on in Section 2.5.

2.3 A brief history of monetary economics in Britain

Monetary debate in England can be traced at least to the discussions leading up to the establishment of the Bank of England. Commentators in the late seventeenth century looked to the Netherlands and to Italy and saw an unambiguous link between banking, money, low interest rates and prosperity. At the time, the most high-profile comments were those by the merchant, economist and governor of the East India Company, Sir Josiah Child. In his *Brief Observations Concerning Trade and the Interest of Money*, he examined the prosperity of the Netherlands. He addressed mainly the role of the rate of interest but also identified the role of banks:

> Their use of BANKS, which are of so immence advantage to them, that some not without good grounds have estimated the profit of them to the Publick to amount to at least one million of pounds sterling per annum.
>
> . . .
>
> [However, discussion focuses on] The Profit That People have received, and any other may receive, by reducing the Interest of Money to a very Low Rate. This in my poor opinion, is the CAUSA CAUSANS of all the other causes of the Riches of that people; and that if Interest of Money were with us reduced to the same rate it is with them, it would in a short time render us as Rich and Considerable in Trade as they are now. (Child, 1668)

Macaulay's *History of England* gives a broader impression of debate at the end of the seventeenth century:

> No sooner had banking become a separate and important trade, than men began to discuss with earnestness the question whether it would be expedient to erect a national bank. The general opinion seems to have been decidedly in favour of a national bank: nor can we wonder at this: for few were then aware that trade is in general carried on to much more advantage by individuals than by great societies; and banking really is one of those few trades which can be carried on to as much advantage by a great society as by an individual. Two public banks had long been renowned throughout Europe, the Bank of Saint George at

Genoa, and the Bank of Amsterdam. The immense wealth which was in the keeping of those establishments, the confidence which they inspired, the prosperity which they had created, their stability, tried by panics, by wars, by revolutions, and found proof against all, were favourite topics. (Macaulay, 1907, p. 291)

Following the 'Glorious Revolution' in 1688, William III may have brought Dutch banking habits to England: 'England was transformed financially as well as politically by the Revolution of 1688' (Homer, 1963, p. 147). The Bank of England was established in 1694; Child's and Macaulay's arguments suggest that the original intention was to go beyond nationalising the sovereign's war debts. Soon after, Robert Walpole, the Whig First Lord of the Treasury and Chancellor of the Exchequer, took giant strides in bringing both the rate of interest and the burden of government debt under control (see Section 2.4).[10]

In terms of theoretical analysis, Schumpeter gives priority to John Law in 1705:

John Law (1671–1729), I have always felt, is in a class by himself.... He worked out the economics of his projects with a brilliance and, yes, profundity, which places him in the front rank of monetary theorists of all times.... Law's performance as a monetary theorist is contained in his tract: *Money and Trade considered, with a Proposal for Supplying the Nation with Money* (1st ed. 1705, 2nd ed. 1720...). (Schumpeter, 1954, pp. 294–5)

Law offered his monetary proposals to the English, Scottish and French governments. He appears to have received the greatest confidence in France where, as Minister of Finance from 1720, he was responsible for a short-lived implementation of his own proposals.[11] English attempts to reduce the interest on the national debt were, in turn, inspired by Law's techniques in France.[12] Some observations from his *Money and Trade Considered* give an idea of his perspective:

Domestick Trade depends on the Money. A greater Quantity employs more People than a lesser Quantity.... Money being in greater Quantity in *Holland*, whereby it is easier borrowed, and at less *use*; He gets Credit for more at 3 or 4 *Per Cent*, ... By a greater quantity of Money and Economy, the *Dutch* monopolize the Trades of Carriage even from the *English*. ... *Some think that if interest were lower'd by Law, Trade would increase, Merchants being able to Employ more Money and Trade Cheaper.* Such a Law would have many inconveniences, and it is much to be doubted, whether it would have any good Effect; Indeed, if lowness of interest were the Consequence of a greater Quantity of Money, the Stock applied to Trade would be greater, and Merchants would Trade Cheaper, from the easiness of borrowing and the lower Interest of Money, without any inconveniences attending it. . . .

The use of Banks has been the best Method yet practis'd for the increase of Money. (Law, 1705, pp. 13–36)

Anticipating the discussion in the next section, throughout the whole of the eighteenth century, the discount rate at the Bank of England was 5 per cent. Interest rates on long-term government bonds ('consols') were broadly between 3 and 4 per cent except during the Napoleonic wars, and between 1885 and 1900 when they fell from 3 to close to 2 per cent. Just as Child and Law had predicted, these low levels of interest rates accompanied the growing prosperity that would quite quickly lead to British commercial and financial supremacy in the world. Adam Smith's *An Inquiry into the Nature and Causes of the Wealth of Nations*, published in 1776, was testament to these achievements. As Schumpeter observed (Section 2.1), Smith was clear about the important role played by banking; nor did he neglect the role of the rate of interest, recording its movements over time. He was, as Keynes observed, 'extremely moderate in his attitude to the usury laws' (*CW* VII, p. 352):

When, therefore, by the substitution of paper, the gold and silver necessary for circulation is reduced to, perhaps, a fifth part of the former quantity, if the value of only the greater part of the other four-fifths be added to the funds which are destined for the maintenance of industry, it must make a very considerable addition to the quantity of that industry, and, consequently, to the value of the annual produce of land and labour.

An operation of this kind has, within these five-and-twenty or thirty years, been performed in Scotland, by the erection of new banking companies in almost every considerable town, and even in some country villages. (Smith, 1812 [1776], p. 236)

In a country, such as Great Britain, where money is lent to government at three per cent. and to private people upon good security at four, and four and a half, the present legal rate, five per cent., is perhaps, as proper as any. (ibid., p. 286)

In the nineteenth century, this appreciation of money was eventually undone by practical developments and Ricardo's economics. The advocates of an international gold standard sought a global financial regime that tied the supply of money to an excessively restrictive supply of gold. The gold 'bullionists' were opposed by those who sought to fully exploit the benefits of banking, the 'banking school'. The debates between the rival factions were of the greatest prominence. In notes for his own lectures, Keynes identified and summed up the major controversies as three 'Grand Discussions':[13]

1st The Bullionist Controversy.

Suspension of cash payments by Bank of England 1796 – the bank being *restrained* from paying in cash, though willing to. (Ricardo held that this was unnecessary.) No serious depreciation until 1809, which was the year of Ricardo's *High Price of Bullion*.

1810 Report of the Bullion Committee, the doctrines of the Report being nearly those of R[icardo]. (cash payments in two years.)

War of pamphlets. Bullionists beaten in the House.

1811 Lord Stanhope's Act making it an offence to deal in guineas for notes above their nominal value.

1819 Bill on Bullionist lines.

1820–1821 Cash payments and Lord Liverpool's reform of the currency (Thornton, Tooke, McCulloch).

2nd The Californian and Australian discoveries gave rise to the second grand discussion amongst economists and even the public – Chevalier, Cairnes, Jevons.

3rd The demonetisation of silver in the Latin Union and Germany, combined with diminished production of gold, gave rise to the bimetallic controversy.

Very voluminous literature.

Marshall's evidence before the G. and S. [Gold and Silver] Commission of 1888.

McLeod, Taussig, Nicholson, Foxwell.
Indian controversy. (*CW* XII, pp. 772–3)

In Schumpeter's terminology, each of these policy debates set monetary theory against real theory and in each case real theory and associated policy conclusions won the day. Ricardo's *On the Principles of Political Economy and Taxation* was actually published during the first controversy (1817) – a context to his theory not usually emphasised. Nevertheless, in each of these debates certain members of the banking school espoused sophisticated monetary analysis despite Ricardo's subsequent conquest of academic economics. Schumpeter's tributes to Henry Thornton (in particular the contrast with Ricardo) and Henry Dunning MacLeod merit a glance:

Henry Thornton (1760–1815) must be saluted at once. . . . His *Enquiry into the Nature and Effects of the Paper Credit of Great Britain* (1802) is an amazing performance. . . . No other performance of the period will bear comparison with it, though several, among them Ricardo's, met with greater success at the time as well as later. (Schumpeter, 1954, p. 689)

[T]he first – though not wholly successful – attempt at working out a systematic theory that fits the facts of bank credit adequately, which was made by MacLeod, attracted little attention, still less favourable attention. [footnote:]

Henry Dunning MacLeod (1821–1902) was an economist of many merits who somehow failed to achieve recognition, or even to be taken quite seriously, owing to his inability to put his many good ideas in a professionally acceptable form. Nothing can be done in this book to make amends to him, beyond mentioning the three publications by which he laid the foundations of the modern theory of the subject under discussion, though what he really succeeded in doing was to discredit this theory for quite a time: *Theory and Practice of Banking* (1st ed., 1855–56; Italian trans. 1879); *Lectures on Credit and Banking* (1882); *The Theory of Credit* (1889–91). (ibid., p. 1115)

In addition, Robert Malthus was vigorous in his criticism of Ricardo's advocacy of gold and sought an economics more in tune with that which would emerge from Keynes, underpinned 'by the notion of an insufficiency of effective demand' (*CW* VII, p. 362). But, as Keynes put it, 'Ricardo conquered England as completely as the Holy Inquisition conquered Spain' (*CW* VII, p. 32). The nineteenth century belonged to the advocates of the gold standard.

2.4 Interest rates and history

In his *A History of Interest Rates*, Sidney Homer (1963)[14] offers five millennia of monetary history:

Students of history may see mirrored in the charts and tables of interest rates over long periods the rise and fall of nations and civilisations, the exertions and the tragedies of war, and the enjoyments and the abuses of peace. They may be able to trace in these fluctuations the progress of knowledge and of technology, the successes or failures of political forms, the long, hard, and never-ending struggle of democracy with the rule of the elite, the difference between law imposed and law accepted. (p. 3)

In my view the book provides unambiguous evidence that, historically, centres of prosperity have followed the development of banking; and the development of banking has been accompanied by low interest rates. The alternative interpretation would be to reverse causality to prosperity as cause and low interest rates as effect. Homer himself, though his concern is primarily the construction of historical record rather than analysis of cause and effect, appears content to take this view. But one is then compelled to find a *real* reason for this historical trajectory of prosperity. On the other hand, the monetary theory asserted in this book, that the effect is prosperity and the cause is the low interest rates permitted by banking, *is* sufficient as well as being supported by the facts.

Ancient civilisations in Sumer, Greece and Rome left detailed records of interest rates that can, in each case, be characterised as falling steadily to a low point (10, 6 and 4 per cent, respectively), holding that low point, and then rising through to the end of the age. Darker ages left no records of interest rates. (If the broader proposition that prosperity and civilisation go hand in hand with low interest rates then a lack of an evidence base might be expected.) Homer leaves the dark ages behind to join 'Medieval and Renaissance Europe' as follows: 'Western European interest rates, when in medieval times they finally again emerge from centuries of darkness, were higher than the highest of the late Greek and Roman rates and very much higher than simultaneous Byzantine interest rate limits' (p. 65).

Taking the thirteenth century as a more formal starting point, Homer characterises that the blossoming of banking and low interest rates are seen first in Italy, then in the Netherlands and then in Britain. After a discussion of the development of banking and bills of exchange centred in thirteenth-to fifteenth-century Genoa and Florence (under the Medicis), Homer looks ahead: 'In the sixteenth century, Lyons and Antwerp developed as financial centres. . . . In the seventeenth century, Amsterdam assumed much of the leadership . . . It was not until the eighteenth century that London became a dominant financial centre' (p. 78).

His record of interest rates after the dark ages begins with the twelfth century; here English rates of between 40 and 120 per cent are contrasted with commercial loans in the Netherlands and Genoa of 10–20 per cent. In the thirteenth century, rates remained very high in England and Germany, but Venetian loan rates for 'States'[15] had fallen substantially to between 5 and 12 per cent. Late in the century, interest rates on Italian commercial loans had fallen to between 8 and 15 per cent.

In the fourteenth century the striking development is the low rates of interest on Italian short-term commercial loans. Homer records rates falling to 5–8 per cent, and then – 'late in the century' (p. 103) – 5 per cent. Rates held these low levels throughout the fifteenth century. By this time, banking appears to have spread to Germany, with the 'Hochsteller' bank paying 5 per cent on small deposits. The sixteenth century then saw lower commercial rates becoming more widespread, with rates of 4–12 per cent in Italy, Antwerp and Lyons. But, at this point, the balance of power shifted: 'Finance supported the great wars of the sixteenth century, and war gave Italian and German bankers great power and led to their ruin. Unpaid mercenaries sacked Antwerp and Rome' (p. 111).

The seventeenth century saw the commercial and financial dominance of the Netherlands. Homer first emphasises that 'State credit became excellent' (p. 114). State rates were reduced gradually from 8⅓ in 1600, to 4 per cent in 1654; following opposition to going as low as 3 per cent in 1665, the rate was reduced to 3⅔ in 1672. War with France then intervened and rates rose. But peace in the period 1679–1700 saw new loans floated at 3 per cent. Alongside the progress on short rates, Homer asserts that 'Modern "easy money" was discovered'. For rates on short-term commercial credit, Homer first cites Child's and Law's observations of Dutch rates of 3 and 3½ per cent. He goes on: 'Finally, at the turn of the eighteenth century the rate of interest on the Amsterdam Exchange was reported as falling to 2 per cent or even to 1¾ per cent. This is the first record of such low rates that we have for northern Europe, although a century earlier even lower rates may have prevailed in Genoa' (p. 129). At this point war interrupted progress again; this time Holland was never able to regain the initiative.

The eighteenth century sees 'England's turn to achieve financial leadership' (p. 147). Homer discusses the trends in long-term government bond yields in two parts:

(a) From 1700 to mid-century, the yields declined most of the time; starting at 6–8% they finally broke through 3%. This first, easy money period culminated in the flotation of the famous British 3% consols in 1751. (b) From 1754 on, consols fell in price, and yields rose in a highly erratic pattern. (p. 155; Figure 2.1)

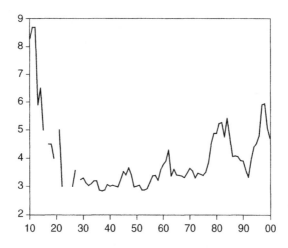

Figure 2.1 Long-term interest rates in Britain, 1710–1800
Source: Homer (1963).

English usury laws were amended in 1714 reducing the maximum rate of interest from 6 to 5 per cent, which became the discount rate for the Bank of England for almost the whole century (notwithstanding 'preferential discount rates of 4½% and then 3%', p. 164).

For much of the nineteenth century, British long-term rates remained at just above 3 per cent (Figure 2.2). But in the 1880s and 1890s progress was made to take long rates below 3 per cent. In 1888 the Chancellor, George Goschen, took the decisive step and converted the national debt to 2½ per cent. By 1897 the new consols yielded 2.21 per cent, the lowest long rate in British history.

Furthermore, for the first time in history, cheap money became a worldwide phenomenon (Table 2.1). Homer describes the period as the 'golden age of easy money' (p. 200) and records an observation by Eugene Von Bohm-Bawerk (1851–1914): 'The higher are a people's intelligence and moral

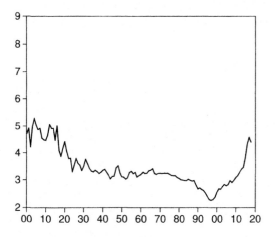

Figure 2.2   Long-term interest rates in Britian, 1800–1918
Source: Homer (1963).

Table 2.1   The lowest national long rates on government debt

	Rate (%)	Year
France	2.96	1897
Holland	2.72	1895
Belgium	2.56	1894
Germany	3.35	1897
Sweden	3.64	1890
United States	2.22	1899

strength, the lower will be the rate of interest' (p. 200).[16] As in Italy and the Netherlands, low English rates were brought to an end by war. The Boer War (1897–1902) saw rates rising back to 2.5 per cent by the end of the century. Ten years later, the First World War brought the 'golden age of easy money' to a decisive and bloody end. Widespread prosperity would prove elusive until after the Second World War; the associated movements in interest rates will be discussed in Chapter 11.

2.5 Money and the class conflict

'[T]he history of all hitherto existing society is the history of class struggles' (*The Communist Manifesto*, Marx and Engels, 1967 [1872], p. 79).

With the wealth owner – capital itself – at threat, Marx's historical imperative suggests that the any transition to banking would be hard fought. In *Capital Volume III* he went into specific detail. He described a conflict between rival capitalists: 'usurers' who owned wealth and those who advocated and then controlled the power that banking offered. The latter interests were closely allied with, or one and the same as, industrial capitalists. For banking offered the low interest rates that would allow industry to flourish.

> The development of the credit system takes place as a reaction against usury. (Marx, 1909, p. 704)

> This violent fight against usury, this demand for the subordination of the interest-bearing under the industrial capital, is but the herald of the organic creations, that establish these prerequisites of capitalist production in the modern banking system, which on the one hand robs usurer's capital of its monopoly by concentrating all fallow money reserves and throwing them on the money-market, and on the other hand limits the monopoly of the precious metals themselves by creating credit-money.
>
> . . .
>
> Against the Bank of England all goldsmiths and pawnbrokers raised a howl of rage.... [T]he goldsmiths ... intrigued considerably against the Bank, because their business was reduced by it, their discount lowered, and their business with the government had fallen into the hands of this antagonist. (ibid., pp. 708–9)

Moreover, his policy goals and associated practical mechanisms involved recognition that to some extent labour would be advantaged by banking:

> Finally, there is no doubt that the credit system will serve as a powerful lever during the transition from the capitalist mode of production to the production by means, of associated labor; but only as one element in

connection with the great organic revolutions in the mode of production itself. (ibid., p. 713)

Over the turn of the century, other socialist scholars would develop this perspective. Rudolph Hilferding (1877–1941) looked to a subsequent stage in the capitalist process – the dominance of 'finance capital':

> In this sense a fully developed credit system is the antithesis of capitalism, and represents organization and control as opposed to anarchy. It has its source in socialism, but has been adapted to capitalist society; it is a fraudulent kind of socialism, modified to suit the needs of capitalism. It socializes other people's money for use by the few. At the outset it suddenly opens up for the knights of credit prodigious vistas – private property – seem to have fallen, and the entire productive power of society appears to be placed at the disposal of the individual. The prospect intoxicates him, and in turn he intoxicates and swindles others.
>
> The original pioneers of credit were the romantics of capitalism like Law and Pereire; it was some time before the sober capitalist gained the upper hand, and Gunderman vanquished Saccard. (Hilferding, 1981 [1910], p. 180)

> Finance capital develops with the development of the joint-stock company and reaches its peak with the monopolisation of industry. Industrial earnings acquire a more secure and regular character, and so the possibilities for investing bank capital in industry are extended. But the bank disposes of bank capital, and the owners of the majority of shares in the bank dominate the bank. . . . As capital itself at the highest stage of its development becomes finance capital, so the magnate of capital, the finance capitalist increasingly concentrates his control over the whole national capital by means of his domination of bank capital. (ibid., p. 225)

> The Hegelians spoke of the negation of the negation: bank capital was the negation of usurer's capital and is itself negated by finance capital. The latter is the synthesis of usurer's and bank capital, and it appropriates to itself the fruits of social production at an infinitely higher stage of economic development. (ibid., p. 226)

As Marx, Hilferding looked to the social goal of Labour's ownership of the means of production:

> While capital can pursue no other policy than that of imperialism, the proletariat cannot oppose to it a policy derived from the period when industrial capital was sovereign; it is no use for the proletariat to oppose the policy of advanced capitalism with an antiquated policy from the era of free trade and hostility to the state. The response of the proletariat

to the economic policy of finance capital – imperialism – cannot be free trade, but only socialism . . . the organization of production, the conscious control of the economy not by and for the benefit of capitalist magnates but by and for society as a whole, which will then at last subordinate the economy to itself as it has been able to subordinate nature ever since it discovered the laws of motion of the natural world. (ibid., pp. 366–7)

Hilferding's argument was preceded by J. A. Hobson's (1858–1940) work. His and A. F. Mummery's *The Physiology of Industry* (1889) marked the start of a building critique of capitalism that would identify, in *Imperialism: A Study* (Hobson, 1902), the wealth-owning capitalist as the root cause of not only economic and social malaise but also 'Imperialist' aggression. He considered that too great a concentration of wealth resulted in under-consumption, which in turn meant under-utilisation of resources. But Hobson was a Liberal who saw a re-distribution of income and wealth within a market economy as sufficient for wider economic and social justice.

Keynes, of course, was also a Liberal. From his earliest days, he believed that the Economic Problem was not inherent to a market economy, but was due primarily to monetary mismanagement. In a December 1923 speech to the Liberal Club, just after the publication of *A Tract on Monetary Reform*, he set out his position in a manner that also serves as a general statement of his lifetime policy perspective:

To begin with a few words about what should be the attitude of Liberalism towards social policy.

We are traditionally the party of *laissez-faire*.

But just as the economists led the party into this policy, so I hope they may lead them out again.

It is not true that individuals acting separately in their own economic interest always produce the best results.

It is obvious that an individualist society left to itself does not work well or even tolerably.

Here I agree with Labour.

I differ from them not in the desirability of state action in the common interest, but as to the forms which such interference should take. Their proposals are out of date and contrary to human nature.

But it is not safe or right just to leave things alone.

It is our duty to think out wise controls and workable interferences.

Now there is no part of our economic system which works so badly as our monetary and credit arrangements; none where the results of bad working are so disastrous socially; and none where it is easier to propose a scientific solution. (*CW* XIX, Vol. I, pp. 158–9)

Keynes's solution to society's ills was perhaps an unrivalled threat to the wealth owner. Keynes did not characterise matters in terms of a class conflict; nevertheless his *General Theory* implicitly re-positioned the nature of that conflict. Capital *was* in conflict with labour but the *General Theory* offered an alternative interpretation of the nature of the conflict. Labour and industry had broadly the same interests, and these were opposed by the interests of finance capital. His theory demonstrated that the interests and preferred policy of finance capital was inimical not only to labour, but also to industry and to economic activity as a whole.

Where Keynes and Marx departed most substantially was in the solution to the class struggle. For Keynes, the solution to the class struggle was not abolition of the market system or private property in Communist Revolution, but the re-positioning of the financial system to serve the interests of industry and labour. The solution to the class struggle was the abolition – with a choice only over the pace – of usury within the market system. In the closing chapter, 'Concluding Notes on the Social Philosophy Towards Which the General Theory Might Lead', he discussed how finance capital (the 'rentier') would be vanquished:

> Now, though this state of affairs would be quite compatible with some measure of individualism, yet it would mean the euthanasia of the rentier, and, consequently, the euthanasia of the cumulative oppressive power of the capitalist to exploit the scarcity-value of capital. Interest to-day rewards no genuine sacrifice, any more than does the rent of land. The owner of capital can obtain interest because capital is scarce, just as the owner of land can obtain rent because land is scarce. But whilst there may be intrinsic reasons for the scarcity of land, there are no intrinsic reasons for the scarcity of capital. . . .
>
> I see, therefore, the rentier aspect of capitalism as a transitional phase which will disappear when it has done its work. And with the disappearance of its rentier aspect much else in it besides will suffer a sea-change. It will be, moreover, a great advantage of the order of events which I am advocating, that the euthanasia of the rentier, of the functionless investor, will be nothing sudden, merely a gradual but prolonged continuance of what we have seen recently in Great Britain, and will need no revolution. (*CW* VII, pp. 375–6)

In this way he saw an end to finance capital, but as a natural stage of the evolution of the free market, capitalist process. For Keynes, the Marxist solution was an incorrect response to the Economic Problem (see also the quotation that opens my Introduction).

Over the 1930s the British Labour Party came firmly to endorse and propound this long-emerging view of the class conflict. Under Hugh Dalton's guidance, with the failures of the inter-war gold standard widely understood (see Chapter 3), the Labour Party became a party of monetary reform. In Dalton's 1935 book, *Practical Socialism for Britain*, 'finance' took centre stage in his critique:

> British public opinion, increasingly impatient at the long continuance of our present disorders, more and more fixes its critical gaze upon finance. . . .
> [T]he economic disasters of the post-war years are mainly due to financial causes and financial mismanagement . . .
> The world-wide crash in the price level since 1929, with all its disastrous consequences, is a financiers' achievement; the continuous deflation of currency and credit in this country from 1920 onwards was a long series of financiers' decisions, taken without public advertisement, or public discussion, or Parliamentary sanction, and imposed upon British industry and agriculture, either unawares or against their will. (Dalton, 1935, pp. 182–3)

Towards the end of the war, the British Labour Party looked to their own post-war financial agenda. In their 1944 paper 'Full Employment and Financial Policy', they offered an unambiguous perspective:

> Blame for unemployment lies much more with finance than with industry. Mass unemployment is never the fault of the workers; often it is not the fault of the employers. All widespread trade depressions in modern times have financial causes; successive inflation and deflation, obstinate adherence to the gold standard, reckless speculation, and over-investment in particular industries . . .
> This view is now widely accepted outside the ranks of the Labour Party, by most economists, by many Government officials, by many businessmen, even by some bankers . . .
> Finance must be the servant, and the intelligent servant, of the community and productive industry; not their stupid master.[17]

The 1945 election perhaps saw the electorate endorsing the reform of the Labour Party that Dalton had achieved. Dalton became Chancellor of the Exchequer and Keynes agreed to stay on as his advisor. The monetary policy of Keynes and Socialist Government were brought together for the first time.

The first act of the first majority Labour Government in British history was of not only symbolic but also economic importance. The nationalisation of the Bank of England formalised the subservience of the Bank to the Government that had followed the departure from gold. Government and Bank monetary policy was then aimed at cheap money, based explicitly on the monetary and debt-management agenda and mechanisms that Keynes

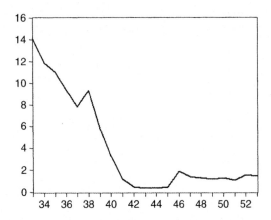

Figure 2.3　British unemployment, 1933–53
Source: Feinstein (1972).

had set out at the National Debt Enquiry, which is discussed in the next chapter.

The Bank of England Bill had its second reading in October 1945; on 7 November 1946 the *Financial Times* reported:

> Cheap money policy, born of a depression, having survived a world war, is now regarded, not as a short lived device to overcome a temporary decline in prosperity, but as a permanent weapon for state regulation . . . So long as the government remains determined to push its cheap money policy to the limit, long-term prospects for the rentier are anything but cheerful.

For the first time in history low interest rates were the explicit aim of government policy.

The policy culminated in an attempt to hold long-term rates at 2½ per cent, from which the Government would eventually retreat.[18] Yet this 'failure' should not detract from the more general preservation of cheap money under the Attlee government. Its economic and social achievements arguably stand apart from those of any other government in history. In the wake of post-war debt and currency instability, the economic growth and unemployment performance (Figure 2.3) were outstanding.

But the Labour Government lost office in the wake of infighting caused by the Korean War. The Conservative Party took office, and in November 1951 the re-activation of the discount rate as an instrument of economic policy was symbolic of the end of the monetary policies of the post-depression age.

The Labour Party victory at the 1945 general election had made the financial reform agenda that had been debated for half a century a brief reality. As with Keynes's theory itself, this policy, its successes and failures are largely lost to history. Marx's historical imperative may advise us to expect nothing else.

Notes

1. The validity of this last statement may be seriously doubted at the time of writing in 2006.
2. The 'famous Mr. Law', as Adam Smith (1776, p. 254) calls him, is discussed in Section 2.3.
3. Banks' cash is often defined to include banks' operational deposits with the central bank.
4. The quantity known as the velocity of money, if it is calculated based on cash in circulation, is in reality a measure of the amount of cash required for economic activity. The speed of circulation of cash is only one of a number of determinants of the cash requirement in a bank-money economy – and probably among the least important.
5. For example, in the United Kingdom the cash in circulation at the end of 2003 was £34 billion and total (retail) deposits at banks and building societies were £743 billion – a cash/deposit ratio of 4.6 per cent (Office for National Statistics, *Financial Statistics*, January 2004, Table 3.1D).
6. The size of the reserve is thus equal to the amount of cash (including settlement accounts at the central bank); all are stocks.
7. The Bank of England (BoE, 2002) description of arrangements in the UK that were used until 2006 is a useful (if detailed) illustration of the type of processes involved (though the arrangements have now been superseded, see MacGorain, 2005). The approach was to discount a wide range of eligible assets in exchange for cash at a rate of interest set by the Monetary Policy Committee. The specific technical processes for discounting involved settlement accounts (SA, formerly bankers' deposits) and repurchase agreements ('repos'). Each commercial bank had a SA at the BoE that was required to be in credit at the end of each day. The daily process saw SAs debited to the value of new cash required by the banks. The resources to zero-set the SAs were provided by BoE purchase of specified eligible assets from commercial banks (these included both long-dated 'gilts' and short-dated 'Treasury bills'). The arrangement was known as a repurchase agreement or 'repo' because the BoE generally bought assets which they agreed to sell back at a specified date (usually two weeks later). The majority of the daily amount of aggregate repos required (the 'shortage') was determined by the sum of new cash demands and any previously maturing repo arrangements. BoE (2002) gives an example showing a £1800 million shortage, consisting of £315 million in notes and £1402 million in maturing repos (the remainder was accounted for by the BoE buying some securities outright). Interest on the repo was charged at the BoE repo rate – the rate set by the Monetary Policy Committee according to their monthly interpretation of economic conditions. The BoE thus set the rate of interest by providing an endogenous supply of cash to banks that in turn allowed banks to lend what they wanted to the public: 'The number of notes issued is ultimately determined by public demand' (*Fact Sheet* on 'Bank Notes' from the

Bank of England website, April 2002). The rate of interest so established, known as the 'repo' rate, was the rate of interest that underpinned lending in the UK economy.

8. Banks' purchases of, for example, Treasury bills are also book transactions. In effect, banks increase credit twice: once to purchase the bill and once through the actual extension of private credit.

9. Anticipating the discussion in Chapter 9, such a conclusion is an example of liquidity-preference reasoning. Furthermore, as described here, the extension of credit sets up a demand for eligible assets. In order to extend the *supply* of credit, banks *demand* eligible assets and cash. This aspect of bank balance sheets allows the application of liquidity preference theory to the demand for money as a means of exchange alongside the demand for money as a store of value.

10. See, for example, Dow and Smithin (1992) for a discussion of the development of banking in Scotland.

11. Janet Gleeson's (1999) *Millionaire* offers an enjoyable account of this colourful genius.

12. As noted by Antoin E. Murphy in his 1994 edition of Law's *Essay on a Land Bank*; whether Law had any influence on the development of the Bank of England is not known.

13. It is unclear whether this characterisation and terminology is due to Keynes; Skidelsky (1992, p. 169) uses it, but attributes it neither to Keynes nor to anybody else. He also refers to 'great' rather than 'grand'.

14. All references in this section are to the 1963 first edition of Homer's work; an updated edition is still in print today.

15. The Republic of Venice floated long-term loans called 'Prestiti' that the wealthy were obliged to take up in proportion to their wealth.

16. The reference is ' . . . quoted by J. A. Schumpeter in *Ten Great Economists* (New York: Oxford University Press, 1951), p. 182'.

17. National Executive Committee of the Labour Party (June 1944), *Full Employment and Financial Policy*.

18. Keynes was not content with the initiatives that led to this failure – some of which appeared to originate with the Bank of England itself. Dalton was sympathetic to Keynes's arguments but Keynes died, and from then on the advice of Treasury officials and the BoE was dominant. A fuller analysis of this episode is necessary.

3
JMK and the Fourth Grand Monetary Discussion

3.1 Introduction

Keynes was a monetary economist concerned above all with monetary policy. His specific objectives have been well described by E. A. G. Robinson:

> Indeed it is difficult not to be impressed by the consistency of his main strategic objectives: the full employment of resources; the achievement of balance of payments for all countries by methods that would not be inconsistent with full employment; as a means to this, a system of exchange rates that would combine the short-term virtues of fixity and predictability with the long-term virtues of flexibility; and, as a means to full employment, low interest rates. (Robinson 1947, p. 45)

All these policy and theoretical initiatives were part of a *coherent strategic whole*. This coherent whole was the basis of the fourth of the grand monetary discussions that Keynes himself had first identified and characterised (see Section 2.3). As he and Schumpeter both observed, 'There have been in the last hundred years three principal crises in the history of currency; and the main developments of monetary theory have been in connection with these' (*CW* XII, p. 772); 'Once more the bulk of the vast literature on money and related subjects, which the period under survey produced, grew out of the discussions of current problems' (Schumpeter, 1954, p. 1074).

Keynes motivated and, for a brief period, dominated the fourth grand discussion. Against a backdrop of a changing role for gold in India, the widespread suspension of internal gold standards during the First World War, the hardship of the 1920s both during the preparation for and following the return to gold in Britain, and then the worldwide great depression itself, Keynes gradually built the most forceful and intellectually cogent case for monetary reform, and against gold and the financial establishment, that the world had seen before or has seen since.

As Alfred Marshall had seen before him, from before the First World War Keynes recognised that the gold standard could lead to monetary action at odds with domestic policy requirements. He advocated exchange mechanisms based on *currency management*; where central banks preserved a parity for a currency through purchases and sales in the market rather than through interest rate action. While he consistently held to these principles, his view of the appropriate domestic monetary policy, given the autonomy permitted by currency management, changed over time. Up to and including his *Tract on Monetary Reform* (1921), Keynes advocated aiming monetary policy at stable prices through the control of credit creation with Bank rate. But when Britain left gold, and with his *Treatise on Money*, he began gradually to see domestic policy differently. Instead he began to advocate a *cheap-money policy*, which would involve direct policy action to set interest rates at a low level across the spectrum of liquidity. By the time he had published his *General Theory*, he regarded cheap money as the secular policy described in the Introduction. Moreover, under this policy, Bank rate was redundant. During the 1930s his strategic objectives were largely achieved; in the most sweeping sense, he oversaw:

- the transformation of the global financial system from the gold standard to the managed currencies of the 1930s (and later the watered-down Bretton Woods Agreement);
- the shift of monetary authority from private central banks that reflected the interests of what Hilferding (1981 [1910]) labelled 'finance capital' to democratically elected governments that represented wider interests; and
- the aiming of domestic monetary policy at the *cheap money* that he saw as necessary to prosperity.

These achievements were hard fought. Britain led the way, but in the United States President Roosevelt pursued the agenda with the most uncompromising vigour. Over the first half of the 1930s, the world fractured into a gold bloc and a group of monetary reform nations. Only with the 1935 election of a socialist government in France did the gold bloc finally collapse. At that point only the totalitarian economies rejected Keynes's agenda for monetary reform.

Alongside these practical developments, Keynes's theory developed from recognition that the classical gold standard denied the existence of credit, to the full theory of a monetary economy underpinned by the liquidity preference theory of interest in the *General Theory*. While the discussion in this chapter aims primarily to characterise the policy perspective and does not examine the theory in any detail, it does seek to re-interpret the essential conclusions of the theory in the context of this monetary whole.

Finally, while the Second World War is regarded as interrupting the academic debate of his theory and policy conclusions, it provided instead the opportunity for a fuller practical test of those conclusions. By the end of the war, Keynes had established a full debt-management framework that had enabled the authorities to set interest rates across the spectrum of liquidity. Furthermore, with the encouragement of President Roosevelt, he had prepared his International Clearing Union currency proposals for the post-war era.

3.2 Background to Keynes's monetary analysis and policies

3.2.1 The gold standard

As Keynes began his work the economic policy environment reflected the triumph of Ricardo and the financial establishment. The most fundamental legacy of the first grand discussion was the gold standard of the 1844 Bank Act. As Keynes later described, the Act formalised a specific process for control of the creation of bank money by controlling the issue of currency:

> The British Bank Act of 1844 prescribed a method of regulation which had some logic behind it at the time when it was introduced – the method (as it is called) of the 'fixed fiduciary issue'. It requires that the amount of the note issue shall not exceed the amount of the gold reserves by more than a stated amount fixed by law (but capable of revision, of course, from time to time). The idea was to cover the fluctuating margin of the note issue with gold, so that there would always be gold available to redeem all the notes that were at all likely to be presented in any normal circumstances; . . . (*CW* VI, p. 237)

The gold standard was first an *internal* or *domestic* policy mechanism. However, it had equally important international implications. First, there was an implicit exchange rate between two countries on domestic gold standards. Following from this, exchange rate movements for trade or other purposes might have effects that could impact on the domestic management of the standard and *vice versa*. While the standard arose from money management requirements at a national level, these international implications came to dominate its operation and its eventual downfall; and these were the matters that Keynes concerned himself with.[1]

The political context was a broader international tendency towards the gold standard in the last quarter of the nineteenth century. In the wake of the Franco–Prussian War, the newly created German Empire replaced its silver-based monetary system with the gold standard. Over the next years, the United States, France and the Latin Monetary Union all did likewise. As Laidler (2001, p. 13) put it, 'there began a twenty year period of slow deflation in gold standard countries' that set the 'background to the controversies between advocates of the restoration of bimetallism on one hand, and defenders of gold monometallism on the other'. International conferences in 1878, 1881 and 1892 resolved little. In Britain the *Report* of the 1888 Gold and Silver Commission saw Alfred Marshall looking to alternative systems, but there was no agreement. While the controversy marked the end of bimetallism as an alternative practical approach, this was only because a new and more substantial opponent for gold began to emerge. The old controversy was upstaged by the development of *gold-exchange standards* as described later by Keynes:

> The gold-exchange standard may be said to exist when gold does not circulate in a country to an appreciable extent, when the local currency is not necessarily redeemable in gold, but when the government or central bank makes arrangements for the provision of foreign remittances in gold at a fixed maximum rate in terms of the local currency, the reserves necessary to provide these remittances being kept to a considerable extent abroad. (*CW* I, pp. 21–2)

Ultimately, and despite the resistance of the financial establishment, the development of international gold exchange standards led to the end of both the domestic gold standard and to any formal international role for gold. This was the fourth grand monetary discussion.

3.2.2 Alfred Marshall

Keynes attributed his own immersion in and understanding of these issues to his teacher, Alfred Marshall, whose lectures on 'Money, Credit and Prices' he attended in 1905 (Moggridge, 1992, p. 95). He later accorded Marshall a good deal of priority in the development of monetary thought; he outlined Marshall's contributions in his 1924 biographical essay (published as Marshall's obituary in the *EJ*):[2]

> Since *Money* was from the early 'seventies onwards one of his favourite topics for lectures, his main ideas became known to pupils in a general way, with the result that there grew up in Cambridge an oral tradition, first from Marshall's own lectures and after his retirement from those of Professor Pigou, different from, and (I think it may be claimed) superior to, anything that could be found in books until recently.…

> Marshall printed nothing whatever on the subject of Money previous to the Bimetallic controversy, and even then he waited a considerable time before he intervened. His first serious contribution to the subject was contained in his answers to a questionnaire printed by the Royal Commission on the Depression of Trade and Industry in 1886. This was followed by his article on 'Remedies for Fluctuations of General Prices' in the *Contemporary Review* for March 1887, and a little later by his voluminous evidence before the Gold and Silver Commission in 1887 and 1888. In 1899 came his evidence before the Indian Currency Committee. But his theories were not expounded in a systematic form until the appearance

of *Money, Credit and Commerce* in 1923. By this date nearly all his main ideas had found expression in the works of others. (*CW* X, pp. 189–90)

The essay went on to identify what Keynes regarded as Marshall's significant contributions to monetary theory (I have excerpted only the headings, and dropped the italics):

(1) The exposition of the Quantity Theory of Money as a part of the General Theory of Value....
(2) The distinction between the 'real' rate of interest and the 'money' rate of interest, and the relevance of this to the credit cycle, when the value of money is fluctuating....
(3) The causal train by which, in modern credit systems, an additional supply of money influences prices, and the part played by the rate of discount....
(4) The enunciation of the 'Purchasing Power Parity' Theory as determining the rate of exchange between countries with mutually inconvertible currencies....
(5) The 'chain' method of compiling index-numbers....
(6) The proposal of paper currency for the circulation (on the lines of Ricardo's *Proposals for an Economical and Secure Currency*) based on gold-and-silver symmetallism as the standard.... (ibid., pp. 191–3)

In 1926, two years after Marshall's death, Keynes edited a collection of those of Marshall's official papers that he regarded as important contributions to monetary theory. A notable analysis, not emphasised by Keynes, was a tentative description of the money multiplier process contained in the 'minutes of evidence' for the 1887–88 Royal Commission on the Values of Gold and Silver:

The relation which the amount of bankers' money bears to the amount of currency has to be discussed as a part of a larger inquiry as to the influence which is exerted on prices by the methods of business; . . . I should consider what part of its deposits a bank could lend, and then I should consider what part of its loans would be redeposited with it and with other banks and, *vice versa*, what part of the loans made by other banks would be received by it as deposits. Thus I should get a geometrical progression; the effect being that if each bank could lend two-thirds of its deposits, the total amount of loaning power got by the banks would amount to three times what it otherwise would be. If it could lend four-fifths, it will be five times; and so on. The question how large a part of its deposits a bank can lend depends in great measure on the extent on which the different banks directly or indirectly pool their reserves. But this reasoning, I think, has never been worked out in public, and it is very complex, and I should not wish to tender evidence upon the subject. (Marshall, 1926, p. 37)

The analysis, however, portrayed a process where deposits created loans. Schumpeter pinpoints the discovery of the correct causality, alongside an overview of the extent of the understanding of monetary processes at this time:

> Nevertheless, it proved extraordinarily difficult for economists to recognize that bank loans and bank investments do create deposits . . . And even in 1930, when the large majority had been converted and accepted that doctrine as a matter of course, Keynes rightly felt it necessary to re-expound and to defend the doctrine at some length, [footnotes a reference to Crick (1927)] and some of its most important aspects cannot be said to be fully understood even now . . . For the facts of credit creation – at least of credit creation in the form of banknotes – must all along have been familiar to every economist. Moreover, especially in America, people were freely using the term Check Currency and talking about banks' 'coining money' and thereby trespassing upon the rights of Congress. Newcombe in 1885 gave an elementary description of the process by which deposits are created through lending. Towards the end of the period (1911) Fisher did likewise. He also emphasised the obvious truth that deposits and banknotes are fundamentally the same thing. And Hartley Withers espoused the notion that bankers were not middlemen but 'manufacturers' of money . . . [After MacLeod] came Wicksell, . . . in the United States . . . Davenport, Taylor and Phillips may serve as examples. But it was not until 1924 that the theoretical job was done completely in a book by [Albert] Hahn [*Volkswirtschaftliche Theorie des Bankkredits*], and even then the success was not immediate. Among English leaders credit is due primarily to Professors Robertson and Pigou . . . (Schumpeter, 1954, pp. 1114–16)

Not only for Keynes but also for many others, Marshall had re-invigorated the science of monetary theory.

3.2.3 Keynes at Cambridge

Just as several of these contributions were published, Keynes had inherited Marshall's teaching at Cambridge. Table 3.1 reproduces his schedule as compiled by Moggridge (CW XII, p. 689).

Extracts from Keynes's own notes for some of these courses are published in Volume XII of *Collected Writings*. While these reproductions are incomplete, sufficient detail is included to gain a relatively clear idea of his perspective. He builds a theory of prices based on the quantity theory of money, but a theory where the money term is understood as a consequence of credit creation and the transmission mechanism is of importance:

Table 3.1 Keynes's early lectures

Money, Credit and Prices	1908/09–1909/10
The Stock Exchange and the Money Market	1909/10–1913/14
The Theory of Money	1910/11–1913/14
Company Finance and the Stock Exchange	1910/11–1912/13
Currency and Banking	1910/11–1913/14
The Currency and Finances of India	1910/11
Money Markets and Foreign Exchanges	1910/11–1912/13
Principles of Economics	1910/11–1913/14
The Monetary Affairs of India	1912/13

The use of the name, 'Quantity theory', however, has certainly tended to overemphasise the influence of supply as compared with that of demand; . . . The total exchange value of the money in circulation is *not independent* of the demand for money. (*CW* XII, pp. 693–4)

The level of prices depends, as we have seen, mainly upon the supply of gold, the volume of trade, and the system of banking and credit. (*CW* XII, pp. 703–4)

There is little in the published lecture notes detailing actual credit creation mechanisms, although one brief extract illustrates a relatively sophisticated understanding of the processes involved:

The proportion of subsidiary currency to standard currency
Dependent upon:

(1) the habits and tastes of the people
(2) the development of banking
(3) the degree of confidence felt in the subsidiary currency
(4) the strength of the motive (chiefly on the part of financiers and bankers and sometimes on the part of Govt) to economise the use of standard currency

(1) This and (2) are in general the dominating influences, e.g. the use of the rupee in India; and the use of notes in Austria, in Brazil.
(2) The use of cheques turns partly on custom, but largely upon the spread of banking facilities, the number of bank branches and their willingness to take and manage small accounts without making charges.
    General in English-speaking countries – England, Canada, Australia, USA., S. Africa.
    Notes, on the other hand, usual in Russia, Germany and Latin countries.
    Metal in oriental countries.

> I shall deal more fully with this when I come to systems of currency and systems of credit and gold reserves. (*CW* XII, p. 757)

Keynes made his contributions to economics against this backdrop. In his 1912 lectures, he looked to a possible fourth grand discussion that is ultimately the subject of my work:

> We may possibly be on the brink of a fourth grand discussion. The recent rise of prices has caused discontent and embarrassed governments in many parts of the world. Several are at the moment conducting investigations into the recent rise in the cost of living; and a project of an International Commission of Enquiry has been launched. (*CW* XII, p. 773)[3]

3.3   India and gold-exchange standards

Keynes's early written work comprised mainly applications of monetary theory to current practical policy; his own theoretical contributions were limited to a running commentary on the fast developing science of monetary theory (in review articles in the *EJ*, which he edited from 1911).

Keynes chose to begin his Civil Service career in the India Office because the dominant economic policy issues of the day were the monetary developments in India in the wake of the bimetallist controversy. In 1893, India had suspended its silver standard and adopted an innovative exchange policy:

> In the course of the 1890s, ... the Government pegged the rupee to gold and left a token silver and paper currency in circulation ... the main method used by the Government of India to peg the exchanges was the maintenance of sterling balances in London, which rose and fell as the authorities sold or purchased rupees for sterling to keep the rupee exchange within the gold points ... (Moggridge, 1992, pp. 201–2)

Keynes identified the importance of these developments as the first substantial manifestation of *gold-exchange-standard* systems. The rupee was not convertible to gold internally, but was convertible into other currencies at a fixed exchange rate in terms of gold. The exchange rate was held at this level by the authorities' purchases and sales of currency as described by Moggridge above. Fundamentally, in terms of future policy development, these *currency management* arrangements did not involve the manipulation of interest rates.

Keynes's contributions to economics, therefore, began on this theme. His first major *EJ* article, 'Recent Economic Events in India', was published in March 1909 (*CW* XI, pp. 1–22). At the same time he began a lifelong correspondence with national newspapers, making his ideas both accessible and widely known. In May 1910, he gave a series of six lectures to the London School of Economics (LSE) that would become his first book: *Indian Currency and Finance.* His prominence was such that, on 9 May 1911, he was reading a summary of his policy stance to the Royal Economic Society:

> I will endeavour to give reasons for thinking that this existing system, to which the name of gold-exchange standard has been given, is something much more civilised, much more economical, and much more satisfactory than a gold currency. I should like to see it openly established in India on a permanent basis and all talk of an eventual gold currency definitely abandoned. (*CW* XI, p. 69)

Indian Currency and Finance set the developments in India in the context of the history of the gold standard. As the centre of global finance, he gave front place to England:

> The history of currency, so far as it is relevant to our present purpose, virtually begins with the nineteenth century. During the second quarter of this century England was alone in possessing an orthodox 'sound' currency on a gold basis. Gold was the sole standard of value; it circulated freely from hand to hand; and it was freely available for export. Up to 1844 bank notes showed a tendency to become a formidable rival to gold as the actual medium of exchange. But the Bank Act of that year set itself to hamper this tendency and to encourage the use of gold as the medium of exchange as well as the standard of value. This Act was completely successful in stopping attempts to economise gold by the use of notes. But the Bank Act did nothing to hinder the use of cheques, and the very remarkable development of this medium of exchange during the next fifty years led in this country, without any important development in the use of notes or tokens, to a monetary organisation more perfectly adapted for the economy of gold than any which exists elsewhere . . . With the growth of the stability of banking, and especially the growth of confidence in this stability amongst depositors, these occasions [bank runs] have become more and more infrequent . . . Gold Reserves, therefore, in Great Britain are no longer held primarily with a view to emergencies of this kind. The uses of gold coin in Great Britain are now three – as the medium of exchange for certain kinds of out-of-pocket expenditure, such as that on railway travelling, for which custom requires cash payment; for the payment of wages; and to meet a drain of specie abroad. (*CW* I, pp. 11–12)

His point was that England thrived *in spite of* the gold standard, because financial developments, in particular the use of cheques, meant that restrictions (i.e. the requirement to be able to convert currency into gold) were not binding. On the other hand, without such developments the gold standard would not be so benign:

> But foreign observers seem to have been more impressed by the fact that the Englishman had sovereigns in his pocket than by the fact he had a

cheque-book in his desk; and took more notice of the 'efficacy' of the bank rate and of the deliberations of the court of directors on Thursdays, than of the peculiar organisation of the brokers and the London money market, and of Great Britain's position as a creditor nation. (*CW* I, p. 14)

He characterised the diminution of the role of gold around the world, in particular in those countries that were commonly identified with the gold standard:

In Germany the policy of 1876 has been deliberately reversed by a recent revision of the Bank Act, and 20-mark notes are now issued with the deliberate object of keeping as much gold as possible in the bank and wasting as little as possible in circulation. This new policy is likely to be extended in the future.

. . .

In other countries, where actual currency is the principal medium of exchange, the attempt to introduce gold as the medium passing from hand to hand has been for the most part abandoned. A great part of the new gold has flowed, during the last ten years, into the reserves of the state banks, and a comparatively small amount only can have found its way into circulation. In Austria-Hungary, for example, after the currency reform of 1892, attempts were made to force gold into circulation just as they were in India. They luckily failed. . . . The same kind of thing occurred in Russia. After establishing with difficulty a gold standard, they began with the theory, and have since abandoned it, that a gold currency was the natural corollary. Other examples could be given. A gold standard is the rule now in all parts of the world; but a gold currency is the exception. The 'sound currency' maxims of twenty or thirty years ago are still often repeated, but they have not been successful, nor ought they to have been, in actually influencing affairs. (*CW* I, pp. 49–50)[4]

Ultimately, he supported the role of gold as 'an international, but not a local, currency' (*CW* I, p. 21), and dismissed the local role in clear terms:

Let the Indian public learn that it is extravagant to use gold as a medium of exchange, foolish to lessen the utility of their reserves through suspicion of the London money market, and highly advantageous to their own trade and to the resources of their own money market to develop the use of notes; and their financial system may soon become wonderfully well adapted to the particular circumstances of their situation. (*CW* I, pp. 136–7)

His practical stance was supported by a theoretical argument that was underpinned by recognition and understanding of the nature and importance of what he would later label *bank-money* systems. It was not appropriate to tie domestic bank-money systems to a fixed exchange parity in terms of gold in the way that it might be for commodity-money systems. The practical effect would be that Bank rate action to preserve the exchange rate might often be at odds with the requirements of the domestic economy.

Keynes stressed that the apparent historical success of the gold standard in Britain was due to the development of banking mechanisms offsetting any constraint on credit through the link to gold.[5] He argued that such gains, as well as fortuitous discoveries of gold, could not be relied on indefinitely:

It is not likely that we shall leave permanently the most intimate adjustments of our economic organism at the mercy of a lucky prospector, a new chemical process, or a change of ideas in Asia. (*CW* I, p. 71)

Even at this early stage, Keynes was regarded as an expert in these matters. In 1913, just as he was finalising his book for publication, he was invited to be the Secretary of the Royal Commission on Indian Currency and Finance. Elizabeth Johnson, the editor of the early volumes of Keynes's *CW*, sums up the final report as follows: 'The report was a vindication of the gold-exchange standard system; it left no doubt that in the minds of the commissioners the much-urged adoption of a gold currency would not serve the best interests of India' (*CW* XV, p. 269). Although this was no small triumph for the 30-year-old Keynes, it was short-lived. 'The war of 1914–18 put to one side all the Commission's recommendations' (*CW* XV, p. 151).

3.4 The First World War and its aftermath

While the First World War brought monetary progress in India to an abrupt halt, it led to developments in British monetary policy in accord with Keynes's views. Keynes was personally involved in these developments as a senior civil servant in HM Treasury. Britain (as well as other countries) modified its internal gold standard; and the foreign exchange policy turned to exchange management. From 1915, J. P. Morgan was instructed to buy and sell sterling in order to preserve an exchange rate of $4.76.[6] Despite his interest in exchange *mechanisms*, Keynes attached immense importance to the preservation of the sterling–dollar exchange *rate* as the cornerstone of allied finance for the duration of the war. The J. P. Morgan arrangements meant that the short-term rate of interest was freed from its role in preserving the exchange parity, and could, in theory at least, be operated more in accord with the requirements of domestic/wartime policy. He witnessed, for the first time, conflicting views between HM Treasury and the Bank of England about exactly what that policy should be.

At the end of the war, Keynes was put in charge of financial issues for the Versailles peace conference. These responsibilities appear to have left him in the background for the British monetary policy developments at this time: the unpegging of the dollar exchange value of sterling and the introduction of an embargo on gold exports (on 20 March and 1 April 1919 respectively).[7] His official involvement in *any* policy ended with his resignation at the end of the Versailles Conference in June 1919. From then until the start of the Second World War he became a commentator on events and an influential agitator for fuller reform.

Throughout history, financial policy has been prominent in post-war policy debate. The Versailles Conference foreshadowed conferences at Brussels and Genoa, which set in motion a movement towards the re-establishment of a global gold standard.[8] In Britain, the 1918 Cunliffe Committee had already recommended that the UK return to gold at the pre-war parity of $4.86.

3.5   *A Tract On Monetary Reform*

On 11 December 1923, Keynes published his own views on these profoundly important matters as *A Tract on Monetary Reform*. On the one hand, the work was a polemic against the gold standard.[9] On the other, he propounded a positive agenda for domestic and international monetary policy in the light of monetary developments before, during and after the war. The Preface set out his challenge for monetary reform:

We leave saving to the private investor, and we encourage him to place his savings mainly in titles to money. We leave the responsibility for setting production in motion to the business man, who is mainly influenced by the profits which he expects to accrue to himself in terms of money. Those who are not in favour of drastic changes in the existing organ-isation of society believe that these arrangements, being in accord with human nature, have great advantages. But they cannot work properly if the money, which they assume as a stable measuring-rod, is undepend-able. Unemployment, the precarious life of the worker, the disappoint-ment of expectation, the sudden loss of savings, the excessive windfalls to individuals, the speculator, the profiteer – all proceed, in large measure, from the instability of the standard of value.

It is often supposed that the costs of production are threefold, corres-ponding to the rewards of labour, enterprise, and accumulation. But there is a fourth cost, namely risk; and the reward of risk-bearing is one of the heaviest, and perhaps the most avoidable, burden on production. This element of risk is greatly aggravated by the instability of the standard of value. Currency reforms, which led to the adoption by this country and the world at large of sound monetary principles, would diminish the wastes of risk, which consume at present too much of our estate. Nowhere do conservative notions consider themselves more in place than in currency; yet nowhere is the need of innovation more urgent. One is often warned that a scientific treatment of currency questions is impossible because the banking world is intellectually incapable of understanding its own problems. If this is true, the order of society, which they stand for, will decay. But I do not believe it. What we have lacked is a clear analysis of the real facts, rather than ability to understand an analysis already given. If the new ideas, now developing in many quarters, are sound and right, I do not doubt that sooner or later they will prevail. I dedicate this book, humbly and without permission, to the Governors and Court of the Bank of England, who now and for the future have a much more difficult and anxious task entrusted to them than in former days. (*CW* IV, pp. xiv–xv)

After a discussion of the 'evil consequences of instability in the standard of value' (*CW* IV, p. 61) and an examination of exchange rate theory and developments, Keynes turned to policy. He emphasised that the techniques he was advocating were similar to systems that had already developed in an *ad hoc* manner: '. . . a good constructive scheme can be supplied merely by a development of our existing arrangements on more deliberate and self-conscious lines' (*CW* IV, p. 147).

He dismissed the use of gold as an internal standard in no uncertain terms:

Those who advocate the return to a gold standard do not always appreciate along what different lines our actual practice has been drifting. If we restore the gold standard, are we to return also to the pre-war conceptions of bank rate, allowing the tides of gold to play what tricks they like with the internal price level, and abandoning the attempt to moderate the disastrous influence of the credit cycle on the stability of prices and employment? Or are we to continue to develop the experimental innovations of our present policy, ignoring the 'bank ratio' and, if necessary, allowing unmoved a piling up of gold reserves far beyond our requirements or their depletion far below them?

In truth, the gold standard is already a barbarous relic. All of us, from the Governor of the Bank of England downwards, are now primarily interested in preserving the stability of business, prices, and employment, and are not likely, when the choice is forced on us, deliberately to sacrifice these to the outworn dogma, which had its value once, of £3 17s 10½d per ounce. Advocates of the ancient standard do not observe how remote it now is from the spirit and the requirements of the age. A regulated non-metallic standard has slipped in unnoticed. *It exists.* Whilst the economists dozed, the academic dream of a hundred years, doffing its cap and gown, clad in paper rags, has crept into the real world by means of bad fairies – always so much more potent than the good – the wicked ministers of finance. (*CW* IV, pp. 137–8)

Instead, for internal policy, he advocated the use of *credit control*: 'Thus the tendency of today – rightly I think – is to watch and to control the creation of credit and to let the creation of currency follow suit, rather than, as formerly, to watch and to control the creation of currency and to let the creation of credit follow suit' (*CW* IV, p. 146). Implicit in this statement and explicit elsewhere in his book was the ability of the authorities to effect this control: 'In my opinion the control, if they choose to exercise it, is mainly in their own hands' (*CW* IV, p. 144). Cash would, as a consequence, be disengaged from gold:

> The volume of the paper money, on the other hand, would be consequential, as it is at present, on the state of trade and employment, bank-rate policy and the Treasury bill policy. The governors of the system would be bank-rate and Treasury bill policy, the objects of government would be stability of trade, prices, and employment and the volume of paper money would be a consequence of the first (just – I repeat – as it is at present) and an instrument of the second, the precise arithmetical level of which could not and need not be predicted. (*CW* IV, pp. 153–4)

He then looked to *exchange management*:

> I believe that we can go a long way in this direction if the Bank of England will take over the duty of regulating the price of gold, just as it already regulates the rate of discount. 'Regulate', but not 'peg'. The Bank of England should have a buying and selling price for gold, just as it did before the war, and this price might remain unchanged for considerable periods, just as bank rate does. (*CW* IV, pp. 149–50)

The international picture was completed as a world of currency management, with the United States adopting the same arrangements as the United Kingdom; 'other countries' would then base their currencies on sterling or the dollar:

> Their wisest course could be to base their currencies either on sterling or on dollars by means of an exchange standard, fixing their exchanges in terms of one or the other (though preserving, perhaps, a discretion to vary in the event of a serious divergence between sterling and dollars), and maintaining stability by holding reserves of gold at home and balances in London and New York to meet short-period fluctuations, and by using bank rate and other methods to regulate the volume of purchasing power, and thus to maintain stability of relative price levels, over longer periods. (*CW* IV, pp. 159–60)

The role of gold in all countries would thus be as an international reserve. He saw these developments as inevitable for a monetary economy: '[a]nd – most important of all – in the modern world of paper currency and bank credit there is no escape from a "managed" currency, whether we wish it or not; . . . ' (*CW* IV, p. 136). Just as bank money required domestic control, it also required international control.

For Keynes, the agenda of the Cunliffe Committee and other supporters of the gold standard was long dead: 'The Cunliffe Report belongs to an extinct and an almost forgotten order of ideas. Few think on these lines now; yet the Report remains the authorised declaration of our policy, and the Bank of England and the Treasury are said still to regard it as their marching orders' (*CW* IV, p. 153).

3.6 The failed return to gold

The sureness and optimism of his analysis were quickly shattered. Between January and December 1924 the Labour Party formed a government for the first time in British history. One of their first acts was to implement the recommendations of the Cunliffe Committee. Notwithstanding a change of government, on 28 April 1925 Winston Churchill, as Chancellor, took Britain back on a full internal gold standard. Notes would be exchangeable for gold according to the historic rate of £3 17s 10½d per ounce. As Keynes predicted, preserving the exchange rate required a sustained high Bank rate which meant high unemployment for the rest of the decade.

The final throes of British gold standard membership are well known: the publication of the Macmillan Report (see Section 3.7), the July 1931 European banking crisis, the publication of what has become known as the 'alarmist' May Committee Report demanding public expenditure cuts of £97 million,[10] the fall of the Labour Government and the advent of the 'National' government on 24 August. Despite his previous stance, throughout these events, Keynes held to gold. But on 10 September 1931, in an *Evening Standard* article, Keynes went public '. . . devaluation, which I personally now believe to be the right remedy' (*CW* IX, p. 242). On 26 September, under the title: 'The end of an epoch', *The Economist* described the suspension of British membership of the gold standard:

It is safe to predict that Monday, September 21, 1931, will become a historic date; the suspension of the gold standard in Great Britain on that day, after six years of painful effort which followed the country's return to gold in 1925, marks the definite end of an epoch in the world's financial and economic development.

On 5 April 1932, in the Preface to the foreign edition of his *Treatise on Money*, Keynes dismissed gold in decisive terms:

Since the publication of the English edition of my book in the autumn of 1930, sensational events have occurred in the world of affairs. The historic gold standard, which had been restored after the war at such heavy pains and costs, has been broken into fragments, and it is unlikely that it will ever be put together again in the old mould. When I wrote my book I was far from optimistic, but thought it right to pay due deference to the *de facto* arrangements of the world. I felt that the leading central banks would never voluntarily relinquish the then existing forms of the gold standard; and I did not desire a catastrophe sufficiently violent to shake them off voluntarily. (*CW* V, p. xx)

As Keynes wrote this, policymakers had finally begun to follow policies that accorded with his advice. This was the true era of Keynes's policy.

3.7   The development of Keynes's theory to the *Treatise*

While the *Treatise* did develop Keynes's policy proposals from the position set out in the *Tract*, it was more important as the start of his substantial theoretical analysis. Keynes at last recognised that his policy initiatives lacked theoretical justification: 'The new book on Monetary Theory which I have in preparation will, I am hopeful, throw much new light on my fundamental arguments in favour of the dogmas to which I have rashly given utterance without sufficiently substantiating them.' [11]

Up to the *Treatise*, Keynes's contributions had been limited to a commentary on the development of monetary theory and an articulation of policy consequence. This work showed him to be Marshall's true successor in two basic ways. First, he dedicated himself to pursuing the monetary theories and practical application that he considered Marshall had begun to open up. Second, while giving front place to these monetary developments, Keynes remained wedded to an underlying Marshallian or classical 'long run'.

Both of these perspectives are illustrated by his commentaries in the 1910s. One of his earliest contributions was a review of Irving Fisher's *The Purchasing Power of Money* (1911). In part, Keynes gave high praise for the articulation of the processes of credit that he considered had only been expressed orally in England. But Keynes did not shirk criticism and controversy, and argued that a fuller treatment of the transmission mechanism between credit and prices was required:

Professor Fisher's book is marked, as all his books are, by extreme lucidity and brilliance of statement. It is original, suggestive, and, on the whole, accurate; and it supplies a better exposition of monetary theory than is available elsewhere....

The most serious defect in Professor Fisher's doctrine is to be found in his account of the mode by which through transitional stages an influx of new money affects prices. The following is an abbreviated account (in his own words, though the italics are mine) of the theory which he presents in Chapter IV: – Let us begin by assuming a slight initial disturbance such as would be produced by an increase in the quantity of gold. *This, through the equation of exchange, will cause a rise in prices* ... Professor Fisher ... is content with showing by the quantity theory that the new gold *must* raise [prices] somehow (*CW* XI, pp. 376–7).

On the other hand, Keynes was abruptly dismissive of those such as Hobson and A. Mitchell Innes who claimed that the changed nature of money altered fundamental classical 'truths':

> One comes to a new book by Mr Hobson with mixed feelings, in hope of stimulating ideas and of some fruitful criticisms of orthodoxy from an independent and individual standpoint, but expectant also of much sophistry, misunderstanding, and perverse thought. In some of his books the first elements greatly predominate. In his latest work now before us [*Gold, Prices, and Wages*, 1913, London, Methuen], the latter prevail almost throughout. (*CW* XI, p. 388)[12]

> In his theory of money the author of this pamphlet[13] is a follower of H. D. McLeod. The fallacy – if I am right in thinking that this theory of the effect of credit *is* a fallacy – is a familiar one, and it will not be worthwhile to discuss it in this review. (*CW* XI, p. 404)

The *Tract* was a practical work and proposals were justified in the context of an analysis of the undesirable effects of price stability. Very much as many do today, Keynes saw the cycle as inevitable, albeit driven by credit, to be at best mitigated by an appropriate monetary policy. The theoretical substance constituted mainly a re-statement of the quantity theory in the light of credit creation. After publication, Keynes succinctly summed up the crucial points of his argument in a rejoinder to a critique by the LSE economist Edwin Cannan (1924):

> Let me repeat the quantity equation in the form in which I stated it in *A Tract on Monetary Reform* (p. 77 [*CW* IV, p. 63]):

$$n = p(k + rk')$$

> where n = number of units of 'cash' in circulation (defined on p. 83 [*CW* IV, p. 67] as being, in the case of Great Britain, 'note circulation *plus* private deposits at the Bank of England').

p = price of each 'consumption unit', or in other words the index number of prices.

k = number of consumption units, the monetary equivalent of which the public find it convenient to keep in 'cash'.

k' = ditto which the public find it convenient to keep in bank balances available against cheques.

r = the proportion of their potential liabilities (k') to the public which the banks keep in 'cash'.

Now, the old-fashioned doctrine used to be that if n could be kept reasonably steady, all would be well. My object was to point out that if k and k' were capable of violent fluctuation, steadiness of n might be positively harmful and must be reflected in an extreme unsteadiness of p – this being, in fact, what h as generally happened in booms and depressions of trade (*CW* XI, p. 416).

From the theoretical perspective, the *Tract* took the existence of credit and the credit cycle as given or commonly known. In the *Treatise* he then took a step back and sought to explain and formalise them. The first book contained a detailed and precise analysis of the evolution and nature of money through time. In particular, Keynes discussed in some detail the existence and implications of the evolution from commodity to bank money; he also defined the latter more fully as 'representative money'.[14] In the light of his new terminology, he then offered the unambiguous statement of the intent and perspective of his economics that was reproduced at the start of Chapter 2. He recognised that classical economics was relevant only to a commodity money economy; a new theory was necessary for a credit economy.

Keynes's theoretical objective was to build a model of a representative money economy, and to use this to draw practical conclusions for macro-economic management. In terms of the actual theoretical scheme, Keynes argued that the role of credit and the banking system was in the determination of investment: 'By the scale and the terms on which it is prepared to grant loans, the banking system is in a position, under a regime of representative money, to determine – broadly speaking – the rate of investment by the business world' (*CW* V, p. 138). In this way, the short-period outcome of an economy depended on monetary policy. The underlying or long-run Marshallian world was underpinned by a natural rate of interest (that he attributed to Wicksell): 'Thus, the natural rate of interest is the rate at which saving and the value of investment are exactly balanced, so that the price level of output as a whole (Π) exactly corresponds to the money rate of the efficiency earnings of the factors of production' (*CW* V, p. 139). The key processes underpinning the credit cycle were then the behaviour of saving and investment:

Thus, the long-period or equilibrium norm of the purchasing power of money is given by the money rate of efficiency earnings of the factors of production; whilst the actual purchasing power oscillates below or above this equilibrium level according as the cost of current investment is running ahead of, or falling behind, savings. (*CW* V, p. 137)

Even as the book was published, this was all about to change.

3.8 The *Treatise* and official advice

As the end of the British membership of the gold standard unfolded, Keynes had become well positioned to offer his advice on any new policy agenda. From a theoretical perspective, he had formulated and published (October 1931) his *Treatise on Money*. From a more practical angle, official channels for his advice had opened up through the Macmillan Committee and the Economic Advisory Council (EAC).

The Macmillan Committee was set up (in June 1929) by the second Labour Government against the backdrop of the economic depression of the 1920s and the associated political pressures:

> There had for years been a demand for such an enquiry, and this had not been confined to Labour circles. From the moment of Keynes's onslaught in *The Economic Consequences of Mr. Churchill*, the gold standard policy had been widely held to have sacrificed the interests of industry and trade, if not actually to the benefit of the financial community, at least for the sake of a fetish of that community. This criticism was voiced for example by Sir Alfred Mond, a leading industrialist who had been one of Lloyd George's Ministers. In 1928 Mond with the Trade unionist Ben Turner took the lead in an unofficial but significant 'Conference on Industrial Reorganisation and Industrial Relations', and this conference urged the Chancellor to institute an enquiry into monetary policy. The suggestion was from 1927 onwards ventilated by McKenna in speeches and in his *Midland Bank Review*, especially in the context of the legislation then in process on amalgamation of the note issue. (Sayers, 1976, p. 360)

On 5 November 1929 the Chancellor of the Exchequer appointed the 'Committee on Finance and Industry' with the following terms of reference:

> To inquire into banking, finance and credit, paying regard to the factors both internal and international which govern their operation, and to make recommendations calculated to enable these agencies to promote the development of trade and commerce and the employment of labour. (*CW* XX, p. 17)

As Sayers (1976, p. 360) puts it, '. . . the Bank for the first time in living memory faced a public enquiry into the full range of its activities'. The membership of the Committee drew on leading figures from finance, academia, journalism, politics, industry and the trade union movement.[15] The first meeting was on 21 November 1929. Keynes was to have the starring role; his own presentation to the Committee of the argument that was emerging in his *Treatise* began on 24 February 1930 and lasted several days.

In the *Treatise*, Keynes had already moved away from the notion that the gold standard was the root cause of all economic ills. In terms of practical policy, the analysis of the *Treatise* finally gave front place to the rate of interest, both as cause and as solution to the problems facing Britain and the world.

> I am writing these concluding lines in the midst of the world-wide slump of 1930...
>
> Thus I am lured on to the rash course of giving an opinion on contemporary events which are too near to be visible distinctly; namely, my view of the root causes of what has happened, which is as follows.
>
> The most striking change in the investment factors of the post-war world compared with the pre-war world is to be found in the high level of the market-rate of interest. (*CW* VI, p. 377)

His argument was that the level of investment activity depended on the long-term rate of interest, over which the authorities had a degree of control. This control followed because a divergence could open up between market and classical 'natural' rates of interest; under such conditions policymakers could and should act to bring the market rate back into line. The flaw of the gold standard remained that it restricted the room for domestic monetary policy manoeuvre; *but the appropriate domestic monetary policy action had now been more accurately identified.*

In terms of specific domestic action Keynes suggested that long-term rates of interest could be brought down by central bank purchases of securities *à outrance* (*CW* VI, p. 331). For international action he continued to recommend and build on his argument for currency management.

His presentations of his theory impressed fellow members of the Committee and, as Sayers (1976, p. 363) puts it, 'the printed evidence and report show it was dominated by Keynes'. Towards the end of the drafting, comments from his fellow Committee member Robert Brand led to an important response by Keynes (dated 7 April 1931) – perhaps offering his sharpest and most concise analysis of the Economic Problem to date:

> This memorandum brings home to me what I was beginning to forget, namely that I have nowhere introduced into my draft chapters in any clear or emphatic form what *I* believe to be the fundamental explanation of the present position. I felt, I think, when I was drafting that this was rather a personal theory of my own and that some members of the Committee might be more inclined to agree with my practical conclusions than with my fundamental reasons. Hence, what has resulted is a semi-suppression of the latter. But Brand points out in effect how lame the result is. For unless my general explanation is more or less on the right lines, it is not clear that it is feasible for central banks to do what I am asking them to do ...

My fundamental explanation is, of course, that the rate of interest is too high, – meaning by the 'rate of interest' the complex of interest rates for all kinds of borrowing, long and short, safe and risky. A good many of Brand's factors I should accept as part of the explanation *why* interest rates are high, e.g. effects of the War, post-war instability, reparations, return to gold, mal-distribution of gold, want of confidence in debtor countries etc., etc....

Next comes the question of how far central banks can remedy this. In ordinary times the equilibrium rate of interest does not change quickly, so long as slump and boom conditions can be prevented from developing; and I see no insuperable difficulty in central banks controlling the position ... The drastic reduction of the whole complex of market-rates of interest presents central banks with a problem which I do not expect them to solve unless they are prepared to employ drastic and even direct methods of influencing long-term investments which, I agree with Brand, they had better leave alone in more normal times....

But I should not be surprised if five years were to pass by before hard experience teaches us to get hold of the right end of the stick. (*CW* XX, pp. 272–3)

While the Report inevitably involved some compromise, and a number of addendum reports were added by various sub-groups of the Committee's members, the overall direction was clear:

[In] the case of our financial, as in the case of our political and social, institutions we may well have reached the stage when an era of conscious and deliberate management must succeed the era of undirected natural evolution. (Cmd. 3897, p. 5, para. 9)

The other channel for Keynes's advice opened up in parallel to the Macmillan deliberations. The Council of Economic Advisers was established following Ramsey MacDonald's invitation to a number of leading figures to submit memos and then to meet to discuss (on 2 December 1929) 'the current industrial situation and ways of improving the advice available to government' (*CW* XX, p. 17). The group met for a second time on 9 December and this time their deliberations centred 'much more on the type of body and the kinds of economic advice the Government needed' (*CW* XX, pp. 22). Keynes set out proposals in a memorandum, *Economic General Staff* (*CW* XX, pp. 22–7); these proposals underpinned the formal creation of the EAC. On 22 January 1930, the Prime Minister formally announced the creation of the EAC with the following remit:

To advise His Majesty's government in economic matters, to make continuous study of developments in trade and industry and in the use of national and imperial resources, of the effect of legislation and fiscal policy at home and abroad and of all aspects of national, imperial and international economy with a bearing on the prosperity of the country. (*CW* XX, p. 28)

Over the next years, an extensive sub-committee structure evolved. It was through this structure that Keynes put forward his explicit policy advice and, more generally and substantially, that the hegemony of economic policy passed from the hands of the Bank of England to HM Treasury. The sub-committee of longest-lasting importance was the Committee for Economic Information (CEI); but the most important immediate issues fell to the sub-committee on Financial Questions.

3.9   The post-gold advice

On 26 November 1931, Keynes was brought into the sub-committee on Financial Questions. The immediate context was the sharp rising of Bank rate that had been perceived as necessary to support sterling following the departure from gold. There were four lines of policy response: exchange policy (3.9.1), Bank rate policy (3.9.2), long-term interest rate policy (3.9.3) and capital control (3.9.4).

3.9.1   Exchange policy

The most important discussions first concerned exchange policy. Keynes set events in motion following a specific request from F. W. Leith-Ross.[16] His memorandum of 16 November 1931, 'Notes on the Currency Question', constituted a detailed discussion of exchange policy and formed the basis for committee and wider HM Treasury discussions. The end result was the announcement in the April 1932 Budget of the Exchange Equalisation Account (EEA) which put into effect the currency management policies that Keynes had long advocated. Under its arrangements, the sterling exchange rate was to be managed by intervention in the foreign exchange markets rather than by manipulation of Bank rate. On the day following the announcement, Keynes published an article in the *Evening Standard*:

> The Chancellor's announcement of the Exchange Equalisation Account was the most interesting and important thing in his speech. His proposal furnishes a means, supplementary to the Issue Department of the Bank of England, for acquiring resources for the management of the sterling exchange.
> It also makes it clear that the ultimate profit or loss from the managing a fluctuating exchange is the affair of the Treasury and not of the Bank of England, which is entirely as it should be.

The plan is excellent and should make us once more master in our own house, which in some recent weeks we were not.

The Macmillan Committee pointed out that the resources of the Bank of England might not prove large enough in an emergency for dealing with the huge globus of loose money, pertaining to exchange speculators and international safety-firsters, which flops about the world in these days, embarrassing now this banking system and now that.

But the Chancellor of the Exchequer's supplementary fund of £150,000,000[17] should enable us to maintain the sterling exchange at whatever figure we deliberately decide to be in our best interest, and not according to the whim of the foreign speculator. (*CW XXI*, p. 104)

Over the next months, the 'Sterling Area' came into existence as country after country left the gold standard, adopted currency management arrangements and pegged their exchange rates to sterling. Even as early as June 1932, Richard Hopkins[18] was observing how the 'greater part of the world' had 'managed exchange currencies'.[19]

3.9.2 Bank rate

In parallel to the exchange discussions, and even before the EEA was established, Keynes had already begun to advocate interest rate cuts – this would become known as the *cheap-money policy*. On 10 February 1932, he contributed 'Supplementary Draft Paragraphs' for the Report of the Committee on Financial Questions. The memorandum proposed a summary paragraph, commencing as follows:

31. We may summarise our conclusions as follows:
(i) we are of opinion that the position of sterling is fundamentally sound, and that it is likely to develop considerable latent strength in the near future.
(ii) we are of opinion that the time has come when a policy of gradually reducing Bank Rate might safely and advantageously be pursued.[20]

On 18 February 1932, a cut of Bank rate to 5 from 6 per cent marked the start of the cheap-money policy and the start of Keynes's material impact on economic policy. With the freedom of domestic monetary action permitted by the EEA, further Bank rate cuts followed rapidly. As Figure 3.1 shows, economic activity in the 1930s and 1940s was subsequently conducted at a Bank rate of 2 per cent.

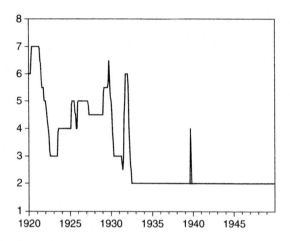

Figure 3.1   British Bank rate, 1920–50

3.9.3   Long-term interest rates

Keynes's theoretical analysis gave the greatest importance to the long-term rate of interest. In July 1932, the authorities' faith in this notion was indicated by the great conversion of the war debt from 5 to 3½ per cent.

It is not known whether the action was originally proposed by Keynes or by officials. The action had a precedent: between 1887 and 1889 the Chancellor, Goschen, converted Consols from 3 to 2¾ per cent and then to 2½ per cent. Other sources are not particularly helpful. Skidelsky (1992, p. 433) appears to depict Keynes as a spectator: 'He applauded Chamberlain's conversion of £2 bn of 5 per cent war loan . . . '. Keynes certainly offered advice and presumed that such an operation would take place. First, in his 16 November 1931 sterling paper, he argued that the burden of national debt should be rejected as a valid criterion for the setting of the sterling rate: ' . . . partly because it would be so much more satisfactory to deal with it mainly by conversions based on a fall in the rate of interest' (*CW* XXI, p. 25).[21] Second, in his *Evening Standard* piece on the EEA, he went on to discuss the conversion: 'But I am not sorry that Mr Chamberlain has refrained from putting out a definite conversion project as a feature of his Budget. For there is more to be lost by the Treasury being premature in this matter than by its waiting too long' (*CW* XXI, p. 106).

The operation was announced in the House of Commons on 30 June (it was accompanied by the final cut of Bank rate to 2 per cent and by the introduction of an embargo on overseas loans – see Section 3.9.4). Keynes produced an analysis of the operation for the CEI that was later reproduced in the September 1932 *EJ*. This analysis effectively constituted Keynes's first statement to the academic community on the development of the cheap-money policy. He applauded the conversion and emphasised the importance of action on the long-term rate:

A reduction of the long-term rate of interest to a low level is probably the most necessary of all measures if we are to escape from the slump and secure a lasting revival of enterprise. The successful conversion of the War Loan to a 3½ per cent basis is, therefore, a constructive measure of the very first rate importance. For it represents a direct attack upon the long-term rate, much more effective in present circumstances than the indirect attack of cheap short-term money, useful and necessary though the latter is. (*CW* XXI, p. 114)

Keynes went on to recommend other measures aimed at ensuring that the effect of the conversion was not just a 'flash in the pan'. In particular, Keynes argued for the extension of the range of securities that the Government issued: 'It is important that the market should be supplied with securities of different types and maturities in the proportions in which it prefers them' (*CW* XXI, p. 115); specifically he advocated the issue of '. . . a short-dated bond at a lower rate of interest than 3½ per cent some time in the autumn or winter' (*CW* XXI, p. 116). These proposals were vital elements of a debt-management policy aimed at lowering the rate of interest by providing securities in order to keep the public as liquid as it chose to be. The degree of consensus that the cheap-money policy had achieved was illustrated by the response of *The Economist* (1 October 1932): '. . . we find ourselves in agreement with Mr Keynes' expectations of very "cheap" money for some time to come'.

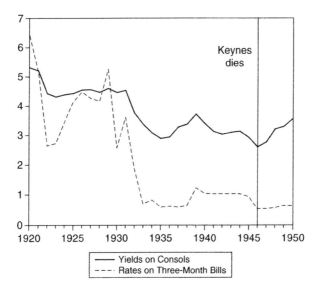

Figure 3.2 Interest rates on British Government bonds and bills, 1920–50
Source: Friedman and Schwartz (1982, Table 4.9).

Over the next years, policymakers began an *ad hoc* (and not wholly enthusiastic or consistent) reduction of interest rates across the range of maturities (Figure 3.2).

3.9.4   Capital control

Lastly, the manoeuvres on long-term rates of interest were supported by what was known at the time as the 'embargo on overseas loans'. This capital control policy remained in force for roughly the next 50 years. As will be elaborated later, the issue of a low interest rate long-term bond in Britain was aided by preventing British investors purchasing higher-rate instruments issued by other countries.

3.10   Worldwide monetary reform

During the Great Depression, Keynes's arguments for monetary reform reverberated across the world. As in Britain, economic and political developments went hand in hand. The start of the story for the major economies – namely Europe and the United States – was a dogmatic adherence to gold.

The first developments of great significance were in Germany: 'Germany was the first country to be hit by the depression; she reached her post-war industrial peak in 1929 . . . she already had two million unemployed in 1929, which grew to six million by the end of 1931' (Moggridge in *CW* XVIII, p. 351). German discount rates were reduced following the Wall Street Crash, as in other major economies, but the currency turmoil of the early 1930s forced interest rates back up (Figure 3.3). The discount rate briefly reached a peak of 12 per cent, and then was pulled back only as far as 8 per cent.

On 7–8 December 1931, the 'Bruning Emergency Decree', proposing reductions in both interest rates and wages, was enacted by President Von Hindenberg. A month later (on 6 January 1932) Keynes gave a lecture to the International Economic Society of Hamburg, not only in the wake of this decree but also as British cheap money and currency management plans were taking shape. Against the backdrop of a global debt crisis and the trend towards protectionism ('Where and how is this ghastly internecine struggle to stop?') he propounded his agenda for monetary reform; he saw Germany leaving gold as an inevitability:

> If Great Britain had somehow contrived to maintain her gold parity, the position of the world as a whole today would be considerably more desperate than it is, and default much more general.
>
> Moreover, I consider it most probable that further currencies will join the sterling group in the course of 1932. In particular, South

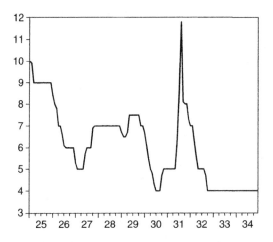

Figure 3.3 German discount rate, 1925–34

Africa, Germany and the Central European countries, and quite possibly . . . Holland . . . At any rate, when the various negotiations now afoot have reached their conclusions, some mitigation of the present strain of deflation and taxation upon the German people will surely be unavoidable. (*CW* XXI, pp. 41–3)

On 11 January, Keynes had a one-hour interview with Chancellor Heinrich Bruning (*CW* XXI, p. 48). Moggridge implies that Keynes spoke against the deflationary wage policies that had accompanied the first rate cut:

At the meeting, according to his memoirs, Bruning tried to convince Keynes that 'an "inflationary" programme would shake the foundations of any reasonable finance programme in Germany'. (*CW* XVIII, p. 364)

German discount rate cuts resumed in March 1932; and by February 1933 the discount rate had fallen to 4 per cent. But at this point, after a prolonged period of intrigue, Hitler came to power (in April 1933). There would be no more interest rate cuts; and Germany seemingly disengaged itself from the agenda of global monetary reform just as it was about to receive its greatest impetus.

This impetus followed from Franklin Delano Roosevelt's victory in the November 1932 US election. Taking office in March 1933, his inaugural address set out a bold agenda for monetary reform:

Values have shrunken to fantastic levels; taxes have risen; our ability to pay has fallen; government of all kinds is faced by serious curtailment of income; the means of exchange are frozen in the currents of trade; the withered leaves of industrial enterprise lie on every side; farmers find no markets for their produce; the savings of many years in thousands of families are gone.

More important, a host of unemployed citizens face the grim problem of existence, and an equally great number toil with little return. Only a foolish optimist can deny the dark realities of the moment.

Yet our distress comes from no failure of substance. We are stricken by no plague of locusts. Compared with the perils which our forefathers conquered because they believed and were not afraid we have still much to be thankful for. Nature still offers her bounty and human efforts have multiplied it. Plenty is at our doorstep, but a generous use of it languishes in the very sight of the supply. Primarily this is because rulers of the exchange of mankind's goods have failed through their own stubbornness and their own incompetence, have admitted their failure, and have abdicated. Practices of the unscrupulous money changers stand indicted in the court of public opinion, rejected by the hearts and minds of men.

True they have tried, but their efforts have been cast in the pattern of an outworn tradition. Faced by failure of credit they have proposed only the lending of more money. Stripped of the lure of profit by which to induce our people to follow their false leadership, they have resorted to exhortations, pleading tearfully for restored confidence. They know only the rules of a generation of self-seekers. They have no vision, and when there is no vision the people perish.

. . .

Our greatest primary task is to put people to work. This is no unsolvable problem if we face it wisely and courageously. It can be accomplished in part by direct recruiting by the Government itself, treating the task as we would treat the emergency of a war, but at the same time, through this employment, accomplishing greatly needed projects to stimulate and reorganise the use of our natural resources.

. . .

Finally, in our progress toward a resumption of work we require two safeguards against a return of the evils of the old order: there must be a strict supervision of all banking and credits: and investments, so that there will be an end to speculation with other people's money; and there must be provision for an adequate but sound currency. (First Inaugural Address of Franklin D. Roosevelt, 4 March 1933)[22]

Without delay he began a dual programme for the restoration of confidence in the financial system and its transfer from private to public control.[23] His first act was to declare a three-day bank holiday (from 6 to 9 March 1933). Under the Emergency Banking Act (which became law on 9 March), the Reconstruction Finance Corporation[24] was given expanded powers over each bank in the United States to investigate and regulate them and ultimately declare solvency or insolvency. On 20 April 1933, Roosevelt took the United States off the gold standard (see below). Institutionally, he began to centralise power within the Federal Reserve System, but brought that power under Government control. Under the Glass-Steagall Banking Act of 16 June 1933:

- exchange control was vested in the Federal Reserve Board;
- Federal Reserve System banks were required to report on the character and amount of all investments and loans to the Board;
- the payment of interest on demand deposits was forbidden;
- the Federal Reserve Board was granted power to set a maximum rate of interest on time deposits;
- commercial banking was separated from investment banking with commercial banks forbidden to underwrite issues or deal in securities other than those issued by state or local governments; and
- a deposit insurance scheme was introduced. Later this was administered by the Federal Deposit Insurance Corporation (FDIC), which also had regulatory powers.

As Roosevelt took hold of the US situation, preparations were underway for a World Economic Conference. Keynes saw the conference as an opportunity to revive more fully the international economy. He attempted to influence the official British approach through the EAC Committee on International Economic Policy which was set up to prepare for the conference. In public he maintained the momentum for monetary reform, first through the November 1932 publication of his *Essays in Persuasion* (a compilation of his public articles). Second, he published a version of the EAC deliberations as part of a series of articles in *The Times* between 13 and 16 March 1933,[25] and then again as his pamphlet *The Means to Prosperity* (*CW* IX, pp. 335–72). His basic aim was an arrangement as follows:

[B]ank credit should be cheap and abundant. This is only possible if each central bank is freed from anxiety by feeling itself to possess adequate reserves of international money. (*CW* IX, p. 353)

The task of this Conference, as I see it, is to devise some sort of joint action of a kind to allay the anxieties of central banks and to relieve the tension on their reserves, or the fear and expectation of tension. . . . We cannot, by international action, make the horses drink. That is their domestic affair. But we can provide them with water. (ibid., pp. 356–7)

But he was unsuccessful. The official proposals the British delegation brought to the conference were based on the alternative 'Kisch Plan'.[26]

Nevertheless, the conference was outstanding for the confrontation of the financial establishment's undimmed support for gold and Roosevelt's outright rejection of gold. Even before the conference, Roosevelt had thrown the financial establishment into turmoil by his taking the United States off gold in April 1933.[27] But on Friday 30th June 1933 the World Economic Conference issued a document for Roosevelt's signature. The opening article was as follows:

I. The undersigned Governments agree that:
(a) it is in the interests of all concerned that stability in the international monetary field should be attained as quickly as practicable;
(b) that gold should be re-established as the international measure of exchange value . . .
II. The signatory Governments whose currencies are on the gold standard re-assert that it is their determination to maintain the free working of that standard at the existing gold parities within the framework of their respective international monetary laws. (Reproduced in *The Economist*)

On Monday 3rd July 1933, President Roosevelt issued the following message:

I would regard it as a catastrophe amounting to a world tragedy if the great Conference of nations, called to bring about a more real and permanent financial stability and a greater prosperity to the masses of all nations, should, in advance of any serious effort to consider these broader problems, allow itself to be diverted by the proposal of a purely artificial and temporary experiment affecting the monetary exchange of a few nations only. . . . [O]ld fetishes of so-called international bankers are being replaced by efforts to plan national currencies with the objective of giving to those currencies a continuous purchasing power which does not greatly vary in terms of the commodities of modern civilization. (Reproduced in *The Economist*)

Keynes recognised in Roosevelt's action the beginning of a new financial order for the world. The following day he wrote in the *Daily Mail* under the title 'President Roosevelt is magnificently right':

It is important that the general public should understand the broad outline of what has happened in the last week. The story begins with the European attempt to drive a wedge between ourselves and the United States and to link our fortunes to those of the European gold standard countries, by threats of breaking up the Conference.

If common report is correct, the representatives of the Dominions and of India, fortunately at hand in London, immediately waited on the Chancellor of the Exchequer to warn him of the disastrous consequences, so far as they were concerned, of any such commitment . . .

But the President's message has an importance which transcends its origins. It is, in substance a challenge to us to decide whether we propose to tread the old, unfortunate ways, or to explore new paths; paths new to statesmen and to bankers, but not new to thought. For they lead to the managed currency of the future, the examination of which has been the prime topic of post-war economics. . . .

But on the broad political issue – on the things which it should be the business of Presidents and Prime Ministers to understand – he is magnificently right in forcing a decision between two widely divergent policies. The Economic Conference will be a farce unless it brings this divergence to a head. If the opposed parties are not inclined to join issue in public on the fundamental choice which America has presented to the world in unambiguous form, it is much better that the Conference should adjourn.

On the one side we have a group of European countries of great political and military importance, but increasingly segregated from the currents of world trade. They disbelieve in official expansionist policies as a means of restoring economic life. They cling fanatically to their gold perches, though most of them are poised there precariously. . . .

On the other side, the United States of America invites us to see whether without uprooting the order of society which we have inherited we cannot, by the employment of common sense in alliance with scientific thought, achieve something better than the miserable confusion and unutterable waste of opportunity in which an obstinate adherence to ancient rules of thumb has engulfed us. . . . (*CW* XXI, pp. 274–6)

The closing paragraph above emphasised how the world had been driven into two: the so-called 'gold bloc' and those that should be described as the 'monetary reformers'. Moggridge (1992, p. 577) records how later the same day (on 4 July): 'Keynes was to be found at the American Embassy working with Walter Lippmann, Herbert Swope and Raymond Moley on a statement which would justify the President's actions, yet perhaps keep the conference alive and rally the countries outside the gold bloc.' *The Economist* published the telegram that was issued on 5 July:

in the hope of that the United States may be of help to the conference, to whose success and friendly co-operation the President continues to attach the greatest importance . . . There is nothing in our policy inimical to the interest of any other country and we are confident that no other country would seek to embarrass us in the attainment of economic ends required for our economic health.

But the gold bloc simply re-affirmed its faith in the established order, and Roosevelt turned again to domestic policy. The most decisive moves in US financial policy were to follow a Keynes initiative. In December 1933 he wrote a famous 'open letter to the President', which was published in the *New York Times* (on 31 December 1933) and *The Times* (on 2 January):

Dear Mr President,
You have made yourself the trustee for those in every country who seek to mend the evils of our condition by reasoned experiment within the framework of the existing social system.

If you fail, rational change will be gravely prejudiced throughout the world, leaving orthodoxy and revolution to fight it out.

But if you succeed, new and bolder methods will be tried everywhere, and we may date the first chapter of a new economic era from your accession to office . . .

. . .

Thus, as the prime mover in the first stage of the technique of recovery, I lay overwhelming emphasis on the increase of national purchasing power resulting from governmental expenditure which is financed by loans and is not merely a transfer through taxation, from existing incomes. Nothing else counts in comparison with this . . .

. . .

These criticisms do not mean that I have weakened in my advocacy of a managed currency or in preferring stable prices to stable exchanges. The currency and exchange policy of a country should be entirely subservient to the aim of raising output and employment to the right level . . .

. . .

Lastly, you can announce that you will control the dollar exchange by buying and selling gold and foreign currencies at a definite figure so as to avoid wide and meaningless fluctuations, with a right to shift the parities at any time, but with a declared intention only so to do either to correct a serious want of balance in America's international receipts and payments or to meet a shift in your domestic price level relative to prices abroad . . .

. . .

I put in the second place the maintenance of cheap and abundant credit, in particular the reduction of the long-term rate of interest. The turn of the tide in Great Britain is largely attributable to the reduction in the long-term rate of interest which ensued on the success of the conversion of the War Loan . . .

. . .

... I see no reason why you should not reduce the rate of interest on your long-term government bonds to 2½ per cent or less, with favourable repercussions on the whole bond market, if only the Federal Reserve System would replace its present holdings of short-dated Treasury issues by purchasing long-dated issues in exchange. (*CW* XXI, pp. 289–97)[28]

Moggridge cites a letter from Walter Lippmann to Keynes that illustrates the impact of Keynes's initiative:

> I don't know whether you realise how great an effect that letter had, but I am told that it was chiefly responsible for the policy which the Treasury is now quietly but effectively pursuing of purchasing long-term Government bonds with a view to making a strong bond market and to reducing the long term rate of interest. (*CW* XXI, p. 305; see Figure 3.4).

Two weeks after the publication of the letter, on 15 January 1934, President Roosevelt took measures to stabilise the value of the dollar: 'He asked Congress for legislation 'to organise a sound and adequate currency system'. Amongst his proposals was that the President should be empowered to fix the gold value of the dollar at between 50 and 60 per cent of its old value' (Moggridge in *CW* XXI, p. 309). On 30 January 1934 the Gold Reserve Act was passed by Congress, empowering an exchange management fund (of $2600 millions[29]) and fixing the value of the dollar at $35 per ounce (a devaluation of 59 per cent). *The Economist* of 27 January 1934 noted that the measure 'has been described as the most important since the Civil War'.

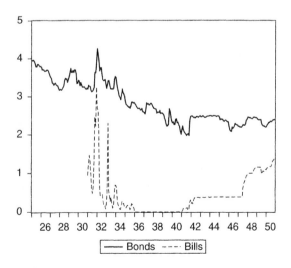

Figure 3.4   Interest rates on US Government debt
Source: NBER macro history database.

At the end of 1934, Roosevelt consolidated his institutional reforms. His own appointee Marriner Eccles took charge of the Federal Reserve on 15 November 1934 (the original Chairman Eugene Meyer had resigned on 10 May 1933 and Eugene R. Black took over in the meantime).[30] Eccles remained at the head of a greatly reformed Federal Reserve System until shortly after Roosevelt's death. The US Banking Act of 1935 was the culmination of the institution of Government control of banking, interest rate and exchange policy:

> The Federal Reserve Board was reconstituted as the Board of Governors of the Federal Reserve System, with the majority of its members being political appointees. Most important was the increase in powers given to the Board. From 1935 the Board had mandatory authority to set the rediscount rate, to change member bank reserve requirements and to regulate loans on securities. The Federal Open Market Committee, which had been established in 1933, was scrapped and a new body, with the same name, but a different membership replaced it. This Committee had complete control over open market operations for the entire banking system ... The power of the Federal Reserve System over monetary policy was centralised and strengthened, as was the power of government over the system. (Fearon, 1987, p. 221)

The Board was entirely replaced by political appointees who mainly took office on 3 February 1936.

In the meantime, on the global stage, the gold standard had begun to unravel completely. On 1 March 1934, Keynes described events in Czechoslovakia in a letter to Walter Case:

> I am told on fairly good authority that they [the gold bloc countries] had a meeting together a few days ago, renewed their oaths and roped themselves together even tighter than before, to give one another mutual support and encouragement to maintain the *status quo*.
>
> . . .
>
> I still, however, think that taking a longer view the gold bloc countries are getting themselves into an untenable position. Sooner or later domestic political events in one or other of the countries will force their hands. The recent devaluation in Czechoslovakia involved the resignation of Pospiscil, the Governor of the State Bank, and all his board, they having nailed their colours to the gold mast. But that did not prevent political pressure from prevailing. So I feel it is bound to be sooner or later with one or other of Holland, Switzerland, Italy, Belgium or France. . . .
> (*CW* XXI, pp. 317–18)

Belgium came off gold in March 1935. This led to an international conference between 11 and 13 July 1935 sponsored by the Antwerp Chambers of Commerce. Keynes attended this conference and took an active role. He helped refine a draft report by Bertil Ohlin, described by Moggridge (*CW* XXI, p. 356) as 'designed to allow the gold bloc countries to follow Belgium's example and devalue successfully, as well as join a world of fixed but adjustable exchange rates'. He chaired and made a speech at the final session; his notes commence as follows:

> Belgian example great impression on world
> Calmness, moderation and skill of Belgian transition
> Not surprising
> Currency changes much easier than usually supposed
> Indian example
> Effect on gold bloc
> Stupid and obstinate old gentlemen at the Banks of Netherlands and France crucifying their countries in a struggle which is certain to prove futile. (*CW* XXI, p. 356)

Keynes took these events as background for his next commentary on the global monetary scene, which was published in the October 1935 *Lloyds Bank Monthly Review* under the title 'The future of the foreign exchanges'. He re-iterated his arguments for currency management and also advocated a degree of capital control:

> A strict, though not pedantic, control of the rate of new foreign lending, so as to avoid a strain arising out of a serious disproportion between such lending and the accruing foreign balance on income account. Only by this means can we retain a sufficient autonomy over the domestic rate of interest ... Circumstances may well arise in future when that control may have to become stricter, if we accept a very low domestic rate of interest as the only means of preserving full employment in a wealthy community. (*CW* XXI, p. 365).

Equally he emphasised what policy should not involve:

> The reader should notice that I have expressly excluded from my devices changes in Bank rate and in the volume of domestic credit, which were the main instruments of pre-war policy. It is the outstanding lesson of our post-war experience that these methods must be entirely discarded as a means of regulating the exchanges ... It is essential that they should be employed in future with exclusive regard to internal conditions and, in particular, the state of employment. (*CW* XXI, pp. 365–6)

The final chapter of the international gold standard began with the election of Leon Blum's Popular Front government in France. *The Economist* of 9 May 1936 reported their pre-election monetary and banking policies:

The reform of the credit system by means of a new control of banking, an improvement of the public returns made by banks and commercial companies, and a reform of the Bank of France through suppression of the 'Regents,'[31] the nomination of a council representing producers (agriculture, industry and trade), and the creation of new Bank of France stock.

As in the United States, the Governor of the Bank of France M. Tannery 'retired' and M. Labeyrie (previously the Procurator General of the Court of Accounts, a civil servant) replaced him. In July the Regency Council was abolished and a new Board of Governors was drawn that represented society more widely, taking members from the civil service, industry, pressure groups, unions and so on. *The Economist* of 22 August 1936 reported from the first meeting of the new General Council: 'M. Labeyrie ... stressed the duty of the Bank to assure to the full extent of its powers the stability of the Franc and the lowering of interest rates for the benefit of French industry ... [T]he main duty of the Bank will be to carry out and not inspire the Government's monetary policy.'

On 26 September 1936 the French government announced that it planned to devalue the Franc and establish an Exchange Equalisation Fund of 10,000 million francs. *The Economist* of 3 October 1936, under the banner 'the gold bloc falls', noted: ' ... it had been made possible by an act of international co-operation: for the French Government only took the plunge on receiving assurances from Britain and the United States ... that British and American resources would be used to prevent undue exchange disturbances'. The French announcement was accompanied by announcements in the British and United States finance ministries; together these announcements have become known as the *Tripartite Agreement*. The British Statement was as follows:

His Majesty's Government, after consultation with the United States Government and French Government, join with them in affirming a common desire to foster those conditions which will safeguard peace and will best contribute to the restoration of order in international economic relations, and to pursue a policy which will tend to promote prosperity in the world and to improve the standard of living ... His Majesty's Government ... declare their intentions to continue to use the appropriate available resources so as to avoid as far as possible any disturbance of the basis of international exchanges resulting from the proposed readjustment ... [they] desire and invite the co-operation of other nations to realise the policy laid down in the present declaration. (Reproduced in *The Economist*, 3 October 1936)

With the gold bloc leaderless, its total collapse was now inevitable. On 26 September the Swiss Federal Council declared that a decision was taken in favour of devaluation. On 28 September, Dr Colijn from the Bank of the Netherlands announced the establishment of a managed currency and equalisation fund and devalued the Guilder by 15–20 per cent. Similarly the Greek, Latvian and Turkish Governments announced that they had decided to devalue and link their currencies to Sterling. Germany remained outside; Schacht, the President of the Reichsbank, announced that he did not intend to devalue the German currency nor join the Tripartite arrangement.

The collapse of the gold standard was complete; Britain and the United States were at the centre of a new managed exchange and monetary policy system that was subservient to Government and aimed primarily at domestic employment policy.

3.11 The *General Theory* of monetary reform

The *General Theory* was in part a new statement of the theoretical case for monetary reform. The collapse of gold and the subsequent policy initiaftives detailed above reflected the growing influence of Keynes's ideas, but there were many who resisted. In Britain, the financial community and the Bank of England, as well as a number of academic economists, Treasury economists, Treasury civil servants and fellow members of the EAC were less than wholehearted in their response to Keynes's initiatives. On the global stage, as discussed in the previous section, countries only left gold when political pressure became overwhelming. A hard core, the 'gold bloc', was resolute until 1935; France only devalued after the election of the Popular Front government in 1936. From an even wider economic policy perspective, fascism might be regarded as an extreme economic solution to the failure of gold and the global economic crisis. Keynes explicitly presented fascist policy as rival to his own discussion: '[t]he authoritarian state systems of today seem to solve the problem of unemployment at the expense of efficiency and freedom' (*CW* VII, p. 381).

Here was Keynes as rationalist. He believed that he had merely to convince his critics of the rightness of his theoretical case in order for his practical position to prevail.

In theoretical terms, the main innovations of the *General Theory* arose from the rejection of the classical theory of interest. The detail of Keynes's analysis waits until Part II of this book. Here the differences between the classical and liquidity preference theories of interest and activity are sketched in only elementary outline.

The classical theory has the rate of interest determined by saving and investment:

Rate of interest determines equilibrium between savings and investment. If people become more willing to save and therefore willing to accept a lower rate of interest, a corresponding increase of investment takes place. Thus a greater willingness to save causes and is indispensable to more investment. Here virtue of saving. (*CW* XXVII, p. 388)

Keynes's theory of liquidity preference has the rate of interest determined as an equilibrium between the demand for money as a store of value (or liquidity preference schedule) and the supply of money as a store of value.[32] The level of investment was then determined by the marginal efficiency of capital (MEC) schedule and the rate of interest. In Keynes's theory, the determination of interest and investment was sequential, not simultaneous as it was (and is) in the Classical theory. Finally, the level of investment was incorporated into a theory of aggregate demand that explained output and employment through the multiplier and the conditions of supply.

From the secular monetary policy perspective, this theory demonstrated that a low rate of interest was necessary for a high level of activity and employment, as well as to mitigate the effects of the economic cycle. Critical to the *General Theory* was the notion of uncertainty: the MEC and liquidity preference schedules would shift with changing expectations of the future.

The practical conclusion of the theory of liquidity preference was that the authorities could intervene in the market for liquidity in order to manipulate the rate of interest to the desired low level. In practice this control depended on debt-management, monetary and international policies that the British authorities had been experimenting with throughout the 1930s. The wider policy conclusion of the *General Theory* went beyond that of his *Treatise*. Cheap money was no longer a necessity of circumstance, but *the essential ingredient* for prosperous economic activity.

While Keynes continued a voluminous private correspondence with the vast range of commentators on the *General Theory*, his published response was very measured. There were only three substantial theoretical initiatives in the first two and a half years after publication. The first was a paper that began as a lecture 'Further reflections on liquidity preference' to the Stockholm Economic Club in autumn 1936. In 1937, it was published as 'The theory of the rate of interest' in *The Lessons of Monetary Experience: Essays in Honor of Irving Fisher* (*CW* XIV, pp. 101–8). The second was the February 1937 *Quarterly Journal of Economics* article that much later became the basis of the post-Keynesian emphasis on uncertainty (*CW* XIV, pp. 109–23). Third, Keynes entered into a debate about the difference between loanable funds and liquidity preference theories of interest in the *EJ* between 1937 and 1938 – the 'alternative theories' debate (loanable funds was the rival neoclassical theory advocated by Robertson and then the 'Keynesians'; it is examined in detail in Chapters 4 and 7). As will be discussed in Chapter 5, Keynes did not dwell on policy implications of his argument in the *General Theory*. Similarly, the subsequent theoretical initiatives almost entirely avoided policy implications except insofar as they were primarily concerned with the interest rate dimension of his theory. Instead, Keynes addressed policy through more public channels: first through his annual speeches as Chairman of National Mutual Life Assurance and then in a series of articles in *The Times* that then formed the basis for a Committee of Economic Information Report.

The necessity for further consolidation of cheap money was the central message of all of Keynes's National Mutual speeches. Different speeches gave emphasis to different policy mechanisms. For example, in both 1936 and 1937 his concern was the need for the authorities to issue shorter-term bonds:

> But it is confidence in the future of short-term rates which is required to bring down long-term rates. Now the policy of the Treasury is not calculated to promote such confidence. They seem reluctant to issue bonds of from five to 10 years' maturity and anxious to reduce the short-term debt, in spite of the extraordinary cheapness with which it can be carried. (19 February 1936, *CW* XXI, p. 375)

His *Times* series (published between 12 and 14 January 1937) was entitled 'How to avoid a slump'. His subject was the prevention of excess demand under the new conditions with the rejection of the traditional monetary weapon. In two passages that have been quoted earlier in Chapter 1, he asserted the fundamental points that dear money should be avoided like 'hell-fire' and that the monetary authorities could be 'masters' of the long-term rate of interest.

Moggridge (1992, p. 605) notes that the recommendations in this article then went on to 'serve as the basis for the Committee of Economic Information's 22nd report of February 1937, "Employment policy and the maintenance of trade activity"'. Sir Richard Hopkins, the Permanent Secretary to the Treasury, added the following handwritten observation to the front of a minute concerning this Report by another Treasury official: 'It is interesting to see how profoundly the EAC committee diffused among themselves Mr Keynes's thesis that the Treasury can continue to govern the general state of interest at its will.'[33]

In May 1937, Keynes had the first of his heart attacks, and his official and public policy interventions were much reduced (although by no means did they cease). On 23 February 1938, he made one of his first public appearances for what would be his last speech as the Chairman of the National Mutual. He focused on the rise in long-term rates that had occurred while he was indisposed (see Figure 3.2). His philosophy of action that closed the speech is of much importance:

> A great deal is at stake. We are engaged in defending the freedom of economic life in circumstances which are far from favourable. We have to show that a free system can be made to work. To favour what is known

as planning and management does not mean a falling away from the moral principles of liberty which could formerly be embodied in a simpler system. On the contrary, we have learnt that freedom of economic life is more bound up than we previously knew with the deeper freedoms – freedom of person, of thought, and of faith. (*CW* XXI, p. 446)

3.12   The Second World War and after

As war approached, Keynes fixed his attention on the financial policy necessary to support the anticipated great increases in public expenditure. In April 1939 he wrote two articles for *The Times* arguing that the Chancellor should not borrow at a rate of interest in excess of $2^1/_2$ per cent and should be willing to accept a large increase in the share of floating debt. At the end of May 1939, he sent a developed version of the argument to the Chancellor and the Governor of the Bank of England; although at this stage he was advocating 3 per cent (*CW* XXI, pp. 533–46). In July 1939, he published two more articles in *The Times* outlining the debt-management techniques that would be necessary to effect the setting of rates (*CW* XXI, pp. 551–64).

With the end of the 'phoney war', Keynes returned to the Treasury for the first time since the Versailles Conference and became directly involved with the policy that he had advocated (the agreed rate was 3 per cent). Over the next years, the authorities developed the specific instruments, arrangements and polices that permitted the full control that Keynes had long seen as possible:

- the 'tap issue' policy for government debt sales and extending the range of securities on offer. Rates of interest and maturities were announced but no limits were set to the cash amount of any issue. The 'tap' of any bond was held open so that individuals and institutions could purchase when and whatever quantities they desired (a notice read 'subscriptions will be received on Tuesday, 25th June, 1940, and thereafter until further notice . . .'). The method was first introduced for the June 1940 wartime issue of $2^1/_2$ per cent medium-term bonds (known as National War Bonds), and then for the next issue of 3 per cent long-term bonds (known as Savings Bonds).[34]
- a change in attitude to the floating debt and also an extension of the instruments on offer. As will be discussed in Chapter 7, setting rates of interest meant accepting a large increase in the volume of floating debt. The Treasury developed Treasury Deposit Receipts (TDRs), which had a six-month maturity and slightly higher interest rate than Treasury bills. These were not reservable against cash at the central bank, and hence helped the authorities control credit creation in spite of an increase in floating debt.
- Bank rate remaining unused as an instrument of day-to-day monetary policy.

In the international context, domestic monetary policy was supported by the ongoing embargo on overseas loans and full exchange control. The authorities managed the 'three per cent war' with ease. Keynes's theory had been vindicated: it had been proven that the rate of interest could be controlled; and, furthermore, that control had been achieved under the most severe financial conditions imaginable. Equally, the classical notion of 'crowding out', that high government borrowing would lead to high rates of interest, was proven false.

The wartime developments formed the background to Keynes's most substantial formalisation of his domestic monetary and debt-management policies at the April/May 1945 National Debt Enquiry (NDE). This enquiry arose as the Coalition Government began to look to economic policy after the war; the specific issue being the measures available for reducing the post-war burden of national debt interest. But the scope was much wider: at these meetings, Keynes was offered the opportunity to discuss all aspects of post-war policy, in particular the continuation of cheap-money policy:

> Hopkins was soon persuaded that there was a case for an early inquiry by a committee of officials and economists, which would also consider the future of the cheap money policy. On the last subject, Hopkins noted, 'Lord Keynes has promised to produce ... some far-reaching proposals.' (Howson, 1993, p. 45, by permission of Oxford University Press)

At these meetings, Keynes outlined his economic theory and put forward a complete framework of practical debt and money management measures, based on the mechanisms developed in war, that would facilitate a cheap-money policy after the war. He set out specific proposals for rates of interest across the spectrum as follows:

(c) ... 5-year Exchequer Bonds at $1\frac{1}{2}$ per cent and 10-year Bonds at 2 per cent on tap, a new series to be started annually;

(d) 3 per cent Savings Bonds on tap, a new series to be started annually, with an option to the Treasury to repay after 10 years and with, preferably, no final maturity (or, if necessary, a fixed latest date of repayment 35 years hence). (*CW* XXVII, p. 399)

These proposals went on to underpin the cheap-money policy of the post-war Labour Government under its successive Chancellors: Hugh Dalton, Sir Stafford Cripps and Hugh Gaitskell. The official report of the enquiry (by Hopkins) constitutes the handbook of practical policy measures that the *General Theory* deliberately was not (it is reproduced as Appendix 3.1).

Turning to international policy, on the one hand the Second World War had interrupted the development of the currency management approach.

But on the other, it seemingly offered the opportunity to start from first principles. In the course of international summits relating to post-war economic
policy, President Roosevelt offered Keynes the opportunity to develop a
financial architecture for the world 'that excluded nothing in advance'.[35]
A few weeks later, Keynes described his plans to the head of the British Civil
Service, Sir Horace Wilson:

> I have been spending some time since I came back in elaborating a truly
> international plan . . . we should do well to start from some such proposal
> as that which I have prepared or a variant of it, even though we may feel
> that it is probably too international and too Utopian to take form just in
> that shape in the real world. (19 September 1941, *CW* XXIII, p. 209)

The essential mechanism of his plan for an 'International Clearing Union'
was outlined in a letter to the Governor of the Bank of England:

> The *essence* of the scheme is very simple indeed. It is the extension to
> the international field of the essential principles of *banking* by which,
> when one chap wants to leave his resources idle, those resources are not
> therefore withdrawn from circulation but are made available to another
> chap who is prepared to use them – and to make this possible without
> the former losing his liquidity and his right to employ his own resources
> as soon as he chooses to do so. Just as the domestic situation was trans-
> mogrified in the eighteenth and nineteenth centuries by the discovery
> an adoption of the principles of local banking, so (I believe) it is only
> by extending these same principles to the international field that we can
> cure the manifest evils of the international economy as it existed between
> the two wars, after London had lost the position which had allowed her
> before 1914 to do much the same thing off her own bat. (*CW* XXV,
> pp. 98–9)

The wartime arrangements also led to a formalisation of the closely related
strand of policy on capital control. Official policy in this area had been *ad
hoc* and subject to change; Keynes's own role in any arrangements is not
well documented, but his perspective is clear. At the end of the First World
War, an 'embargo on overseas loans' was in place; this was only repealed
6 months after the return to gold. As noted in Section 3.9, the embargo
was then put back in place for the conversion of the war loan in 1932 and
remained in place from then on. Keynes regarded such capital controls as
essential to his domestic monetary policies for the post-war world:

> You overlook the most fundamental long-run theoretical reason. Freedom
> of capital movements is an essential part of the old *laissez-faire* system and
> assumes that it is right and desirable to have an equalisation of interest

rates in all parts of the world. It assumes, that is to say, that if the rate of interest which promotes full employment in Great Britain is lower than the appropriate rate in Australia, there is no reason why this should not be allowed to lead to a situation in which the whole of British savings are invested in Australia, subject only to different estimations of risk, until the equilibrium rate in Australia has been brought down to the British rate. *In my view the whole management of the domestic economy depends upon being free to have the appropriate rate of interest without reference to the rates prevailing elsewhere in the world.* Capital control is a corollary to this. Both for this reason and for the political reasons given above, my own belief is that the Americans will be wise in their own interest to accept this conception, even though its immediate applicability in their case is not so clear. (*CW* XXV, p. 149, my emphasis)

As he suspected, his proposals were too Utopian for the real world. While the Clearing Union was put forward as the official proposal of the British Government, the primary 'inspiration' for the Bretton Woods Agreement was the rival US Treasury proposals for a 'stabilisation fund'. Keynes's leading role in the negotiations did ensure that the final agreement offered economies a degree of autonomy and flexibility for the post-war era; in particular, Article VI of the Agreement permitted member countries to put into place, or keep in place, capital controls. But Bretton Woods was not the Clearing Union.

The Clearing Union was the culmination of Keynes's work: it applied his *General Theory* and associated practical experience in the widest possible context. These proposals may have been rejected on political grounds; they were *never* rejected or disputed on economic grounds. Indeed the comments on his scheme showed a unanimity of support entirely denied to the *General Theory* – as illustrated by comments from Dennis Robertson and Lord Catto (who would later become Governor of the Bank of England):

I sat up late last night reading your revised 'proposals' with great excitement – and a growing hope that the spirit of Burke and Adam Smith is on earth again to prevent the affairs of a Great Empire from being settled by the little minds of a gang of bank-clerks who have tasted blood (yes, I know this is unfair!). (Robertson to Keynes, 27 November 1941, *CW* XXIII, p. 67)

Now that it has been published, I want to congratulate you on your Clearing Union. I have avoided adding myself to the critics. I felt sure your basic principles were sound and unalterable. I was content to let others, with greater theoretical knowledge than I have, do the criticising. As I expected, the final document does not differ at all in essentials (nor much even in detail) from your very early drafts which I was privileged to see and, if I may say so, to encourage. (Catto to Keynes, 30 April 1943, *CW* XXIII, p. 236)

The proposals remain a legacy for a global market economy that is untested and virtually unknown.

Appendix 3.1 Copy of the National Debt Enquiry Report

The report was drafted by Sir Richard Hopkins, who was about to retire as Permanent Secretary to HM Treasury and be succeeded by Sir E. Bridges (the chair of the Committee passed from the former to the latter with the second meeting). According to the minutes of the meetings, the other civil servants on the Committee were Sir W. Eady, Sir H. Brittain, Sir C. Gregg, Mr Chambers and, as joint secretaries, Mr Cockfield and Mr Shillito; the academics were Lord Keynes, Professor Robbins and Mr Meade.

The copy used for reproduction here was on Treasury file T230/95; it belonged to 'Mr Meade' according to handwriting on front page and was dated 'May 15th 1945' in the same handwriting.

N.D.E. First Report

TOP SECRET

NATIONAL DEBT ENQUIRY – FIRST REPORT
THE QUESTION OF FUTURE GILT-EDGED INTEREST RATES
(For the Chancellor's eye only)

I

1. The matters dealt with in this report are very much in the province of the Bank of England (who have inter alia to manage the market) as well as the Treasury. There should be the greatest possible community of view between the two and we do not contemplate that any of our suggestions in this report should be determined without careful prior consultation.

II

2. We were asked to define more closely an appropriate Treasury policy in regard to cheap money with particular reference to statements in the White Paper on Employment Policy.

3. *Employment White Paper references.* The principal reference in the White Paper is as follows:

"58. In ordinary times the volume of capital expenditure is influenced by movement in the rate of interest. If the cost of borrowing money is high, some projects which are not profitable at that rate will be held back. When it falls again, those projects will be brought forward and others will also be taken in hand.

59. For some time after the end of the war it will be necessary, as explained in paragraph 16, to maintain a policy of cheap money. Thereafter, the possibility of influencing capital expenditure by the variation of interest rates will be kept in view. The experience gained

since 1931 of co-operation in this field between the Treasury and the Bank of England and the Joint Stock Banks will make it possible to operate a concerted and effective monetary policy designed to promote stable employment.

60. Monetary policy alone, however, will not be sufficient to defeat the inherent instability of capital expenditure. High interest rates are more effective in preventing excessive investment in periods of prosperity than are low interest rates in encouraging investment in periods of depression."

4. Paragraph 16, referred to in paragraph 59, includes the following:

"(d) The use of capital will have to be controlled to the extent necessary to regulate the flow and direction of investment. Heavy arrears of capital expenditure on buildings, plant and equipment have to be overtaken, and construction on new development must begin. Without control, therefore, there would be a scramble to borrow, leading to a steep rise in rates of interest. The Government are determined to avoid dear money for these urgent reconstruction needs. In this period, therefore, access to the capital market will have to be controlled in order to ensure the proper priorities."

5. In these passages the emphasis is mainly, though not exclusively, on the rate of interest for long term loans as opposed to Treasury Bill rate and the rates for short term money generally, and the question of engineering a fluctuation of rates after an initial period in the interests of stable employment is tentatively raised.

6. *General desirability of low rates.* There is a wide measure of agreement, though not complete unanimity, in the present Committee in the view that on the whole, subject to the qualification dealt with in paragraphs 11 to 15 below, the desirable ideal for this country for a long time to come is not merely the continuance but even the reduction of the existing relatively low levels of interest rates both for long term and for short.

7. This view is based on two grounds, one economic and the other budgetary.

8. The Economic ground, stated briefly, is as follows. With the passage of time it may become increasingly difficult to match the amount of new investment with the country's will to save at a point sufficiently high to secure good employment. But the amount of new investment will be stimulated – and in a variety of regions materially stimulated – if loan money is cheap and share capital easily attracted on other than onerous terms.

9. The budgetary ground is a simple one. The real burden of the debt is represented – especially from the point of view of the taxpayer who is

primarily concerned, – not by the figure representing its capital amount, but by the annual burden of the interest charge. A rise in the annual burden of interest as a result of increases in rates materialises as debt matures for repayment or new borrowing takes place, but a large part of the increased interest returns to the Government either in the form of income tax or surtax or as interest on national debt which is itself held by public departments. Assuming, for the purpose of this calculation, a total further net borrowing before 1950 of, say, £4,000 millions, a rise in the rate of interest of $1/2\%$ per annum from 1945 onwards on all forms of Government borrowing which would be affected might involve a net additional burden on the budget of the order of £35 millions a year by 1950 and £50 millions a year by 1955.

10. On these two grounds if they stood alone it might come to pass in the course of time that there was no limit, short of an almost nominal figure, to the level to which the desirable rate of interest at any rate on long term might fall. Nevertheless a definitive lower limit might then be set by social and psychological considerations such as the need to foster the habit of thrift – a principle long recognised in the specially favourable terms extended to small savers – and to allow to individuals and to certain types of institutions that measure of independence which an income from interest ensures and which could not conveniently be assured in any other way.

11. *The question of fluctuations.* If it be agreed that low rates are generally to be desired there remains the question whether the low rates should remain as rigid as possible or whether on the contrary within the limits of a range which may be definitely described as low (and even above that limit in certain conditions) fluctuations should be permitted or engineered to act as a brake on temporary economic tendencies whether in an upward or downward direction. If so the further question arises whether these fluctuations would be better confined to the short term issues including the floating debt or should affect also the long term issues.

12. The transition period will be a period in which highly inflationary tendencies will be at work from causes already established. The problem will be increased by the large, though gradual, flood of new purchasing power represented by war gratuities and ultimately by the repayment of the post-war income tax credits. Against the dangers of inflation the measures available are the price and physical controls inherited from wartime, high taxation and high interest rates. In fact the issue ultimately turns of the first of these. If either by misjudgement or owing to the pressure of an unintelligent public opinion the physical controls are prematurely relaxed or if by reason of practical difficulties in new and difficult conditions they fail of their object, the flood gates become open.

13. In these circumstances higher taxation though serving a certain purpose would be inadequate as an alternative defence. Already the prospect held out of modest relaxations has been welcomed with an avidity, and interpreted with a liberality, which is itself disturbing. The excess of the level of taxation which a Government might in gravely inflationary conditions feel obliged to maintain over what it would wish to maintain would not, in the immediately ensuing conditions of extreme liquidity, yield a figure capable of having a sufficient effect. The same applies in considerable measure to high interest rates which moreover, like high taxation, act blindly and without discrimination and, unlike high taxation, with an ill Budgetary effect. Any sharp increase in long term rates involves also a very marked fall in the quotation of existing long-dated stocks. Nor must the psychological effect upon war time savers be omitted from consideration.

14. This argument suggests a certain measure of caution in choosing the time for any important downward steps. Our proposals are set out in paragraphs 30 and 35.

15. In the more distant future after the transitional period the question both as regards taxation and interest rates will arise differently. The physical controls inherited from wartime will no longer be in existence and conditions may arise in which fluctuations particularly in the short term rates are necessary or minor fluctuations generally are intrinsically unavoidable. This is a matter which, it seems, must be handled by trial and error when the time arrives: it is unsuitable for present public discussions unless in very vague and general terms.

16. *Practical possibilities of securing low rates.* While the general desirability of low interest rates may be agreed, the power to secure them may seem much more doubtful. As regards short money the passing of the gold standard and the contemplated permanent control of external capital movements remove the necessity for the use of the short term domestic money rate to maintain the gold stock. Apart from overseas holdings mentioned below, very short money is now chiefly lent by banks and similar large financial institutions, and the history of the past fifteen years, and particularly of the war period, sufficiently indicates the advent of a new era in which the central authorities, given close understandings with the banking and financial world, can expect to exercise control over the rate.

17. Thus the short-term rates on the floating debt in the hands of domestic holders need, subject to these necessary understandings, be no higher (except on the occasions when a stiffening of short-term rates is deemed to be a useful adjunct to other policies, e.g. to a policy of rationing the volume of credit) than is required to give a return adequate to meet

the costs (with an appropriate profit margin) of market and banking machinery. If a special short term rate is required on overseas funds in London this could be arranged as was done at the end of the last war.

18. The long term rate is a more difficult question. It is understood that the following extract from Lord Keynes' work, The General Theory of Employment, Interest and Money (1937 [sic]) page 203, would now command a wide measure of agreement among economists:

> "A monetary policy which strikes public opinion as being experimental in character or easily liable to change may fail in its objective of greatly reducing the long-term rate of interest, because (the amount of cash held to satisfy the 'speculative' motive)[36] may tend to increase almost without limit in response to a reduction in (the rate of interest) below a certain figure. The same policy, on the other hand, may prove easily successful if it appeals to public opinion as being reasonable and practicable and in the public interest, rooted in strong conviction, and promoted by an authority unlikely to be superseded'.

> "It might be more accurate, perhaps, to say that the rate of interest is a highly conventional, rather than a highly psychological[,] phenomenon. For its actual value is largely governed by the prevailing view as to what its value is expected to be. *Any* level of interest which is accepted with sufficient conviction as *likely* to be durable *will* be durable; subject, of course, in a changing society to fluctuations for all kinds of reasons round the expected normal."[37]

19. This passage must be read subject to the underlying assumption that the policy is well within the limits not only of public acceptability (as the text declares) but also of economic commonsense (as the text may be inferred to assume). On this basis the Committee feel justified on the evidence before them in taking the passage as a working guide, and they do so the more readily both because it appears to have been consistent with recent experience in varying conditions and because they know of no other general theory which begins to hold out the same prospect of achieving a very important objective.

20. If this be rightly judged, it will clearly be less difficult to exercise control when the State is a continuous and substantial borrower than when it is not, for in the former case it will be actively setting the pace in the terms which it has continuously on offer. The State has recently assumed extensive new obligations to raise capital required by Local Authorities; it will need to borrow for other purposes connected with employment policy; and there are many large maturities to be dealt with in the next ten years. For all these reasons it is likely that the State will be a large and continuous borrower for at any rate a long time to come.[38]

21. *The question of the method of issuing loans and in particular the funding question.* It does not appear to the Committee that the general objective of controlling the rate of interest would be readily attained, if attained at all, through the issue at varying intervals of large loans for immediate subscription. Rather they consider that for borrowing purposes, usually but not necessarily always including conversion purposes, the technique of tap issues of loans with differing maturities should be continued into peace time.

22. By this method the preference of the public rather than of the Treasury determines the distribution of new debt between different terms and maturities and the proportions in which maturing debt passes into a longer, a shorter or a similar class of security are determined by the public preference in the conditions of the time.

23. Accordingly an important departure from pre-war practice (followed in very different conditions) is involved. In past times it has been a pre-occupation of the authorities to fund short term and floating debt on to a long term basis, more especially until recently because of the difficulty of controlling the market in floating debt (at that time fairly widely held) in gold standard conditions. Today (as already noted) the domestic floating debt other than that held by the Government is in the main firmly held by banking and other financial institutions.[39] The dangerous character of this type of debt disappears if there are adequate understandings with the financial world (including, it may be, appropriate regulations for continuing into the future the system of Treasury Deposit Receipts) to ensure the continuous holding of a large, and even increasing, floating debt in all circumstances.

24. At the same time the whole development of this matter would require to be carefully watched. The market and the public – and the House of Commons – are probably accustomed to looking upon the floating debt as the more dangerous kind of debt, partly for reasons already indicated, partly also because of the immediate and heavy effect on the Budget of any large increase in the short term rate if operating on great sums. Thus, material increases of floating debt, unless accompanied by explanations of policy as may be necessary, might give rise to serious distrust.

25. *General Conclusion.* We have been led to form a series of views not completely consistent with the brief references to the matter in the Employment White Paper. Rather we say that the White Paper ought to mean that, subject to uncertainties as to the extent to which and the conditions in which moderate fluctuations should be admitted (which uncertainties need not be brought too much into the open), the object of Government should be to maintain low interest rates, long and short,

for as far ahead as can reasonably be the subject of discussion – certainly far beyond the transitional period. We do not however suggest that dogmatic conclusions should be laid down here and now for a long future about the rates of interest appropriate to different maturities. They should be fixed from time to time in the light of experience and should pay attention primarily (a) to the effects of Government policy on the market for borrowing by private institutions, companies and individuals and on the problem of controlling and maintaining the desired rate of investment at home and abroad, (b) to social considerations in the wider sense and (c) perhaps especially to the burden of interest charges on the Exchequer and other State funds and on Local Authorities. The terms of the issues should be such as to preserve the maximum degree of flexibility and freedom for future policy.[40] But continuity of policy and gradualness of changes should be aimed at unless in exceptional circumstances and for grave cause.

26. Accordingly in the next section of this note we set out suggestions for a programme of procedure. It is primarily a programme of initial procedure only but is designed to set a standard suitable to be generally followed. In doing so we make these observations.

27. Firstly, a general assumption underlying many recent discussions of financial policy is that this country can be largely insulated from the effects of financial conditions overseas by a control of external capital movements, assumed to be made permanent and assumed to prove adequately effective in the absence of postal censorship. For example, conditions of serious distrust in this country, if they ever arose, might lead to a break in the control. The Committee take the view however that, among the circumstances which might lead to such a failure of the control, a level of interest rates lower here than elsewhere would be relatively of small – perhaps almost insignificance – importance as an inducement to law-breakers or law-evaders[.] It is rather the case that the failure of the control would endanger much more than the recommendations in this report than the recommendations in this report endanger the control.

28. Secondly, as in the White Paper on Employment (paragraph 80), we plead that there is many a slip 'twixt the cup and the lip. In the whole of this matter we enter a field "where theory can be applied to practical issues with confidence and certainty only as experience accumulates and experiment extends over untried ground. Not long ago the ideas embodied in the present proposals were unfamiliar to the general public and the subject of controversy among economists".

29. Thirdly, contrary to the course pursued in the White Paper we do not advocate that there should be any preliminary and detailed

announcement of a new settled policy. It happens that the measures about to be recommended represent no more than a continuance and development of existing policies and we think it better that, in the main at any rate, the public should learn by practical experience rather than by exposition.

III

30. We suggest the following programme of initial procedure – the date of its introduction is discussed below.

(a) Treasury Bill rate to be brought down to $^1/_2$% and Treasury Deposit Receipts to carry $^5/_8$%; probably a special rate of 1% (broadly the present rate) to apply to overseas money now in Treasury Bills and the like.

(b) Subject to action on (a), 5 year Exchequer Bonds at $1^1/_2$% and 10 year Bonds at 2% to be issued on tap, a new series to be started annually.

(c) 3% Savings Bonds to be issued on tap, a new series to be issued annually, with an option to the Treasury to repay after 10 years with, preferably, no final maturity (or if necessary a fixed latest date of repayment after 35 years).

(b) follows upon (a); (c) could either follow (a) or precede it.

31. No change would be made in the present terms affecting Tax Reserve Certificates, Savings Bank Deposits and Savings Certificates, but after an interval a worsening of the yield on Defence Bonds should be considered.

32. As regards (a) $^1/_2$% was roughly the Treasury Bill rate for several years before the war. It is not thought however that the rate for overseas balances could be brought down below 1% at any rate until the whole complex of questions surrounding them has been settled.

33. As regards (b) there is no social reason requiring a relatively liberal rate of interest on five or ten year bonds, nor any ground for offering those investors who have funds to put away for long periods an easy alternative of investing short with little sacrifice of interest. The gap therefore between the short bonds and the long term issue should be fairly wide.

34. The proposal (c) differs from the existing 3% issue in that the final date of maturity is more distant (or there is no final date) while the date of optional redemption (so far from moving further into the future pari passu with the final date, as has been the course followed during the war) – is moved backward to 10 years. The conditions of the suggested offer are therefore more favourable to the Exchequer than at present. The general grounds for making no more advanced proposal are:

(i) that it would be premature to try to move to a lower rate at a time when the opportunities for investment are exceptionally abundant

and before the conditions normal to the post-war epoch have been established;
(ii) that the return to the investor and the cost to the Exchequer of a 3 per cent Bond is modest so long as direct taxation remains at or near its present level;
(iii) that at the same time the option of early redemption safeguards a future liberty of action.

35. It has been indicated above (paragraph 14) that there are grounds for caution in deciding when to take steps towards lower levels. One of the factors to be considered is the effect of action in regard to Treasury Bill rates upon the negotiations with the Dominions and India. Consequently we do not suggest that any action should be taken on (a) before the autumn, when the matter should be reviewed again before a final decision is taken, and (b) therefore also remains in suspense. On the other hand we see no reason why (c), which is free from the overseas complication and represents only a modest deviation from the present issue, should not be adopted at any convenient time in the course of this year.

36. The necessity soon to withdraw the present $1\frac{3}{4}\%$ offer leaves a gap to be filled (or perhaps left for a time unfilled) before action on the lines of (b) could be taken; the nature of any new offer in this interval is left for discussion with the Bank of England.

IV

37. In this section we add some reflections on developments which may come as time goes on in regard to issues that may be on offer.

38. If, at any time, the terms offered result in an increasing preference on the part of the public for the shorter-dated securities, the resultant saving in the interest cost may up to a point be welcomed, and, unless the ruling conditions at the time (as they quite likely may) indicate a different conclusion, opportunity may be taken for a further economy in interest cost by a lowering of short-term rates.

39. If, on the other hand, the terms offered result in an increasing preference for the longer-term securities, consideration should be given whether the social and other advantages of the existing terms as affecting the habit of thrift outweigh the cost to the Exchequer; and, if not, the rate of interest on them should be reduced if it appears that these market conditions are likely to continue. If the prevailing long-term tap rate, say 3 per cent, becomes chronically too high, in the sense that it attracts to the Exchequer an excessive volume of funds in that form and the supply of new investments expected to yield a corresponding return is running short, on the reduction of the rate other means could be sought, if necessary, to provide the social incentives and advantages which a lower rate might be inadequate to afford.

40. Illustrations of such other possible means are:

(a) the further development of the existing facilities already available up to a limited amount for an individual holder, such as the Post Office and Trustee Savings Bank deposits, Savings Certificates and Defence Bonds;
(b) the acceptance by the Treasury of deposits from Charities and the like (perhaps including Life Offices) at a preferential rate;
(c) possibly also the offer of annuities on joint lives, calculated on the basis of a low rate of interest, but favourable to the holder in other respects, especially the principle on which the annuity is taxed.

41. If the prevailing long-term tap rate becomes chronically too low, in the sense that it encourages new capital formation on a scale tending to inflation, the rate should, in general, be raised. We are also disposed to take the view, though this is a matter in which the Bank of England may be specially interested to advise, that tap issues of short and intermediate-term debt should be, in general, on terms of repayment at a fixed date; and that (under the general system proposed), where optional dates of redemption exist in the case of past issues, advantage should be taken of the option to repay if, otherwise, the bonds would be standing at a premium (thus indicating that the rate of interest they carry has become too high to be appropriate to the term of maturity they have now reached), unless there appear to be special reasons at the time to the contrary.

Notes

1. And to this day the gold standard is primarily regarded as an international architecture.
2. An essay of 'unsurpassable brilliance' according to Schumpeter (1954, p. 834).
3. Skidelsky (1992, p. 169) agrees that the 'First World War can be seen as introducing the fourth great monetary discussion'. He does not, however, specify the nature of this discussion.
4. The terminology in Keynes's discussion here is confusing, as he used gold standard to mean gold exchange standard and gold currency to mean gold standard.
5. That is, falls in the reserve ratio were offsetting the impact of restricting the supply of cash.
6. A devaluation from the pre-war level of $4.86.
7. No commentary by Keynes is recorded on either development.
8. Opinions appeared to differ whether this was the full internal gold standard as preferred by the Bank of England and as later implemented in Britain or a gold exchange standard as implied by resolutions of the conferences.
9. Much of the material was re-working of articles that had been published in 'Reconstruction Supplements' of the *Manchester Guardian Commercial*, mainly in April 1922.
10. 2.6 per cent of 1931 GDP of £3785 million.

11. Skidelsky (1992, p. 164); he gives the reference: 'KP: NS/1/1. JMK to Prof. Kurt Singer, 23 April 1925'. The item is not included in *Collected Writings*.
12. Later the *General Theory* would contain a substantial tribute to Hobson and other monetary 'heretics'.
13. 'What is Money?' (1913) *Banking Law Journal*, New York.
14. Bank money is representative money if/when the State 'undertakes to accept [it] in payments to itself or to exchange [it] for compulsory legal-tender money' (*CW* V, p. 6).
15. Moggridge (*CW* XX, p. 17) provides a source for the membership. *Chairman*: H. P. Macmillan, a Scottish judge; *Members*: Sir Thomas Allen, of the Co-operative Wholesale Society; Ernest Bevin, of the Transport and General Workers Union; Lord Bradbury formerly of the Treasury; R. H. Brand of Lazards, the merchant bankers; Professor T. E. Gregory of the London School of Economics; J. M. Keynes of Cambridge University; Lennox Lee of the Federaton of British Industries; Cecil Lubbock of Whitbreads the brewers and a former Deputy Governor of the Bank of England; Reginald McKenna of the Midland Bank and a former Chancellor of the Exchequer; J. T. Walton-Newbold editor of *The Social Democrat*; Sir Walter Raine, a coal exporter; J. Frater Taylor of Armstrong Whitworth; R. G. Tulloch of the District Bank.
16. HM Treasury Deputy Controller of Finance, 1925–32, and the Chief Economic Advisor to the Government, 1932–46.
17. 4 per cent of 1931 GDP.
18. Richard V. N. Hopkins; at the time the Second Secretary to HM Treasury; Permanent Secretary to HM Treasury from 1942–45.
19. Source: The National Archives: Public Record Office (PRO) file T 175/157.
20. Source: PRO file CAB58/169.
21. He footnoted views on technicalities: 'My own view on the latter is a little different from that usually put forward. I believe that if we pursue a right policy very great economies will be obtainable in due course from conversions. But we shall only get the full advantage if the Chancellor of the Exchequer is exceptionally patient and always thinks more of his successor than of himself' (*CW* XXI, p. 25).
22. http://www.yale.edu/lawweb/avalon/presiden/inaug/froos1.htm
23. The detail of these events is taken from Fearon (1987, pp. 218–22).
24. Hoover initially established this organisation in January 1932 to lend to banks, with capital provided by Government. Eugene Meyer, the Governor of the Federal Reserve Board, was put in charge. As Fearon (1987, p. 116) notes 'It was unable, however, to prevent the failure of the banking system'.
25. In his letter to the editor that originally proposed the series, Keynes noted that the international aspect of the series was '. . . not really my own, but has been evolved by a group which, for your private information, includes H. D. Henderson of the Economic Advisory Council, Stamp, Layton, Salter, Blackett and Sir Alfred Lewis of the National Provincial Bank' (22 February 1933, *CW* XXI, p. 163).
26. Sir Cecil Kisch was a Civil Servant (Harrod, 1972 [1951], p. 150).
27. This followed moves from smaller countries as recorded by Keynes in the *Daily Mail*: 'Country after country abandons, or moves farther away from, the gold standard – South Africa, New Zealand, Denmark, Canada within the last few weeks' (*CW* XXI, p. 230).
28. He also addressed the argument that output could be increased simply by increasing the money supply: 'Some people seem to infer from this that output

and income can be raised by increasing the quantity of money. But this is like trying to get fat by buying a larger belt' (*CW* XXI, p. 294).
29. 1.7 Per cent of 1934 US GNP, which is estimated at $154.3 billion.
30. From the Federal Reserve website.
31. *The Economist* on 26 July explained: 'the Regency Council merely recruited itself by co-option. The example is cited of one seat on the Council which, ever since the creation of the Banque by Napoleon in 1800, has been held without interruption by the same family – that of MM. Mallet, the bankers'.
32. Stated this way the role of transactions demand is ignored; the issue is discussed in Chapter 7.
33. Source: PRO file T 177/38, dated 13/3/1937.
34. Source: Howson (1988, p. 252).
35. Roosevelt's words, cited by Moggridge in *CW* XXIII, p. 228.

Footnotes to the Report of the National Debt Enquiry

36. 'In the text the words in brackets are represented by symbols. In this transcription the meaning of the symbols has been substituted.'
37. 'It will be noted that on the whole the tenor of the passage is against permitting *important* fluctuations round a general norm.'
38. 'This must not be taken to imply that the State will continuously be a *net* borrower. While it is borrowing for productive and quasi-productive purposes, not only local authorities but also the State may be purchasing and redeeming securities on a large scale. The questions surrounding the Budget Sinking Fund are reserved for a separate report. In the transition period however problems may be created by competition for money among industrial concerns and to meet this the technique of the Capital Issues Control will require to be adapted from time to time as may be necessary.'
39. 'The present floating debt of some £m6,000 may be divided into three roughly equal parts; one-third is held by Government Departments or their equivalent and is in the nature of a book entry; one-third represents overseas sterling balances; the remaining third is held almost entirely by financial institutions. Publication of estimates of these separate elements appears to be practicable and might go far to allay any public apprehensions concerning the volume of this class of debt.'
40. 'For the present also effects upon the Savings Campaign should be considered.'

4

The Origins of 'Keynesian' Economics

4.1 Introduction

As seen in the previous chapter, Keynes's primary aim and policy goal was monetary reform. In the 1930s, it was mainly other economists as well as policymakers who gave more emphasis to fiscal policy and other *ad hoc* – generally, non-market – measures, and called these measures 'Keynesian'.

Such policies are not radical. Throughout history, policymakers, as exemplified by George W. Bush, have not hesitated to retreat from professed free-market ideals in the wake of domestic economic difficulties. While conventional wisdom has Keynes's fighting a futile battle over the merits of fiscal policy in the 1930s, the reality was that, at the time, with the Labour Government out of office, a broad section of the British Establishment turned to advocating 'Keynesian' measures. One of the advocates was the future British (Conservative) Prime Minister, Harold Macmillan, for whom the policies constituted 'economic nationalism'.

Correspondingly, and again contrary to conventional wisdom, economists across the world were equally willing to jettison previously dearly held classical theory in the wake of the failure of the global economy. Their approach was wholly different to that of Keynes. An attempt was made to modify – in a crude way – the classical theory to allow 'money' or government demand to change output, particularly under conditions of spare capacity. Ralph Hawtrey made some of the early running; but Dennis Robertson was the most important neo-classical economist and made the key contributions in the years between the *Treatise* and the *General Theory*. The most substantially debated (but by no means the only) differences between this and Keynes's own theory were the treatment of the relation between saving and investment, and the distinction between the loanable funds and liquidity preference theories of interest.

It is my contention that Hicks's and others' simultaneous equation models were developments of Robertson's not Keynes's approach (see also the quotations in Chapter 1). The economics profession wholeheartedly embraced this initiative and advocated its development and adoption from the moment the original contributions were made. This promotion was conducted in a coherent manner throughout the world, in particular, in the United Kingdom, in the United States, in Sweden and at the League of Nations (LoN).

When the *General Theory* was published, those that entered into any dialogue with Keynes did so from the perspective of this new developing approach. During the war the 'Keynesian' model was modified; with Modigliani's (1944) version there was no role for monetary considerations. In parallel the agenda of the British Government *Employment White Paper (EWP)* (Cmd. 6527) was more in the spirit of Macmillan's initiatives than the monetary perspective of Keynes. In a sleight of hand of staggering implication, 'Keynesian' theory and policy were simply substituted for Keynes's own.

4.2 'Keynesian' policy in the 1930s

Throughout most of the 1930s, 'Keynesian' policies were vigorously advocated and commanded support in Britain and the United States. While Keynes was primarily concerned with international and domestic monetary reform, a cross-section of the Establishment turned to a more radical retreat from market mechanisms. That is not to say that Keynes opposed such measures; he lent his support to arguments for both tariffs and public works expenditure. The subtle and unspoken, yet fundamental, distinction was that Keynes saw these measures as *supplementary* to monetary reform; it seems that others saw the measures as *alternative* to monetary reform.

In Britain, a significant movement in the retreat from market mechanisms occurred in 1930, when leading city bankers signed a resolution supporting protectionism:

> While we retain the hope of an ultimate extension of the area of free trade throughout the world . . . we believe that the immediate step for securing and extending the market for British goods lies in reciprocal trade agreements between the nations comprising the British Empire. (Kynaston, 1999, p. 204)

In February 1933 the new (Conservative) Chancellor Neville Chamberlain announced a 10 per cent general tariff.

While in 1931 the Labour Government had been destroyed in the wake of widespread demands for cuts to public expenditure, such demands were apparently short-lived. On 17 October 1932, A. C. Pigou and D. H. MacGregor – professors of political economy at Cambridge and Oxford respectively – headed the signatories to a letter to *The Times* advocating public works expenditure.[1] The other signatories were Arthur Salter, Walter Layton, Josiah Stamp and Keynes himself (all would become members of the EAC). Stamp (1880–1941) was a statistician (Vice Chairman, 1925–32, and Chairman, 1935–41, of the Royal Statistical Society) and industrialist

(Secretary and Director of Nobel Industries, 1919–26; and President of the London, Midland and Scottish Railway, 1926–41), who also took a number of public roles (e.g. British representative on the Dawes and Young Committees on German reparations). He was a vociferous supporter of Keynes (reviewing the *Treatise* for the *EJ*). He was made a Baron in 1938 but was killed in an air raid in 1941. Salter and Layton would be important figures in the post-war world. Salter was variously a bureaucrat (in the British civil service and as a LoN official), academic (the Gladstone Professor of Political Theory and Institutions at Oxford and a fellow of All Souls) and a politician (Member of Parliament for Oxford University, 1937–50, and as a member of the Conservative Party, 1951–53). He became a Baron in 1951. Layton was an academic (economics at Cambridge University and then University College London), and then the editor of *The Economist* from 1922 to 1938; *The Dictionary of National Biography* adds that Layton 'worked for Anglo-American understanding, European Unity, and the United Nations'. He became a Baron in 1947.

In 1933 Harold Macmillan, one day to become British Prime Minister, set himself up as figurehead for the campaign for what he referred to as 'economic nationalism'. The preface of his book, *Reconstruction: A Plea for a National Plan*, explained cause, motive and means:

> We must realise the essential contradictions of *laissez-faire* even while we may appreciate the energy and drive of a rugged individualism. The policy we are seeking will only be satisfactory if it goes *deep* enough to correct the maladjustments and reconcile the disharmonies from which our problems arise. But, if revolutionary violence is to be avoided, it must also make its appeal to a sufficiently *broad* strip of public opinion to secure the support for its adoption. It must be at once radical and popular. (Macmillan, 1933, pp. 6–7; his italics)

Macmillan then emerged alongside Clifford Allen as leaders of the 'Next Five Years Group' (NFYG; Skidelsky, 1992, p. 438). Reflecting the cross-party nature of the initiative, Allen was a leading Fabian and member of the Labour Party (he took MacDonald's side when the Labour Party split in 1931). After issuing two pamphlets, a fuller manifesto was published as *The Next Five Years: An Essay in Political Agreement* (1935). The 'Foreword' includes a list of 152 signatories drawn from across the British Establishment ('drawn from different parties and schools of thought'). The list also indicates those signatories that were members of the 'drafting Committee': Allen, W. Arnold-Forster, A. Barratt Brown (the Principal of Ruskin College, Oxford), Geoffrey Crowther (soon to succeed Layton as editor of *The Economist*), Macmillan and Salter.

The manifesto foreshadowed much of what was to become the post-war agenda. Chapter 1 was titled 'Economic Planning':

The *motive* of profit-making has already, to a greater extent than is commonly realised, ceased to be the mainspring of economic activity in this country: and we think it safe to assume that this tendency will continue in the future, . . .

. . . [W]e believe that the State will find it increasingly necessary to intervene in order to set the *direction* of the economic activity of the community. . . .

We assume, then, that the functions of government in relation to economic activities are increasing and will increase, both in range and complexity. . . .

We need more economic planning. (Liberty and Democratic Leadership, 1935, pp. 11–12)

Chapter 5 turned to 'Banking and Finance'; monetary reform was rejected:

The importance of monetary policy, though great, can easily be exaggerated.

. . .

But money is not all-powerful. Many years ago Jevons wrote: "There are men who spend their time and fortunes in endeavouring to convince a dull world that poverty can be abolished by the issue of printed bits of paper. I know one gentleman who holds that exchequer bills are the panacea for the evils of humanity. Other philanthropists wish to make us all rich by coining the national debt, or coining the lands of the country, or coining everything." The forms of these beliefs have grown more subtle, and more plausible in the process, since Jevons' day. But the root-belief is still the same: that by a few simple book-keeping transactions a flood of wealth hitherto pent up by an imperfect monetary system can be released to sweep poverty from the face of the earth.

We do not share these beliefs. (ibid., pp. 97–9)

The most promising suggestion is that currencies should be re-linked to gold, but at parities which could be changed from time to time. (ibid., p. 111)

In the longer run, the task of the Central Bank in regulating credit policy should, as far as it is compatible with its international currency policy, aim at preserving stability. This somewhat vague requirement can perhaps best be envisaged as meaning the stability of the general price-level . . . (ibid., p. 113)

Chapter 8, under the title 'Social Justice', looked at what was to become known as the welfare state (extracted from the summary in the 'contents' section):

The Social Services. The policy of a National Minimum. . . . (1) Unemployment. . . . The Means Test to be purged of its harshness. (2) Old

Age.... the urgent need for a State organised system of superannuation allowances.... (3) Education.... an increase in the school leaving-age is essential... (4) Nutrition... beginning with milk....

Taxation and Equity.... Possible future sources of tax revenue: the increment in land values; increased surtax rates on 'unearned income'; increased death duties. (ibid., pp. x–xi)

Leon Keyserling has similarly observed how 'Keynesian' policy commanded widespread support in the United States long before Keynes had written his *General Theory*.

[R]epeated public works bills.... stem[med] in turn from Senator Wagner's Economic Stabilization Act of 1929, which proposed increased public works spending as private indexes of economic activity fell. The proposal that the government spend more to employ people when unemployment is very high, and thus run a deficit, came well before Keynes was in vogue, and cannot be attributed to any one man or school. (Keyserling *et al.*, 1972, p. 134)

More recently, Esteban Pérez Caldentey has studied how the Chicago School were in the vanguard of professional economists taking this stance (though Laidler and Sandilands (2002) show that these views may well have originated with Lauchlin Currie, Paul Theodore Ellsworth and Harry Dexter White in Harvard):

As a group Chicago economists advocated on more than one occasion an increase in aggregate demand to revamp a stagnant economy. In January, 1932, twenty-four economists participating at a conference at the University of Chicago urged President Hoover to pursue more aggressively open market operations and to continue the Government's public works program. Later on in April, 1932, at the request of Congressman Samuel B. Pettengil (Republican of Indiana), Chicago economists drafted and signed a statement urging a public work program financed by having resort to the printing press. As they put it,

"Recovery can be brought about, either by a reduction in costs to a level consistent with existing commodity prices, or by injecting enough new purchasing powers so that much larger production will be available at existing costs. The first method is conveniently automatic but dreadfully slow.... The second method... only requires a courageous fiscal policy on the part of central Government (Quoted in Tavlas, 1997, p. 164)." (Caldentey, 2000, p. 10)

4.3   Dennis Robertson's neo-classical economics

Underpinning the policies touched on in the previous section was a more pragmatic view of the operation of a free-market economy than is implied by the basic classical model. At the very least the implication was that policy intervention had a real effect in a short run. Nor was such a perspective new to the mainstream economics profession. The standard notion of an underlying or long-run equilibrium has tended to co-exist with an acceptance of a short-run output fluctuation since at least Hume's 'Of Money' in 1752:

> In my opinion, it is only in this interval or intermediate situation, between the acquisition of money and the rise in prices, that the increasing quantity of gold and silver is favourable to industry... The farmer and gardener, finding that their commodities are taken off, apply themselves with alacrity to the raising of more... It is easy to trace the money in its progress through the whole commonwealth; where we shall find that it must first quicken the diligence of every individual, before it increases the price of labour. (Hume, 1955 [1752])

As noted in Chapter 1 of this book, Keynes would label this position 'neo-classical'. Over the 1930s, neo-classical economists would develop and refine this position and ultimately would present their developments as rival to Keynes's own contributions. In the post-Second World War period, simultaneous equation versions of these models would become known as 'Keynesian' economics.

In the twentieth century these models originated first with the work of Ralph Hawtrey and Dennis Robertson. Initially, they saw credit creation as the factor that led to a divergence from classical conclusions. Hawtrey's 1919 *Currency and Credit* offered the following approach:

> If industry is employed up to capacity, the credit expansion is felt mainly in a rise of prices. On the other hand, if there is a considerable margin of productive power unemployed, the main effect will be to increase production. If all producers were employed below capacity to the same proportional extent, there might be for a time no rise in prices at all. ...Nevertheless it is the case that, at a time when industry is underemployed, the rise of prices caused by an expansion of credit is less. The rise of prices and the increase of production are, to a great extent, *alternatives*. (Hawtrey, 1919, pp. 49–50; his italics)

But the most important advocate of the neo-classical model was Dennis Robertson. Robertson's role in the theory that eventually would become attributed to Keynes is of great importance, for Robertson was opposed to Keynes in almost every way. Philosophically, Keynes's Liberalism and optimism contrasts with what Gordon Fletcher (2000, pp. 24, 26 and 98) has described as Robertson's deep conservatism and 'profound sense of the harshness of human destiny' and 'devotion . . . against the folly of trying to do too much'.

In terms of economics, Robertson devoted himself to the study of money, but seemingly did so in order to *deny* it any fundamental importance. Fletcher describes his approach through an interpretation of his first three books. In *A Study of Industrial Fluctuation* (1915), Robertson set out a 'real theory of the trade cycle' with an underlying perspective that might be referred to as 'Schumpeterian'. He concluded:

> that the apparent chaos of *laissez-faire* produced growing prosperity; that the nature of modern technology-led, capitalistic production gave rise to fluctuations as an integral part of the growth process; that the human urge to benefit descendents led to an unreflecting compulsion to sacrifice present consumption in favour of future abundance. (Fletcher, 2004, p. 7)

In *Money* (1922):

> Robertson had glimpsed the power of money to seriously upset the conclusions of the *Study* (1915) and of the assumptions of Classical (Cambridge) orthodoxy to which he was so deeply attached. In brief, Robertson had discovered that money possessed the ability not only to oil the wheels of economic life but significantly to amend his real theory of the cycle, by supplementing and supplanting in importance the supply of saving made available by voluntary means. (ibid., p. 6)

And then in *Banking Policy and the Price Level* (1926):

> Robertson attempted a definitive demonstration of his conviction that, though money plays an important role in the economy, it alters nothing fundamental and can be so regulated that the economy will function as though money did not exist: that is, money is rendered neutral. (ibid., p. 7)

Nevertheless the mechanisms Robertson grappled with – in particular the relationship between money, saving and investment – would be critical points of departure for both Keynes's own theory and the 'Keynesian' theories.

Two years after the publication of the *Treatise*, Robertson responded in two *EJ* articles. Fletcher argues that Robertson 'recast his theory in interest-rate terms as a means of replying to an initiative of Keynes' (Fletcher, 2000, p. 288). Equally these contributions were taking critical steps towards the 'Keynesian' model.

The first article, 'Saving and Hoarding', opened by articulating his aim: 'In a future article I hope to examine certain aspects of the relation between saving, the rate of interest, and the course of industrial fluctuation' (Robertson, 1933, p. 399). The specific context was a prolonged dialogue between Keynes and a number of his critics over his treatment of the relation between saving and investment in the *Treatise*. As a consequence, one of two rejoinders (rejecting the position Robertson was taking) was by Keynes himself (in the December 1933 *EJ, CW* XIII, pp. 327–30).

Robertson's second contribution, 'Industrial Fluctuation and the Natural Rate of Interest', was published in December 1934. The work was introduced as follows:

> The following paragraphs are an attempt to bring together (1) the concept of Saving developed in my article in the *Economic Journal*, Sept. 1933, and (2) the attempts which have been made to analyse cyclical fluctuation in terms of a divergence between the 'natural' and 'market' rates of interest. (Reprinted in Robertson, 1940, p. 83)

The article followed *Banking Policy and the Price Level* and depicted economic activity as an interaction between real phenomena and the lending behaviour of banks. But much of the discussion was based on a diagrammatic centrepiece, reproduced below as Figure 4.1; it was described by Robertson as follows:

> [We] have a curve *DD'* representing the declining marginal productivity of new lendings in industrial uses, . . . And we have a curve *SS'* representing the rate of new available savings per atom of time – . . . [I]n equilibrium the rate of interest *PM* is the rate at which the new lendings which can be absorbed by industry . . . and the new available savings . . . are equal . . .

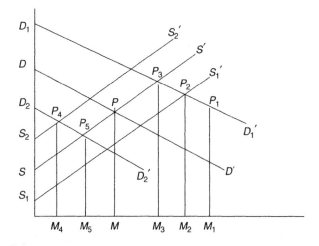

Figure 4.1 Robertson's diagram (1)

Now, owing to the discovery of the Diesel engine, South America, or what not, an industrial expansion sets in, and DD' is raised D_1D_1'. If the banks keep the rate of interest right down at PM ($= P_1M_1$), the initial rate of *lendings* per atom of time will exceed the rate of available new *savings*, and the whole of the excess MM_1 . . . will consist of newly created bank-money. . . . There is now a *quasi-natural* rate of interest P_2M_2 which would equate industrial requirements and available new savings under the new conditions, towards which the actual rate is likely to rise, . . . (Robertson, 1940, pp. 85–6)

In essence, the model developed a distinction between the rate of interest defined by the 'old' savings–investment equilibrium, which concerned real resources, and a rate of interest that was related in some way to the credit policy of the banking system. The diagram was the first step towards what would become known as Hicks's *IS-LM* model. Robertson sought a graphical representation of the ability of credit expansion to supplement saving. More broadly, it was Robertson's first attempt to 'generalise' the classical savings–investment equilibrium. The theory of interest that would emerge would be known as loanable funds. Chick's explanation of the loanable funds perspective seems exactly right:

At least the neoclassical theory brought money into the picture. However, the theory was so designed that the conclusions or implications of Classical theory still held.

In particular, saving was still *prior* to investment. Investment could however be financed out of dishoarding or from new money as well as from 'saving proper' – i.e. saving in the Classical sense. Sources and uses of funds are fundamental to this theory, hence its designation as Loanable-Funds Theory. Sources and uses may be indicated by an equation:

$$I + H = S + \Delta M$$

where the new symbol, H, is net hoarding (i.e. the accumulation of cash balances by surplus units less dishoarding by others.)

. . .

It is probably best to view loanable-funds theory as an attempt to preserve a Classical outlook on interest, saving and investment while adapting the theory to a monetary economy. (Chick, 1983, pp. 178–9)

A variant of Robertson's diagram would next appear in the *General Theory* itself (p. 180; reproduced here as Figure 4.2). The original proposal for the inclusion of the diagram was made by Roy Harrod in the course of his dialogue with Keynes over the galley proofs of the *General Theory* (CW XIII, pp. 526–65). Harrod argued that Keynes's rejection of the classical theory

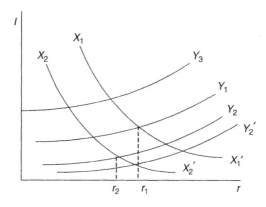

Figure 4.2   Keynes's/Harrod's diagram

of interest should be portrayed as an alleged indeterminacy of the classical perspective and offered the following clarification of what he had in mind:

> Let y_1, y_2 etc. be rates of interest and Y_1, Y_2 etc. incomes corresponding to them (Y_1 being derived from y_1 via marginal efficiency of cap. and the multiplier). For each value of Y draw classical supply curves, of which *each* curve shows amount of saving corresponding to various values of y at a given level of Y. Then according to you it will be found that the value of y at which the curve appropriate to income Y_r intersects the demand curve is in fact y_r, where y_r represents any given rate of interest whatever. The so-called supply curve in the passage from your letter which I have quoted is the locus of points on the classical supply curves for that value of y corresponding to the level of income on the assumption of which each was drawn. (*CW* XIII, pp. 556–7)

In this version of the diagram, the classical saving (Y) and investment (X) curves have been replaced by a family of curves based on different levels of incomes. My inclination would be to refer to it as the income-generalised saving–investment diagram. Keynes did not indicate any awareness of the similarity with Robertson's diagram during the actual exchange with Harrod. But in the *General Theory* he added the following footnote: '[t]his diagram was suggested to me by Mr R. F. Harrod. Cf. also a partly similar schematisation by Mr D. H. Robertson, *EJ*, December 1934, p. 652' (*CW* VII, p. 180). As will be discussed in Chapter 6, the insertion of this diagram – which was not part of the wider scheme of the *General Theory* – was a vital step for the identification of the 'Keynesian' model with the *General Theory* itself.

In parallel to Robertson's work, LoN initiatives in the 1930s sought to endorse the emerging neo-classical approach and, more specifically, the loanable funds theory of interest. This work originated in a resolution adopted in September 1930. Funding was provided by the Rockefeller Foundation, according to the following mandate:

> The key word was 'consensus', since the Rockefeller Foundation expected as one of the results of its five-year grant to the League of Nations, that "the divergence of views among economists as to the nature and the means of controlling the business cycle will be appreciably lessened", which would be an "essential preliminary to the unification of national policies for dealing with the business cycle". (Boianovsky and Trautwein, 2004, p. 28, citing a memorandum by a Rockefeller Foundation employee)

Gottfried Haberler, an economist originally of the 'Austrian school', took the lead in developing the 'consensus'. His emerging work was presented in a meeting of economists in June/July 1934. According to LoN records, the following economists were present: Robertson, Haberler, O. Anderson, J. M. Clark, L. Dupriez, A. Hansen, O. Morgenstern, B. Ohlin, C. Rist, L. Robbins, W. Röpke and J. Tinbergen.[2] The verbatim note of the meetings records the perceived need for coherence with Robertson's recent contributions:

> Ohlin suggested that a more detailed discussion of the saving–investment mechanism should be provided, including recent contributions by Robertson (1934). According to Ohlin, this could show how a higher level of expenditure in public works brings about "unintentional savings" able to finance the public deficit (pp. 30–1). There was general agreement that "we must have period analysis in the way indicated by Mr. Robertson". (Boianovsky and Trautwein, 2004, p. 19)

Even this short quotation indicates an appearance of fiscal policy considerations and introduces the notion of period analysis, another technique that would come to be identified with Keynes (and is discussed in Chapter 6).

4.4   The classical and neo-classical reception of the *General Theory*

4.4.1   The classical reviews

The neo-classical theory – including the LoN work – would emerge more substantially through a number of published academic reviews of the *General Theory* itself. The discussion in this section seeks to distinguish these contributions from the more vigorous critiques made by those that Keynes considered classical economists (see Chapter 1).

Under the overall editorship of Andrew Pyle, the excellent *Contemporary Responses* series reproduces the published responses to major academic works as they were released. Part 21 of this series provides the *Contemporary Responses to the General Theory*. Editor Roger Backhouse divides the reviews

into the following categories: 'newspapers', 'general, literary and professional' and 'specialist academic journals'. In his introductory section, Backhouse sums up the stance of the academic reviewers:

> Whilst all bar one reviewer (Beckhart, [1936] *Political Science Quarterly*,
> [51(4), Dec.] p. 602, who thought the book likely to remain 'but an inter-
> esting exhibit in the museum of depression curiosities') considered it an
> important book, it was subjected to strong criticism. Enthusiasm was gener-
> ally muted, Harris (1948, p. 29) going so far as to say that not a single enthu-
> siastic review had come to his attention. (Backhouse, 1999, p. 12)

This state of affairs was not new to Keynes. His theoretical developments had
been opposed by prominent members of the academic economics profession
from the moment that he had begun to make contributions to the discipline.
The most vigorous early critic was Edwin Cannan of the LSE. Cannan opposed
Keynes's emerging policy conclusions simply by denying the fact that banks
created money. The most public of these disputes was over Keynes's rejection
of the gold standard in his *Tract on Monetary Reform*.[3] With Cannan's death,
the main critics of his *Treatise on Money* were those who would oppose Keynes
for the rest of his life: R. G. Hawtrey and D. H. Robertson. Also prominent among
the critics of the *Treatise* was Friedrich A. von Hayek; Hayek was, however,
silent on the later matter of the *General Theory*.

The nature of the outright opposition to the *General Theory* must be
emphasised, but need not be dwelled on. It is well illustrated by Keynes's
comments in response to reviews and commentaries by the 'senior' British
economists, Hawtrey, H. D. Henderson, W. Beveridge and A. C. Pigou:

> I find your letter of April 3rd rather shattering. For, after reading it, I am
> now convinced that nothing that I can say will open your eyes – I do
> not say to the truth of my argument – but to what the essence of my
> argument, true or false, actually is. . . .
>
> . . .
>
> . . . I have been conscious that you have never made any reference to
> about 75 per cent of my book, and I have been bothered by this, because
> whilst, on the one hand, silence in such a long correspondence would
> seem to give consent to it, yet your observations on other passages lead
> me to doubt whether you will be in agreement. (Keynes to Hawtrey, 15
> April 1936, *CW* XIV, pp. 23–4)

> Hubert [Henderson] came to the Marshall Society yesterday, with Dennis
> in the chair, to read his paper against my book. I was astonished at the
> violence of his emotion against it: he thinks it a poisonous book; yet
> when it came to the debate there was very little of the argument which
> he was really prepared to oppose. . . . One got the impression that he was
> not really much interested in pure economic theory, but much disliked
> for emotional or political reasons some of the practical conclusions to

which my arguments seemed to point. As a theoretical attack there was almost nothing to answer. (Keynes, in a letter to Lydia Keynes, 3 May 1936, *CW* XXIX, p. 218)

[T]he general nature of your points is such as to convince me that I have really had a total failure in my attempt to convey to you what I am driving at. (Keynes to Beveridge, 28 July 1936, *CW* XIV, p. 56)

I was distressed by the Prof's [Pigou's] review and even more so that you should think it worthy of him. I have felt it something about which the less said the better. . . .

But indeed I thought the Prof's review profoundly frivolous in substance. Surely I deserve to be taken a little more seriously than that. (Keynes in a letter to Robertson, 20 September 1936, *CW* XIV, p. 87)

At the time, Pigou was the President of the Royal Economic Society; Kahn refers to his review in *Economica* as 'bitter and sarcastic' (Kahn, 1984, p. 125).

But the reviews from neo-classical economists were more subtle and less unequivocal in their dismissal of the *General Theory*. In general terms these economists argued that developments already underway to classical theory were adequate to deal with the question that Keynes was concerned with. The approach played down the achievement and impact of the work. Matters of theoretical substance were addressed, but the authors argued that differences between Keynes and the neo-classical approach were slight. A particular line of argument was that differences were issues of terminology and definition rather than substance. In terms of characters, the dialogue drew in those who would become known as the Keynesian economists; first through reviews and then through the subsequent contributions that would become known as the origin of 'Keynesian' economics. The only distinction between these new 'Keynesians' and Robertson appears to have been a greater desire to stress the feasibility and desirability of reconciling the two theories (see Robertson quote in Section 4.4.4).

In terms of theoretical detail, the two main contested areas were the nature of the relationship between saving and investment, and the distinction between loanable funds and liquidity preference theories of interest. The bulk of the discussion on these specific issues waits until Chapter 7; but matters are covered in broad terms here.

4.4.2 The neo-classical reviews

John Hicks opened the neo-classical approach to the *General Theory* with his review in the June 1936 *EJ*. It concluded with the downplaying that was typical of the approach:

The technique of this work is, on the whole, conservative: more conservative than in the *Treatise*. It is the technique of Marshall, but it is applied to problems never tackled by Marshall and his contemporaries. . . . Thus, we have to change, not so much our methods of analysis, as some important elements in the outlook that we have inherited from the classics... (Hicks, 1936, p. 253)

On specific theoretical detail he referred to the saving–investment identity as 'merely a change in definition' (Hicks, 1936, p. 239) and asserted a version of the equivalence of loanable funds and liquidity preference: 'This latter method is the method of Mr Keynes. It is a perfectly legitimate method, but it does not prove other methods to be wrong' (ibid., p. 246).

Fittingly, Hicks's review was closely followed by Alvin Hansen's piece in the October 1936 *Journal of Political Economy*. Hansen would be identified as the leading US 'Keynesian' as Hicks would be in the United Kingdom. The review is notorious for this closing passage, which was later amended when reproduced in a collection of his work (Hansen, 1938):

> We are living in a time when economics stands in danger of sterile orthodoxy. The book under review is not a landmark in the sense that it lays a foundation for a 'new economics'. It warns once again, in a provocative manner, of the danger of reasoning based on assumptions which no longer fit the facts of economic life. Out of the discussion and research will come bit by bit an improved theoretical apparatus (Keynes's interest rate theory contains promising suggestions) and a more accurate appreciation of social psychology (the brilliant chapter on long-term expectation) and of the precise character of the economic environment in which humans act as individuals and in groups. The book is more a symptom of economic trends than a foundation stone on which a new science can be built. (Hansen in the *Journal of Political Economy*, October 1936, reproduced in Backhouse, 1999, pp. 176–7)

On specific points of detail he attacked Keynes's new 'terminology' for saving and investment as 'by no means wholly satisfactory' (Backhouse, 1999, p. 167); and recommended instead the use of Robertson's definitions.

The next review of importance was Robertson's own. The outlet for these comments was not a British journal, but the November 1936 edition of the US *Quarterly Journal of Economics* (*QJE*), where his was one of four reviews of the *General Theory*. In private correspondence, Robertson had previously indicated a largely unrepentant opposition to Keynes's new work: 'I've spent a lot of time this summer on the said book. It's no use pretending I like it much better, or that I don't agree more or less with the Prof.'s [Pigou] review...' (Robertson to Keynes, 28 September 1936, *CW* XXIX, p. 163). While this comment indicates a fundamental opposition, his public comments adopted a less controversial and confrontational tone; he opened his review as follows:

> I am grateful for the opportunity to publish these notes in a setting which will make it plain that they are not an attempt to appraise Mr. Keynes'

book as a whole, or to discuss properly the high matters of judgement and policy on which it bears – matters on some tho not all of which I am, I think, more nearly in agreement with Mr. Keynes than the reader of these notes might suppose! (Robertson, 1936, reproduced in Backhouse, 1999, p. 206)

Again the review dwelled on the relationship between saving and investment. But he also used the review to develop his own theory, and ultimately to complete the groundwork for the 'Keynesian' model. In his critique of Keynes's discussion of the rate of interest he introduced a diagrammatic representation ('. . . we may illustrate Mr. Keynes' propositions diagrammatically as follows', Robertson, 1936, p. 181) in order to emphasise the loanable funds aspects of Keynes's theory. His new diagram is reproduced here as Figure 4.3; and is followed by Robertson's description.

At a given level of money income people will wish to hold an amount of money OM' for "transaction, etc." purposes, and, if the rate of interest is $P'N'$, a further amount $M'N'$ for "speculative" purposes. At a certain higher level of money income they will wish to hold OM' for "transaction, etc." purposes, and, if the rate of interest is $P'N'$, a further amount $M'N'$ for "speculative" purposes. LL_1 is the locus of P, $L'L_1'$ of P'. (In the simple case illustrated, $L'L_1'$ is simply LL_1 shifted to the right by a distance MM', i.e. the conditions of what I will call "liquidity preference proper" are assumed unchanged.) (Robertson, 1936, pp. 181–2)

Ultimately his complaint against the *General Theory* was that it was not a loanable funds theory: 'Even so . . . the rate of interest will be rather a co-determinee with income and saving–investment than a determinant thereof ' (Robertson, 1936, p. 186).

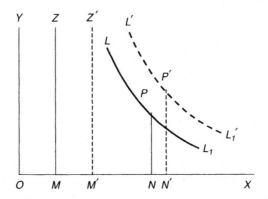

Figure 4.3 Robertson's diagram (2)

4.4.3 *IS-LM* emerges

From the broader perspective, Robertson had now set out the diagram in (M, r) space that would accompany his earlier diagram in (S, I, r) space. The models that have become known as 'Keynesian' initially did little more than bring together these two diagrams as a set of simultaneous equations and look to their resolution. They remained 'loanable-funds' models to the extent that higher activity required a higher quantity of money that would push up the rate of interest, and saving continued to play an important role. While Hicks's *IS-LM* model is the most famous, a number were produced by different economists all with seemingly close links to Robertson. Three versions – Hicks's, Harrod's and Meade's – were put together specifically for the 26 September 1936 Econometric Society symposium on the *General Theory* at Oxford University. This conference has achieved notoriety as the conference from where 'Keynesianism' emerged.

In his excellent *Interpreting Mr Keynes: The IS-LM Enigma*, Warren Young (1987) examines the similarity between the three models put to the conference. He poses the question: 'If the equational representation of Keynes's system in all three IS-LM papers is identical, how did this come about?' (p. 32). According to the argument here, this coincidence came about because all three young economists were tackling the same problem: the algebraic depiction of Robertson's diagrams. Young also cites a letter from Hicks to Meade that indicates the collaboration between the economists:

Dear Meade,

Harrod has asked me to send his paper on to you, and I take the opportunity of returning your own paper at the same time. I am sorry not to have returned your paper before, but I was waiting till I saw Harrod's before I decided what to write myself, and I didn't know how much of yours I should want until then. Now I have got a good deal of my paper done, and can manage without that from now on. I am taking up a number of Harrod's points, but making my paper on the whole rather critical of Keynes. I have got some maths in my paper, and have been careful to use your symbols, so as not to cause unnecessary confusion.

As I am just going away for a holiday, I am afraid I shan't get my paper done until about 2 days before the meeting; consequently I shall be obliged to produce it out of a hat and not circulate it first. I am sorry for this, but it is not altogether my fault.

Yours, John R. Hicks (Young, 1987, p. 33)

While all three models were similar, it was Hicks's *IS-LM* diagram that captured the profession so completely. Furthermore, he was already the most prominent of the 'Keynesians', and his most recent work had a distinct Keynes flavour (although, prior to this, his 1932 *Theory of Wages* set him against the theoretical and practical initiatives of the monetary theorists at the peak of the great depression). His 1935 paper, 'A Suggestion for Simplifying the Theory of Money', set out a theory of interest based on demands for money derived from asset balances. It therefore anticipated the not-yet-published theory of liquidity preference. In his much later *Economic Perspectives* (1977), Hicks records Keynes's comments on this work (not included in *CW*): 'When I sent that (in proof) to Keynes, I got this postcard, dated December 24, 1934: "Many thanks for the proof of your article. I like it very much. I agree with you that what I now call 'Liquidity Preference' is the essential concept for Monetary Theory"' (Hicks, 1977, p. 142). Hicks speculates that the article was the main reason for his being offered the opportunity to review the *General Theory*: 'It was no doubt because of "Simplifying" that I had this difficult honour conferred upon me' (ibid.).

Hicks's equations and famous *IS-LM* diagram (Figure 4.4; at this stage, it was known as *SILL*) represent Robertson's two diagrams and then a picture of their possible resolution respectively.

The equations in Hicks's paper represent Robertson's 1934 diagram as follows:

- *DD'*, 'the declining marginal productivity of new lendings in industrial uses', becomes $I_x = C(i)$, where i is the rate of interest; and
- *SS'*, 'representing the rate of new available savings per atom of time', becomes $I_x = S(I)$.

Hicks expresses both in terms of I_x, 'income earned in investment trades' (Hicks, 1937, p. 148), through his use of the equation 'Investment = Saving' (ibid., p. 149). I denotes the 'Total Income' (ibid., p. 148).

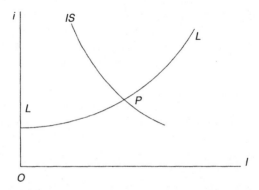

Figure 4.4 Hicks's diagram

The *IS* curve is then defined as the locus of solutions to this diagram: 'The curve *IS* can therefore be drawn showing the relation between Income and interest which must be maintained in order to make saving equal to investment' (ibid., p. 153).

Robertson's *QJE* review depiction of the liquidity preference schedule, 'LL_1, the locus of *P*', is represented by Hicks as $M = L(I, i)$. Hicks derives *LL*, the locus of solutions to this diagram, by taking a given money supply: 'Against a given quantity of money, the first equation, $M=L(I, i)$, gives us a relation between Income (*I*) and the rate of interest (*i*). This can be drawn out as a curve (*LL*) which will slope upwards, since an increase in income tends to raise the demand for money, and an increase in the rate of interest tends to lower it' (Hicks, 1937, p. 153).

Hicks turned Robertson's diagrams into a set of five simultaneous equations in five variables (in later notation: *Y*, *I*, *S*, *i*, *M*). However, as is widely recognised, he did not stop here:

In order to elucidate the relation between Mr. Keynes and the 'Classics,' we have invented a little apparatus. It does not appear that we have exhausted the uses of that apparatus, so let us conclude by giving it a little run on its own.

With that apparatus at our disposal, we are no longer obliged to make certain simplifications which Mr. Keynes makes in his exposition. We can reinsert the missing *i* in the third equation, and allow for any possible effect of the rate of interest upon saving; and, what is much more important, we can call in question the sole dependence of investment upon the rate of interest, which looks rather suspicious in the second equation. Mathematical elegance would suggest that we ought to have *I* and *i* in all three equations, if the theory is to be really General. Why not have them there like this:

$$M = L(I, i), \ I_x = C(I, i), \ I_x = S(I, i) \text{ (Hicks, 1937, p. 156)}$$

Through this 'mathematical elegance' – rather, inserting a variable into an equation that was not previously a function of that variable – Hicks claimed that he 'generalised' the model. According to the standard interpretation, Hicks's *IS-LM* thus showed that both the *General Theory* and classical theory could be reconciled as individual special cases of an even wider framework – a ' "generalised" General Theory' (as, for example, Skidelsky, 1992, p. 622, puts it).

The discussion above suggests that this is not how the generalisation evolved. The model began as a separate and rival model that preceded the *General Theory*; the generalisation was a trivial algebraic manoeuvre (though

one with far-reaching consequences). Furthermore, Hicks's actual presentation of the *IS-LM* model is not consistent with the standard interpretation.
Hicks stated his objective as *comparison*, not generalisation:

> Professor Pigou's theory runs, to a quite amazing extent, in real terms...
> But if, on behalf of the ordinary classical economist, we declare that he
> would have preferred to investigate many of those problems in money
> terms, Mr. Keynes will reply that there is no classical theory of money
> wages and employment. It is quite true that such a theory cannot easily
> be found in the textbooks. But this is only because most of the textbooks
> were written at a time when general changes in money wages in a closed
> system did not present an important problem. There can be little doubt
> that most economists have thought that they had a pretty fair idea of what
> the relation between money wages and employment actually was...
>
> If we can construct such a theory, and show that it does give results
> which have in fact been commonly taken for granted, but which do
> not agree with Mr. Keynes' conclusions, then we shall at last have a
> satisfactory basis of comparison. We may hope to be able to isolate
> Mr. Keynes' innovations, and so to discover what are the real issues in
> dispute.
>
> Since our purpose is comparison, I shall try to set out my typical clas-
> sical theory in a form similar to that in which Mr. Keynes sets out his
> own theory;... (Hicks, 1937, pp. 147–8)

In particular, he aimed to bring to bear a newly defined 'classical theory
of money wages' (achieved in three pages) and his simultaneous equation
version of the *General Theory* on a specific issue: 'how does Mr. Keynes come
to make his remarks about an increase in the inducement to invest not
raising the rate of interest?' (ibid., p. 154). Two paragraphs later he implies
that the increase in the inducement to invest that he has in mind is one due
to public spending '(Mr. Keynes in 1936 is not the first Cambridge economist
to have a temperate faith in Public Works)' (ibid., p. 154). He concludes,
of course, that an increase in 'the inducement to investment' might not
increase the rate of interest if the *LM* schedule is flat. This conclusion is driven
by his characterisation of the fixed *LL* curve as follows: 'It will probably
tend to be nearly horizontal on the left, and nearly vertical on the right'
(ibid., p. 154).

If a framework can *illustrate* the differences between two theories in the
context of a specific problem, it does not follow that the framework encompasses and supersedes those two theories. Nor does Hicks make this claim
in the paper; the closest he comes is as follows: '[t]hese, then, are a few
of the things we can get out of our skeleton apparatus. But even if it may
claim to be a slight extension of Mr. Keynes' similar skeleton, it remains a

terribly rough and ready sort of affair' (ibid., p. 158). Furthermore, if this were genuinely the achievement of the paper it would be a feat demanding the highest accolade. No such accolade was forthcoming from Keynes.

Roy Harrod's and James Meade's contributions to 'Keynesianism' were published respectively in the January 1937 *Econometrica* and February 1937 *Review of Economic Studies*. In amongst Harrod's algebra were the standard claims:

> The stress which he lays on expectations is sound, and constitutes a great improvement in the definition of marginal productivity. This improvement, however, might be incorporated in traditional theory without entailing important modifications in its other parts. (Harrod, 1937, p. 77)

> It appears to me that the achievement of Mr. Keynes has been to consider certain features of traditional theory which were unsatisfactory, because the problems involved tended to be slurred over, and to reconstruct that theory in a way which resolves the problems. (ibid., p. 84)

> In my judgement Mr. Keynes has not affected a revolution in fundamental economic theory but a re-adjustment and a shift of emphasis. (ibid., p. 85)

4.4.4 Wider endorsement

While Robertson's role in the development of 'Keynesian' theory remains unrecognised, at the time the closeness of their respective positions was both public and portrayed as a virtue. In his private correspondence with Keynes, Robertson used Harrod's and Hicks's work as support for his own:

> Both over the *Treatise* and this book I have gone through real intellectual torment trying to make up my mind whether, as you often seem to claim, there is some new piece on the board or rather a re-arrangement, which seems to you superior, of existing pieces. It has been an intellectual relief to me to find Hicks (e.g. review pp. 246–8) and Harrod (*Econometrica* paper) both taking the latter view, though agreeing far more with you than me about the merits of the re-arrangement. (Robertson to Keynes, 29 December 1936, *CW* XIV, p. 95)

More publicly, Robertson acknowledged Hicks's contribution in his *QJE* review:

> After numerous discussions of this book and these notes I am in the usual difficulty – how to acknowledge indebtedness without compromising the acknowledgee. Especially from Professor Pigou, Mr. Henderson, Dr. Bode, Mr. Hicks and above all from Mr. Sraffa, . . . (Robertson, 1936, reproduced in Backhouse, 1999, p. 206)

Finally, just after the three 'Keynesian' papers were published, in June 1937 Haberler's work for the LoN was published. Under the title *Prosperity and Depression: A Theoretical Analysis of Cyclical Movements*, Haberler reiterated the case for the general neo-classical approach.[4] The book was in two parts. The first part sets out summaries of existing theories of the cycle, according to the following categorisations: monetary, over-investment, changes in cost efficiency, under-consumption, psychological and 'harvest'. Keynes's work was included as a 'psychological' theory, with elaboration in a footnote:

> In recent years, it has become fashionable to lay stress on the element of expectation. Keynes' "General Theory of Employment, Interest and Money" is conceived in terms of expectation; and, at an earlier date, the conception of economic expectation was interpreted and developed by the Swedish school . . . (Haberler, 1937, p. 135)

In the second part of the book, Haberler sets out his 'synthesis'. The underlying approach and the specific approach to the *General Theory* were in line with Robertson's perspective. A combination of classical and neo-classical theories could explain the problems that the League had concerned itself with; Keynes made no great advance, but merely pointed towards the necessary areas where synthesis was required:

> In the course of this analysis of existing theories, it became apparent that many of the seeming differences of doctrine were due rather to the use of different terminologies than to any more fundamental causes.
>
> The measure of agreement which appeared to exist between those who have devoted special attention to the problem of the trade cycle seemed to justify an attempt to make from their theories even at this early stage of the work the general synthesis which constitutes the second part of this volume. This synthesis, however, is more than a simple patching together of the theorems of others: it is an attempt to create a living and coherent, if incomplete, theory on the basis of the knowledge at present available. (ibid., pp. iv–v)

In specific theoretical terms, the book set out a loanable funds approach to interest, adopted Robertson's interpretation of the savings–investment relationship and advocated the accelerator theory of investment.

4.5 Alternative theories of the rate of interest

At this point, the neo-classical economists began to focus specifically and intensively on the theory of interest. They argued that loanable funds was an 'alternative theory' of the rate of interest that was compatible with liquidity preference. The detail of the theoretical case is examined in Chapter 7; here the debate is examined to illustrate the joined-up nature of the opposition as well as the equivalence in the approaches of the 'Keynesians' and Robertson. Keynes's original response to Robertson's *QJE* article picked up the ill-defined and underdeveloped nature of the theory that his own work was being set against:

> When you say that 'it is not as a refutation of a common-sense account of events in terms of supply and demand for loanable funds, but as an alternative version of it' that my account is to be regarded, what 'common-sense account' have you in mind? Where is it to be found? Can you give me the references? (Keynes to Robertson, 13 December 1936, *CW* XIV, p. 92)

Robertson's eventual response to these questions was published in the *EJ*. Keynes arranged a debate between himself and the advocates of loanable funds under the title, 'Alternative Theories of the Rate of Interest' (henceforth, 'alternative theories'). These articles were perhaps the most substantial debate provoked by the *General Theory*. Robertson's first contribution explained the evolution of loanable-funds theory:

> Mr. Keynes complains that, in comparing his theory of interest with "a common sense account of events in terms of supply and demand for loanable funds," I have given no indication of where an example of the latter is to be found. In point of fact, I am afraid I was referring primarily to the account which I had just attempted to give myself [his *QJE* review, 1936] . . . No doubt I had also in mind the more elaborate analysis of Dr. Haberler, which was not, I admit, generally accessible [footnote: Now published in *Prosperity and Depression* pp. 191 ff.]. But these accounts are both, I think, merely attempts to give a rather pedantic precision to the ordinary view enshrined in the well-known studies of the capital and credit markets as those of Lavington and Hawtrey, . . . (Robertson, 1937a, p. 428)

Robertson thus claimed that loanable funds theory was first set out in his own review and second in the work by Haberler that was at the time unpublished. Robertson went on to use Hicks's (1937) *Econometrica* presentation (five months after its publication) to support a concession to Keynes that would become known as the liquidity trap: 'And I am prepared, too, with Mr. Hawtrey and Mr. Hicks,[5] to concede to Mr. Keynes that so-called 'liquidity' considerations might in certain conditions set a limit to the practicable fall in the long-term rate of interest, . . . ' (Robertson, 1937, pp. 433–4).

Yet for the purposes of the *EJ* debate, the loanable funds argument was not presented by Robertson, Haberler or Hawtrey. Instead, the case was set out by the Swedish economist Bertil Ohlin in two contributions entitled 'Some Notes on the Stockholm Theory of Savings and Investment' (March and June 1937). On receipt of the second instalment of Ohlin's article, Keynes wrote:

> I am very glad that you have been able to put down in a way I can understand the theory of the rate of interest as established by the demand and supply for credit. This is an idea which is widely held outside Sweden, e.g. to some extent by Dennis Robertson and Hicks. For my part, I am not convinced by it and consider it fundamental heresy.... So far from its being an alternative version of my theory, my first impression is that this and mine are wholly irreconcilable. (3 February 1937, *CW* XIV, pp. 185–6)

The debate continued through to the September 1938 edition of the *EJ*. In April 1938, Robertson (1938c) wrote an additional overview piece for the *Manchester School*. Keynes described Robertson's final *EJ* contribution as 'completely worthless and, what is more, intolerably boring' (*CW* XXIX, p. 168).

In parallel to the 'alternative theories' debate, the June 1938 *American Economic Review* (*AER*) contained a paper by M. Millikan under the title 'The Liquidity-Preference Theory of Interest': 'This paper is an expansion of some remarks delivered before a Round Table on General Interest Theory at the Fiftieth Annual Meeting of the American Economic Association in Atlantic City, December 29, 1937' (Millikan, 1938, p. 247). At the start of the paper, Millikan acknowledges that 'specific criticisms here advanced are derived almost entirely from the work of others'; a footnote elaborates: 'especially' Robertson's *QJE* review, Robertson's and Ohlin's contributions to the 'alternative theories' debate and both Hicks's review of the *General Theory* and his just-published *Econometrica* article. After some discussion, Millikan precisely predicts the terms on which the economics profession would accept liquidity preference. These terms were according to an 'equilibrium theory' as follows:

> It is this equilibrium concept that will, I suspect, ultimately come to be taken as the substance of Mr. Keynes's theory of interest,... Drawn up subject to the strict assumptions outlined above and stripped of the inconsistencies... the theory can, I think, be made formally perfectly valid. Mr. Hicks has shown us what it looks like when we subject it to this overhaul...
>
> In Mr. Hicks's formulation the dependence of i on all these factors is clearly brought out and hence the two curves which appear as proximate determinants of i (the *IS* curve and the *LL* curve) satisfy at least to a considerable extent the Criterion of Evident Dependence [simply that the theory should include the 'Evident' variables]. (ibid., p. 257)

In his 'Summary and Conclusion', Millikan looked to the more complex presentations of 'Keynesianism' that would emerge later:

> I think most modern economists would reject as emphatically as does Mr. Keynes the theory that *i* is determined solely or proximately by the supply of real savings and the demand for real capital for investment. I think they would agree that a *complete* theory of interest is to be found only in a many-dimensional formula involving a number of variables in addition to those specified in Mr. Hicks's generalised version of *The General Theory.* (ibid., p. 259)

In 1939 the LoN then issued a second edition of Haberler's book. A new 'Preface' explained some modification in the light of criticism and the main innovation: a chapter which 'deals with the very rich literature on the subject which has come into existence since the completion of the manuscript of the first edition' (Haberler, 1939, p. iii).

In this new chapter, Haberler explained 'The greater part of the literature to be discussed in this chapter emanates from, and centres around, Mr. KEYNES' *General Theory of Employment, Interest and Money'* (ibid., p. 197). However, the interest was not in the *General Theory* in its own right, but in the need to incorporate it and the subsequent literature – in particular, the alternative theories debate – into the LoN synthesis. As before, standing in the way of this reconciliation were merely exaggerations of differences and terminological difficulties:

> [T]hese theories suffer from the fact that their authors have not been able to make clear in all cases whether apparent differences between their views and those of other writers rest on different empirical assumptions or only on a different usage of terms; in other words, whether differences are of a material kind or of a purely terminological nature.
>
> There can be no doubt that, in recent years, the discussions on saving and investment and the possibility of their being unequal, on hoarding, liquidity-preference and the rate of interest, and similar topics, have made it increasingly evident that purely verbal misunderstandings and slight differences in the definition of terms have played a very great role . . .
>
> Even in those instances where the new theories amount to nothing more than a terminological innovation and cannot be said to be in material contradiction to the traditional views, they have sometimes served a useful purpose, by bringing to light hidden implications in the older theoretical schemes and forcing the propounders of 'rival' theories to make all their assumptions clear and explicit. (ibid., p. 205)

Haberler then cited explicitly and approvingly Robertson's and Hicks's work:

> Professor Robertson has recently made an attempt at separating terminological from substantial differences. *Cf.* "A Survey of Modern Monetary Controversy" in *The Manchester School*, Vol. 9, No. 1, April 1938 as well as Hicks's 'Mr Keynes and the Classics . . . ' (ibid.)

While most of Keynes's senior colleagues commented on the *General Theory* and then withdrew from controversy, Robertson's opposition to the *General Theory* in public and in private never ceased. Eventually, Keynes's and Robertson's relationship broke down.[6] In 1938 Robertson moved to LSE. Two years later he published a vicious and unrepentant assault on the *General Theory*. This assault, 'Mr. Keynes and the Rate of Interest', was the only new work in a book of re-printed articles *Essays in Monetary Theory* (although it was mainly drawn from his *QJE* review and other arguments he had put to Keynes in the years since publication). In the 'Preface' he sought to explain his actions:

> In the badinage of correspondence, Mr. Keynes has accused me of being a bad snake, unapt at sloughing its old skins; while I have presumptuously claimed in reply to be a good glow-worm, shedding its feeble light fairly consistently and impartially on all the phenomena in its neighbourhood, by contrast with the powerful searchlight which launches a penetrating but distorting beam on a number of different objects in succession, obscuring the rest in temporary darkness. And there we must leave it. (Robertson, 1940, p. ix)

Again, Robertson applauded Hicks's contribution:

> In this long and intricately worked terrain, the problem of acknowledgement has become a nightmare. I have tried to solve part of it *ambulando* in the text, but much remains. Among the many published appraisals of Mr. Keynes' latest work, I have, I think, derived most benefit from those by Mr. Hawtrey and Mr. Hicks; among many conversations on the same theme, those with Mr. Sraffa stand out in memory as most inevitably ending in theft. (ibid., p. viii)

If Keynes responded to the book it has not been recorded. Furthermore, no correspondence or report of contact exists until official work brought them together at the end of the Second World War. On the other hand, Hicks offered Robertson fulsome praise:

> The reviewer of Professor Robertson's *Essays*, especially when (as is the present case) he comes to his task a year after its publication, is confronted

with something different from the usual task of reviewing. Either in their collected form, or as originally published, these essays will already be familiar to most persons who are likely to read a review in ECONOMICA. They have already won an assured place in economic literature, which in this instance is English literature too; for may we not say that Robertson at his best is unmatched this side of Adam Smith for the combination of profound wisdom with literary charm? The present volume contains a larger proportion of these best things than any of its predecessors; their clarity and humanity would be superfluous to praise. My own favourite is that Harvard address, characteristically entitled "The Snake and the Worm". I do not know how often I have read it; I shall go on reading it until I know it by heart. (Hicks, 1942a, p. 53)

In the course of the review, Hicks explicitly endorsed Robertson's approach to the savings–investment relationship and to the theory of liquidity preference:

[S]ince the time of the *General Theory* the need for definitions [of saving and investment] of the Robertsonian sort has been increasingly felt . . .

. . .

The search for the ideal definitions of Saving and Investment has now been narrowed down, and narrowed down to something in the near neighbourhood of Professor Robertson's original definitions. (ibid., pp. 54–5)

He has no difficulty in showing that the theory of Liquidity Preference is a very rough and ready description of the way the forces governing interest work; . . . (ibid., pp. 55–6)[7]

4.6 Pigou's Keynesianism

An alternative presentation of the 'Keynesian' model next emerged late in 1937, with the prestige of a Royal Economic Society Presidential Address. The initiative saw Pigou pursuing the theme of a neo-classical 'theory of money wages', and taking steps towards the notion of a 'Keynes effect'. The latter limited the role of the rate of interest to explaining the transmission mechanism between a cut in wages and lower unemployment.

Keynes was ill when Pigou's (1937) paper was accepted for publication. On recovery, he attempted to halt its publication (see *CW* XIV, p. 234); failing to do so, he wrote a two-page rejoinder for the next issue of the *EJ*. While Keynes rejected Pigou's argument on the grounds of faulty logic, the same *EJ* also contained a more generous response to Pigou's article by Nicholas Kaldor (then at the LSE). Kaldor did not dispute Pigou's conclusion, but argued that it could be better stated in terms of a number of macroeconomic functions: $M = f(r)$, $S = \psi \{r, x\}$ and $V = \phi \{r, I/wx\}$, with V, velocity, w, money wages, x, total employment and others obviously defined. The primary analytical technique was a discussion of the size and sign of various partial derivatives. *IS-LM* made its appearance at the end of the article, in a footnote of the second to last page:

> This proposition could be best illustrated by the type of diagram used by Dr. Hicks [shown below as Figure 4.5].... Measuring real output (or employment) along *OX*, and the rate of interest along *OY* the curve *IS* (determined by the *I* and *S* functions) shows the various levels of real output at which savings are equal to investment, at different rates of interest. The *LL* curve, depending on the *M* and *V* functions, shows the money rates of interest consistent with different levels of output. A reduction in money wages cannot affect the position of the *IS* curve, but it will shift the *LL* curve to the right; for, by reducing the size of "working balances" at a given level of real income, it enhances the size of "idle balances," and thus reduces the interest rate consistent with that level of output. Its effect therefore is exactly the same as that of an increase in the quantity of money or a reduction in liquidity preference. It is, in fact, nothing more than an alternative way of increasing the quantity of money in terms of wage units (cf. Keynes, *General Theory*, p. 267). If the banking system pursues a policy aiming to keep the rate of interest constant, the *LL* curve will be horizontal and the effect on employment will be nil. If dM/dr is large, the effect on employment of any reduction in wages can only be small. (Kaldor, 1937, p. 752)

Pigou rejected Keynes's critique: 'I have not been able to follow the reasoning of Mr. Keynes' short note' (Pigou, 1938, p. 134); but he accepted Kaldor's argument: 'As Mr. Kaldor has shown, it is possible to extend an

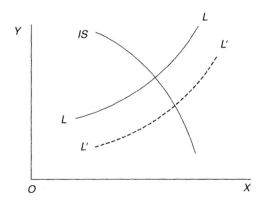

Figure 4.5 Kaldor's diagram

algebraic analysis of the type used in the study of our model to conditions nearer to real life' (ibid., p. 138).

Robertson was involved in both the preparation of Pigou's original article and its publication.[8] His correspondence with Keynes indicates that he supported both Kaldor's and Hicks's techniques:

> The argument requires re-stating, as it has been re-stated by Kaldor (p. 4, top), as a *reductio ad absurdum*. As thus re-stated, it proves what it sets out to prove, viz. that the new equilibrium position is one of increased employment. (*CW* XIV, p. 252)

> As we approach the real world, the considerations advanced by Viner (*Q.J.E.* Nov. '36, p. 161) and Hicks (*Econometrica*, Ap. '37, p. 156 [the page that first depicts the 'generalised' model]) appear to me to assume governing importance. But that, again, is another story. (ibid., p. 254)[9]

Pigou continued to develop his approach. In 1941 he issued a book: *Employment and Equilibrium – A Theoretical Discussion*. It was greeted with rapturous applause on both sides of the Atlantic – Samuelson's and Kaldor's reviews well capturing the true neo-classical nature of the work as well as betraying their own prejudices:

> [T]his is one of the most important books of recent years. Moreover, it reveals with remarkable force the extent to which the Keynesians all along have been speaking classical prose, at the same time that "classicists" have thought in Keynesian poetry. (Samuelson, 1941, p. 552)

> But the book is more than just a confirmation of Mr. Keynes' propositions reached by a different and more "classical" route. For in the course of the investigation Professor Pigou develops a technique which is eminently suited for a systematic treatment of problems relating to the general level of activity and its fluctuations; ... (Kaldor, 1941, p. 459)

4.7 Modigliani's 'synthesis'

In the light of macroeconomic debate today, the neo-classical contribution of by far the greatest importance was that of Franco Modigliani (1944) (based on his PhD thesis). The contribution strengthened the 'neo-classical synthesis', virtually eliminated the role of the theory of liquidity preference and the rate of interest from economic discourse, established the 'rigid wage' interpretation of the *General Theory*, and at the same time moved the centre of gravity of economic debate to the United States.

Modigliani's 'Keynesian' model claimed Hicks (1937) as predecessor: 'In reconsidering the Keynesian system we shall essentially follow the lines suggested by J. R. Hicks in his fundamental paper, "Mr. Keynes and the 'Classics' ". Our main task will be to clarify and develop his arguments, taking into account later theoretical developments' (Modigliani, 1944, p. 48). He took Hicks's five equations in their generalised form, and merged the model with four more equations and four more variables (below) to give nine equations in nine variables. The equations he added were respectively a nominal/real output relation, a production function, a labour demand function and a function reflecting 'Keynesian assumptions concerning the supply-of-labor schedule' (ibid., 1944, p. 47).

$$Y = PX$$

$$X = X(N)$$

$$W = X'(N)P$$

$$W = \alpha w_0 + \beta F^{-1}(N)P$$

where Y was now the notation for 'money income'; P, 'price level'; X, 'an indicator of physical output'; N, 'aggregate employment'; and W, 'money wage rate'. The fourth of these equations introduced, for the first time, an algebraic depiction of wage 'stickiness'.

The paper is also notable for a further alternative development of 'Keynesian' economics, purportedly making the model dynamic. This elaboration was achieved by a seemingly arbitrary allocation of time subscripts to a seemingly arbitrary subset of equations from his nine-equation model. The need to solve this dynamic system in turn intensified the level of mathematics required for macroeconomics. No justification for the economic validity of this step was offered.

In the course of his analysis the – by then wholly accepted – device of distinguishing between the so-called 'Keynesian' case and the 'generalised system' allowed Modigliani to reject two of the fundamental conclusions of Keynes's economics:

> The liquidity-preference theory is not necessary to explain under-employment equilibrium; it is sufficient only in a limiting case: the "Keynesian case" [the liquidity trap]. In the general case it is neither necessary nor sufficient; it can explain this phenomenon only with the additional assumption of rigid wages. (ibid., pp. 75–6)

> In conclusion, then, the statement that unemployment is caused by lack of investment assumes implicitly that every possible economic system works under the special conditions of the "Keynesian case"; and this is clearly unwarranted. (ibid., p. 77)

Given the rejection of the role of liquidity preference, Modigliani's explanation for unemployment centred on wage behaviour:

I. As long as wages are flexible, the long-run equilibrium rate of interest is determined exclusively by real factors, that is to say, essentially by the propensity to save and the marginal efficiency of investment . . .

II. If wages are rigid it is still true that the long-run equilibrium rate of interest is determined by the propensities to save and to invest but the situation is now more complicated; for these propensities depend also on money income and therefore on the quantity of active money which in turn depends itself on the level of the rate of interest . . . We want however to stress again that the dependence of the rate of interest on the quantity of money does not depend on liquidity preference. (ibid., p. 88)

This conclusion is perhaps hardly surprising, given his imposition of a classical labour market onto the 'Keynesian' model. We see here the emergence of the short-run 'sticky wage' and long-run 'flexible wage' position that has remained the mainstream interpretation of Keynes's economics right up until today:

Most macroeconomists believe that the crucial difference between the short run and the long run is the behaviour of prices. *In the long run, prices are flexible and therefore can respond to changes in supply or demand. In the short run, however, many prices are "stuck" at some predetermined level.* Because prices behave differently in the short run than in the long run, economic policies have different effects over different time horizons. (Mankiw, 1992, p. 215, his emphasis)

In Romer's *Advanced Macroeconomics* textbook, first published in 1996, a virtually identical copy of Modigliani's model is set out as alternatively the 'standard' or 'textbook' 'Keynesian model'. Only the sticky wage aspect is explicitly attributed to Keynes: 'The aggregate supply portion of the model in Keynes's *General Theory* (1936) begins with the assumption that the nominal wage is rigid (at least over some range): $W = \overline{W}$ (Romer, 1996, p. 215).

It is unclear if Keynes was aware of the existence of Modigliani's assault; no written comment has been published. Under the entry for 'IS-LM analysis' in the *New Palgrave*, Leijonhufvud has written: 'Thus, the debate came to the distinctly odd conclusion that Keynes had revolutionised economic theory by asserting the classical platitude that when money wages are too high for equilibrium in the labour market unemployment is the result' (Leijonhufvud, 1987, p. 1003).

Modigliani's article marks the point where substantial theoretical contributions to 'Keynesian' economics ceased. 'Keynesian' economics, therefore, culminated in a position that emphasised as strongly as possible its rejection of the central theoretical and practical component of Keynes's theory. Modigliani's position remains today as the modern depiction of the 'Keynesian' position.

The validity of Modigliani's conclusions depend entirely on four very substantial theoretical steps – what might be called the 'necessary propositions of "Keynesian" economics': (i) Hicks's simultaneous-equation depiction of the *General Theory* is a wholly complete depiction of the *General Theory*; (ii) Hicks's depiction of the classical theory is similarly complete; (iii) the mathematical generalisation of the two depictions into the simultaneous five-equation model is a valid generalisation in the economic, in contrast to the mathematical, sense; and (iv) the grafting of a classical model onto the generalised *IS-LM* model is also a valid technique in the economic sense. The reality of modern 'Keynesian' economics is that it has never addressed the theory from this perspective; it has simply chosen to accept the propositions without acknowledging that such a step has been taken. The only justification for this abandonment of analysis, investigation and rigour is the notion that Keynes accepted 'Keynesian' economics. This claim is analysed in detail in Chapter 9.

It is of profound and central importance to the exposition in this book that *any* 'Keynesian' 'reconciliation' between the thinking of Keynes's senior colleagues with Keynes's model took place at the expense of the nature and theoretical substance of Keynes's economics. Explaining the specific ways in which the two approaches are opposed is one of the main pre-occupations of Parts II and III of this book. In all its main points the 'Keynesian' framework accorded with the complaints of Keynes's senior colleagues despite Keynes's protest against these complaints.

4.8   Neo-classical and 'Keynesian' policy

As Backhouse observes, virtually all of the academic reviews ignored Keynes's broader policy and social conclusions: 'Where the "popular" reviews focused on Keynes's chapter on the social philosophy implied by the general theory, this received far less attention in the specialist reviews' (Backhouse, 1999, pp. 12–13). Equally, all of the theoretical contributions discussed in the previous sections were almost meticulous in their avoidance of policy issues. The contributions to the 'Keynesian' theory rarely addressed Keynes's policy conclusions; they simply addressed contrived practical pre-occupations of their own: the effect of increases in government expenditure, the 'Pigou effect' and the 'liquidity trap'. Furthermore, any discussions of policy tended to be abstract, with policy conclusions often incidental or at least secondary to a tortured exposition of theory. Explicit statements of policy were rare and, when they came, were equivocal. For example, Hicks's review only offered 'Even if his theory is generally accepted, there will still be room for wide differences of opinion about the consequences of particular policies' (Hicks, 1936, p. 242). Harrod's Keynesian piece (1937) was highly oblique, and while Meade (1937) addressed a number of different policy situations, he did so in an abstract manner. Towards the end of the war, however, through comments by Hicks and Meade, the Keynesian stance was increasingly revealed as opposed to Keynes when it came to interest rates.

Robertson's theoretical contributions also avoided policy. But, like Keynes, he separately made a number of policy pronouncements (although generally through academic rather than newspaper outlets). Two key statements were a speech in Harvard University in September 1936 and a year later a paper in the *Lloyds Bank Review*. The former speech was given under the title 'The State and Economic Fluctuations'. His conclusion exactly encapsulates his whole discussion:

> The advocates of energetic State action against developed depression have had in all countries a hard fight to wage against the forces of apathy and despair. Let us salute them everywhere, in their victories or in their honourable defeats: but let us beg them, whether flushed with success or saddened with failure, to think again before concluding that cheap money and Government deficits, still less trade restriction and exchange manipulation, are the right diet for all phases of the trade cycle or the right remedy for all the economic ills of the world. (Reproduced in Robertson, 1966, p. 94)[10]

To the extent he approved of the monetary measures, he did so *only* to aid escape from slump.

A year later he made a more direct attack on cheap-money policy, in his paper 'The Trade Cycle – an Academic View' (1937).[11] The work was motivated in part by an article by Lionel Robbins in a previous number of the journal. Robbins was at that time head of economics at LSE, the post previously held by William Beveridge, who had moved to Oxford in 1936. LSE economics was of course notoriously at loggerheads with Cambridge economics. Robbins himself had opposed virtually all of Keynes's theoretical and practical initiatives since he first emerged as an economist of stature. In his own article, Robbins's position was the antithesis of Keynes's position: rejecting monetary reform, preferring gold and advocating dear money under normal circumstances. Robertson positioned himself between the two views as follows:

> There is nothing in Professor Robbins's pages about the rate of interest with which in practice I disagree – neither in his defence of low money rates in the early phases of the present recovery, nor in his contention that the normal tendency of rates, both short and long, to harden as expansion proceeds should not now be resisted and may have to be actively reinforced. All the same, I am conscious of a certain difference of emphasis in my mind, both from Professor Robbins and from those who, diagnosing differently from himself, have reached precisely the opposite conclusion

that an increase in interest rates should be avoided like hell-fire. For both these parties are convinced that the rate of interest is supremely important . . . The one party finds the ultimate villain of the piece in the extravagance of the human race, the other in its passion for keeping money safe; and their recipes for monetary policy diverge accordingly. 'Let rates rise now,' says Professor Robbins, 'to prevent unwise planning; for the desire to spend is sure to make them rise later.' 'Keep rates down now,' say his opponents, 'lest if once you let them rise the desire to hoard prevent you from ever getting them down again.' My judgement is, on the whole, with Professor Robbins; yet, even if he has his way, I hope for no great things. (Robertson, 1966, p. 98)

In the same article, Robertson also introduced a theme that would recur in subsequent contributions; he referred to the monetary measures as 'authoritarian':

Even in the democratic countries we live under a degree of authoritarianism which would have been inconceivable thirty years ago. The power of Governments over Central banks, and the influence of Central Banks over their financial communities, have grown beyond all knowledge. (Robertson, 1966, p. 95)

He closed his 1938 *Manchester School* paper in a similar manner:

Can the Authoritarian State solve that problem of periodic painless transition from a higher to a lower level of fixed capital formation which liberalistic capitalism has failed to solve, and if so is the achievement worth the price? . . . To suspect that from a long run point of view Cheap Money may prove a broken reed and Liquidity Preference a bogey man is not necessarily to suppose that all is for the best in the best of all possible worlds. (Roberston, 1938c, p. 19)

As with Modigliani's theoretical contribution, developments in the war sought to resolve, and to a great extent did resolve, the policy debate. In Britain this was effected through the *EWP* (Cmd. 6527, 1944) and Beveridge's (1944) *Full Employment in a Free Society*, which most still regard as setting the planning/'Keynesian' agenda for the post-war world. The conventional wisdom of a conversion to 'Keynesianism' is perhaps based on these developments. However, the reality of the nature of any conversion is wholly different to that associated with the conventional wisdom. Instead, the preparation for post-war employment policy saw the LSE advocates of *laissez-faire*, Beveridge and Robbins, as well as the great supporter of austerity, Hubert Henderson (see below), not only converted to but leading the development of post-war planning agenda. Nobody was converted to Keynes; these economists, his most outspoken rivals, merely adopted the economic nationalism agenda set out by Harold Macmillan and the NFYG.

The *EWP* emerged from the Economic Section of the British Government Cabinet Office. This unit appears to have been set up during the war, perhaps in part as a successor to the EAC and as a counter-balance to Keynes's influence though his wartime role in HM Treasury. Lionel Robbins became director in 1941. James Meade produced both the preparatory material for and then the first draft of the *White Paper* itself (in March 1943), which Robbins then redrafted.[12]

Skidelsky (2000, p. 279) notes that '...Keynes was not importantly involved in its preparation' and Moggridge (1976, p. 132) that '...Keynes's drafting contributions to the White Paper which followed were few, because of his involvement in an extensive official and ministerial debate on post-war external economic policy and his illness during March and April 1944, the months of heaviest drafting'. Furthermore, Skidelsky (2000, p. 282) records that Hubert Henderson was involved in the preparation of the final draft. Henderson rivalled Robbins for his relentless opposition to Keynes's work and practical initiatives. Keynes's response to his assault on the *General Theory* was noted above. Skidelsky offers an insight into Henderson's policy perspective:

Henderson was a Schachtian[13] ... Contrary to what he called the 'Chatham House' view, which blamed inter-war economic evils on economic nationalism, he viewed economic nationalism as an inevitable response to changes in the world economy. He did not believe that the old system of complementary international trade between manufacturing centres and primary producers, fuelled by rapid population growth and international lending, could be restored.... Henderson was convinced that the system of planned trade pioneered by Schacht, and copied by Britain in the war, was tailor-made for both Britain's 'secular' and its short-term balance of payments problem... Henderson believed that Britain needed to cling on at all costs to the imperial remnants of its once global position.... In point of theory, Hubert Henderson was a Schachtian because he was not a Keynesian. He believed that Britain's economic problems lay on the supply not the demand side. But, unlike the Thatcherites of the 1980s, he thought that very little could be done about them – that is, he had little faith in market mechanisms or the possibility of restoring them. This being so, Britain should grab as much of the world's supply as possible – by exploiting its imperial position to plan its trade to its advantage. This sounded very much like the 'rational' division of labour Funk[14] planned for occupied Europe.... He is accurately described as an Economic Nationalist – the British equivalent of Hjalmar Schacht. (Skidelsky, 2000, pp. 200–1)

In a footnote to the end of this passage, Skidelsky offers the following additional information on 'economic nationalism':

Economic Nationalists, too, can be divided into two camps – National Capitalists and National Socialists. Henderson fits the first, his protégé Thomas Balogh the second. One must, of course, distinguish the economic doctrines of the latter from the politics of Hitler's national socialists.

In parallel, Beveridge was preparing his *Full Employment in a Free Society* (1944). Beveridge had been opposed to Keynes's economics from as early as the *Economic Consequences of the Peace*. Between 1919 and 1937 he was the director of the LSE; and then between 1937 and 1944 he was the master of University College, Oxford. He moved from the School that most strongly opposed Keynes's ideas throughout the 1930s to the University that was at the centre of the 'Keynesian' revolution. His leaving speech between the two posts was notable for his vicious assault on both Keynes's theory and practice, described by Dimand (1999, pp. 222 and 228) as follows:

Beveridge devoted his farewell lecture, upon leaving the LSE for the mastership of University College, Oxford, in 1937, to a denunciation of abstract economic theorizing as exemplified by Keynes's *General Theory*. At the same time, Beveridge published a series of three articles on 'An analysis on unemployment' in *Economica* (1936–37), reformulating and restating his own approach.

Beveridge's remarkable valedictory address had a second theme: he deplored the excessive involvement of university teachers, especially social scientists, in public affairs, seeking to change society as well as study it, as a menace to the objectivity and neutrality of science.

In spite of these views, he emerged from the war as what Dimand (1999, p. 222) describes as a 'militant Keynesian'. His book effectively set out a more extreme economic nationalist agenda; at the same time fostering a debate, not about the *necessity*, but about the *extent* of state control.

Like Robertson and the NFYG, both post-war documents took a low-key approach to monetary considerations. The *White Paper* was non-committal: '59. For some time after the end of the war it will be necessary, . . . to maintain a policy of cheap money. Thereafter, the possibility of influencing capital expenditure by the variation of interest rates will be kept in view' (Cmd. 6527, 1944). While Beveridge did have a fuller discussion of monetary issues, this was positioned in Annex C – hardly central to the main discussion. Any notion that monetary failure was the cause of the Economic Problem was absent from both reports.

In terms of those who would later be specifically identified as 'Keynesians', Meade's view on monetary policy might be inferred by the *Employment White Paper*. Later at the NDE he would clash with Keynes on the mechanisms for post-war monetary policy. As Howson (2000, p. F132) notes, Meade 'found himself defending interest-rate flexibility against Keynes' and '[he] personally never really gave up the idea of using variations in the rate of interest as one of the macro-economic controls'. Hicks seemingly only once intervened on monetary policy, in the course of debate concerning the relevant interest rate during the war. Following the publication of Keynes's argument for a $2^1/_2$ per cent rate of interest in *The Times* of 3 October 1939, Hicks responded:

> During the war this saving is very convenient to the State. But it leaves a problem for the aftermath. One would feel more convinced by Mr Keynes's prescription of low interest rates if he would tell us how he would deal with that problem.

Keynes replied:

> We must be at cross-purposes. My point is that low interest rates will alleviate the problem of the aftermath, compared with high interest rates, as effectively as a very high burden of immediate taxation. He does not want more taxes, and he clearly cannot mean that high interest rates will help. So I am perplexed. (*CW* XXII, p. 32)

Hicks then pursued matters in private correspondence:

> I feel I must rather apologise to you for butting in to The *Times*, particularly since it is clear I have done it so badly! I now feel it would have been much better to have written to you privately; at least so far as the present matter is concerned. On the other hand, I shall no doubt have benefited from a little experience in the difficult art of newspaper correspondence; perhaps I may do it better another time. May I now try to explain my difficulties more fully? They are not by any means 100 per cent divergences from your position, but rather particular difficulties, which I think you might be able to help me out of. I dare say they are partly due to my lack of opportunity for discussing these matters up here; but I expect there are other people in the same position as myself. (*CW* XXII, p. 32)

On the key issue of the rate of interest he noted:

> My point about the aftermath was evidently too elusive. It is not the long-run problem which troubles me – there I am of course completely in agreement with you. What I am bothered about is the immediate post-war problem, the problem of the post-war boom. The more saving and

the less private investment there is in wartime, the greater will be the release of effective demand the moment the war is over; there is every reason to expect this to happen long before public expenditure can be contracted very vigorously. This is the stage when (am I right?) even you become a deflationist, for it is at this stage, when people are naturally impatient of controls, that the danger of really runaway inflation is much the most serious. Although I am quite in agreement with you about the pros of keeping interest rates down during the war, I cannot help feeling that that policy has the considerable disadvantage of piling up liquid funds in the hands of the public, which is likely to make the problem of controlling the post-war boom even more intractable. I probably rate this danger higher than you do, but I do not think you will deny its existence. I am not saying that this is a decisive argument against the policy of low interest rates – I do not regard it as such myself. But I do feel (as I said in my letter) that the low interest policy would be more convincing if it were combined with some prescription for this particular trouble which it is likely to induce. (*CW* XXII, p. 34)

Keynes responded on the rate of interest issues, elaborating his thinking and arguing that Hicks's concerns were not matters for the rate of interest.

About the problem of the aftermath, I am still perplexed as to what you mean. The amount of effective demand released after the war would not, I should have thought, be materially affected by the question whether what had been borrowed during the war had been borrowed at a high or a low rate of interest. If you are right in expecting a post-war boom like last time, the long-term rate of interest will be for the time being of only secondary importance. Whether or not, however, you are right in expecting such a boom, I should be inclined to predict that it would only be an event of a few months and that our real post-war problem would be inadequate effective demand. The difficulty will be to find any continuing successor to war expenditure. That indeed is an important part of the reason why I want to end up the war with a low rate of interest. During the war this policy will limit the burden we put on the future tax-payer and, after the war is over, it will facilitate the transition to peace-time capital expenditure. The problem of how to control a short time immediate post-war boom, due to replenishments of stocks and restoration of damage, appears to me to lie largely outside this problem. (*CW* XXII, p. 34)

For reasons of space, the discussion here has primarily focused on events from the British perspective. As with the development of the 'Keynesian' theory, there was a very significant international dimension to 'Keynesian' policy. In particular there were parallel domestic policy initiatives in the United States. While echoing almost entirely those in Britain, in a sense these were more fundamental to future developments because the centre of gravity of the economics profession would transfer from Britain to the United States after the war. This was achieved for theory in 1944 by Modigliani; his Nobel autobiography describes the work as integrating 'the "Keynesian revolution"... with the mainstream of classical economics'.[15] In institutional terms, US Keynesianism was based in Harvard; Haberler arrived from the LoN in 1937; Hansen arrived in time for his celebrated conversion to 'Keyensianism' around the same time; and Samuelson (at MIT) began to emerge as 'the incarnation of the economic establishment'.[16]

In the United States the debate was plainly and simply focused on fiscal policy. Hansen set out the 'Keynesian' agenda in his 1941, *Fiscal Policy and the Business Cycle*:

> It is at this point that depression policy emerges in a new role as an important element in a positive governmental program. But an economic minimum cannot be insured by reliance exclusively upon monetary policy. (Hansen, 1941, p. 74)

> There is thus emerging a new aim of fiscal policy, vigorously assailed by some and staunchly defended by others – the aim of ensuring full employment of the factors of production. This policy involves greatly enlarged governmental expenditures. (ibid., p. 117)

> The public debt is an instrument of public policy. It is a means to control the national income and, in conjunction with the tax structure, to regulate the distribution of income. (ibid., p. 185)

Two years later, S. E. Harris (1943) set out the 'Keynesian' case in his book, *Postwar Economic Problems*:

> Most of the participants – though not all – have been influenced by the writings of Lord Keynes; they are, therefore, disposed to put much emphasis on the measures which must be taken to maintain demand, particularly the contributions to full employment of an improved distribution of income – and hence a rise in the propensity to consume – and public investment.... Keynesian influence will be especially evident in the parts of the volume devoted to the discussion of full employment and fiscal policies. (Harris, 1943, p. 5)

Echoing developments in Britain the US policy would culminate in the Employment Act of 1946, which mandated the Federal Government to do all in its authority to achieve full employment; employment was established as a right guaranteed to the American people. The stage was set for the 'Keynesian' revolution in policy. Policy debate was positioned on fiscal policy; monetary policy fell into the background.

Notes

1. Later Keynes famously expressed frustration with Pigou's supporting public works while adhering to (or seeming to adhere to) a theory under which such spending would be ineffective (*CW* XIV, p. 259).
2. Conspicuous by their absence were the Cambridge economists – except Robertson.
3. See Skidelsky (1992, pp. 162–5).
4. The text stresses that 'the manuscript of Part I of this book was substantially completed by December 1935; that of part II, by May 1936. An attempt has, however, been made to refer, at least in footnotes, to some of the important publications which have appeared after the completion of the relevant parts of the manuscript' (Haberler, 1937, p. 2).
5. Footnoted: '*Capital and Employment*, p. 214: *Econometrica*, April 1937, pp. 154–5'. The 'liquidity trap', along with the 'Pigou effect', were debated as central issues by future Keynesians. They were not central to the *General Theory*.
6. So too did Robertson's mental health according to Moggridge (e.g. 1992, p. 601).
7. Hicks later looked back at this review: 'The first thing which has to be said is that by that time I was feeling myself to be much closer to Robertson than to any other economist who was my senior. Most of the papers which have gone before in this collection had been criticised by him, before or after their publication; I owed him quite a debt. I felt myself to be temperamentally much closer to him that I was to the Keynesians [meaning presumably Kahn and the Robinsons], from whom he had separated himself so sharply after 1936, or a bit earlier. But my position was on the Keynes side of his. I regretted the feud, for such indeed it had become. I really wrote the review for him, to persuade him to turn away from the polemics which I felt had become sterile, and to turn to more constructive work, on the basis of what I felt he had already achieved' Hicks (1965, p. 127, by permission of Oxford University Press). The new essay did not retract the position on the more detailed technical issues.
8. See dialogue between Keynes and Austin Robinson (*CW* XIV, p. 239) and Pigou's published acknowledgement to Robertson (Pigou, 1937, p. 422).
9. Young (1987, p. 111) also discusses Robertson's approach to Kaldor's paper.
10. Later published under the title 'The Snake and the Worm' in Robertson (1966).
11. Also published in Robertson (1966).
12. Howson (2000, p. F129).
13. Schacht was Hitler's economic adviser and the head of the German Central Bank.
14. Schacht's deputy and later, successor.
15. Source: Nobel Foundation website: http://nobelprize.org/economics/laureates/1985/modigliani-autobio.html.
16. Source: CEPA New School website: http://cepa.newschool.edu/het/profiles/samuelson.htm.

Part II
Theory

5
Theory: Preliminary Discussion

5.1 The *General Theory* and practical policy

In emphasising policy, the statement of Keynes's theory here differs substantially from both Keynes's own presentation and subsequent post-Keynesian interpretations. Keynes stated that the focus of the *General Theory* was theory, not practice:

> its main purpose is to deal with difficult questions of theory, and only in the second place with the applications of this theory to practice. (*CW* VII, p. xxi)

> It would need a volume of a different character from this one to indicate even in outline the practical measures in which they might be gradually clothed. (ibid., p. 383)

He sought to foster a debate about the validity of the classical theory. And the order of presentation of his theory was largely dictated by the theory that he sought to challenge rather than following more naturally from his own theoretical discoveries.

I take the opposite approach: I am concerned primarily with the theoretical justification for Keynes's secular cheap-money policy. My aim is to first show how cheap money *can* be set, and then to show why cheap money *must* be set. This leads not only to ordering the structure of the argument differently from the order of the *General Theory*, but also, different degrees of emphasis being given to the detailed components of the theory.

In addition, I am not greatly concerned with the detailed differences between Keynes's and the classical theory. But instead, in the light of the events outlined in Chapter 4, I do dwell a little on the neo-classical/'Keynesian' theory that has become identified with Keynes and look to Keynes's specific responses to the imposter in terms of the detailed theoretical argument.

It is my view that Keynes's decision to state his theory in the way he did, though logical in terms of his contemporaries' understanding and concerns, was extremely unfortunate and ultimately destructive of his message. Perhaps it was his own rationalism that demanded that he justify in meticulous detail why he no longer adhered to the theory that he had previously held to be true:

> I have been much pre-occupied with the causation, so to speak, of my own progress of mind from the classical position to my present views, – with the order in which the problem developed in my mind. What some people treat as an unnecessarily controversial tone is really due to the importance in my own mind of what I used to believe, and of the moments of transitions which were for me personally moments of illumination. You don't feel the weight of the past as I do. One cannot shake off a pack one has never properly worn. And probably your ignoring all this is a better plan than mine. For experience seems to show that people are divided between the old ones whom nothing will shift and are merely annoyed by my attempts to underline the points of transition so vital in my own progress, and the young ones who have not been properly brought up and believe nothing in particular. The portholes of light seen in escaping from a tunnel are interesting neither to those who mean to stay there nor to those who have never been there! I have no companions, it seems, in my own generation, either of earliest teachers or of earliest pupils; I cannot in thought help being somewhat bound to them, – which they find exceedingly irritating! (to R. F. Harrod, 30 August 1936, *CW* XIV, pp. 84–5)

The evidence of experience is that this concern of Keynes obscured the practical applications of the theory and made the relative emphasis that should be accorded to different components of the theory exceedingly difficult to judge. In particular, as with the basic premise of my book, the pivotal role of the rate of interest has been lost. Of course, Keynes's audience at the time would have been in no doubt of its importance. As seen in Chapter 3, his advocacy of monetary reform was highly public and gaining momentum each year. The review of the *General Theory* published in *The Times* exemplifies this reception: 'Mr. Keynes appears in this book, therefore, as a champion ... of the cheap money policy that has always been associated with his name' (Anonymous, *The Times*, 10 March 1936, Backhouse, 1999, p. 49). His academic audience would have regarded him as a monetary economist, responsible for the important contributions to the theory and analysis of credit that had been most comprehensively stated in the *Treatise*. Furthermore, those who were following his theoretical contributions at the time would have also seen his moving towards greater and greater emphasis on the role of the rate of interest. In the *Treatise* he finally arrived at the importance of cheap-money policy towards the end of the book. Similarly, Keynes's correspondence with the Macmillan Committee members indicates the circumstance of his arrival at this point of view.

After the publication of the *Treatise* on 31 October 1930, Keynes gave prominence to the rate of interest in his June 1931 Harris Foundation lectures in the United States (see Chapter 10). Here he argued that rate of interest was the *cause* of the depression:

> We are today in the middle of the greatest economic catastrophe – the greatest catastrophe due almost entirely to economic causes – of the modern world. . . . I see no reason to be in the slightest degree doubtful about the initiating causes of the slump . . .
> The leading characteristic *was an extraordinary willingness to borrow money for the purposes of new real investment at very high rates of interest* – rates of interest which were extravagantly high on pre-war standards, rates of interest which have never in the history of the world been earned, I should say, over a period of years over the average of enterprise as a whole. This was a phenomenon which was apparent not, indeed, over the whole world but over a very large part of it. (*CW* XIII, pp. 343–5, my emphasis)

Then, in December 1931, an *Economic Journal* article by H. Somerville hailed Keynes's work as 'a vindication of the Canonist attitude to interest and usury!' (Somerville, 1931, p. 647). He introduced at the same time the notion that '*interest is the villain of the economic piece*' (ibid., my emphasis). The work prompted a symposium on 'Savings and Usury' in the next issue. Three of the four contributions, by Edwin Cannan, B. P. Adarkar and B. K. Sandwell, rejected very strongly any condemnation of usury. Keynes's contribution, while agreeing some theoretical points, 'on one main issue [came] to the support of Mr Somerville' (*CW* XXIX, p. 16). His concluding words foreshadowed his future work:

> Personally I have come to believe that interest – or, rather, too high a rate of interest – is the 'villain of the piece' in a more far-reaching sense than appears from the above. But to justify this belief would lead me into a longer story than would be appropriate in this place. (*CW* XXIX, p. 16)

Over the next years his theoretical contributions were very limited as he put together his *General Theory*. His lecture courses,[1] however, provide another perspective on the development of his argument. The presentation in the lectures is closer to the presentation in this book than to that of the *General Theory*. In his October/November 1932 course, entitled 'The Monetary Theory of Production' (Rymes, 1989, pp. 47–84):

- the first lecture outlined 'The Characteristics of a Monetary Economy';
- the second and third looked at macroeconomic quantities: output, cost and profit, leading up to the saving–investment identity;

- the fourth was 'On interest, Its Rate and Its Determination' (continued in the fifth);
- the sixth was 'Monetary and Neutral Economy in Long and Short Periods', including a theory of investment demand;
- the seventh was entitled 'Equations are Symbolic Rather Than Algebraic'; and
- the eighth and final lecture took a broad historical view of the importance of the rate of interest to investment and output:

There was a conviction that the rate of interest should be controlled and that a higher rate of interest is injurious. The Church was against usury. Efforts were formerly made to control the rate of interest by law. Adam Smith realised that savings did not always find their way into investment and figured that if the rate of interest was too high investment would be prevented and money would flow into [unproductive, spendthrift consumption] debts. Bentham disagreed and violently attacked this passage. (Rymes, 1989, p. 82)

As he neared the end of preparing his book, Keynes made a contribution to a radio debate in which a number of economic experts contrasted their various diagnoses and proposed cures to the Economic Problem. He summarised his views in *The Listener* of 21 November 1934. The article looked to the specific point of theory that was of most concern (the practical dimension of this debate is addressed in Chapter 9):

There is, I am convinced, a fatal flaw in that part of the orthodox reasoning which deals with the theory of what determines the level of effective demand and the volume of aggregate employment; the flaw being largely due to the failure of the classical doctrine to develop a satisfactory theory of the rate of interest. (*CW* XIII, p. 489)

But, as noted, the *General Theory* did not pivot so clearly on the rate of interest. The theoretical argument was built up through a contrast with the classical theory, and, in great part, according to the logic of the classical theory. Policy was by no means ignored but was addressed only as suggestive points after the substance of the theoretical argument was laid out; he often pre-supposed knowledge of what was being referred to. Even in the following categorical statement, Keynes's argument is in the negative: that previous policy thwarted a sensible interest-rate policy, rather than a positive assertion of what that sensible policy should be:

Thus, the weight of my criticism is directed against the inadequacy of the *theoretical* foundations of the *laissez-faire* doctrine upon which I was brought up and which for many years I taught; – against the notion that the rate of interest and the volume of investment are self-adjusting at the optimum level, so that preoccupation with the balance of trade is a waste of time . . .

Under the influence of this faulty theory the City of London gradually devised the most dangerous technique for the maintenance of equilibrium which can possibly be imagined, namely, the technique of bank rate coupled with a rigid parity of the foreign exchanges. For this meant that the objective of maintaining a domestic rate of interest consistent with full employment was wholly ruled out. Since, in practice, it is impossible to neglect the balance of payments, a means of controlling it was evolved which, instead of protecting the domestic rate of interest, sacrificed it to the operation of blind forces. Recently, practical bankers in London have learned much, and one can almost hope that in Great Britain the technique of bank rate will never be used again to protect the foreign balance in conditions in which it is likely to cause unemployment at home. (*CW* VII, p. 339)

It is equally difficult to understand how such a statement could have been confused with fiscal policy for so long.

The *General Theory* was published in February 1936. The decision to aim the book at theorists did not appear to lead to any misunderstanding at the time. Backhouse's collection of reviews of the *General Theory* (1999) illustrates how most commentators (at least those not writing in 'specialist academic journals') accurately reflected Keynes's primary emphasis on monetary policy with fiscal policies in support:

State control of investment, with as one of its main objectives the forcing down of the rate of interest to a level difficult or impossible to achieve under conditions of uncontrolled investment, is an essential condition of a permanent solution of the problem of unemployment. . . . Alongside of his examination of the rate of interest . . . Mr. Keynes urges therefore the necessity for measures to increase consumption. (Francis Williams, *Daily Herald*, 4 February 1936, in Backhouse, 1999, pp. 21 and 25)

Mr. Keynes is more emphatic than ever that in the long run the trend of evolution will point towards a further considerable decline in interest rates . . . Mr. Keynes would like to see an increased degree of State intervention . . . Mr. Keynes declares that it is the policy of an autonomous rate of interest, unimpeded by international preoccupations, and of a national investment programme directed to an optimum level of domestic employment, which is calculated to help ourselves and our neighbours at the same time. (Anonymous, *Financial News*, 4 February 1936, in Backhouse, 1999, pp. 29–31)

If, then, left to itself, the economic system cannot provide work for all who want it a deus ex machina must be invoked. The State must stimulate consumption by redistributing incomes through taxation (as urged by Mr. Hobson), by forcing down the rate of interest, ... (T. S. Ashton, *Manchester Guardian*, 24 February 1936, in Backhouse, 1999, p. 38)

The main contention of the book as a whole, crudely and bluntly summarised, is that the criterion of monetary policy should be neither gold values nor exchange rates, nor even price levels, but the abolition of unemployment. Full employment, Mr. Keynes contends, can only be achieved by a correct monetary policy. ... Mr. Keynes appears in this book, therefore, as a champion not merely of the cheap money policy that has always been associated with his name, but also of the expansion of social service expenditure as a necessary part of economic as well as social policy. (Anonymous, *The Times*, 10 March 1936, in Backhouse, 1999, p. 49)

The very important conclusion, therefore, emerges that when cyclical unemployment exists interest rates should be forced down, and held down until 'full' or 'normal' employment is reached. ... He also realises that interest rates alone cannot always achieve everything, and that in some cases effective demand must be maintained by increased consumption and not increased investment. (Douglas Jay, *The Banker*, April 1936, in Backhouse, 1999, p. 58)

He hopes his scheme would eliminate unemployment and he believes that driving the rate of interest down to almost zero would result in a tremendous multiplication of equipment within a generation, at the same time eliminating the rentier class.

Aside from the question as to whether a positive rate of interest is the main factor in keeping us poor, it is worth pointing out that Keynes' vagueness about state control of investment has saved him from showing that under it anything of laissez-faire is left. (Virginius Coe, *Canadian Forum*, Vol. 16, May 1936, in Backhouse, 1999, p. 65)

Thus, the state should use taxation to curtail private saving; it should supplement private consumption and investment with its own spending; and it should force down and keep down the rate of interest to promote new enterprise. At times the author seems to suggest outright fixing of the volume of investment and of the rate of interest by the government. (Henry C. Simons, *Christian Century*, Vol. 53, 22 July 1936, in Backhouse, 1999, p. 67)

He wants the State to control the supply of money so as to secure its adequacy for maintaining full employment; and this involves a repudiation of the gold standard, or of any fixed international monetary standard, and also a decisive repudiation of all those economists who wish to stabilise the supply of money. Secondly, he wants the State to control the rates of interest (mainly by adjusting the supply of money) in order to keep these rates down to a point which will make investment worth while up to the level of 'full employment'. This involves a complete repudiation of the orthodox view that interest rates are self-adjusting to a 'natural' level. Thirdly, he wants the State largely to take over, or at any rate control, the amount and direction of investment, with the object of maintaining full employment on the basis of a balanced economic development. (G. D. H. Cole, *New Statesman and Nation*, Vol. 11, no. 15, February 1936, in Backhouse, 1999, pp. 104–5)

5.2   Re-stating the *General Theory*

Keynes was clearly dissatisfied with the manner in which he had presented matters. And much emphasis has already been given to Keynes's intention to re-state his *General Theory*. Indeed Moggridge's 'Editorial Introduction' to the reprint of the book (*CW* VII), rather than being concerned with the rich and radical nature of the theory, is concerned with the transition from the *Treatise* and then with this intention. But Keynes was not rejecting any of his own reasoning in expressing this desire. My view is that he saw a need to restate from two perspectives: first, to tighten up the presentation of specific components; and second, and more importantly, to divorce the statement of the theory from what he regarded as the classical economics.

The General Theory of Employment, Interest and Money was not a complete or flawless theory of activity in a free-market economy. It was, however, a most substantial contribution to such a theory and a very significant advance on classical theory. Furthermore, taken in their broadest sense, its central theoretical propositions and its basic policy conclusions were, according to the present author, correct. This contrast between the rightness of the broad perspective and potential flaws in the detail was one that Keynes fully recognised:

> I am more attached to the comparatively simple fundamental ideas which underlie my theory than to the particular forms in which I have embodied them, and I have no desire that the latter should be crystallised at the present stage of the debate. If the simple basic ideas can become familiar and acceptable, time and experience and the collaboration of a number of minds will discover the best way of expressing them. (*CW* XIV, p. 111)

After publication, Hugh Townshend[2] made a number of helpful and important contributions to the debate and in particular advocated a restatement.

In the course of a June 1937 review of Hawtrey's *Capital and Employment*, he argued that Keynes needed to pull further away from the classical theory towards broader notion of a 'general theory of economic activity':

> It must, I think, be admitted that Mr. Keynes' excavations into the foundations of classical economics are still (in *The General Theory*) rather encumbered with their own debris. We have, I suggest, to distinguish between Mr. Keynes' less general and his more general theory. There is surely a good deal in Mr. Keynes' book which represents, not quite the most general form of his thesis, but rather earlier stages of his thought before he arrived at a self-consistent new theory of value, subsuming the new theory of interest at which he had originally been aiming. If this view be correct, the theoretical critic who wants to be constructive must approach the book from the standpoint that in it Mr. Keynes is *leading up* himself and his readers to a general theory through a series of partial applications of his central ideas. (Townshend, 1937, p. 324)

Townshend offered additional justification for the restatement: that Keynes was writing the theory as he discovered it. The point is augmented by the widely recognised urgency with which Keynes viewed his task – he feared the totalitarian response to the great depression, a threat that was very real in much of continental Europe and perhaps no less in Britain itself. As a consequence, Keynes was taking major theoretical steps but never giving himself the time fully to understand and incorporate each of them. Keynes was in complete agreement:

> I am conscious that this, like a good deal else in the book, is largely the product of the old associations of my mind, the result of always trying to see the new theory in its relation to the old and to discover more affinities than really exist. When one has entirely sloughed off the old, one no longer feels the need of all that. I should like some day to endeavour to restate the whole matter, not controversially or critically or in relation to the views of others, but simply as a positive doctrine. (*CW* XXIX, pp. 246–7)

In my opinion this positive doctrine would, as here, be focused on the secular monetary policy. As noted above, the statement of the theory as Keynes taught it in his lecture courses was closer to such a statement than the *General Theory* itself. Then finally, the presentation of his theory at the 1945 National Debt Enquiry (NDE), while brief, was essentially this positive doctrine.[3] The positive doctrine is obtained by adopting the order of presentation in these versions of his theory, supplemented with theoretical detail from the *General Theory* itself, monetary background from the *Treatise*, practical discussions of policy from his writings throughout his life, and finally later arguments of others and of the present author.

5.3 The theoretical background to the *General Theory*

In this section, issues of methodology and perspective are examined, in preparation for the statement of the theory that is the subject of the next three chapters. The material is deemed necessary in part because of the far-reaching confusion that has been caused by the 'Keynesian' interpretation. Three issues are covered: the method of Keynes's economic reasoning, in particular given his recognition of the importance of uncertainty; the monetary foundations of the *General Theory*; and the relation of the nature of the economy described in the *General Theory* to that of the classical theory.

5.3.1 Methodology

Keynes described his methodological technique as follows:

The object of our analysis is, not to provide a machine, or method of blind manipulation, which will furnish an infallible answer, but to provide ourselves with an organised and orderly method of thinking out particular problems; and, after we have reached a provisional conclusion by isolating the complicating factors one by one, we then have to go back on ourselves and allow, as well as we can, for the probable interactions of the factors amongst themselves. This is the nature of economic thinking. . . . It is a great fault of symbolic pseudo-mathematical methods of formalising a system of economic analysis, . . . , that they expressly assume strict independence between the factors involved and lose all their cogency and authority if this hypothesis is disallowed; . . . Too large a proportion of recent 'mathematical' economics are merely concoctions, as imprecise as the initial assumptions they rest on, which allow the author to lose sight of the complexities and interdependencies of the real world in a maze of pretentious and unhelpful symbols. (*CW* VII, p. 298)

His analysis was discursive. The *General Theory* did not utilise the mathematical approaches associated with Ricardo and Walras and instead adopted the path of Smith, Malthus and Marshall. But the above extract motivates his methodological technique through interdependencies. In his celebrated 1937 *QJE* article Keynes instead chose to emphasise the existence of *uncertainty*.

For post-Keynesians, the definition and treatment of uncertainty is recognised as a critical component of Keynes's theoretical scheme. His *QJE* definition is worth repeating:[4]

By 'uncertain' knowledge, let me explain, I do not mean merely to distinguish what is known for certain from what is only probable. The game of roulette is not subject, in this sense, to uncertainty; nor is the prospect of a Victory bond being drawn. Or, again, the expectation of life is only slightly uncertain. Even the weather is only moderately uncertain. The sense in which I am using the term is that in which the prospect of a European war is uncertain, or the price of copper and the rate of interest twenty years hence, or the obsolescence of a new invention, or the position of private wealth owners in the social system in 1970. About these matters there is no scientific basis on which to form any calculable probability whatever. We simply do not know. (*CW* XIV, pp. 113–14)

Keynes saw that this uncertainty allowed economic activity to be dictated by the expectations – and 'animal spirits' – of economic actors.[5] More specifically, uncertainty underpinned both the MEC and liquidity preference schedules. As a consequence, the level of investment and the rate of interest were determined partly by expectation.

But preceding the *QJE* quotation is a link between methodology and uncertainty:

The whole object of the accumulation of wealth is to produce results, or potential results, at a comparatively distant, and sometimes *indefinitely* distant, date. Thus the fact that our knowledge of the future is fluctuating, vague and uncertain, renders wealth a peculiarly unsuitable subject for the methods of the classical economic theory. This theory might work very well in a world in which economic goods were necessarily consumed within a short interval of their being produced. But it requires, I suggest, considerable amendment if it is to be applied in a world in which the accumulation of wealth for an indefinitely postponed future is an important factor; . . . (*CW* VII, p. 113)

So here Keynes connects the liquidity and investment decisions in the face of an uncertain future to his choice of methodological technique.

More recently, Chick has explored Keynes's methodological technique in detail. In *Macroeconomics After Keynes* she emphasised, as well as interdependencies, that Keynes's reasoning should be ordered in a manner that reflects real-time events:

Keynes's method is something of a compromise, using the partial equilibrium method to analyse a market taken in isolation, then feeding the result back into the mainstream of economic events, which were themselves moving meanwhile. There is a distinct time-stream of events, in sharp contrast to general equilibrium, where everything happens at once, or partial equilibrium, where everything happens in the market being analysed and nothing is allowed to happen in other markets, while the economist's back is turned. (Chick, 1983, p. 15)

The aim here is to follow the same methodological principles and to adhere to both the existence of uncertainty and to some specific compartmentalising and ordering of the theory. As discussed in Section 5.1, the secular monetary policy perspective provides a structure for an order of presentation of the theory different from that adopted by Keynes but that continues to be in accord with the notion of a distinct time-stream of events (this order is detailed in the last section of this chapter). Following Keynes, key phenomena are compartmentalised, enabling their separate treatment but without losing the essential interdependence of the economic system. Under conditions of uncertainty, each 'compartment' has distinct supplies and demands that can be 'solved' as an equilibrium to determine key economic quantities. The compartmentalisation reveals three key markets: interest, investment and production. Any change to the equilibrium in one market has repercussions on equilibria through all other markets. While it may be that no explicit single-valued algebraic solution to the system is possible, the method allows the *relative* effects of different circumstances – and in particular different policy initiatives – to be analysed. In practical terms, the technique is sufficient to draw the most profound conclusions.[6]

Finally, I consider that ordering the theory in this way has an importance that goes beyond the notion of a time-stream of events. There is a broader logical dimension to Keynes's theory of the economy: 'It seems to me that economics is a branch of logic, a way of thinking' (Keynes to R. F. Harrod, 4 July 1938, *CW* XIV, pp. 296–7). Each of the following chapters constitutes self-contained arguments, but they fit together as consecutive components of the *General Theory*. Each sets up a proposition that, if accepted, leads to the next step in the following chapter. The argument as a whole has validity insofar as each logical step is accepted as valid.

5.3.2 Monetary considerations

In the 1960s it was a commonplace, still too widely held, that 'money did not matter' in the *General Theory*. As discussed in Chapter 2, Keynes's contributions to economics constituted a gradually more sophisticated and comprehensive analysis of a monetary economy. From the monetary perspective, the fundamental innovation of the *General Theory* was the liquidity preference theory of interest. Here Keynes shifted the emphasis of monetary theory from analyses of credit or exchange (flows), to the theory of money as a store of value (stocks). Schumpeter goes even further (too far perhaps): 'It was gradually realised that these two functions are *separable* and that their theories are *different*' (1954, p. 297, my emphasis).

Yet the *General Theory* is widely regarded as a retrograde step in monetary analysis. This has partial roots in 'Keynesianism', with its adoption of an exogenous supply of money. But others have fostered this view explicitly – for example, Schumpeter himself:

> There is, however, a sequel to Lord Keynes's treatment of the subject of credit creation in the *Treatise* of 1930 of which it is necessary to take notice in passing. The deposit-creating bank loan and its role in the financing of investment *without any previous saving up of the sums thus lent* have practically disappeared in the analytical schema of the *General Theory*, where it is again the saving public that holds the scene. Orthodox Keynesianism has in fact reverted to the old view according to which the central facts about the money market are analytically rendered by means of the public's propensity to save coupled with its liquidity preference. I cannot do more than advert to this fact. Whether this spells progress or retrogression, every economist must decide for himself. (Schumpeter, 1954, pp. 1114–15)

More recently, Basil Moore has perhaps been most responsible for perpetuating this view:

> After reading these passages in the *Treatise*, where the endogeneity of credit money is so clearly recognised, it is difficult to understand how Keynes only six years later could have assumed the money stock to be exogenously determined by the monetary authorities. (Moore, 1988, p. 195)[7]

The reality is that the *General Theory* was the culmination of Keynes's search for a theory of a representative money economy – what he now called a 'monetary theory of production'. A statement of intent written in late 1932 for a *Festschrift* appears unambiguous:

> The theory which I would desiderate would deal, in contradistinction to this, with an economy in which money plays a part of its own and affects motives and decisions and is, in short, one of the operative factors in the situation, so that the course of events cannot be predicted, either in the long period or in the short, without a knowledge of the behaviour of money between the first state and the last. And it is this which we ought to mean when we speak of a *monetary economy*. (CW XIII, pp. 408–9, Keynes's emphasis).

What has perhaps caused the confusion is the change in the *priority* of credit. With the emphasis on the theory of money as an asset, the existence and role of credit in generating the supply of money was put to one side. It is however an error – an astonishing error and a great insult that to my mind charges Keynes with imbecility – to think that credit had been forgotten.

Keynes even discussed this very point in the *General Theory*, although perhaps not as clearly as he might have. In the Preface to the British edition (*CW* VII, p. xxi), he outlined 'the relation between this book and my *Treatise on Money*'. The contrasting roles of money are addressed as follows: '... whilst it is found that money enters into the economic scheme in an essential and peculiar manner, technical monetary detail falls into the background' (*CW* VII, p. xxii). While the shift in emphasis from means of exchange to store of value is not mentioned, this text certainly does not amount to a rejection of his earlier position that the existence of credit creation has profound implications for economic activity.[8] In addition, as will be obvious from Chapter 12, his theory of aggregate demand requires or assumes a supply of credit that responds (endogenously) to effective demand. Under this theory, demand is determined by the interaction of the MEC, the rate of interest and the MPC. Credit is assumed to be generated to meet any demand for borrowing on the part of business not already met from the existing stock of money. Chick and Dow have made the same point, while still using the terminology that Keynes took money as 'given'.[9] In making this simplification Keynes was not repudiating the importance of such monetary details. In modern language, in the case of the theory of effective demand, Keynes was assuming that money was endogenous, responding automatically to the level of demand in the economy. In the case of the theory of liquidity preference, Keynes's theory could assume a given quantity of bank money because, sequentially, store-of-value considerations were relevant *after* money has been created. These simplifications are wholly opposed to the monetarist notion of exogenous money, which in practice reflects an assumption that the quantity of bank money is determined by the monetary authorities rather than the level of demand. However, Keynes's theory does not preclude the authorities having at least a degree of control. The assumption of a given money supply might be relaxed to examine the authorities asserting pressure on the supply of bank money through the discount rate, the supply of Treasury bills or even the supply of cash. The motivation for such actions and processes through which they might influence the money supply are however much more complex than the monetarist theory might imply. These issues are developed in Chapter 7.

This is not to say that Keynes's treatment is comprehensive. In giving priority to liquidity preference, he did not state his assumptions about credit creation or tackle what would happen if they did not hold (except in the case of a government deficit; see *CW* VII, pp. 200–1). From our own vantage point this is clearly problematic, perhaps disastrous. We must remember, though, that Keynes was writing for an economics profession who, with very few exceptions, recognised the critical role of credit in economic activity. The true state of affairs is surely that he considered he could take the role of bank credit as understood by all and explained in detail in his own earlier works. Finally, after the publication of his book, he recognised these issues as shortcomings. He sought to address them as an element of the alternative theories debate with Dennis Robertson and Bertil Ohlin that was raised in Section 4.6 and will be developed in Chapter 7.

No matter how prominent this issue has become in terms of the subsequent development of academic debate, in my view, it is a side issue that has detracted from the truly great innovation of the *General Theory*. Keynes's treatment of money as a store of value through the theory of liquidity preference was an advance of monetary theory, with implications of the most profound significance.

5.3.3   The multiple nature of the long-run equilibrium

Up to and including the *Treatise*, Keynes's understanding of the economic system was based on the commonplace distinction between the short and long runs. Then, as now, economists drew a distinction between the operation of the economy in the short run and a long-run state of affairs; Marshall defined the latter as follows:

> This is the real drift of that much quoted, and much-misunderstood doctrine of Adam Smith and other economists that the normal, or "natural," value of a commodity is that which economic forces tend to bring about *in the long run*. It is the average value which economic forces would bring about if the general conditions of life were stationary for a run of time long enough to enable them all to work out their full effect. (Marshall, 1920 [1890], Book V, Chapter III, para. 23)

In classical economics, real factors defined that long run (the hallmark of this long run was of course monetary neutrality); but the day-to-day operation of an economy could and would diverge from that situation as a short-run outcome. In particular, short-run 'disturbances' were caused by monetary factors.

As discussed in Section 4.3, it is a great error to attribute precedence for such a distinction to the Keynes of the *General Theory*. His contributions in *Indian Currency and Finance*, *A Tract on Monetary Reform* and the *Treatise* were based on this perspective on economics. Indeed, the *Treatise* might be regarded as Keynes's attempt to reconcile theoretically the short run and the classical long run. From a practical perspective, he had realised that prior to this point his policy insights had not been adequately substantiated in theory. He, therefore, sought to explain how an economy could 'malfunction' for a prolonged period (as with the British economy in the 1920s), given his acceptance of the notion that a free-market economy has a unique long-run equilibrium. The mechanism he proposed was based on a divergence between saving and investment that led to a divergence between 'market' and 'natural' rates of interest, the latter being the manifestation of the underlying long-run equilibrium of classical economics.

With the *General Theory*, Keynes finally abandoned his classical roots. In his own words:

> The composition of this book has been for the author a long struggle of escape, and so must the reading of it be for most readers if the author's assault upon them is to be successful, – a struggle of escape from habitual modes of thought and expression. The ideas which are here expressed so laboriously are extremely simple and should be obvious. The difficulty lies, not in the new ideas, but in escaping from the old ones, which ramify, for those of us brought up as most of us have been, into every corner of our minds. (*CW* VII, p. xxiii)

More specifically, with the *General Theory*, the classical long run was gone. Instead, Keynes saw a free-market economy as a *multiple*-equilibrium system. According to my interpretation, this meant that not only the short-run equilibrium but also the long-run equilibrium of an economy could be at any level of employment. Monetary factors remained important in the long run, and money was never neutral.

However, Keynes also adopted an analytical distinction between the short and long run. Adopting the terminology 'period', the short-period analysis was based on the assumption of fixed capital stock (but not fixed production of capital goods); for longer-period analysis, the capital stock could change. Amadeo (1989, pp. 14–15) makes the same distinction and reminds us of its origins in Marshall:

> as regards short periods . . . [t]he supply of specialised skill and ability, of suitable machinery and other material capital, and of the appropriate organization has not time to be fully adapted to demand; but the producers have to adjust their supply to the demand as best as they can with the appliances already at their disposal. (Marshall, 1920 [1890], Book V, Chapter V, para. 33)

> In long periods on the other hand all investments of capital and effort in providing that material plant and organization of a business . . . have time to be adjusted to the incomes which are expected to be earned by them. (ibid., para. 7)

The role of aggregate demand is widely understood as the feature which distinguishes between the classical system and Keynes's system. While extremely important, emphasis on aggregate demand has resulted in a concentration on the short-period aspect of Keynes's theory, in particular in connection with the role of government expenditure, or the impact of inappropriate exchange rate policies as restricting aggregate demand. From the secular perspective with which my interpretation is primarily concerned, the more relevant aspect is the long period, as the time frame of relevance to the analysis of the causes and consequences of changes to the capital stock. In this time frame the most important governor of aggregate demand and the long-period equilibrium is the long-term rate of interest.

Keynes did not explore the distinction between the classical long run and the analytical long period. My tentative resolution is that long-period analysis retains a place for an underlying equilibrium, but this equilibrium depends on a number of additional considerations that go way beyond the classical real factors, namely the rate of interest, the MPC and the level of government demand.

In operating according to this framework, Keynes was modifying and extending the classical theory rather than rejecting the classical theory in its entirety. Equally, he was not rejecting all aspects of classical policy doctrine. He saw his policy arrangements as necessary to facilitate the effective operation of a free-market economy. But given the implementation of these policies, classical forces of supply and demand should be allowed to hold sway. In his famous House of Lords speech defending the Bretton Woods and war loan agreements, Keynes argued the proposals constituted '... an attempt to use what we have learnt from modern experience and modern analysis, not to defeat, but to implement the wisdom of Adam Smith' (18 December 1945, *CW* XXIV, p. 621). In his final (and posthumously published) *EJ* article, he appears to me to be pleading to those who continued to draw even further away from classical doctrine:

> I must not be misunderstood. I do not suppose that the classical medicine will work by itself or that we can depend on it. We need quicker and less painful aids of which exchange variation and overall import control are the most important. But in the long run these expedients will work better and we shall need them less, if the classical medicine is also at work. And if we reject the medicine from our systems altogether, we may just drift on from expedient to expedient and never get really fit again. The great virtue of the Bretton Woods and Washington proposals, taken in conjunction, is that they marry the use of the necessary expedients to the wholesome long-run doctrine. (*CW* XXVII, p. 445)[10]

In theoretical terms he saw the classical theory as the special case of his general theory, relevant to the special case of equilibrium at full employment: 'I shall argue that the postulates of the classical theory are applicable to a special case only and not to the general case, the situation which it assumes being a limiting point of the possible positions of equilibrium' (*CW* VII, p. 3).[11]

But his theory depicted a very different reality to that of the classical theory. Even given an underlying acceptance of equilibrium states of affairs, these were still such that matters might be dictated by something so elusive as expectations:

A monetary economy, we shall find, is essentially one in which changing views about the future are capable of influencing the quantity of employment and not merely its direction. But our method of analysing the economic behaviour of the present under the influence of changing ideas about the future is one which depends on the interaction of supply and demand, and is in this way linked up with our fundamental theory of value. We are thus led to a more general theory, which includes the classical theory with which we are familiar, as a special case. (*CW* VII, p. xxii)

5.4 The presentation of the *General Theory* in three chapters

In terms of the sequential structure of Keynes's theory, each of the following chapters sets up propositions that – if accepted – lead to the next steps in the following chapter and so on. The foundation for the theory is the treatment of bank money that has here been set out in Chapter 2 and in Section 5.3.

Chapter 6 deals with what, it is argued, should be regarded as *the* first step to the *General Theory* from the *Treatise*: the recognition that, in a bank-money economy, the relationship between the macroeconomic aggregates, saving and investment, was identity rather than equilibrium. Recognition of this relationship opened the path to recognition of the multiple-equilibrium nature of the economic system, re-enforced the leading role for investment and led to the decisive rejection of the classical theory of interest. Linking this development with the first, the release of the saving constraint on economic activity through the existence of bank money was finally recognised to affect not only prices in the long run – as Keynes thought up to and including the *Treatise* – but also output and employment in the long run and the short.

Chapter 7 deals with the central monetary component of the *General Theory*: the liquidity preference theory of interest rate determination. In logical terms, the saving–investment identity dismisses the classical theory of interest and, as Keynes put it in 1937, leaves the rate of interest 'in the air' (*CW* XIV, p. 212). An alternative theory of interest is, therefore, required. His theory put credit to one side and gave centre stage to phenomena arising from the use of money as a store of value. Analysis of these phenomena led Keynes to his conclusion that there was no reason that the rate of interest prevailing in a free-market economy should be the rate appropriate for full employment. The liquidity preference theory then led to the prospect of using debt-management to manipulate interest rates, and the chapter draws heavily on his later proposals to the 1945 NDE to achieve this end.

Chapter 8 deals with the interaction between the monetary theories developed in Chapters 2, 6 and 7 and the 'real' economy. As with the monetary theory, the central component is the rate of interest. The level of activity in a market economy is explained by the theory of effective demand, and the level of effective demand is underpinned by the effect of the rate of interest on the level of investment. The fuller theory of investment demand as an interaction between the rate of interest and the MEC that reflects businesses' expectations of the yield on investment in an uncertain future can then be used to explain the economic cycle. The discussion attempts to incorporate Keynes's theory of the economic cycle more formally into the argument as a whole. In the *General Theory*, this latter theory is presented using tools of the previous chapters, but it is not rigorously extended and incorporated into the broader framework. Furthermore, it is not discussed in terms of any notion of 'equilibrium'. It is argued here, going beyond the *General Theory*, that the notion of a 'correct MEC' helps to develop the cyclical aspects of his theory. The 'correct MEC' is regarded as defining an underlying (perhaps long-period) equilibrium against which any short-period outcome determined by the theory of effective demand must be understood. This equilibrium-based framework can then be used to elaborate the economic cycle process. It is proposed that, following Fisher (1933), in a 'boom' an underlying equilibrium exerts its pressure through an unsustainable build-up of debt which leads eventually and inevitably to financial and real collapse. The transmission mechanism between credit facilitated short-period outcomes and an underlying or long-period equilibrium, in part determined by a monetary rate of interest, is seen to be excessive debt. The case for cheap-money policy is then brought forward more fully than in the *General Theory*. First, Keynes's rather throwaway argument that a low rate of interest can prevent the economic cycle is elaborated. Second, the role of the authorities in economic activity is identified as the ability to manipulate the underlying equilibrium. Chapter 8, therefore, takes two approaches: the first elaborating the *General Theory*, the second going beyond it.

Notes

1. See T. K. Rymes's invaluable compilation of notes taken by Keynes's students during the crucial period of development between 1932 and 1935 (*Notes of a Representative Student*, 1989).
2. Townshend worked for the Post Office; Keynes tutored him for the Civil Service examinations (see Chick, 1987).
3. Indeed it is through the NDE Report and Keynes's notes that the present author came to the interpretation set out here.
4. This passage has been emphasised by Davidson (e.g. 1972), before him, Shackle (e.g. 1968) and, after him, Carabelli (1988).
5. Hicks (1936, pp. 239–40) emphasised the importance of 'expectations of the future' to Keynes's theory in his review; unfortunately, in *IS-LM* he did not adopt this method.
6. Keynes did not aid understanding by the use of graphical techniques; 'I know you fight shy of diagrams' (Colin Clark to Keynes, 16 January 1933, CW XXIX, p. 59). As will be discussed in Chapter 10, the only graph he used in the *General*

Theory explained the failings of classical theory; it was not part of the theoretical scheme of the *General Theory*. Nevertheless, in my view, graphical illustrations can usefully be adopted and I have done so.

7. While acknowledging that the change in position is 'difficult to understand', Moore does not go on to look for any explanation. Given that Moore's own theoretical argument is based on the paramount importance of credit, some sort of explanation for Keynes's alleged error on so fundamental a point is surely a necessary element of a serious study.

8. Davidson has made a similar point: 'Since these technical details have been dealt with at great length in his *Treatise*, Keynes' willingness to suppress these complications to make this point is understandable, although from hindsight it is regrettable' (Davidson, 1978, p. 49).

9. For example: Chick, 1983, p. 184, and 2001, p. 9, and Dow, 1997. More recently Dow has connected the confusion between 'given' and 'exogenous' with closed-system thinking.

10. Though he uses the terminology 'run' here; and I do not think that he ever fully explored the distinction between the two notions.

11. He also elaborated his attitude to the classical theory in the course of a discussion about the theory and policy of the mercantilists in Chapter 23: 'Regarded as the theory of the individual firm and of the distribution of the product resulting from the employment of a given quantity of resources, the classical theory has made a contribution to economic thinking which cannot be impugned. It is impossible to think clearly on the subject without this theory as part of one's apparatus of thought. I must not be supposed to question this in calling attention to their neglect of what was valuable in their predecessors' (*CW* VII, pp. 339–40).

6
The Saving–Investment Identity and the Transition from the *Treatise* to the *General Theory*

6.1 Introduction

In late 1932, Keynes recognised that the nature of the relationship between the macroeconomic aggregates saving and investment was one of identity rather than equilibrium. The central argument of this Chapter is that this was the 'discovery' that set Keynes away from the *Treatise* and became the foundation for all his subsequent theoretical arguments. The nature, cause and consequence of the saving–investment relationship are crucial components of any statement of Keynes's *General Theory* as a positive doctrine.

The corollary of this argument is that, as with the monetary nature of his economics, neo-classical/'Keynesian' economics has diverted economic science away from this 'discovery'. The diversion began virtually the moment that the discovery was made. Robertson put forward an alternative definition of saving that was more compatible with his loanable funds perspective as rival to both Keynes's *Treatise* position and his developing position. Robertson's assault was relentless and is judged here to have been aided by inadequacies in Keynes's treatment of the relation both in the *General Theory* and in his response to his critics. After the war, a relationship between saving and investment that owed more to Robertson than Keynes emerged as a central component of the 'Keynesian' model. But, while there was inevitably some common ground, the nature, cause and consequence were wholly different from Keynes's version. Indeed, in the Keynesian version, the relationship became the central component of the theory rather than a point of departure for an alternative theory. While Keynes's relationship was finally restored by post-Keynesian economists, its position in the *General Theory* itself has not been fully recognised.

This chapter, therefore, first examines each of the nature, cause and consequence of the identity in the context of the positive statement of the *General Theory* that Keynes never made. The discussion then goes on to examine the historical context of Keynes's actual discovery of the identity, how it influenced his theoretical development and how others interpreted, criticised and ultimately lost this fundamental logical step.

6.2 Nature, cause and consequence

In the *General Theory*, the relationship between saving and investment is a relationship between macroeconomic aggregates in monetary or nominal terms. The *nature* of this relationship is that, in any period, the aggregate flow of saving is exactly and necessarily equal to the aggregate flow of investment. This position stands in contrast to classical theory where the relationship between saving and investment is an equilibrium between real resources (most famously, corn for consumption versus corn for planting); saving is equal to investment, but this equality arises through the rate of interest equilibrating the supply of and demand for saving. Keynes did not use the term 'identity' himself, but it is used here to draw a clear distinction between the two types of equality – one arising through equilibrium and the other through necessary equality. This relationship was not a matter of definition adopted for convenience, but a profound 'discovery' with cause and consequence. However, Keynes did not give sufficient justification for his appeal to and use of the identity. He tended to argue from macroeconomic equations, and did not fill in the underlying mechanisms that are microeconomic and monetary in nature.

Turning to cause, the identity is essentially a *monetary phenomenon*. This fundamental connection between the theories of saving and investment and monetary considerations has been exposed most fully in Chick's work. The analysis follows from her characterisation of the evolution of banking in 'stages'. The second of five stages is characterised by widespread acceptance of deposits as money for transactions. '[T]he banking system can now lend to a multiple of reserves, subject to a conventional or imposed reserve requirement; deposits are a consequence' (Chick, 1992, p. 195; see also 1983, Chapter 9). The conclusion is as follows:

> With the arrival of Stage 2 banking, investment could precede saving; . . . Subsequent banking developments have not changed that process; they have intensified it. . . . From Stage 2 onwards, 'savers' have no influence over the volume of banking business or the volume of deposits. (Chick, 1992, pp. 199–200)

The identification of the *causal priority for investment* is the first of a two-part argument. At this point, with investment no longer constrained by the amount of current income set aside as saving, the classical model of an equilibrium relationship between savings and investment must be rejected. Instead, investment is an autonomous variable, determined by a demand unrelated to aggregate saving (see Chapter 8). The second part of the story is that investment, as Keynes later put it, 'always drags [saving] along with it at an equal pace' (*CW* XIII, p. 276).

The demonstration that follows uses both macroeconomic and micro-economic arguments. From a macroeconomic perspective, the relation has traditionally been demonstrated using a national-accounts-type presentation: $Y \equiv C + I$ and $Y \equiv C + S$, $\therefore S = I$. However, this only shows that the two variables are equal; it does not distinguish between equality, equilibrium and identity, and pays no attention to the underlying causal processes that allow the identity to be asserted. With the recognition of the relation's monetary nature, it is an altogether more powerful proposition. From 'Stage 2' an increase in investment no longer requires a decrease in consumption as in the fixed-output world of classical economics. Instead, with consumption unchanged, *an increase in investment leads directly to an increase in income*. The national accounts presentation could be enhanced by considering two periods: 1 and 2 with C, I and Y obviously defined.

$$C_1 = C_2 = C$$
$$I_1 = I$$
$$I_2 = I + \Delta I$$
$$Y_1 = C + I$$
$$Y_2 = C + I + \Delta I = Y_1 + \Delta I \tag{6.1}$$
$$\text{given} \quad S = Y - C$$
$$S_2 = Y_1 + \Delta I - C$$
$$\Rightarrow S_2 = I + \Delta I = I_2 \tag{6.2}$$

In this way, saving is *kept* equal to investment (Equation 6.2) by the increase in income (Equation 6.1). It should be emphasised at this point that the discussion is in terms of *income* rather than *output*; the identity is a monetary or nominal proposition. Keynes's theories of effective demand and the determination of output and price emphatically see an increase in output following an increase in demand, but price too is likely to move. In the context here, an increase of investment demand will increase income through increasing both output and price.

From the microeconomic perspective, Chick has made the crucial connection between saving, investment and bank-money creation: 'the matching saving in the first instance is the new bank deposits resulting from loan expansion to support the investment' (Chick, 1992, p. 199). Any credit created to finance investment creates deposits to exactly the same value. At any subsequent point in the economic process these deposits are some-body's savings. The act of spending the deposit simply transfers the deposit to somebody else. From the perspective of the recipient, the transfer of the deposit is income, and if they do not spend the income in the period of account, with saving defined as income not spent, the deposit is saving. Even if the deposit is spent several times over in the period of account, some of it may be saved by each set of hands that it passes through and the rest will always be held idle at the end of the period of account. In this way, a constant and increased level of saving is preserved from the moment the credit is created. (This argument has clear parallels with a 'process analysis' of the new spending based on the multiplier; the technique is addressed in Section 6.7.)

There were also two other approaches to the saving–investment relationship that were based primarily on the micro perspective. One that came to prominence immediately after publication of the *General Theory* adopted the concept of *ex ante* and *ex post* saving that Ohlin originally introduced in the course of the 'alternative theories' debate. In each period, a flow of *ex ante* saving can be identified as due to the level of investment and activity in the previous period. The loanable funds perspective gives emphasis to the requirement for credit or 'finance' as the difference between *ex ante* and *ex post* saving (discussed in more detail in Section 6.7). The second was the notion of voluntary and involuntary saving. *Ex post* saving could be distinguished between existing *ex ante*, or voluntary, saving and the new saving created by new activity and price change which could be described as involuntary. Involuntary saving is, therefore, a macroeconomic consequence of an increase in investment activity. Both perspectives elaborate the underlying processes, but it should be stressed that those who were concerned to discuss matters in these terms were also concerned to preserve some degree of causal priority to saving in the determination of the rate of interest. This stance was at least in part due to a predisposition to loanable funds. For Keynes, saving ceased to have any causal significance in the basic economic processes that he was interested in exposing.

The first *consequence* of the identity was not a logical consequence, but its role in the historical development of Keynes's own thought. In the *Treatise*, Keynes was concerned with establishing the link between (i) a short-run process characterised as a disequilibrium investment cycle (facilitated by credit); and (ii) a long-run classical equilibrium. The centrepiece of his analysis was the relationship between saving and investment. The long run was defined in classical terms as an equilibrium between saving and investment at Wicksell's 'natural rate of interest'. The short-run process saw saving and investment move out of line as a result of a divergence between the market rate of interest and this natural rate (*CW* V, pp. 138–42). Long-run equilibrium was restored through relative price changes in consumption and investment goods. Keynes, therefore, adhered to the underlying equilibrium relationship of the classical case, but a disequilibrium between the two quantities provided the basic dynamic of the economic cycle. The consequence of Keynes's 'discovery' of the identity between saving and investment undermined the characterisation of events in the *Treatise*. This evolution was a, and in my view *the*, historical development that set Keynes towards the *General Theory*. As Section 6.6 will demonstrate, within about a year from the recognition of the identity, the significant theoretical steps towards the *General Theory* had been achieved. In turn, these significant steps arose largely from the logical consequences of the identity that will now be addressed.

The second consequence of the identity was to re-enforce Keynes's developing attitudes to the priority of investment and to the desirability of individual or collective acts of saving, that were opposed to the classical theory. The *Treatise* had recognised that an act of saving did not necessarily increase investment:

> In short, the increase or decrease of capital depends on the amount of investment and not on the amount of saving.
>
> That saving can occur without any corresponding investment is obvious, ... There is no increase of wealth in any shape of form corresponding to the increase of saving – the saving has resulted in nothing whatever except a change and change-about between those who consume and between those who own titles to wealth. (*CW* V, p. 156)

Keynes's identity fatally undermined the classical causal nexus. Investment was seen to lead to a necessarily equal amount of saving rather than increased saving being necessary for increased investment. The recognition of the identity, therefore, helped explain and re-enforce this specific point from the *Treatise* (despite throwing the wider analysis into doubt). In the *General Theory*, the classical position was ultimately completely reversed. Through the theory of effective demand, an increase in attempted saving at the microeconomic level would be reflected as a reduction in the MPC and a reduction in aggregate income via the multiplier. High consumption, not high saving, led to high investment and high income.

The third consequence of the identity was fatally to undermine the depiction of long-run equilibrium in his *Treatise* and perhaps too of the classical analysis. Working from the position of the *Treatise*, if saving was identical to investment, the variables could no longer define a unique position of equilibrium. With saving identical to investment at any level of employment or output, the long-run position of the economic system itself was no longer defined. Ultimately therefore, and in a manner not wholly clear from available published material, the identity led Keynes from the single-equilibrium system of the classical theory and the *Treatise* to the multiple-equilibrium system of the *General Theory*. The proposition that, given the usual 'real factors', a free-market economy does not have a unique equilibrium, is surely *the* fundamental theoretical distinction between the *General Theory* and the classical theory. This is addressed further in Chapter 8.

Fourth, with investment identical to saving, there was no longer a theory of interest. The identity, therefore, provided the logical opening for the liquidity preference theory of interest. This is the subject of Chapter 7.

There is a substantial degree of inter-relation between each of these theoretical consequences. But each consequence reflects a difference of the most substantial importance when considering the relation between the *General Theory* and the classical theory. Each consequence is in fundamental opposition to the propositions and theory of the classical economics.

6.3 The saving–investment debate

The relationship between saving and investment quickly came to dominate the debate after the publication of the *Treatise*. While Hawtrey's detailed critique, eventually published as *The Art of Central Banking* (1932), was very important to the change in Keynes's perspective, ironically the midwife to the identity was Robertson. The debate appears to have started with a letter from Robertson in May 1931; this contained a document that was essentially Robertson's critique of the *Treatise*.[1] Following receipt of the paper, there was a prolonged exchange of views between Keynes and Robertson that also drew in J. A. Hobson, Kaldor, Pigou, Sraffa and Hayek, with Kahn involved in advising Keynes throughout. Robertson's paper, 'Mr Keynes' Theory of Money', and a rejoinder by Keynes were published in the September 1931 *EJ*.

From the perspective of this chapter, the important point in Robertson's published critique concerned the definition of income that Keynes had adopted in the *Treatise*:

> 8. I pass on to another distinctive feature of Mr. Keynes' work – the sharp distinction which he draws between "incomes" and "profits." "Incomes," it will be remembered, include the normal earnings of the entrepreneur, whether these are in fact being earned or not; and "profits," positive or negative, are composed of the difference between the *actual* net receipts of the entrepreneur per unit of time and these theoretical "incomes." "Incomes" are usually assumed not to alter during the short transitional periods with which, in the study of the trade cycle, we are concerned. "Savings" can only be made out of "incomes," so that if an entrepreneur spends his "profits" on the purchase of new machines, he is not "saving," while if he refrains from spending on consumption a normal income which he has never received, he is deemed to be "saving."
>
> I do not think there is any question that his terminology is extremely confusing, and will be liable to lead even practised thinkers into error unless they are continually on their guard. (Robertson, 1931, pp. 406–7)[2]

After discussing what he saw as the substance of their respective positions, Keynes's published response turned to what he referred to as Robertson's 'other comments'. The penultimate of these addressed what was, at this stage, regarded as a definitional issue:

> I will consider what Mr Robertson says about nomenclature in his [section] 8. I think I might do better than in my *Treatise*, but it is not very easy... [I]f, as he suggests, we were to define 'income' to mean 'earnings *plus* profits' ($E + Q$ in my notation) and 'saving' to mean the difference between income thus defined and expenditure on consumption ($S = E + Q - PR$), then it would follow that savings and the value of new investment would always be exactly equal (for $Q = PR + I - E$, so that $S = I$). Does Mr Robertson, in practice, mean by 'savings' exactly the same as what he means by 'the value of new investment'? (*CW* XIII, pp. 234–5)

Keynes and Kahn discussed the detail of the two papers prior to publication. Kahn's critique hinted at the solution that was shortly to emerge, with his comments illustrating that he saw sense in Robertson's definition: 'But surely Dennis is merely adopting a perfectly simple-minded and natural definition of saving – receipts minus expenditure – though it is true that it involves him in the difficulty to which you allude?' (15 August 1931, *CW* XIII, p. 238).

Skidelsky discusses a letter of 1 October 1931 that shows Keynes pursuing this line of thought in order to help address shortcomings that Hawtrey had raised in his critique of the *Treatise*:

> I could further re-express my theory in your language... by saying that... whenever there is increased capital expenditure then, other things being equal, consumers' income is increased by an equal amount. And again, whenever anyone saves money, other things being equal, that has the effect of reducing consumers' income by an equal amount. (Skidelsky, 1992, p. 446)[3]

Hayek's involvement came through his two-part review of the *Treatise* that was published in *Economica*. The first instalment was published in August 1931, thus coinciding precisely with the above debate (the second was published in February 1932). Keynes was very unhappy with the review, and published a response in the November 1931 *Economica*. In the course of this response, Keynes used the definitional identity in a more positive manner:

> Has he, moreover, apprehended the significance of my equation $S + Q = I$, namely that savings *plus* profits are always exactly equal to the value of

new investment? It follows from this that, if we define *income* to include profits, and savings as being the excess of income thus defined over expenditure on consumption, then savings and the value of investment are identically the same thing. He appears to conceive of savings and investment as not being identical and yet shrinks from defining them accordingly. (*CW* XIII, p. 251)

After a limited amount of follow-up correspondence, Keynes called a halt in March 1932. He wrote to Hayek (as he had already done to Kaldor – Hayek's research assistant at the time): 'I am trying to re-shape and improve my central position, and that is probably a better way to spend one's time rather than in controversy' (*CW* XIII, p. 266).

True to his word to Hayek, Keynes sent a long paper to Robertson on 22 March 1932 entitled 'Notes on the Definition of Saving'. A covering letter began: 'I have been trying recently to avoid controversy and to get back to the beginning in restating the point of view which I seem to have put inadequately in Book Three of my *Treatise*' (*CW* XIII, p. 275). The position set out in the paper reflects a substantial development in thought and is very important in the history of the transition.

The paper opened with a re-statement of the definition of income along the lines recommended by his critics:

Let E be the amount of earnings or cost of current net output, i.e. the sum of fixed and variable costs and of entrepreneur's inducement.

Q the net profits of entrepreneurs, i.e. the amount of their actual net receipts in excess of entrepreneurs' inducement. So that $E + Q = E'$ which is total income in Hawtrey's, Hayek's and D. H. R.'s sense, and in the sense to which I have now bowed the knee. (*CW* XIII, p. 275)

Keynes then turned to the relationship between saving and investment. He began with definitional issues and then looked to issues of causality and of practical implication:

... Thus, the S' definition of savings works out to be identical with the value of current investment. And this is the justification for the old-fashioned 'common-sense' view that savings and investment are, necessarily and at all times, equal, – being, indeed, the same concept looked at from opposite points of view.

On the other hand the implications of this use of language are decidedly different from what 'common-sense' supposes. For S' always and necessarily accommodates itself to I. Whether I consists in housing schemes or in war finance, there need be nothing to hold us back, because I always drags S' along with it at an equal pace. S' is not the voluntary result of virtuous decisions. In fact S' is no longer the dog, which common sense believes it to be, but the tail . . .

. . .

. . . Thus, whilst it remains true that an increase of savings S' must increase the value of investment, it does not follow that a decreased expenditure on consumption will increase S'. The mistake of the 'common-sense' view lay not in the belief (using words as it chose to use them) that an increase of savings S' necessarily means an increase in the value of investment. The mistake lay in supposing that a decreased expenditure on consumption leads (*cet. par.*) to an increase of S' . . .

. . .

The two matters of primary importance to the community are the aggregate of real output and the increment of real capital. Therefore, it is of great significance to show that a decreased expenditure on consumption does not necessarily lead to an increment of real capital even if aggregate real output is unchanged; . . . Indeed it is easy to conceive circumstances in which a decreased expenditure on consumption leads to a decrease both of real output and of real investment. (*CW* XIII, pp. 276–9)

The importance with which he regarded these developments was emphasised by his 'Preface' to the Japanese edition of *Treatise*; this was dated 5 April 1932, 18 months after the publication of the British edition and only a few weeks after he sent his paper to Robertson. After a discussion of the highly significant events set in motion by the collapse of the gold standard, he turned to 'matters of purely theoretical interest which I would wish to take this opportunity to mention' (*CW* V, p. xxii). The first of these was the 'distinction between *saving* and *investment*'. He set out the new position that the debate had led him to:

The difference begins, I think, with a lack of clearness in former definitions of the meaning of *saving* or of *voluntary saving*. My definition of *income* is thought paradoxical because I exclude from it (as explained below) windfall profits and losses, and my definition of *saving*, being the excess of income thus defined over expenditure on consumption, corresponds to my definition of *income*. But those who object to these definitions have not, I think, followed out to the end the consequences of rejecting them. For if windfall profits and losses are included in income, i.e. if income is defined as being not E, but $E + O$ . . . and saving as the excess of income thus defined over expenditure on consumption, it follows that saving is in all cases exactly equal to the value of current investment. That is to say the total volume of saving ceases to be a factor having any independent existence. Its amount cannot be affected by the voluntary decision of the various recipients of income as to how much of their income they will spend on consumption; and it solely depends on what the value of current investment happens to be. This seems to me not less paradoxical than my use of these terms, . . . (*CW V*, p. xxiii)

At this stage he presents the identity as helping to clarify the position and aiding subsequent debate of the *Treatise* rather than setting the way to the far-reaching consequences. He closed the Preface as follows: 'It is not, however, my intention to revise the existing text of this *Treatise* in the near future. I propose, rather, to publish a short book of a purely theoretical character, extending and correcting the theoretical basis of my views as set forth in Books III and IV below' (*CW V*, p. xxvii).

Keynes's lecture notes written just after the Preface to the Japanese edition of the *Treatise* show things moving on. *Collected Writings* XXIX records '[t]yped and handwritten fragments from which Keynes appears to have lectured, 2 May 1932' that dwell on the distinction between the *Treatise* and his latest position:[4]

Thus, we are left with the remarkable generalisation that, in all ordinary circumstances, the volume of employment depends on the amount of investment, and that anything which increases or decreases the latter will increase or decrease the former . . .

The general upshot of this and the previous chapter seems to be that the fluctuations of output and employment for a given community over the short period, within the ranges of fluctuations which certainly occur, depend almost entirely on the amount of current investment – not indeed with logical necessity but with a high degree of probability in practice. This goes beyond the contention of my *Treatise*, where it was meant to depend on the amount of Investment *relatively* to Saving – which has the advantage of logical necessity, apart from the results of temporary miscalculation or of a policy which deliberately ignored considerations of profit. (*CW* XXIX, pp. 40–1)

The position cited indicates that over the course of April and May 1932 Keynes had begun to include the identity as part of his own positive analysis. Kahn incorporated it into his own work as well, re-iterating Keynes's original statement of the identity in the September 1932 *EJ*:

But in the simple-minded sense of the term, savings are *always and neces-sarily* equal to investment: that is a mere truism, which emerges at once, as Mr. Keynes has demonstrated [a year earlier in the *Economic Journal*], from the simple-minded definition of savings. Whatever the level of invest-ment, funds are always available to pay for it. (Reprinted in Kahn 1972, p. 101)

6.4   The consequences of the identity

As can be seen from the above extracts, Keynes first used the identity to re-enforce the *Treatise* position that investment dominated matters and that increased saving was not helpful to higher output. His Preface to the Japanese edition suggests that the basic long-run/short-run distinction of the *Treatise* remained in place. Matters were to change swiftly. The main period of theoretical development was between the Japanese edition of the *Treatise* and the end of 1933.

Unfortunately, virtually nothing relating to these developments is reproduced in either of the relevant volumes of *CW* (XIII and XXIX). Table 6.1 details the published private correspondence from the March 1932 paper that he sent to Robertson through to the preparation of the proofs of *General Theory* (published articles and pages of early draft chapters are omitted). There are only *13* short series of correspondence over this crucial *three-year* period.

The evidence cited here that Keynes made his great leap forward in this period is a single extract from *CW* and two entries in Rymes's compilation of lecture notes. While slight, the extracts show unambiguously that Keynes had moved from the unique equilibrium system of the *Treatise* to the multiple-equilibrium system of the *General Theory* and had brought the savings–investment identity to bear on the theory of interest. In addition, as Table 6.1 indicates, any slightness of evidence must be seen in the context of the wider lack of published correspondence in this period.[5]

The transition to multiple equilibrium is seen from Keynes's perspective in lecture notes reproduced in *CW* XXIX. Moggridge reproduces what he refers to as a '[t]yped and handwritten fragment from which Keynes appears to have lectured, 14 November 1932':

> For the root of the objection which I find to the theory under discussion, if it is propounded as a long-period theory, lies in the fact that, on one hand, it cannot be held that the position towards which the economic system is tending or the position at which it would be at rest or the *optimum* position . . . whichever of these tendencies we have in view, is entirely independent of the policy of the monetary authority; whilst, on the other hand, it cannot be maintained that there is a unique policy which, in the long run, the monetary authority is bound to pursue.
>
> Thus, I conclude that this theory is not really dealing with a generalised doctrine of the long period, but is concerned rather, *with a special case*; i.e. with a long-period position corresponding, in some or all of the senses of this term, to a *particular* assumed policy on the part of the monetary authority.
>
> On my view, there is no unique long-period position of equilibrium equally valid regardless of the character of the policy of the monetary

authority. On the contrary there are a number of such positions corresponding to different policies. Moreover there is no reason to suppose that positions of long-period equilibrium have an inherent tendency or likelihood to be positions of optimum output. A long-period position of optimum output is *a special case* corresponding to a special kind of policy on the part of the monetary authority. This conclusion will be developed in subsequent chapters. [Moggridge then notes: 'although the pagination is consecutive, some words are missing at this point'] (*CW* XXIX, pp. 54–5)

Table 6.1 Correspondence during the transition published in the *Collected Writings*[1]

Volume/pages	Date	Between	Subject
XIII 289–320	March 32–November 33	*DHR/Keynes	S/I
XIII 376–380	May 32	*J. Robinson/Keynes	S/I and output adjustment
XXIX 42–48	May 32	Robinson et al.	S/I and output adjustment
XXIX 58–62	January 33	*Keynes/Clark	estimates of the multiplier
XIII 419	May 33	Keynes to J. Robinson	two sentence note on the rate of interest
XIII 412–418	September 33	*Kahn/Giblin/Keynes	brief exchange on the multiplier following publication of *Essays in Persuasion*
XIII 321–326	September/October 33	*Shove/Keynes	Pigou's 'The Theory of Wages'
XXIX 120–122	March 34	from Kahn	definitional issues
XIII 422	April 34	to Kahn	half page note on definition of effective demand
XXIX 122–131	November/December 34	Lindahl/Keynes	S/I (includes Lindahl's seven page paper)
XIII 492	January 35	Keynes to Bernard Shaw	impact of his theory
XXIX 131–151	July 35	*Bryce/Keynes	Bryce's 19 page 'monetary theory of employment' and Keynes's one-page response
XXIX 157–161	undated	*Keynes/Sraffa	discussion of wage cut

Notes: 1. Pages 211, 214, 218, 266, 271, 294, 306, 419 and 477 of *CW* XIII contain explicit references to missing material.
* Indicates series of correspondence.

While the extract above and fuller published version do not use the identity as a motivating force, the text is a categorical statement about the nature of the economic system that Keynes has in mind. Chronologically, the lecture came only a few months after his fuller development of the identity. The same passage can also be seen from the student perspective under a very important title: Rymes (1989, p. 73) reproduces a 'Sixth Lecture: 14 November 1932', 'Monetary and Neutral Economy and Long and Short Periods'.

The *only* early published reference to the theory of the rate of interest during the key period of transition is in Rymes's compilation of lecture notes. The relevant statement comes from a lecture on 27 November 1933, one year after the above extract. In this lecture, the saving–investment identity is the motivating force for the rejection of the classical theory of interest:

> For the community, aggregate saving and investment must be equal. One 'can't discover where a point is by having two names for it'. Saving and investment balance at any rate of interest, therefore any analogy with demand and supply analysis doesn't work. The analogy is like trying to deduce the price from the equality of *buyers* and *sellers*...
>
> The ordinary theory of interest is the one which I was brought up on, and I think I taught it once, a certain number of years ago, but it doesn't hold one drop of water. It is the idea that the rate of interest is determined by the point of intersection of two supply and demand curves, that of Saving and that of Investment...
>
> But we have just seen that these curves run parallel, or rather are coincident, because Investment and Saving are merely two names for the same thing. You cannot find were a point lies merely by having two names for it. The curves rise and fall together, not in opposite directions. (Rymes, 1989, pp. 121–2)

From the broadest theoretical perspective, these and other lecture notes show that by the end of 1933 Keynes had in place the beginnings of the MPC, a theory of investment demand and the liquidity preference theory of interest. It must be emphasised that the lack of published correspondence means that there is basically no public record of what Keynes saw as the implications of each of these discoveries as he made them.

6.5 Dispute prior to the *General Theory*

While Keynes's fuller treatment of the saving–investment identity would not see the light of day until the publication of *General Theory*, the continuation of the dialogue with Robertson and an initiative due to Roy Harrod ensured that the identity was publicly aired and debated, and hence criticised, before 1936.

Robertson's own theoretical development at this time is noteworthy in itself. As seen, Robertson's critique was a significant factor in the development of Keynes's new position. But as soon as Keynes articulated this position, Robertson was immediately dissatisfied and retreated to develop a new position of his own. Apart from the March 1932 paper, Keynes also sent Robertson copies of his lecture notes on this topic (*CW* XIII, p. 294). The two exchanged correspondence in May 1932; Robertson then wrote a holding reply on 21 June 1932 and fell silent for about 10 weeks. On 2 September 1932 he sent Keynes a very short paper, 'Some Revised Definitions of Saving and Allied Concepts', that he described as 'the product of a lot of reflection' (*CW* XIII, p. 302). Keynes's response to Robertson's new position is not recorded: 'at this point a further gap appears in the Keynes–Robertson correspondence' (Moggridge in *CW* XIII, p. 306). The next published paper from the dialogue with Robertson is dated May 1933.

This stage of the debate ended with new *EJ* articles. Robertson's 'Saving and Hoarding' appeared in the September 1933 *EJ*, alongside rejoinders by Keynes and Hawtrey. Robertson published a re-rejoinder in the December 1933 issue. This debate essentially saw Robertson 'get in first'; he offered his new definitions of saving: 'A man's disposable income ... is ... the income received not on that day but on the previous one. A man is said to be *saving* if he spends on consumption less than his disposable income' (Robertson, 1933, p. 399). Keynes disputed the usefulness and relevance of Robertson's construct; and Hawtrey offered a critique on points of detail. In the course of his response, Keynes set out the new position he was developing:

> If we define savings as the excess of income during a period over expenditure on consumption during that period, it follows that savings are exactly equal to the value of output added to accumulated wealth, i.e. to investment. The sense of saving in which it is necessarily equal to investment, i.e. the excess of current income over current consumption, let us, for the present, call *surplus*. In my *Treatise on Money* I gave a definition of savings which was not the same as surplus and was, therefore, not necessarily equal to investment. Mr Robertson also feels a need for a conception of savings which is not identical with surplus and proposes one in the above article. I do not like his conception any more than he likes mine. (*CW* XIII, p. 327)

Following a discussion of the two positions, Keynes left 'the reader to decide' (ibid.).

Harrod's part in the saving–investment debate arose from a paper in *Economica* and an article in *The Economist*. Both were primarily concerned with criticising Hayek's theories. However, his paper, 'The Expansion of Credit in an Advancing Community', involved a definition of saving in accordance with Keynes's new definition:

> The rate at which credit must be expanded in order to maintain the system, is equal to the rate at which aggregate income is increasing . . . The savings of the community in any period may be defined as the difference between the value of its total income and the value of the consumable goods purchased therewith. (Harrod, 1934, p. 297)

In the next issue of *Economica*, Robertson addressed Harrod's article in a peculiar manner. He labelled the relationship the 'Grand Monetary Tautology' and implied that it had long been understood:[6]

> Mr. Harrod seems to me . . . to have succumbed to the charms of the Grand Monetary Tautology, which, long found useful by bankers as a cloak for their misdeeds, is now being rediscovered with alarming frequency by theoretical economists. The bank's balance-sheet always balances: *alias* Savings always equal Investment: *alias* all money which is anywhere must be somewhere. (Robertson, 1934, p. 473)

At the end of the short piece, he articulated his main concern that one should not build a theory on this foundation:

> But the preservation of what I will still venture to call equilibrium between real Saving and Investment is, at the least, one consideration among others . . . But I feel pretty sure that we shall get no way at all if all kinds of progress are to be smothered up together in the blanket of the Grand Tautology! (ibid.)

In this way, Robertson argued that the saving–investment identity should not be used as the foundation for a theory just as Keynes was doing exactly that. And he re-asserted the classical ('real') saving–investment theory of interest. The dialogue was, in effect, a pre-emptive strike at the *General Theory*.

Harrod's work prompted a wider dialogue that drew in Kahn as well as Haberler and Karl Bode.[7] Kahn's comments in the course of the dialogue make perfectly clear his and Keynes's understanding of the identity:

> In all these matters I take my standpoint on the fundamental truism that savings are always and in every situation equal to investment . . . [C]ould anything be simpler and more beautiful than this truism and all that goes with it. (Kahn to Harrod, 22 October 1934, Harrod, 2003, letter 382)

[T]he truism "savings = investment" points to some important truths, e.g.
(i) investment is always self-financing: there need never be any question
of "where the money comes from" . . .
(ii) All references to "forced saving", etc. are meaningless.
(iii) It makes no difference what part the banking system is playing in
supplying credit or taking charge of hoarded funds.
(iv) The rate of interest cannot be determined by the "supply and
demand of savings". (Kahn to Harrod, 1 November 1934, Harrod, 2003,
letter 391)

Nevertheless, Robertson continued to pursue the same point on reception
of the galley proofs of the *General Theory*, writing on 3 February 1935:

I'm afraid I haven't altered my view that equations of the type of those on
p. 63 [Vol. XIV, p. 424] are unsuitable for application to heterogeneous
slices of time within which income is changing, because they obscure
the time element. (I never liked Kahn's s[hort]. p[eriod]. method in his
public works article: but it did at least allow *time* (though unspecified in
amount) for the 'savings', corresponding to an act of investment financed
(e.g.) by new bank money, to be elicited: whereas now, since there is no
limit to the shortness of time over which we are at liberty to apply your
equations, they are simultaneous and identical.) It seems to me that the
rehabilitation of the Grand Tautology takes us all back to the pre-Withers,
pre-Wicksell days, and obscures instead of clarifying what happens when
an act of investment takes place. But you have made your mind up on
this! (*CW* XIII, p. 497)

Keynes's response specifically addressed this point:

The grand tautology has either to be accepted or disposed of. I think it is
important because it clears away lots of very subtle muddles which seem
to take almost everyone in. They think that they can use the terms with
their natural senses and yet escape the tautology. One might call $2 + 2 = 4$
a grand tautology. Indeed it is, but that would not dispose of it. (*CW* XIV,
p. 512)

Robertson's arguments left Keynes unmoved. However, in creating his own
definition of saving, Robertson set out a position that in general terms could
challenge Keynes's version, and more specifically could be taken as implying
that the relation was a matter of definition rather than a causal proposition
of theoretical substance. In my view, Keynes never adequately dealt with
this definitional *versus* causal issue.

6.6 The nature and consequence of the identity in the *General Theory*

Foreshadowing his response to his critics, Keynes's treatment of the identity in the *General Theory* did not set out the identity as a central logical proposition, but was more low-key. The title of Chapter 6, where the identity was first mentioned, was rather inappropriate: 'The Definition of Income, Saving and Investment'. The first actual presentation of the identity also had a definitional flavour. Keynes expressed the relationship using the national-accounts-type identities:

> Whilst, therefore, the amount of saving is an outcome of the collective behaviour of individual consumers and the amount of investment of the collective behaviour of individual entrepreneurs, these two amounts are necessarily equal, since each of them is equal to the excess of income over consumption. Moreover, this conclusion in no way depends on any subtleties or peculiarities in the definition of income given above. Provided it is agreed that income is equal to the value of current output, that current investment is equal to the value of that part of current output which is not consumed, and that saving is equal to the excess of income over consumption – all of which is conformable both to common sense and to the traditional usage of the great majority of economists – the equality of saving and investment necessarily follows. In short –
>
> Income = value of output=consumption + investment
> Saving = income–consumption
> Therefore, saving = investment.
>
> Thus, *any* set of definitions which satisfy the above conditions leads to the same conclusion. It is only be denying the validity of one or other of them that the conclusion can be avoided. (*CW* VII, p. 63)

The definition is *ex post*, in the sense that Keynes is talking about macroeconomic aggregates that have already been determined. After further discussion, he only briefly addresses the identity from an *ex ante* perspective:

> Saving, in fact, is a mere residual. The decisions to consume and the decisions to invest between them determine incomes. Assuming that the decisions to invest become effective, they must in doing so either curtail consumption or expand income. Thus, the act of investment in itself cannot help causing the residual or margin, which we call saving, to increase by a corresponding account. (*CW* VII, p. 64)

The key point that income is not constrained by saving is identified but not given due emphasis. Furthermore, he does not use credit processes to aid the exposition. Credit is only discussed – and somewhat obliquely – in Chapter 7, 'The meaning of saving and investment further considered'. The analysis comes in the course of a discussion of the treatments of saving and investment attributable to Robertson, Hayek, Hawtrey and Robbins. Section V discusses the 'prevalence of the idea that saving and investment, taken in their straightforward sense, can differ from one another . . . ':

> It is supposed that a depositor and his bank can somehow contrive between them to perform an operation by which savings can disappear into the banking system so that they are lost to investment, or, contrariwise, that the banking system can make it possible for investment to occur, to which no saving corresponds. But no one can save without acquiring an asset, whether it be cash or a debt or capital-goods; and no one can acquire an asset which he did not previously possess, unless *either* an asset of equal value is newly produced *or* someone else parts with an asset of that value which he previously had . . .
>
> The notion that the creation of credit by the banking system allows investment to take place to which 'no genuine saving' corresponds can only be the result of isolating one of the consequences of the increased bank-credit to the exclusion of the others. If the grant of a bank credit to an entrepreneur additional to the credits already existing allows him to make an addition to current investment which would not have occurred otherwise, incomes will necessarily be increased and at a rate which will normally *exceed* the rate of increased investment. (*CW* VII, pp. 81–2)

The argument is in the negative: Keynes demonstrates that the creation of credit is not inconsistent with the existence of identity. As with Chick in the discussion above, a positive statement of matters would explain the identity by means of the credit-creating process.

However, the identity may have been more critically undermined by Keynes's diminution of the consequence of the identity rather than his inadequate explanation of the cause. The extract from his 1933 lecture (Section 6.4) saw Keynes use the identity to dismiss the classical theory of interest. He continued to use the identity in this way in the early drafts of *General Theory*. But Keynes did not use the identity as motivation for the theory of liquidity preference in the published version of the *General Theory*.

The record of the early drafts of the *General Theory* (in the annex of *CW* XIV) shows the extent of the changes to Chapter 14, 'The Classical Theory of the Rate of Interest'. Following a statement of this theory of interest, the text '[n]ow the analysis of the previous chapters will have made it plain that this account of the matter must be erroneous' (*CW* VII, p. 177) is common to both the second and the third drafts. The second draft goes on to reject the classical theory of interest as follows:

> The amount of "saving", in the sense undoubtedly intended in the above, is the same thing as the amount of investment, looked at from a different standpoint. The amounts of saving and investment are not two distinct variables which tend to move in opposite directions in response to a change in the rate of interest; they necessarily and always move in the same direction, just as the value of the sales of any commodity always moves in the same way as the value of the purchases. It is impossible that a rise in the rate of interest can at the same time increase the excess of income over consumption and decrease the amount of current investment. At *any* rate of interest, however arbitrarily determined, there will be equality between the two. The amount of "saving" is not something determined by an independent set of causes from those determining the amount of investment. The dichotomy offered by Walras, by Marshall or by Cassel between the causes determining the supply of waiting as set forth in chapter so-and-so and the quite different causes determining the demand for waiting as set forth in chapter such-and-such is a nonsense dichotomy, if we mean by the "supply of waiting", not the "propensity to wait", but the actual excess of income over expenditure. The analogy with the demand and supply for a commodity at a given price is a false analogy. For whereas it is perfectly easy to name a price at which the supply and the demand for a commodity would be unequal, it is impossible to name a rate of interest at which the amount of saving and the amount of investment could be unequal. Whatever determines the one, determines the other at the same time. The analogy would be to describe price as the providential factor which ensures that the amount actually bought is kept equal to the amount actually sold. (*CW* XIV, pp. 475–6)

The rejection in the third draft did not utilise the identity and presented matters instead according to what has been referred to as the 'income-generalised saving–investment diagram', with origins in Robertson's work (Section 4.3). According to this presentation, the classical theory of interest is rejected because it is undefined.

> For the assumption that income is constant is inconsistent with the assumption that these two curves can shift independently of one another. If either of them shift, then, in general, income will change; with the result that the whole schematisation based on the assumption of a given income breaks down. (*CW* VII, p. 179)

I believe this to be a very fundamental factor in the loss of Keynes's own theory. Not only does the presentation neglect the role of the identity, but it also contains the seed corn for the Keynesian 'output-adjustment' perspective that is discussed in more detail in the next section. It appears that Keynes rejects the classical theory because it fails to take into account income changes. This facilitates a transition to the *IS-LM* perspective where matters are 'repaired' with the introduction of output (not income) into the two classical schedules. This change of presentation followed persuasion from Harrod, who began a critique of the galley proofs shortly after Robertson and Keynes broke off their dialogue.[8,9]

6.7 The output-adjustment interpretation, the multiplier and the standard interpretations of the 'transition'

Robertson's definition of saving as 'the difference between *previously received* income and current expenditure on consumption' (Robertson, 1940, p. 6) should be understood in the context of the loanable funds perspective. In this theory, the most important determinant of the rate of interest was the gap between saving according to this definition and current investment (equal to the requirement for finance). Loanable funds considerations were no less important to the 'Keynesian' variant; in addition, the model placed the saving–investment relationship at the centre of a wider theoretical structure. As in Keynes's *Treatise*, the two quantities could diverge and were equal only in long-period 'equilibrium'. The mechanism by which equilibrium was restored was a change in *output*. In algebraic terms, this was effected through adding output or real income to saving and investment functions. The basic Keynesian model hence not only departed from the notion of identity, but also permitted the restoration of the relationship to the classical *real* perspective.[10] The model has in turn become known as the output-adjustment model.

The differences between this 'Keynesian' model and the *General Theory* are at the same time substantial and subtle. First, in the *General Theory* the nature of the relationship was an identity between monetary variables; in the 'Keynesian' model the nature was equilibrium between real variables. Second, in the *General Theory* the cause of the identity was monetary. In 'Keynesianism', the cause, insofar as it existed, involved rejecting the assumption of constant output (or full employment) in the classical model. But it is in its consequence that the difference is most profound. In the 'Keynesian' approach the whole model revolved around the saving–investment relationship in the context of the new adjustment to allow for variable output. In the *General Theory*, the saving–investment identity was only the springboard to the theories of liquidity preference, effective demand and the cycle as a whole.

Despite these profound differences, the 'Keynesian' version of the relationship has been attributed to Keynes. It is of importance to examine a little further how this came about.

References to output adjustment can be found in Keynes's writings in this period. His treatment has the change in income preserving, rather than restoring, the identity; therefore, for a less than careful reader, the notion of output change is in the air at this point. Furthermore, he was also engaged in a debate with Hawtrey and (later) the Cambridge 'Circus' over a specific point in the *Treatise* where he had assumed that output did not change in the wake of a change in consumer demand. The (three-page) observations of the latter group have become known as a 'manifesto' and by some have been accorded a crucial role in the transition: 'It was the so-called "manifesto" of April 1932, an open criticism of Keynes's lectures, that made the crucial shift from price to quantity adjustments, which laid the basis of the *General Theory*' (Pasinetti, 1994, p. 4).[11] In general terms, this argument ignores the fact that all neo-classical theories allowed output to adjust in the short run. Eric Davis has pointed out the more specific problem with Hawtrey's theories: ' . . . it was Hawtrey, not Keynes, who first introduced output changes in an equilibrating role and the concomitant identification of quasi-equilibrium positions to economic theory' (Davis, 1980, p. 722). In the light of the wider interpretation of this book, if Hawtrey has precedence it is for aspects of the 'Keynesian' model not for the *General Theory*.

The other key issue that has become synonymous with the common view of the transition between the *Treatise* and the *General Theory*, and at the same time is related to the saving–investment relationship, is the multiplier. The multiplier is portrayed as providing the critical theoretical justification for the validity of public works policies in a depression.

Moggridge's presentation of the transition in *CW* provides a good and obviously influential illustration. He opens by emphasising the practical government expenditure proposals set out in *Can Lloyd George Do It?* Next, output adjustment is emphasised: 'Moreover, the bulk of the formal analysis of the *Treatise* placed the emphasis on changes in prices rather than output. The concern with output changes was clearly secondary' (*CW* XIII, p. 338). From this position, he argues that three developments 'mov[ed] changes in output to the centre of the stage which they were to occupy in the *General Theory*': (i) the building intensity of the great depression and associated demands for public spending policies; (ii) (what Moggridge regards as) the critical reception given to the *Treatise* and associated debates; and (iii) the 'discussions in Cambridge'. The discussion of (iii) emphasises the role of the Cambridge 'Circus' and finally on Kahn's (1931) multiplier article that 'gave much greater precision to the line of thought that had already emerged in *Can Lloyd George Do It?*' (*CW* XIII, p. 340).[12]

According to my interpretation of the transition, the saving–investment identity was the key step and Keynes did not use the multiplier to establish this relation. Instead, at this point, the multiplier and the associated technique of sequence/process analysis were drawn into the debate by advocates of the output-adjustment model. However, once this and associated confusions are recognised and set aside, it is possible that the original development of the multiplier did become helpful to Keynes in this transition period, and can usefully aid explanation.

The multiplier (in its sequential form) was first drawn into the debate on the proofs of the *General Theory* by Robertson. This is seen first in the quotation in Section 6.5 from 3 February 1933, where he demands a role for *time* in the saving–investment relationship. In the 1936 private correspondence, Robertson took a stronger position: 'The "multiplier" only becomes interesting when, in Hicks' phrase, it has wings, i.e. is used to analyse a dynamic process' (*CW* XIV, p. 97). In his later (1940) *Essays in Monetary Theory* he sets out a fuller position. In 'Effective Demand and the Multiplier', he portrays Kahn's multiplier analysis as describing an '. . . Authoritarian act of investment of money amount N as generating a series of increments of money income – qN, q^2N, etc. – and a series of increments of saving $(1-q)N$, $(1-q)qN$, etc. – at later dates' (Robertson, 1940, p. 117). He goes on to set out a process analysis in response to his own complaint:

> [I]f, with Mr. Kahn, we are prepared to forget about the period of transition, we can declare the problem of the finance of the process of investment to be self-solving.
>
> For the convenience of those who, like myself, are left uneasy by this last step, and who prefer a more explicitly temporal method of analysis, I venture to retell the story in my own language and in tabloid form as follows, . . . (Robertson, 1940, pp. 117–18)

Again his concern emanates from loanable funds considerations; Robertson is stressing a temporal dimension to the need for finance. Such 'dynamics' later became part of the 'Keynesian' depiction. But the use of process analysis and the assumption of constant prices have overshadowed the actual dynamics of the *General Theory*. For Keynes, the multiplier was primarily an instantaneous relationship in the context of the theory of aggregate demand (see Chapter 8):[13]

> It is obvious that an initiative of this description [an increase in the output of the capital-goods industries] only produces its full effect on employment over a period of time. I have found, however, in discussion that this obvious fact often gives rise to some confusion between the logical theory of the multiplier, which holds good continuously, without time-lag, at all moments of time, and the consequences of an expansion in the capital-goods industries which take gradual effect, subject to time-lag and only after an interval. (*CW* VII, p. 122)

The process of interest that followed an increase in demand, or more specifically of investment, was the response of other industries to the increase in purchasing power in the economy. These industries are faced with the basic choice of increasing quantity or price, or, with increasing costs, both; these are the choices of relevance to the determination of output and hence employment and potentially the equilibrium of the system. Whatever the resolution, the multiplier relation dictates that income must always be equal to the value determined by this relation. The short-period dynamics of the *General Theory* follow from the dynamics in the allocation of changes in income between output and price over time. Such a dynamic is set into motion not just by an exogenous change in demand but one due to specific changes in the rate of interest, MEC and, to a lesser extent, MPC. Keynes used the multiplier *equation* to derive the change in aggregate demand, given a change in investment and the MPC. The relation, thus, has a fundamental role, but a role that is different from the traditional interpretations. (In terms of the order of presentation adopted in this book, the discussion of aggregate demand and hence the multiplier comes after a discussion of the theory of liquidity preference.)

With the 'Keynesian' version set aside, it is however possible that the multiplier was important to the development of the *General Theory* in a more subtle manner. Kahn's paper (1931) discusses how an increase in public expenditure is self-financing using what he referred to as 'Mr Meade's relation' (see Meade, 1993 for a retrospective view). In this way Kahn and Meade were considering the relation between saving and investment through the perspective of exports and government expenditure and the multiplier, just as Keynes was doing through the perspective of investment. The participants did not contrast the two approaches in public, although two of Kahn's private comments are of interest:

> After all, 'Mr Meade's relation' is the forebear of 'savings = investment'. (Kahn to Harrod, 1 November 1934, Harrod, 2003, letter 391)

> Of course what we had done – but failed completely to realise – was, by a very roundabout method, to establish the identity of saving and investment – if saving is defined on commonsense lines rather than those of the *Treatise*. (Kahn, 1984, p. 99)

Kahn's (1931) paper derived these effects through the geometric progressions that have ended up defining the technique of process/sequence analysis advocated by Robertson, but without the income lag. In recent years, several authors have used these techniques to illustrate how an increase in investment brings about an equal increase in saving. As noted, Meade restated his relationship in the *EJ* in 1993; Chick (1983, pp. 257–63) used the technique to illustrate the role of new deposits in preserving the saving–investment identity; later she showed how the identity is preserved at every stage of the multiplier process (Chick, 1997, p. 177).

6.8 Richard Kent's discovery of Keynes's 1929 multiplier

A recent discovery by Richard Kent offers an alternative interpretation of the place of the multiplier in the development of the *General Theory*. Kent (2005) shows that the arithmetic progression that underlies the multiplier process was first outlined by Keynes himself in May 1929. The demonstration is based on Keynes's notes for a speech supporting his proposals in *Can Lloyd George Do It?* that Kent discovered in the Keynes papers; these notes have not been reproduced in the *CW*.

Keynes, therefore, understood multiplier processes even before he wrote the *Treatise*. This timing provides more evidence to refute the notion that the discovery of the multiplier was so critical to the transition to the *General Theory*.

6.9 Post-publication debate

The saving–investment identity was debated extensively after the publication of the *General Theory*. The nature of the discussion was, however, deeply unsatisfactory; it was more about the assertion of the neo-classical models than an attempt to understand Keynes's own theory. There were two main strands: first, the assertion that the identity was a matter of definition. Such a perspective followed from the claimed equivalence of the loanable funds and liquidity preference theories of interest. If these theories of interest were the same then the different approaches to the saving–investment relationship had no material significance. So the different approaches could be argued to be a matter of definition. The second strand was the bald statement of the neo-classical equilibrium relationship, using output as the adjusting variable, as if it were due to Keynes. The actual validity of Keynes's version of the identity was not explicitly rejected in any review; as a consequence, Keynes had no real critique to get his teeth into. In the main he appears to have left the response to other colleagues, with Kahn, Townshend and Abba Lerner making important contributions (see below and Chapter 10). Ultimately, the nature of the debate was such that no resolution was possible.

Hicks's and E. A. G. Robinson's reviews, for the *EJ* and *The Economist* respectively, illustrate each of the perspectives:

> Probably the most striking, to a casual reader, of the theoretical doctrines of this book is that which proclaims the necessary equality of Savings and Investment. This looks like a decided recantation of one of the most fundamental principles of the *Treatise on Money*, but inspection shows

that it is nothing of the sort. It is merely a change in definition – but a change in definition which marks a very important change in point of view. (Hicks, 1936, reproduced in Backhouse, 1999, p. 142)

In equilibrium, then, saving must equal investment. If these two tend to be unequal, the level of activity will be changed until they are restored to equality. But the restoration of equality does not depend upon any particular rate of interest. If the rate of interest is kept high, so that channels for profitable investment are few, the level to which savings, incomes and output will be forced to descend will be correspondingly lower. The fact that savings tend to exceed investment does not, in Mr Keynes' view, in itself reduce the rate of interest directly, . . . (Robinson, 29 February 1936, reproduced in Backhouse, 1999, pp. 75–6)

No response to Hicks's comment is recorded. Hugh Townshend felt obliged to address Robinson's version in a follow-up letter to *The Economist*:

there is one rather fundamental theoretical point relating to the vexed question of savings and investment which is left a little obscure. Your reviewer says: [as above] . . .

But if investment be defined, as it is by Mr Keynes (pages 62 and 52) as including additions to entrepreneurs' stocks of finished goods (consumption-goods as well as capital-goods), saving is *always* equal to investment, whether in "equilibrium" or not, and cannot "tend" to be unequal to it. (*The Economist*, 21 March 1936)

Keynes and Townshend exchanged correspondence after the publication of Townshend's letter. Keynes's comments clearly illustrate his attitude to the review (as well as attributing the output-adjustment perspective to Hawtrey):

I was uneasy about the passage in *The Economist* review to which you refer and am very glad that you have dealt with it.

The main point with which you are dealing is concerned, of course, with the difference between Hawtrey and myself. I gave a good deal of consideration as to whether I should deal with it explicitly, and perhaps I was wrong to decide not to do so. (*CW* XXIX, pp. 238–9)

In the United States, Hansen took a definitional position and argued further that Keynes's own definitions led him to error. He explicitly set the output-adjustment position against the *General Theory* and went onto argue that Keynes was in error because he did not take into account loanable funds considerations. Furthermore this 'leading Keynesian' explicitly stated that he preferred Robertson's position, footnoting Robertson's 1933 *EJ* article to the following:

> At this point it becomes necessary to inject a brief consideration of terminological difficulties. In the new book Keynes formally abandons his former highly artificial definition of income and saving. But his new terminology is by no means wholly satisfactory. In the writer's opinion his entire exposition would have been very greatly facilitated had he adopted outright Robertson's definitions of income, saving, and investment. This would have made it far easier for him to make clear the factors of disequilibrium. For Robertson's terminology enables one to see very clearly the disequilibrating effects of hoarding and dishoarding and of credit creation and debt cancellation. (Hansen, 1938, pp. 20–1)

Needless to say, Robertson himself was prominent throughout the discussion. While his *QJE* review did not address the *nature* of the identity, he undermined the *role* of the identity by addressing a version of events exactly consistent with the Harrod amendment and hence the output-adjustment perspective:

> 6. One prominent feature in Mr. Keynes' scheme requires further mention – the increased saving generated by the expansion of trade activity . . .
>
> According to Mr. Keynes, it is an error to regard the supply schedule of saving as a determinant of the rate of interest, since the position of this supply schedule itself depends on the level of employment and income, which in turn depends on the position of the demand schedule for saving. There is thus a 'gap' in the classical system, which Mr. Keynes claims to close by introducing the rate of interest, as determined by "liquidity preference" and the quantity of money, from outside as a determinant. (Robertson, 1936, pp. 184–5)

Keynes's response did not comment on this aspect of Robertson's critique. Next, Robertson directly addressed the identity as part of the 'alternative theories' dialogue, arguing (with Hansen) that the identity made Keynes fail to appreciate the importance of loanable funds considerations (this will be discussed further in Chapter 7). The 'alternative theories' dialogue, however, should have helped to clarify the difference between Keynes's and Robertson's positions. Keynes approved of Ohlin's concepts *ex ante* and *ex post* and used them in the course of the discussion; in the *General Theory*, saving was defined as *ex post* saving; Robertson's saving was *ex ante*. In this way, the debate has a definitional aspect, but the choice of definition makes no difference to Keynes's theory of the identity of *ex post* saving and investment.[14]

Meanwhile, as Keynes was engaged in the 'alternative theories' dialogue, Kahn was reviewing Haberler's *Prosperity and Depression* (1937) for the *EJ*. His assessment gave prominence to a rejection of Haberler's treatment of saving and investment:

> There is, however, one fundamental difficulty running throughout this book, . . . We are informed that "the terms 'savings' and 'investment' are used here in the ordinary meaning of the two words" (p. 116 note). If "sums saved are used to liquidate bank credit or are accumulated and hoarded in the shape of cash and idle deposits" (p. 116), there is an excess of saving over investment . . . There is no possibility here of "savings running to waste." Nor can an "excess of investment over saving" be substantiated. Professor Haberler was aware of this difficulty, as is shown by his controversy with Mr. Harrod, published in *Economica* in February 1935, . . . [and] the point was raised by some of those economists to whom, as Mr Loveday mentions in his Preface, a first draft of Part I was sent for their comments and criticisms. But nowhere is the difficulty fairly faced; it is simply brushed on one side. "Mr. Keynes objections," to the doctrine of "forced saving," "are purely verbal" (p. 40 note). "We do not propose to reproduce in great detail these terminological discussions" (p. 197). It is unfortunate that the author has made so little attempt to deal with a difficulty which must prevent many of his readers from attaching any very definite meaning to the views which he is putting forward. (Kahn, 1937, pp. 671–2)

The similarity between Haberler's and Robertson's position was not lost on Kahn:

> It is true that, following the lead of Mr. Robertson (to whose views on this matter, curiously enough, no space is devoted in the earlier portion of this volume), Professor Haberler is here putting forward a definition of saving which, on certain drastic assumptions, is such (though Professor Haberler omits to say so) as to make the difference between saving and investment equal to the change in the quantity of active balances. (Kahn, 1937, p. 675)

In the published response, Haberler simply took the definitional approach:

> If, that is to say, we define both saving and investment as the money value of the unconsumed output of the period, then they are always and under all conditions equal, irrespective of whether people hoard or not, for the simple reason that they are the same thing (two symbols for the

same magnitude). I assume that Mr. Kahn has these definitions in mind, because they are Mr. Keynes' definitions. What I cannot understand, and what is highly symptomatic of the prevailing confusion, is that he does not simply stop there. Why his unfortunate digression into the field of hoarding and dishoarding? Why not simply say: S ≡ I? (Haberler, 1938, p. 326)

A further debate on the issue was published in the *QJE* between August 1937 and August 1939. This series of articles saw a fuller bringing together of the saving–investment relationship and process analysis. The argument was advanced that Robertson's definition of saving was preferable because it allowed matters to be viewed dynamically through this technique. While Lerner made robust contributions on Keynes's behalf (discussed in Chapter 10), the concluding article endorsed this dynamic 'resolution' to the debate: 'Those who think of things as happening in a certain order of time . . . will prefer Robertson's concepts. Those who think of things, not in the process of happening but after the event, will favour Keynes's terminology' (Lutz, 1939). (The wider charge that the *General Theory* described a static system may have originated in Keynes's not adopting process analysis techniques. In my opinion this misrepresents; as discussed earlier, the dynamics are just different.)

Lastly, Robertson introduced one more angle. He argued in his (1940) *Essays in Monetary Theory* that the size of the 'debate' was indicative of the weakness of Keynes's stance:

Since this saving-"investment" identity has played such a large part in the discussions of the last few years, I must be forgiven a brief digression on it here. I wish I could feel that its expositors were *continuously* as conscious as at times they profess themselves to be that it is completely nugatory (to use a favourite work of Mr. Hawtrey's) for purposes of causal analysis as distinct from statistical calculation . . . . Hence they are enabled to close their eyes to the absurdity of even enquiring what the forces are which "ensure equality" between the two magnitudes . . . This lack of firmness in the handling of their own concepts convinces me that Mr. Keynes and his expositors are not altogether comfortable in the terminological garments that they have elected to wear. (Robertson, 1940, pp. 5–6)

As noted in Chapter 3, if Keynes responded to this critique it is not recorded.

6.10   The 'resolution' of the debate

In the 'Preface' to the French edition of his book (dated 20 February 1939), Keynes paid special attention to the relationship between savings and investment. His comments are indicative of a growing recognition of the profound importance of the identity and equally of an emphatic rejection of arguments put by others:

> a relationship is set up between aggregate savings and aggregate invest-ment which can be very easily shown, beyond any possibility of reas-onable dispute, to be one of exact and necessary equality. Rightly regarded this is a banale [sic] conclusion. But it sets in motion a train of thought from which more substantial matters follow. (*CW* VII, p. xxxiii)[15]

His last full statement of his theoretical position (at the NDE) saw Keynes again using the identity to reject the classical theory of interest:

> Rate of interest determines equilibrium between savings and investment. If people become more willing to save and therefore willing to accept a lower rate of interest, a corresponding increase of investment takes place. Thus, a greater willingness to save causes and is indispensable to more investment. Here virtue of saving. Doubt about this due to
>
> (*a*) It did not fit the facts. For in this case there could never be general, as distinct from frictional and seasonal unemployment, i.e. there would always be a sufficiency of jobs offering for it would mean that whatever was earned was spent so that business as a whole would always cover its costs (subtleties here, I will not stop to explain)
>
> (*b*) It was logically pure nonsense for [because] $S = I$ at all rates of investment. Y either definable as $C + S$ or as $C + I$. S and I were opposite facets of the same phenomenon they did not need a rate of interest to bring them into equilibrium for they were at all times and in all conditions in equilibrium. (*CW* XXVII, pp. 388–9)

A year after this statement of his theory, Keynes was dead. With a helping hand from Robertson, his position was lost with astonishing rapidity. Kahn records how Robertson dismissed Keynes's position and re-asserted his own position and in the 'Preface' to the 1949 edition of *Banking Policy and the Price Level*:

> While Keynes must at the time have understood and acquiesced in my step-by-step method, it is evident that it never, so to speak, got under his skin; for in his two successive treatments of the savings–investment theme in his two big books he discarded it completely. This was naturally a great personal disappointment to me; and it is, I think, being increas-ingly recognised that it was also a misfortune for the smooth progress of theory. I do not think that anybody who had really grasped the method of the Appendix to Ch[apter] v of this book need have been puzzling in the head in 1930 over the problem of 'where the savings went to', or have

stood in need of the crowning revelation that 'savings' and 'investment', if defined so as to be identical, are indeed always necessarily equal, – a phenomenon which was the staring-point, not the culmination, of the analysis attempted in this little book! (cited in Kahn, 1984, p. 63)

Writing Keynes's contributions out as 'misfortunes', Robertson hence realigned theory to his own position in 1924.[16] In broad terms, during the 'Keynesian era' the 'Keynesian' interpretation of the relation held sway. As time went by, the 'Keynesian' model was attributed to Keynes himself. With the dismissal of 'Keynesianism', the saving–investment equilibrium adhered to by the classics was restored. Chick's restoration of the identity (originally in 1985), in the context of the evolution of banking, that underpinned the discussion of the nature of the identity in Section 6.2, remains of no interest to the wider profession. Her restoration has followed the fate of the original: not refuted just set aside. With Keynes's theory building from this identity, the effect of setting it aside is to set aside the *General Theory*.

Notes

1. The exact course of events and developments must be partly based on conjecture since Moggridge's notes in *CW* indicate that much of this material during the course of the dialogue is missing. The relevant parts of Volume XIII refer to missing papers on pages 211, 214 and 218.
2. Keynes adhered to Marshall's concept of 'normal' output and prices, a long-period position where only normal profits were made. While the short period of the *Treatise* saw supernormal profits made, Keynes continued to define income with this long-period position in mind and excluded such profits.
3. Skidelsky offers a reference to the Hawtrey papers (RGHP: 11/5); he notes that the piece is 'Omitted from *CW*'.
4. The identity can also be seen from the students' perspective on pages 62, 116, 120 and 167 of Rymes's (1989) book of lecture notes.
5. Many other scholars have examined the transition between the *Treatise* and the *General Theory* (e.g. Clarke, 1988, and Amadeo, 1989). However, these characterisations emphasise different aspects of the transition (see Section 6.7); as a consequence they are less useful sources from the perspective of my own interpretation. Toshiaki Hirai's work (e.g. 2005) is more relevant to my approach to the transition and identifies and emphasises many of the passages that I consider important.
6. Private correspondence between Harrod and Robertson shows the phrase is due to Robertson: '. . . what I have ventured to call the Grand Tautology' (Harrod, 2003, letter 562, 19 May 1936).
7. Bode was an 'Austrian' Economist. He worked at the LoN with Haberler and later was an associate professor in Stanford (1937–45).
8. See Chapter 3. Keynes sent Harrod the papers on 5 June 1935; he terminated the dialogue with Robertson on 14 March 1935.
9. The relevant discussion between Harrod and Keynes is in *CW* XIII (pp. 525–65). A good illustration of this neo-classical perspective is Harrod's claim: 'The essence of your point I feel to be that the *cet. par.* clause of the supply and demand

analysis, which in this case includes the level of income, is *invalid*. The classical theory is invalid but not nonsense' (*CW* XIII, p. 540).

10. Hicks later explicitly attributed the removal of any role for price to Keynes. In his *Capital and Growth*, Hicks reproduced a paper that claimed the fixed price assumption was one of the 'central simplifications ... of the so-called "General Theory"' (Hicks, 1982, p. 230).

11. Keynes's later comments on an article addressing similar issues by Joan Robinson (1933) are unambiguous: 'I think you are a little hard on me as regards the assumption of constant output [in the *Treatise*]. It is quite true that I have not followed out the consequences of changes in output in the earlier theoretical part. I admit that this wants doing, and I shall be doing it in my lectures; though that does not absolve me from being criticised for not having done it in my *Treatise*. But in my *Treatise* itself, I have had long discussions with [?of] the effects of changes in output; it is only at a particular point in the preliminary theoretical argument that I assume constant output, and I am at pains to make this absolutely clear' (*CW* XIII, p. 270). Kahn's *Making of the General Theory* (1984, p. 111) answers the charge that Keynes took output as constant in the *Treatise* by reproducing the same text.

12. As noted in Section 1.4, the saving–investment relation is not presented as relevant to the *General Theory* but instead is presented as part of the discussion of the *Treatise*. In terms of source material, Moggridge's 'Towards the *General Theory*' chapter of *CW* Volume XIII involves virtually no reproductions of useful historical material; and the first seven pages of this chapter record only Moggridge's own commentary. The use of such extensive interpretation rather than source material at this critical juncture might also be regarded as a natural consequence of the invalidity of the standard interpretation.

13. Though Chick (1983; Appendix to Chapter 14) has pointed out that Keynes sometimes spoke of the multiplier in dynamic terms.

14. The following statement in a letter to Hawtrey illustrates Keynes's view on whether there is a definitional aspect to his theory: 'I should entirely and violently dissent from your statement near the bottom of page 3 that the proposition that investment and saving are necessarily equal is an essential step in my train of reasoning. The train of reasoning does not depend in the least on my particular definitions. There is not the slightest difficulty, as you will readily see on reflection, in re-writing the argument in terms of your own definitions' (*CW* XIV, p. 16).

15. Kahn reproduces elements of the same discussion on savings and investment, observing: 'This is a far more fruitful exposition of the meaning of the word "general" – the result of three years of discussion and thought' (Kahn, 1984, p. 121).

16. Though Jan Toporowski tells me that the identity was consistently enunciated in all Kalecki's work relating to investment.

7
The Theory of Liquidity Preference and Debt-Management Policy

7.1 Introduction

The previous chapter explained the importance of the macroeconomic identity between saving and investment. Logically, the next step in the discussion of Keynes's theory is the theory of liquidity preference – the central monetary innovation of the *General Theory*. In this theory, Keynes turned his attention from money as a means of exchange to money as a store of value. His analysis led him not only to the theoretical treatment of uncertainty and expectation, but also to practical conclusions of the most profound importance. Ultimately, the theory turned classical analysis on its head. The rate of interest was the cause, not the passive consequence, of the level of economic activity. Moreover, as a quantity that depended on expectation, the authorities – if they so desired – had full control of the rate of interest that prevailed in a national economy. This control depended on the monetary, debt-management and international financial policies that were outlined in Chapter 3.

While it was possible to trace the development of the saving–investment identity, there is virtually no correspondence or other information concerning the development of the theory of liquidity preference. The main markers have already been discussed: the emphasis on the rate of interest in the *Treatise*, the 1931/32 *EJ* symposium, 'Savings and Usury', the Festschrift for Professor A. Spiethoff concerning the need for a monetary theory of activity as a whole and the November 1933 lecture notes rejecting the classical theory of interest. There is no discussion of the theory as it developed; published correspondence begins after the work was in proof form. Furthermore, the dialogue that does exist is almost entirely concerned with controversy.

Just as liquidity preference was the most important monetary innovation in *General Theory*, it was the central component of subsequent discussion and critique. This began at proof stage and continued through the reviews into the fuller 'alternative theories' debate; the dialogue did not stop until after the war had begun. The argument was two-sided: first, liquidity preference was criticised for inadequately treating 'loanable funds' considerations; and second, the equivalence of loanable funds and liquidity preference was asserted. The critique was at least well aimed. Keynes's theory of liquidity preference was primarily a theory of money as a store of value, but, in the interests of simplicity, Keynes incorporated aspects of money as a medium of exchange. In the 'alternative theories' dialogue, Keynes sought to clarify matters using a distinction between *inactive* and *active* holdings of money.[1] Even then, his treatment was not regarded as entirely satisfactory and it was not the full reconciliation between the theories that his opponents demanded. The subsequent debate led to Keynes making concessions, but he regarded these as only serving to clarify and re-enforce his original theory. However, his rivals did not appear to be interested in Keynes's concessions. And despite confirmation of the theory as a whole with the setting of wartime interest rates at 3 per cent, liquidity preference was set aside. The properties of the treatment of 'liquidity preference' within *IS-LM* were loanable-funds properties. The literature discussed below indicates that this should come as no surprise: Hicks was involved in the critique of liquidity preference from the start.

Even those post-Keynesians who have seen through this charade have not gone far enough with their restoration of liquidity preference. The debate has been excessively skewed to loanable-funds considerations (see Section 7.9). More fundamentally, though, the post-Keynesian restoration of the role of expectations in liquidity preference has not yet seen its way to Keynes's conclusion that expectations can be manipulated and interest brought under control.[2] The positive discussion that follows attempts to set out the theory of liquidity preference, with emphasis on the role of expectation, a fuller treatment of the incorporation of the theory of money as a means of exchange within the same framework, and lastly on practical policy. Inevitably, the negative discussion is an exposition of the 'Keynesian' critique and 'resolution'.

7.2   The demand for and supply of money as a store of value

Keynes argued that the rate of interest was not a reward for parting with *savings* but a reward for parting with *liquidity*. His first discussion of the concept comes in Chapter 13, 'The General Theory of the Rate of Interest':

> But this decision having been made, there is a further decision which awaits him, namely, in *what* form he will hold the command over future consumption which he has reserved, whether out of his current income or from previous savings. Does he want to hold it in the form of immediate, liquid command (i.e. in money or its equivalent)? Or is he prepared to part with immediate command for a specified or indefinite period, leaving it to future market conditions to determine on what terms he can,

if necessary, convert deferred command over specific goods into immediate command over goods in general? In other words, what is the degree
of his *liquidity-preference* – where an individual's liquidity-preference is
given by a schedule of the amounts of his resources, valued in terms of
money or wage-units, which he will wish to retain in the form of money
in different sets of circumstances? (*CW* VII, p. 166, italics in original)

While this definition comes at matters through the perspective of a saving
decision, liquidity preference is a decision that arises after the decision to
save has been made. Liquidity preference is the decision about the degree
of liquidity at which savings should be held. Furthermore, it is a decision
concerning the stock of savings – *wealth* – at any point in time rather than
any new flow of saving alone. The rate of interest is hence not determined
by the supply of and demand for (flows) of saving, but by the supply of and
demand for assets into which holdings of (stocks) of wealth can be placed.
In the theory of money as a store of value, money is one of these assets.

Keynes's first formal definition of the equilibrium for the rate of interest
is as follows:

> The rate of interest is not the 'price' which brings into equilibrium the
> demand for resources to invest with the readiness to abstain from present
> consumption. It is the 'price' which equilibrates the desire to hold wealth
> in the form of cash with the available quantity of cash; (*CW* VII, p. 167)

Later in the book, Keynes puts matters as follows:

> The current rate of interest depends, as we have seen, not on the strength
> of the desire to hold wealth, but on the strengths of the desire to hold
> it in liquid and illiquid forms respectively, coupled with the amount of
> the supply of wealth in the one form relatively to the supply of it in the
> other. (*CW* VII, p. 213)

The first definition is in terms of money as 'cash'. The second quotation,
however, more fully captures the more general nature of liquidity preference
theory (LPT). Liquidity preference should be thought of as reflecting the
demand for assets of various degrees of liquidity, and the rate of interest as
depending on both the demand of and supplies for assets across the whole of
this spectrum. 'Money', however, does have a particularly crucial role; while
it is obvious that illiquid assets offer holders a reward in the form of interest,
the reward for holding money is the essence of liquidity itself. Furthermore,
it was a shortage of 'money' that most stood in the way of the interest rate
policies that Keynes had in mind.

Keynes's discussion emphasises that at first sight the desire to hold wealth
as money was paradoxical: ' . . . why should anyone prefer to hold his wealth

in a form which yields little or no interest to holding it in a form which yields interest ... ?' (*CW* VII, p. 168). He was more emphatic in the 1937 *QJE* paper:

> Money, it is well known, serves two principal purposes. By acting as a money of account it facilitates exchanges without its being necessary that it should ever itself come into the picture as a substantive object. In this respect it is a convenience which is devoid of significance or real influence. In the second place, it is a store of wealth. So we are told, without a smile on the face. But in the world of the classical economy, what an insane use to which to put it! For it is a recognised characteristic of money as a store of wealth that it is barren; whereas practically every other form of storing wealth yields some interest or profit. Why should anyone outside a lunatic asylum wish to use money as a store of wealth? (*CW* XIV, pp. 115–16)

In the *General Theory* the paradox was resolved as follows:

> A full explanation is complex and must wait for chapter 15. There is, however, a necessary condition failing which the existence of a liquidity-preference for money as a means of holding wealth could not exist.
>
> This necessary condition is the existence of *uncertainty* as to the future rate of interest, i.e. as to the complex of rates of interest for varying maturities which will rule at future dates. (*CW* VII, p. 168)

Keynes argued that the necessary condition for liquid holdings of savings was the fact that people did not know what the future rate of interest would be; it was *uncertain*. The nature of uncertainty has already been discussed in Chapter 5, but merits elaboration in this specific context. In the market for liquidity, uncertainty operates through the capital value of assets. A holding of government bonds will change in value as expectations towards the future rate of interest change. In the case of the expected rate of interest rising, the market value of a holding of bonds will fall. The factors that determine this expected rate of interest will be discussed more fully in due course; for the time being it is sufficient to note that (i) no agent knows the value of the future rate of interest with certainty; and (ii) there will be a distribution of opinions at any point in time and this distribution will change over time. Thus, Keynes's famous motives for holding 'money' should primarily be seen as reflecting his interpretation of how uncertainty gave rise to a demand for money. Exactly what was meant by 'money' will also be examined shortly; for the time being it is sufficient to define money in the context of this discussion: as an asset with a certain (or nearly certain) capital value. This is set against a demand for bonds of uncertain future capital value. In the *General Theory*, he summarises the 'three motives' as follows:

> (i) the transactions-motive, i.e. the need of cash for the current transaction of personal and business exchanges; (ii) the precautionary-motive, i.e. the desire for security as to the future cash equivalent of a certain proportion of total resources; and (iii) the speculative motive, i.e. the object of securing profit from knowing better than the market what the future will bring forth. (*CW* VII, p. 170)

While this characterisation is familiar, it offers a first sight of the conflict between the theory of money as a store of value and considerations of money as a means of exchange. Transaction demands arise through exchange not store of value requirements. A more specific aspect of the conflict is Keynes's choosing to treat transactions and precautionary demands together as a single function of income.

The three motives can be analysed to derive the money demand or liquidity preference schedule. The schedule is reasonably shown as a curve convex to the origin with the rate of interest (price) on the *y*-axis and money (quantity) on the *x*-axis (Figure 7.1). While it might usefully be depicted algebraically, doing so is presentational not mathematical. In my view, Keynes did not intend this relation to be manipulated as one of a set of simultaneous equations in the way that it has. This was perhaps only ever broached in Keynes's lectures; Rymes observes that

In this lecture, in almost all the notes we find

$M = A(W, \rho)$

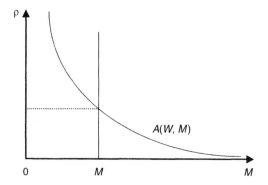

Figure 7.1 Basic liquidity preference

where $A(W, \rho)$ is the demand for money to hold in relation to income and is expressed as a function of the state of the news, W, and the rate of interest, ρ, with M being the stock supply of money.

All the notes concentrate on the three determinants of the rate of interest, A, liquidity preference, itself a function of the state of the news W and the quantity of money, M – that is, A, W and M are being treated as exogenous! Again, the notes reflect the continued inference of Keynes that expressions such as $M = A(W, \rho)$ *are not formal relationships but rather methods of thought*. The listeners were sometimes disconcerted by such philosophical grazing by Keynes. In Tarshis's notes at this point we find: 'What the Hell'. (Rymes, 1989, pp. 24–5, my emphasis)[3]

Using this notation, Figure 7.1 would be an appropriate depiction for the equilibrium determining the rate of interest (I have reversed ρ and M in line with standard supply and demand presentation).

Keynes dropped this notation for *General Theory* and no longer incorporated any shorthand for the state of the news. While it is absurd to argue that his dropping of the shorthand meant that Keynes had disregarded the role of expectations in the theory of liquidity preference, there can be no question, as Kahn later observed (see Section 10.5), that Keynes's occasional use of unqualified algebraic shorthand, and his letting go as others built on this technique, was a serious problem.

In the *General Theory*, Keynes first explained the shape of the liquidity preference schedule through both the speculative and transactions motives (*CW* VII, pp. 171–2). For the time being the role of the transactions motive is left aside, first because of the emphasis on the wealth aspect of liquidity preference; and second because the speculative demand is crucial in terms of the transmission of monetary policy in a way that the transactions is not.

Speculators hold bonds or money according to their expectations about the future rate of interest. If they expect a rise in the rate of interest they are therefore expecting a fall in the price of bonds and they will therefore hold all wealth that they use for speculation as money (which may involve selling holdings of bonds). When they expect the rate of interest to fall again, the same individuals will use inactive speculative money holdings to purchase bonds. Thus, the demand for money changes according to the expectations of the future rate of interest. As noted, uncertainty is involved because market participants do not know – either individually or collectively – what the future rate of interest will be. Participants in the speculative market will only have opinions as to the future rate of interest. While these opinions will be held with varying degrees of conviction (as Chick, 1983, p. 204, has emphasised), the nature of speculation is such that opinion is all that speculators have to act on.[4] The aspect of speculative demand that determines the shape of the schedule is the *distribution* of these opinions at any point in time.

In the *General Theory*, Keynes's exposition has the distribution of views based around a 'safe' rate of interest:

It follows that a given M_2 [the quantity of money held to satisfy the speculative motive] will not have a definitive quantitative relationship to a given rate of interest of r; – what matters is not the *absolute* level of r but the degree of divergence from what is considered a fairly *safe* level of r, having regard to those calculations of probability which are being relied on. (*CW* VII, p. 201, italics in original)

A short discussion led to the conclusion that 'in any given state of expectation, a fall in r will be associated with an increase in M_2' (*CW* VII, pp. 201–2). However, his argument did not depict the process of speculation in theoretical terms. Chick's (1983, pp. 204–8) derivation of the shape of the liquidity preference schedule provides the missing analysis. Rather than a safe rate of interest, her argument centres round a 'normal' rate of interest: '[e]ach speculator, i, has an expectation of a "normal" rate of interest, r_{iN}, toward which the actual rate of interest, r_t, tends to return' (Chick, 1983, p. 204). Individual speculators expect capital gains or losses and hence hold bonds or money depending on the sign of the difference between r_t and r_{iN}:

$$r^e_{i,t+1} - r_t = f(r_{iN} - r_t), f > 0$$

where r^e is the expected future rate. Thus the higher (lower) the current rate, the more are capital gains (losses) expected. The liquidity preference schedule is derived as a cumulative distribution function of individual speculators' expectations of the rate of interest and the funds they have set aside for speculation. The schedule is concave between $r_t = r_{MIN}$, where all wealth holders expect a rise in the rate of interest and hence all speculative resources S_+, and even resources held for long-term investment (normally never held as money), are held as money; and $r_t = r_{MAX}$, where all speculators as well as long-term investors hold bonds (Figure 7.2).[5]

Chick (1983, p. 204) argues that 'Keynes did not discuss how the normal rate was estimated'. She elaborates:

The suggestion that the normal rate is generated by some adaptive learning mechanism based on past interest rates would, I think, be rejected by Keynes. Of course speculators learn from the past, and a long history of low rates is bound to lower the normal rate; but speculators undoubtedly use more than past history to derive r_N [r_{iN}]. (ibid., p. 211)

The central argument of this thesis goes beyond this description: Keynes was pre-supposing action aimed at the manipulation of the rate of interest. Anticipating matters that are more fully addressed later in this chapter, this

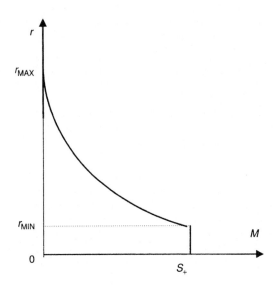

Figure 7.2 The speculative demand for money

action meant attempting to manipulate individuals' normal rates to be in line with a rate on long-term debt that the authorities want to set, r_{policy}. The ideal situation would be that $r_t = r_{\text{policy}} = r_{iN}$, for all i and t. At this point there would be no speculative demand for money (speculative funds would be held as bonds, given the flow of interest income). Setting interest rates does not, however, rely on achieving this equalisation of normal rates, but does rely on ensuring a sufficient supply of money to meet the demand of speculators at r_{policy}.

Before looking in more detail at Keynes's description of expectations and policy, the contribution of the precautionary motive to the demand for money wealth needs to be examined. In the *General Theory*, Keynes offers two motives for the precautionary demand:

> [T]he desire for security as to the future cash equivalent of a certain proportion of total resources; . . . (*CW* VII, p. 170)

> To provide for contingencies requiring sudden expenditure and for unforeseen opportunities of advantageous purchases, and also to hold an asset of which the value is fixed in terms of money to meet a subsequent liability fixed in terms of money, . . . (ibid., p. 196)

These go further than the standard notion of reserving money for unexpected expenditure opportunities (e.g. a bargain home-entertainment system) or necessities (e.g. repairing a leaking roof). The *general* form of the precautionary motive includes the desire to hold money through fear of capital loss on selling a long-term bond before maturity. There are then any number of *reasons* as to why wealth might be required in cash before maturity date. These reasons can be subdivided further according to whether they are for *expected* or *unexpected* events. Examples of unexpected expenditures dominate in the literature; expected expenditures (e.g. school fees in 5 years time)[6] have received less emphasis. The balance between the demands associated with expected and unexpected events is, however, not important for the theory of liquidity preference. What is important is to recognise that, as a consequence of the precautionary motive, there will be a far wider demand for money holdings of wealth than that solely due to speculators. This demand for money in turn must be incorporated into the liquidity-preference schedule.

As noted, Keynes brings together the transactions and precautionary demands as a function of income:

> Let the amount of cash held to satisfy the transactions- and precautionary-motives be M_1, and the amount held to satisfy the speculative-motive be M_2. Corresponding to these two compartments of cash, we then have two liquidity functions L_1 and L_2. L_1 mainly depends on the level of income, whilst L_2 mainly depends on the relation between the current rate of interest and the state of expectation. Thus,
>
> $$M = M_1 + M_2 = L_1(Y) + L_2(r)$$
>
> Where L_1 is the liquidity function corresponding to an income Y, which determines M_1, and L_2 is the liquidity function of the rate of interest r, which determines M_2. (*CW* VII, pp. 199–200)

It is fairly obvious that precautionary holdings of money are likely to be higher with higher income, but not in a manner that is particularly interesting or important – the same is true of speculative holdings. It is therefore sensible, as with the speculative demand, to examine matters with income taken as given. In the *General Theory*, Keynes rules out sensitivity to interest as an assumption ('... assumed to absorb a quantity of cash which is not very sensitive to changes in the rate of interest ...', *CW* VII, p. 171). Kahn (1954, p. 246) examined the matter in some detail and legitimised Keynes's technique.

The more interesting determinant of the precautionary demand is the state of expectation. At times of concern about the future (these might be cyclical or the result of policy ambiguity), there will be a tendency for larger holdings of money; conversely, in stable times, there will be a tendency for larger holdings of bonds. With given income, the precautionary motive shifts the schedule according to changes in the state of expectation. In this way, the schedule of the demand for money as a store of value could be more helpfully depicted as:

$$L(r) = L_S(M, \varepsilon_s | Y) + L_P(\varepsilon_p | Y), \tag{7.1}$$

where the subscripts indicate speculative and precautionary and ε denotes the state of expectation.

To summarise, the precautionary demand is closely related to the speculative demand; holding precautionary assets as money to avoid capital loss is a type of speculative action, although the motivation is different (to avoid loss from *adverse* changes in the future rate of interest rather than to attempt to profit from expected favourable changes in the future rate of interest). Both Kahn (1954) and Joan Robinson (1951) developed the discussion of liquidity preference in this direction after Keynes's death. Much later, Kahn (1984, p. 18) described the distinction between the speculative and precautionary motives as 'very blurred'. It is particularly blurred at low rates of interest, when capital losses are almost universally expected.

Keynes paid less attention to the supply of money than to the demand for money in the *General Theory*. So far here (Section 7.2), the supply of money has been defined as liquid, capital-safe assets into which holdings of wealth can be placed as an alternative to long-term bonds. A fuller discussion requires revisiting the nature and definition of money. In the *General Theory*, Keynes's main discussion was (indicatively) confined to a footnote:

> [W]e can draw the line between 'money' and 'debts' at whatever point is most convenient for handling a particular problem. For example, we can treat as *money* any command over general purchasing power which the owner has not parted with for a period in excess of three months, and as *debt* what cannot be recovered for a longer period than this; or we can substitute for 'three months' one month or three days or three hours or any other period; or we can exclude from *money* whatever is not legal tender on the spot. It is often convenient in practice to include in *money* time-deposits with banks and, occasionally, even such instruments as (e.g.) treasury bills. As a rule, I shall, as in my *Treatise on Money*, assume that money is co-extensive with bank deposits. (*CW* VII, p. 167, n. 1)

The problems are again related to the incorporation of money as a means of exchange into a theory of money as a store of value. At first sight, the supply of 'money' is different according to each of these perspectives. As discussed in Chapter 2, a theory of money as a means of exchange (or of active money) concerns the creation of and day-to-day transactions in bank money. In contrast, the theory of money as a store of value (inactive money demands) concerns matters that occur *after* the creation of bank money (Dow, 1997). Inactive money demands are demands for *liquid assets* into which holdings of wealth can be placed as an alternative to illiquid bonds. In general, the institutions carrying out the majority of such transactions are not households but financial institutions on behalf of households. For financial institutions the most important liquid asset is the *bill* – a short-term security (usually 3 months) of near-certain capital value issued by companies or government. The speculation that Keynes discussed takes place in practice between bonds and bills; an increase in the precautionary demand is reflected, in practice, as an increase in the demand for bills relative to bonds. The supply/stock of 'money' of most importance to the theory of money as a store of value is hence the supply/stock of bills.[7] The role of deposits in the theory of money as a store of value is as the medium through which 'money' is transferred to the issuer or holder of an asset from the purchaser.[8] The issuer of the asset is then in a position to spend the money on real activity; the purchaser holds a liquid savings instrument.

This supply of money in the form of bills can then be seen as part of a broader framework. From the perspective of wealth holders, the supply of bills is a specific component of a wider supply of assets across the whole spectrum of liquidity. From the perspective of the issuer, the supply of assets is a supply of debt. In practice, this debt will be issued by companies and government through various instruments (bills, bonds, equities and derivatives), through which they access household savings. In liquidity preference theory, households *demand* liquidity for their stocks of wealth; while in the classical model, households *supply* a flow of saving. The household *demand* is a demand for liquid or short-term debt instruments that are *supplied* as one element of the borrowing instruments of firms and government. From this perspective, firms and governments need only pay a rate of interest for loans if they supply insufficient short-term assets (leaving aside risk considerations and administrative costs). The reality is that the interaction is mutually beneficial: households need to find an outlet for their savings, and businesses and governments need finance and funding.

In the same way, it is not through the stock of deposits that the authorities are able to manipulate 'the' long-term rate of interest, but through the supply of bills or other contrived liquid assets (e.g. special deposits created by the central bank).[9] The policy regarding the issue of various debt instruments on the part of firms and government is the critical aspect of the supply of 'money' in terms of interest rate policy. And liquidity preference, therefore, leads to debt-management policy. First, however, the supply of and demand for 'money' have to be brought together to give equilibrium.

7.3   Expectation, equilibrium and policy management

In the theory of liquidity preference the rate of interest on bonds is determined by an equilibrium between the existing stock of money and the associated demand. Expectations play a crucial role in the context of both the equilibrium so established and the authorities' ability to manipulate that equilibrium. While the role of expectations has been addressed in order to derive the liquidity preference schedule, the discussion to this point has been static. A liquidity preference schedule has been derived with a given set of views about the future rate of interest in conditions of uncertainty. What has not been fully addressed is why expectation is one thing rather than another. A more general discussion is required, looking at the *determinants of expectation*, and the *dynamics* of liquidity preference in the light of these determinants.

Keynes's main discussion of liquidity preference in the *General Theory* covers both the role of expectation and of policy at the same time. As a consequence, the theoretical properties of liquidity preference were revealed in the course of examples of practical policies without making explicit the properties so revealed. Conversely, the practical policy discussion was primarily theoretical and did not strongly assert these monetary policy interventions as the most important practical conclusions of the theory. He wrote assuming an understanding that policy action should be an action aimed at manipulating the long-term rate of interest as detailed in Chapters 3 and 5. A good illustration of this tendency is on page 164 of the *General Theory*, the last page of his chapter on 'The State of Long-Term Expectation' and the page *before* he first begins his discussion of the theory of the rate of interest. Here Keynes observed that '[o]nly experience, however, can show how far management of the rate of interest is capable of continuously stimulating the appropriate volume of investment'. I consider that this approach resulted in an inadequate depiction of both theory and policy.

Keynes's exposition of the theory of liquidity preference does not re-state the general determinants of the state of expectation. Instead, he relies on the discussion of the determinants of the state of expectation that he set out in the context of the theory of investment demand. This follows his decision to treat the theory of effective demand before liquidity preference in *General Theory*. So while Chapter 12, 'The State of Long-Term Expectation', is motivated primarily by the theory of (capital/real) investment, many passages are of equal importance to liquidity preference. In particular, Keynes emphasises the role of the 'existing situation' as a guide to the future:

> It would be foolish, in forming our expectations, to attach great weight to matters which are very uncertain. It is reasonable, therefore, to be guided to a considerable degree by the facts about which we feel somewhat confident, even though they may be less decisively relevant to the issue than other facts about which our knowledge is vague and scanty. For this reason the facts of the existing situation enter, in a sense disproportionately, into the formation of our long-term expectations; our usual practice being to take the existing situation and to project it into the future, modified only to the extent that we have more or less definite reasons for expecting a change. (*CW* VII, p. 148)

He emphasises the importance of the 'spontaneous optimism' or 'animal spirits' to expectations governing investment demand (*CW* VII, p. 161).

Keynes refers back to this discussion when expectation is addressed in the context of liquidity preference: 'Just as we found that the marginal efficiency of capital is fixed, not by the 'best' opinion, but by the market valuation as determined by mass psychology, so also expectations as to the future of the rate of interest as fixed by mass psychology have their reactions on liquidity-preference' (*CW* VII, p. 170). He does not, however, re-assert the idea that the 'existing situation' is an extremely important governor of the view of the future. Instead, Keynes turns straight to the properties of expectations in the context of policy.

Keynes raises first the distribution of opinion in the context of a policy to manipulate the rate of interest by changing the quantity of money: '... if we are to control the activity of the economic system by changing the quantity of money, it is important that opinions should differ' (*CW* VII, p. 172). The underlying but unstated theoretical proposition is that the distribution of opinion influences the shape of the liquidity preference schedule. Next, developing the same policy, Keynes raises the tremendously important issue of expectations *changing*:

> If, however, we are tempted to assert that money is the drink which stimulates the system to activity, we must remind ourselves that there may be several slips between the cup and the lip. For whilst an increase in the quantity of money may be expected, *cet. par.*, to reduce the rate of interest, this will not happen if the liquidity preferences of the public are increasing more than the quantity of money; ... (*CW* VII, p. 173)

Figure 7.3 illustrates how a change in the money supply from M_0 to M_1 would not reduce the rate of interest if expectations towards the future change and shift the liquidity preference schedule from L to L'; instead, the rate of

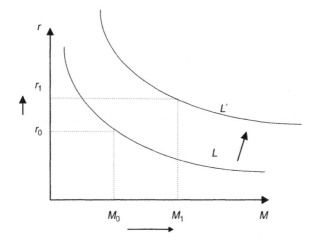

Figure 7.3 Open-market operations and changing expectations

interest increases from r_0 to r_1. Keynes does not describe how this operation takes place. The operation is essentially an open-market operation (OMO), involving the government or monetary authority issuing short-term debt in exchange for long-term debt. The operation changes the nature rather than the amount of the government's liability to the private sector.

To re-iterate, this discussion was the first time the notion of changing liquidity preference was introduced; Keynes takes it as given that such shifts can occur. In retrospect, it is clear that the point demanded more emphasis. In the *General Theory*, Keynes then left his own theory in order to address the classical theory of interest (Chapter 14). He returned to his own theory in Chapter 15, where he addressed the motivations for liquidity in more detail. In the course of a further examination of the speculative motive, he looked again at the theme of shifting liquidity preference in the context of OMOs:

> But it is by playing on the speculative-motive that monetary management (or, in the absence of management, chance changes in the quantity of money) is brought to bear on the economic system. ...
>
> . . .
>
> In dealing with the speculative-motive it is, however, important to distinguish between the changes in the rate of interest which are due to changes in the supply of money available to satisfy the speculative motive, without there having been any change in the liquidity function, and those which are primarily due to changes in expectation affecting the liquidity function itself. Open-market operations may, indeed, influence the rate of interest through both channels; since they may not only change the volume of money, but may also give rise to changed expectations concerning the future policy of the central bank or of the government. Changes in the liquidity function itself, due to a change in the news which causes revision of expectations, will often be discontinuous, and will, therefore, give rise to a corresponding discontinuity of change in the rate of interest. (*CW* VII, pp. 196–8)

Here Keynes talks about the changes in the liquidity function in the context of policy without specifically advocating these policies. The passage may also be partly responsible for wider confusion about Keynes's monetary policy. The emphasis is strongly on OMOs; there is no discussion of direct manipulation of expectations. The discussion might be interpreted as implying that changing expectations are simply 'accidental'. However, his next comments, while still not entirely unambiguous, must surely imply very strongly that changes in expectation might be a response to deliberate manipulation:

> If the change in the news affects the judgement and the requirements of everyone in precisely the same way, the rate of interest (as indicated by

prices of bonds and debts) will be adjusted forthwith to the new situation without any market transactions being necessary.

Thus, in the simplest case, where everyone is similar and similarly placed, a change in circumstances or expectations will not be capable of causing any displacement of money whatever; ... (*CW* VII, p. 198)

Nevertheless, Keynes continued to conflate an implied manipulation of the rate of interest (by 'changing the news') with theoretical effects of changing liquidity preference. He argued that a reduction of the rate of interest from r_0 to r_1 due to a shift in liquidity preference from L to L' that is deliberately encouraged will leave the demand for money unchanged (Figure 7.4).

Keynes draws fundamental conclusions about the role of expectations and the role of the monetary authority at the end of the chapter. At this point he is fairly unambiguous about the nature of policy that he has in mind (I have used underscoring to emphasise positive statements; the italics are Keynes's emphasis):

It is evident, then, that the rate of interest is a highly psychological phenomenon. (*CW* VII, p. 202)

But at a level *above* the rate which corresponds to full employment, the long-term market-rate of interest will depend, not only on the current policy of the monetary authority, but also on market expectations concerning its future policy. (ibid., p. 202)

The short-term rate of interest is easily controlled ... But the long-term rate may be more recalcitrant when once it has fallen to a level which,

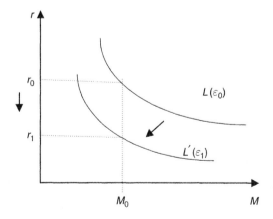

Figure 7.4 A 'change in the news'

on the basis of past experience and present expectations of *future* monetary policy, is considered 'unsafe' by representative opinion. (ibid., p. 203)

Thus, a monetary policy which strikes public opinion as being experimental in character or easily liable to change may fail in its objective of greatly reducing the long-term rate of interest, ... (ibid., p. 203)

It might be more accurate, perhaps, to say that the rate of interest is a highly conventional, rather than a highly psychological, phenomenon. For its actual value is largely governed by the prevailing view as to what its value is expected to be. *Any* level of interest which is accepted with sufficient conviction as *likely* to be durable *will* be durable; subject, of course, in a changing society to fluctuations for all kinds of reasons round the expected normal. (ibid., p. 203)

Public opinion can be fairly rapidly accustomed to a modest fall in the rate of interest and the conventional expectation of the future may be modified accordingly; thus preparing the way for a further movement – up to a point. (ibid., p. 204)

Keynes then brought practical experience to bear. He emphasised his first-hand experience of attempts to reduce the long-term rate of interest in Great Britain through the 1930s:

The fall in the long-term rate of interest in Great Britain after her departure from the gold standard provides an interesting example of this; – the major movements were effected by a series of discontinuous jumps, as the liquidity function of the public, having become accustomed to each successive reduction, became ready to respond to some new incentive in the news or in the policy of the authorities. (ibid., p. 204)

Even at this point, Keynes has covered essentially *ad hoc* methods of manipulating the rate of interest. As has been argued in Part I, practical experience led ultimately to a full policy to manipulate the rate of interest. This policy involved debt-management, manipulation of expectations and the development of banking policy. In Chapter 15 he only hinted at the debt-management policy that his theory pointed to:

If the monetary authority were prepared to deal both ways on specified terms in debts of all maturities, and even more so if it were prepared to deal in debts of varying degree of risk, the relationship between the complex of rates of interest and the quantity of money would be direct. (ibid., p. 206)

Perhaps a complex offer by the central bank to buy and sell at stated prices gilt-edged bonds of all maturities, in place of the single bank rate for short-term bills, is the most important practical improvement which can be made in the technique of monetary management. (ibid., p. 206)

Nevertheless, he looked to a more formal and broader application of policies with which – under his influence and/or explicit direction – the British authorities were already experimenting: 'In Great Britain the field of deliberate control appears to be widening' (ibid., p. 206). Lastly, in addressing the 'limitations on the ability of the monetary authority to establish any given complex of rates of interest for debts of different terms and risks' (ibid., p. 207), Keynes was surely unambiguous about the aim of the monetary policy that he had in mind.

While Keynes's conflating of his discussion of the theoretical nature of liquidity preference with practical policy matters may have served to confuse interpretation of his theory of liquidity preference, once understood, discussing the two dimensions together is really quite natural. Once it has been established that the rate of interest depends on expectations, there are then really only two situations: the 'norm', where past rates of interest dominate expectations, or the 'deliberate policy', where the authorities are seeking to manipulate that expectation. It is perhaps paradoxical that so important a conclusion can be so simply expressed.

Keynes returned to these matters most fully at the NDE (the detail is in Section 7.5). Given the purpose of this enquiry was to consider the rate of interest policy that should prevail after the war, matters were unambiguous: 'The monetary authorities can have any rate of interest they like' (*CW* XXVII, p. 390). His NDE notes dealt briefly but succinctly with the expected rate of return for surrendering liquidity over the long term: 'What determines the return the individual requires to surrender his liquidity for a long or short period. In practice, of course, what some stockbroker who knows nothing about it advises him, or convention based on old dead ideas or past irrelevant experience' (*CW* XXVII, p. 391). He was showing signs of cynicism, arguing that individuals expected the return they were told to expect and that, in the absence of any contrary evidence, such expectations would persist. If individuals had received a high reward in the past they would continue to expect a high reward into the future. But he considered such judgements based to be ideas that were 'dead' and experience that was 'irrelevant'.

To sum up, interest is paid not as a reward for not spending but as a reward for parting with the liquidity of wealth. Firms and government do not need to encourage households to save to gain access to their idle resources. If firms and government are willing to borrow on liquid terms then they would not need to pay *any* reward for access to these resources. The only premium necessary is that required to cover the costs of administering the transaction.

Debt-management policy should permit a sensible and coherent framework for the balancing of firms', government's and households' differing preferences towards holding and borrowing wealth with different degrees of liquidity/illiquidity.

7.4　Liquidity preference and the theory of money as a means of exchange

Chapter 5 addressed and rejected the widespread belief that the *General Theory* overlooked the nature of bank money and argued (with Chick and Dow) that the *General Theory* took bank money as 'given' or predetermined when analysing liquidity preference. But the compatibility between the theory of liquidity preference as a theory of money as a store of value and the theory of bank money as a theory of money as a means of exchange demands attention. With the theories of money delineated in this way, there is no *a priori* reason to expect incompatibility; indeed, they are wholly compatible. Nevertheless, the inadequacy of Keynes's treatment, both in the *General Theory* and in subsequent debate, has led to misinterpretation by some and rejection by others.

According to the discussion in Chapter 2, the central bank is able to set the short-term rate of interest if two conditions are satisfied: first, that banks are supplied with cash according to demand; and second, that there is no shortage of eligible assets to deposit at the central bank in exchange for that cash. Both conditions are liquidity preference considerations: there should be an adequate supply of liquidity in the form of both cash and bills to support the supply of bank money. Examining matters in this way abstracts from the transactions and finance[10] demands that Keynes identified and focuses on a broader demand for bank money/active money as a whole. Furthermore, as with inactive demands, a supply of bills that is under the control of the authorities is key to both. At this point Keynes's simplification through treating inactive and active demands together is seen as justifiable. However, the discussion above equally suggests that the treatment was an oversimplification and that it may have been better to elaborate these processes more fully.

A charge not levelled at Keynes by others, but surely equally valid, is that he also did not address the relationship between the rate of interest in the short-term money market and the long-term rate of interest determined in the capital market (i.e. the banks' lending rate and the reward for parting with liquidity).[11]

Keynes's LPT assumes that the reward for illiquidity is a premium over a *zero* reward for liquidity. In practice there is a reward for liquidity. While money is the liquid asset *par excellence*, as emphasised throughout this discussion, the liquid asset of most importance is the bill. The reward for illiquidity is therefore more fully identified as a spread between long- and short-term government assets. The bill rate on short-term lending to the government is in turn related to the discount rate as the short rate underpinning lending to the private sector. The latter can simply be set so that it is compatible with the desired structure of interest rates in the economy.

The long-term rate of interest depends on the short rate, the liquidity premium and also any risk premia. The latter reflects the premium for lending to companies rather than the government, but also including a premium to reflect the likelihood of default. The risk of default applies to both governments and companies and may, of course, be cyclical.

An alternative statement of the conclusion of Keynes's theory of liquidity preference is that the liquidity premium can be brought under control. With the discount rate under control, the monetary authorities are able to set the spectrum of interest rates. A spectrum from $1/2$ per cent short to $2^{1}/_{2}$ per cent long is feasible and not *a priori* absurd.

7.5 Debt-management and monetary policies

At the NDE, Keynes set out the practical policies that would allow the government to set rates of interest across the whole spectrum of liquidity (as discussed in Chapter 3). These rates would in turn underpin the prices for all other debt. The theory of liquidity preference determines the rate of interest by the interaction of firms', the government's and households' preferences towards holding and borrowing wealth with different degrees of liquidity. Therefore setting the price of securities is simply a matter of allowing the lenders' liquidity preferences rather than those of the borrowers to be paramount: 'Authorities make [the] rate what they like by allowing the public to be as liquid as they wish' (*CW* XXVII, p. 392). The framework for achieving this involved: (i) a new policy of government debt issue; (ii) an international financial framework that permitted capital control; (iii) a number of changes to short-term debt and banking policy; and (iv) abandoning use of Bank rate. Each of these policy areas is examined in turn, with the discussion based mainly on Keynes's speaking notes.[12]

7.5.1 Debt management

Keynes first addressed how traditional policy was the opposite of the desired framework. Historically, the authorities chose to set the quantity of securities and this meant that the market set the price of those securities.

> Now the authorities are only fettered in their policy if they themselves have a counter-liquidity preference. If they are indifferent about funding they can make both the short and long-term whatever they like, or rather whatever they feel to be right having regard to possibilities of under and over-employment and other social reasons.

If, however, they are not indifferent their motivation comes into play.

Historically the authorities have always determined the rate at their own sweet will and have been influenced almost entirely by balance of trade reasons and their own counter-liquidity preference. . . .

Authorities make rate what they like by allowing the public to be as liquid as they wish.

Suppose Tr[easury] say half the debt must be more than 25 years off *or* floating debt must not exceed £*x*mn then it is the public which set the rate of interest. If they require a great inducement to become so illiquid, then rates have to be higher. However it is a vicious circle, dear money provokes expectation of dearer money.

It is the technique of the *tap* issue that has done the trick.

Thus, it is only if the Tr[easury] get rid of the Funding Complex that cheaper money is possible.

The Funding Complex originated in a situation

   (*a*) when there was a fixed fiduciary issue,

   (*b*) Bank rate was the means of preserving the balance of payments,

   (*c*) the rate of interest was used as an instrument of deflation.

With the abandonment of both[13] it becomes completely meaningless. I am not aware of *any* argument in its favour.

On the contrary it is expensive

> it is inconsistent with the avowed policy of cheap money (as Hoppy [14] pointed out) it means losing control of the rate of interest.

(*CW* XXVII, pp. 391–3)

Keynes here referred to the traditional debt-management policy as the 'Funding Complex'. This was the practical manifestation of the authorities' 'counter-liquidity preference', that is, their own preference to issue longer-dated debt (traditionally known as the 'funds') and to limit the supply of shorter-dated debt.[15,16]

According to the theory of liquidity preference, the problem with funding was that if the public's preference for illiquidity was not as strong as the government's preference for long borrowing then rates on longer-term debt would have to be higher in order to encourage the public to accept the longer-term issues. Under such circumstances 'it is the public which sets the rate of interest' – and it was not possible for the authorities to bring the rate of interest under control. His specific example illustrated this point. He also observed that there was a vicious circle whereby increases to the long-term rate of interest to encourage illiquidity would generate further expectations of high rates into the future.

As cheap-money policy meant abandoning the 'funding complex', Keynes examined its original justification. The first two of (a), (b) and (c) were explicitly linked to the existence of the gold standard, and therefore were no longer valid. The third consideration was invalidated by Keynes's wider theory. First, the mechanism through which deflationary monetary policy operated was by reducing demand and hence employment. Second, the NDE notes (just quoted) recorded Hopkins's observation that use of Bank rate was inconsistent with cheap money. This is discussed in the next section, where Keynes's Bank rate proposal is set out.

Given the rejection of the 'funding complex', the practical issue was to find a debt-management technique which facilitated keeping the public as liquid as they would like. Keynes argued that the technique of the 'tap issue' provided such a policy: 'it is the technique of the *tap* issue that has done the trick'.[17] Under the tap system, the Government announced the price and maturity of the bond being issued, but set no limits to the cash amount of that issue. The 'tap' of the bond issue was held open so individuals and institutions could purchase when and whatever quantities they desired.[18] The system, therefore, enabled the public to choose the quantity of debt issued at each degree of liquidity at the price set by the Government (the practical arrangements were discussed in Section 3.12).[19]

The second aspect of Keynes's debt-management policy was to extend the degrees of liquidity available by issuing a wider range of securities. Before the gradual development of Keynes's techniques, the authorities tended to offer only very long-term securities and a limited amount of Treasury bills. At the NDE, and again following wartime experience, Keynes argued that the Government should offer two fixed maturity bonds of five and ten years and a perpetuity as specified in Section 3.12.

The purpose of these arrangements was to cater for medium-term as well as longer-term savings requirements. The offer of extended facilities further relieved pressure arising from the desire to hold precautionary holdings of wealth as money and served to create a more balanced portfolio of asset holdings. Keynes argued that for the longer-term debt 'the option of early redemption safeguards a future liberty of action' (*CW* XXVII, p. 400). This reflected his views on (perhaps very) long-term trends in interest rates. From the macroeconomic perspective, the notion of diminishing returns to capital means that the yield on aggregate capital expenditure will fall over time. With the rate of interest governing the volume of capital expenditure – as of course it does – a monetary policy aimed at stable and high employment would, therefore, have to be managed at not only low but also falling rates of interest. From the debt-management perspective, this meant that terms on any long bond issued should not be superseded by terms on a later issue. It was therefore desirable to avoid, to as great an extent as possible, the situation where previous higher-interest bonds remained in the market as new lower-interest bonds were issued. Overall, his minute of recommendations looked to mechanisms that preserved 'the maximum degree of flexibility and freedom for future policy' (Keynes, *CW* XXVIII, p. 397).

Lastly, the theoretical proposition of diminishing returns to capital also provided a component of the apparatus for cheap-money policy that was likely to be important from the perspective of expectations. With recognition that the long-term rate of interest would move in line with the yield on capital, the public would come to appreciate that movements to the long-term rate of interest would only be in the downward direction. The expectation would be that present terms on longer-term issues would not be superseded by better terms.

7.5.2 Monetary policy

While a number of discussions touched on various practical points, Keynes made no full and formal statement of his monetary policy and the associated theory in the way that he did for debt-management policy. However, much earlier, the February 1937 Economic Advisory Council Report did set out what amounts to a fairly fundamental statement of principles:

> 22. . . . [I]t may be much more possible and desirable for the financial authorities to exercise adequate control over the supply of credit without recourse to the manipulations of short-term rates which are traditionally associated with this objective . . .
>
> 24. . . . We attach far greater importance to the effect of credit policy on long-term interest rates, as expressed by the yield on Government securities . . . (TNA: PRO CAB 58/22)

With active use of the short-term rate of interest ruled out, the authorities' 'quantitative regulation of the basis of credit' (CAB 58/22) was instead effected through control over the issue of eligible assets. By tightening the supply of bills to banks, the authorities could, in theory, restrict the issue of credit. The necessity of such action should depend on the cause – if known – of an increased demand for credit and whether that might be inflationary; even then, this demand might be better addressed more directly (e.g. with taxes). In general, Keynes advised an accommodative stance.

Again the Second World War led to further development of practical policies. Sayers notes that the discounting procedure of the Bank of England was formalised as the 'open back door', 'to which the discount houses could resort . . . [and] turn Treasury Bills into cash at the fixed discount rate of 1 per cent' (Sayers, 1956, p. 223). The most substantial development, however, picked up on the inter-relation between the level of government borrowing and the ability for banks to extend credit. With Keynes advising that the great increase in expenditure for the war effort should be financed in the first place by borrowing from banks, doing so by issuing Treasury bills would have had the paradoxical side effect of permitting an even larger increase in the banks' ability to extend credit. The authorities, therefore, developed the Treasury Deposit Receipt, described by Howson as follows:

> The introduction in July 1940 of Treasury Deposit Receipts (TDRs), by which the major banks were obliged to lend directly to government, added a new instrument to the floating debt, enabling the authorities to borrow on short term without either increasing the Treasury bill issue or having recourse to Ways and Means Advances. Of longer maturity (six months) than three-month Treasury bills and non-marketable, TDRs were less liquid than Treasury bills and carried a slightly higher interest rate (1 1/8%). This wartime expedient[20] was, as Sayers put it, 'concocted . . . [so as] not to disturb the customary relationship [between banks, discount houses, and the Bank of England] and customary "ratios" of the peacetime [banking] system', but it was nonetheless seen as a revolution in fiscal policy, at least in Labour Party circles . . . (Howson 1988, pp. 252–3)[21]

The critical point was that banks were unable to trade in or reserve TDRs to support an expansion of credit. Given their less liquid nature, banks were offered slightly higher interest on TDRs than that paid on Treasury bills (1$\frac{1}{8}$ per cent compared with 1 per cent). At the NDE, Keynes suggested reducing the interest rate on both instruments by $\frac{1}{2}$ per cent.

In this way, policy addressed the concern of 'monetising' government debt and potentially causing inflation by breaking the direct link between floating debt and credit creation. Outside banking mechanisms, any substantial increases to the floating debt as a result of accommodating liquidity preference for shorter-term instruments were due to *savings* not spending considerations and therefore were also not inflationary.

> The dangerous character of this type of debt [floating debt] disappears if there are adequate understandings with the financial world (including, it may be, appropriate regulations for continuing into the future the system of Treasury Deposit Receipts) to ensure the continuous holding of a large, and even increasing, floating debt in all circumstances. (NDE Report, paragraph 23)

During the war, the control of credit was also aided by other aspects of economic policy. Most importantly, aggregate demand was dominated by government expenditure, which should have been more easily regulated than other sources of demand. In addition, consumer demand was implicitly controlled by higher and well-thought-out taxation policies, and investment was potentially controlled by the Capital Issues Committee's management of the new issues market.

Finally, Bank rate itself was of slight importance in the light of wider policy. In his minute of NDE recommendations, Keynes's proposal was as follows: '(a) Bank rate to be reduced to 1 per cent and to govern the rate payable on overseas money in the hands of the Bank of England, so that this rate would remain unchanged' (*CW* XXVII, p. 399).

7.5.3   International financial policies

Keynes's domestic initiatives emerged against a foreign exchange regime for which he had provided the intellectual justification. The over-riding consideration was that exchange policy should not interfere with domestic policy. While wartime initiatives were facilitated by fuller exchange and capital controls, Keynes also looked to more formal international mechanisms after the war. The details of these proposals are highly important aspects of Keynes's overall practical policy, yet have been almost entirely ignored in the context of facilitating domestic policy autonomy. Two key quotations were cited in Chapter 3. It will suffice to re-iterate here that for asset markets Keynes required capital control and for exchange markets he developed his Clearing Union.[22]

7.6   'Keynesian' theories of liquidity preference

The Keynesian or *IS-LM* approach to LPT followed the general argument that the *General Theory* was not a revolution in thought: Keynes's approach to interest theory revealed a necessity to formalise developments to the classical theory that were already well known, if not clearly set out in the literature. In classical theory the rate of interest is determined by saving and investment. Loanable funds theory (LFT) is a variant of this, preserving the importance of saving and investment but moving away from the classical conception of real resources and a real rate of interest to a monetary rate seemingly determined by monetary factors.

The specific argument had two main strands: first, that liquidity preference failed to take active money into account; and second, that LFT not only adequately tackled the issues raised in the context of liquidity preference but also, properly understood, was equivalent to Keynes's theory. Keynes's general approach to his critics waits until the third part of the book; however his specific approach to LFT is examined in some detail here. While he gradually conceded some ground on the first of the two strands, he emphatically rejected the second. Again, the dialogue exemplifies how the old neo-classicals (Robertson) and future 'Keynesians' (Hicks) were exactly in accord.

The public debate began with Hicks's (1936) review:

The rate of interest will be determined at that level which makes the demand for money equal to the supply.
This looks a most revolutionary doctrine; but it is not, I think, as revolutionary as it seems ... The ordinary method of economic theory would be to regard each price as determined by the demand and supply equation for the corresponding commodity or factor; the rate of interest as determined by the demand and supply for loans. ... But we could equally well work in another way. We could allot to each commodity or factor the demand and supply equation for that commodity or factor, as before; but we could allot to the rate of interest the equation for the demand and supply of money ... This latter method is the method of Mr. Keynes. It is a perfectly legitimate method, but it does not prove other methods to be wrong. The choice between them is purely a question of convenience. (p. 246)[23]

Keynes first responded to Hicks in private correspondence. He addressed the claimed equivalence of the interest theories: '3. In summing up what you have to say about liquidity preference you say mine "is a perfectly legitimate method but it does not prove other methods to be wrong". I am not clear in this passage what "other" methods you have in mind' (31 August 1936, *CW* XIV, p. 72). Hicks's reply illustrates his adherence to loanable funds:

3. By talking about 'other methods' when I was discussing liquidity preference, I meant that I still believe that that whole theory could be cast into a more traditional form, and even that this might have some advantages. What you do is determine the rate of interest by the demand-for-money equation – and this means that you have to pack an unconscionable lot into the demand for money. I don't see that there is anything to prevent anyone who chooses to determine the rate of interest by the demand and supply for loans – provided he remembers to pack into them a similar lot of things to those you pack in elsewhere. (*CW* XIV, p. 73)

Keynes followed up quickly, asking for more clarification on 8 September 1936; Hicks replied on 16 October 1936. As Moggridge observes,[24] this letter contained the draft *IS-LM* paper, and thus arguably *IS-LM* was a response to Keynes's attack on LFT.

While Keynes's response (in March 1937) is almost universally regarded as a categorical approval of Hicks's construct, Keynes's response was by no means uncritical. In particular, he raised specifically the loanable funds implications of Hicks's construct, objecting to the implication that an increase in investment (in Hicks's context, in government expenditure) led to a rise in the rate of interest: 'From my point of view it is important to insist that my remark is to the effect that an increase in the inducement to invest *need* not raise the rate of interest' (*CW* XIV, p. 80). Given the coming 'alternative theories' debate, the same letter also asked Hicks directly about his more general 'Robertsonian' tendencies on interest theory:

> In this connection I shall be referring to what you wrote in your review of my book. But you dealt with this very briefly, and I do not really understand what you were driving at. In particular, where you say 'It is a perfectly legitimate method, but it does not prove other methods to be wrong', what exactly are the other methods which you have in mind? (ibid., p. 81)

Hicks's response to Keynes's original letter affirmed the Robertsonian position:

> Over a short period (short enough to neglect interest charges) a person's receipts minus expenditure must equal net lending plus increment in demand for money. (I mean this as no more than a reflection of the two-sidedness of transactions.) It is thus an identity, and it remains an identity when it is aggregated for all persons and firms. Consequently, if we are seeking to determine (*a*) prices, supposed for simplicity to move together, (*b*) the rate of interest, we have three demand and supply equations to determine them (those for 'goods and services', loans, money) one of which follows from the other two. Thus, two of the equations, as you would say, are operative equations; one is a check equation. But it is possible to select any one of the three equations as a check equation, and distribute the operative equations among prices and interest as we choose. Thus, there are six possible alternative 'theories'; but if they are correctly stated, they all mean the same thing, and are all equally right.
> I. Prices determined by effective demand and supply for goods and services; interest by the demand for money; saving and investment a check equation.
> II. Prices determined by the quantity of money; interest by saving and investment; effective demand the check equation.
> And so on; of course I don't deny that some of these theories would be easier to state accurately than others. (ibid., p. 82).

He explained his motivation as follows: 'Of course what lies behind this rather silly business is a desire to separate the essential content of your theory from its formal arrangement. I am a convinced liquidity preference man, but I do covet some freedom of choice about the way (or ways) the doctrine shall be expressed.' (ibid., p. 83)

Keynes replied in a terse letter on 11 April 1937; the note is reproduced in its entirety and is not notable for any accord, or even friendliness, with his alleged greatest interpreter:

Dear Hicks. I do not really understand how you mean interest to be determined by saving and investment under II, near the bottom of your second page. However, I am trying to bring the whole thing to a head by a short article I shall write for the next *Journal*, commenting on Ohlin's exposition of the Swedish theory of interest regarded as determined by the demand and supply for loans, which is being printed in the same issue. I am there accusing you of agreeing with the Swedes in this matter. If this is a calumny, and your theory is really quite different, forgive me. Yours sincerely, J.M.K. (ibid.)

Moggridge records no further correspondence between Hicks and Keynes on this topic following this rebuke. Hicks did not take the opportunity to claim his theory was different from that of Ohlin and Keynes named Hicks as a loanable-funds theorist in his published contribution to the alternative theories debate (see Section 3.3); from this it must be concluded that Hicks was acknowledging that his theory was the same. In this way, Keynes saw Hicks as adhering to a theory of interest that he considered a 'fundamental heresy'. Given that *IS-LM* exhibits the essential property of loanable funds – to re-iterate: that an increase in the inducement to invest raises interest – it is almost certain that Keynes considered his 'alternative theories' critique was relevant to *IS-LM*.

Overlapping with this exchange were Robertson's and Viner's reviews in the November 1936 *QJE*. Viner covered a range of issues. In the course of his discussion he emphasised transactions requirements: 'Whatever its origin, demand for cash for transaction purposes is, dollar for dollar, of equal influence on the rate of interest as demand for cash for hoarding purposes' (Viner, reproduced in Backhouse, 1999, p. 204).[25] Most of Robertson's article was concerned with the loanable funds critique. Objecting specifically to Keynes's theory combining 'those who to desire to *hold* more money and those who desire to *use* it . . . ' (Robertson, 1936, reproduced in Backhouse, 1999, p. 209), he argued that loanable funds considerations had an 'important effect in determining the rate of interest'. As shown in Chapter 3, he set out the groundwork for the *LM* presentation in the course of this critique.

Keynes first responded in a private letter to Robertson. He argued that loanable funds considerations *were* addressed in the *General Theory*:

I have many pages on the theme that increasing investment involves increasing output and that this kicks back on the rate of interest by draining away more money into the active circulation, so that, failing measures to the contrary, a high level of activity carries within it the seeds of its own destruction by raising interest too high. (*CW* XIV, p. 91)[26]

His first formal response came as part of the famous February 1937 *QJE* article. While the paper set out a summary of his whole theory, in the course of the discussion he referred briefly to the loanable funds critique. He first repeated the points he had made privately to Robertson, and second emphasised that his theory of interest concerned money as a store of value:

[the classical economist] has overlooked the precise nature of the difference which his abstraction makes between theory and practice, and the character of the fallacies into which he is likely to be led.

This is particularly the case in his treatment of money and interest. And our first step must be to elucidate more clearly the functions of money.

Money, it is well known, serves two principal purposes. By acting as a money of account it facilitates exchanges without its being necessary that it should ever come into the picture as a substantive object. In this respect it is a convenience which is devoid of significance or real influence. In the second place it is a store of wealth ...

...

The significance of this characteristic of money has usually been overlooked; and in so far as it has been noticed, the essential nature of the phenomenon has been misdescribed. (ibid., pp. 115–16)

The fuller response came through the 'alternative theories' debate. As seen in Section 3.3, both the background correspondence with Ohlin, who was putting the loanable funds case, and the published article showed that Keynes's work was aimed at Hicks and Robertson. Keynes was unequivocal about the incompatibility between the two theories. In his February 1937 letter to Ohlin he wrote that loanable funds was 'fundamental heresy', and that the two theories were 'wholly irreconcilable' (ibid., pp. 185–6). Equally, his published article could not have been clearer. It opened:

There is, I think, a concealed difference of opinion, which is of very great importance, between myself and a group of economists who express themselves as agreeing with me in abandoning the theory that the rate of interest is (in Professor Ohlin's words) 'determined by the condition that it equalises the supply of and the demand for saving ...'

... The alternative theory held, I gather, by Professor Ohlin and his group of Swedish economists, by Mr Robertson and Mr Hicks, and probably many others, makes it to depend, put briefly, on the demand and supply of *credit* or, alternatively (meaning the same thing), of *loans*, at different rates of interest. Some of the writers (as will be seen from the quotations given below) believe that my theory is on the whole the same as theirs and mainly amounts to expressing it in a somewhat different way. Nevertheless the theories are, I believe, radically opposed to one another. (ibid., pp. 201–2)

Robertson refused to accept Keynes's argument. He provided one of three rejoinders in the September 1937 *EJ* (Robertson, 1937a). In the December 1937 *EJ*, Keynes responded with a new article, 'The 'Ex Ante' Theory of the Rate of Interest' (*CW* XIV, pp. 215–23); Robertson (1938a) followed up in 'Notes and Memoranda' of the June 1938 issue: 'Mr. Keynes and "Finance" '; Keynes added a rejoinder at the end of Robertson's article (*CW* XIV, pp. 229–33). Seemingly determined to have the last word, Robertson (1938b) provided a re-rejoinder for the September 1938 issue. Keynes's exasperation is clear from private correspondence at the time (found in the laundry basket, *CW* XXIX, pp. 163–84), describing the June contribution as 'completely worthless and, what is more, intolerably boring' (ibid., p. 168). In parallel, Robertson aired the argument in the *Manchester School* (1938c) and for the last time while Keynes was alive returned to matters in his 1940 book.

Hicks, on the other hand, retreated into the background after Keynes's April 1937 letter. In February 1939 he re-emerged with *Value and Capital* (a second edition was published in July 1946 – 3 months after Keynes's death).[27] In the Introduction, Hicks assesses the necessity of publishing a new book on economics given the existence of the *General Theory*: 'Yet I still think it worth while to produce my own analysis, even if it looks pedestrian beside his. A more pedestrian approach has the advantage of being more systematic; further, I think I have cleared up several important things he left not very clear' (Hicks, 1939a, p. 4). In Chapter 12, 'The Determination of the Rate of Interest', he states his aim as demonstrating equivalence:

I shall hope to show that it makes no difference whether we follow his [Keynes's] way of putting it, or whether we follow those writers who adopt what appears at present to be a rival view. Properly followed up, the two approaches lead to exactly the same results. (Hicks, 1939a, p. 153)

A footnote puts his new position into context:

It appears that my earlier attempt to convince Mr. Keynes that the above is a valid way of approaching his theory was not very successful. (Keynes, 'Alternative Theories of Interest', *EJ*, June 1937, quoting my review article, 'Mr. Keynes's Theory of Employment', *EJ*, June 1936.) I think the obscurity in this article of mine arose mainly from the fact that I was not clear when I wrote about the different properties of a spot economy with short lending and a spot economy with long lending.

Mr. Keynes habitually works with the latter model; I was already, before the appearance of his book, beginning to work out the properties of the former. The device of eliminating the loans (or securities) equation can be used with either model; I had discovered its convenience for my model before Mr. Keynes's book came out. (See my 'Wages and Interest', *EJ*, Sept. 1935, p. 467.) I hope the present chapter will clear up the matter. (Hicks, 1939a, p. 162, by permission of Oxford University Press)

Even at the time, Harrod's (1939) review for the *Economic Journal* was sceptical:

There is, however, a lengthy discussion of interest theory. Professor Hicks finds an ingenious way of reconciling the views of Mr. Keynes and his critics; it is not for a reviewer to intervene between Professor Hicks and Mr. Keynes, but some suspicion must be registered that Professor Hicks has not fully unfolded the whole truth of the matter. (Harrod, 1939, p. 298)

No comments from Keynes on Hicks's new approach are recorded in *CW*. However, Moggridge's biography of Keynes reproduces a letter from Keynes to Kahn (11 April 1939):

I have now finished reading Hicks's book. I don't think I have ever read a book by an obviously clever man, so free from points open to specific criticisms, which was so utterly empty. I did not, at the end, feel a penny the wiser about anything. He seemed able to decant the most interesting subjects of all their contents, and to produce something so thin and innocuous as to be almost meaningless. Yet, in may ways, it is well written and clear, clever and intelligent, and without mistakes. But about nothing whatever. Simple things are made to appear very difficult and complicated, and the emptiest platitudes paraded as generalisations of vast import. A most queer book. (Moggridge, 1992, p. 553)[28]

Chick is one of the few modern scholars to address the validity of Hicks's claims. In her 'Hicks and Keynes on Liquidity Preference: a Methodological Approach' (1991) she argued that attempts at reconciliation 'will remain . . . unsuccessful' (Chick, 1991, p. 309).[29]

Hicks returned to the debate for a last time in a Review of Hawtrey's *A Century of Bank Rate*. He interpreted the work as an empirical challenge to Keynes: 'In other works, in *The Art of Central Banking*, in *Capital and Employment*, he has conducted an assault on the theoretical foundations of Mr. Keynes' doctrine; this is the complementary volume in which the attack is transferred onto the ground of fact, or rather (of course) interpretation of fact' (Hicks, 1939b, p. 21). While Hicks found Hawtrey's own explanation of movements in long-term rates 'unsatisfactory' (ibid., p. 23), he also concluded that 'Mr. Keynes's emphasis on the significance of the long-term rate in monetary policy seems best regarded as a reflection of the peculiar situation of the nineteen-twenties' (ibid., p. 37). In this way he also set up a position pursued after the war – that the *General Theory* was 'depression economics': '. . . Keynes's *General Theory* a piece of model-building in the face of the Great Depression' (Hicks, 1947, p. 151).

Hicks was not the only 'Keynesian' economist concerned with the theory of the rate of interest at this time. In 1939 and 1940, N. Kaldor and M. Kalecki began to advance the 'expectations' perspective, where the long-term rate is a function of expectations of the short-term rate. Kalecki's review of the *General Theory*[30] gave emphasis to means-of-exchange considerations rather than wealth considerations:

> Hence the rate of interest cannot be determined by the demand for and supply of 'capital'. Its level, according to Keynes's theory, must therefore be determined by other factors, namely the supply of and demand for means of payment. If, for instance, a given amount of money is in circulation and social income grows, the demand for the means of payment will increase and the rate of interest will rise as much as it is necessary to bring about the use of the same quantity of money despite the higher level of activity. This is a very general sketch of Keynes's theory of the rate of interest, which we do not want to deal with in detail here. (Kalecki, translated by Targetti and Kinda-Hass, 1999, p. 29)

His own theory of interest, 'The Short-Term Rate and the Long-Term Rate', was published in the fourth issue of *Oxford Economic Papers*: '. . . our theory explains satisfactorily the long-run changes in the long-term rate of interest in the period 1849–1938. In the light of it they appear to be caused by the long-run changes in the short-term rate and by the rise in the "risk coefficient" σ and of r_{max} as a result of the Great War' (Kalecki, 1940, p. 21). Here r_{max} is the yield corresponding to the minimum price, p_{min} defined as follows: 'a certain more or less definite idea based on past experience about the minimum . . . to which this price [of a Consol] may fall, . . . ' (ibid., p. 16). The theory entirely sets aside the notion that interest was the reward for parting with liquidity. The paper neither mentions Keynes nor does it contrast the two approaches. Kalecki's aim is essentially to find retrospectively various 'real' factors to explain away the behaviour of the rate of interest. Kaldor had developed a similar argument in an October 1939 paper, 'Speculation and Economic Stability'. He later described his analysis in the introduction to his 1960 book of re-prints, *Essays on Economic Stability and Growth*: 'It followed . . . that the factors which determine the short rate of interest over longer periods provide a point of anchorage for explaining the whole structure of interest rates, which was missing (according to Professor Robertson's 'bootstraps' argument) from Keynes' presentation' (Kaldor, 1960,

p. 4).[31] There is no recorded comment from Keynes on either of these papers. As will be discussed in Chapter 10, Kahn and Robinson explicitly rejected this approach after Keynes's death.

Lastly, while the properties of the 'Keynesian' theory of liquidity preference were loanable-funds properties, there was of course also a static foundation based on a theory of money as an asset. As Chick has exposed in detail and with rigour, these theories are theories of portfolio preference under conditions of risk rather than uncertainty.[32] Kaldor's *Scourge of Monetarism* provides an example of a two-asset model in which '. . . the idea of liquidity preference – that people's demand for money will be greater the lower the rate of interest' (Kaldor, 1986, p. 21). Without uncertainty, to avoid Keynes's 'lunatic asylum' (Section 7.2), the (usually non-stated) appeal is to a 'shoe-leather' or opportunity-cost argument, with there being less to lose when holding money at a lower rate of interest compared to a higher. The celebrated model is Tobin's (1958) 'Liquidity preference as behaviour towards risk', extending the two-asset portfolio theory to any number of assets. But this is an extension of 'Keynesian' portfolio theory, not Keynes's theory of interest (and seemingly acknowledges the distinction in the title of the paper – though not in the text). These theories merely provide a justification for the existence of a static liquidity preference schedule that is then transformed to 'LM' using LFT. They, as all other 'Keynesian' approaches examined here, are opposed to Keynes's own work.

7.7   The validation of liquidity-preference theory

With no recognition of the fundamental policy conclusion of Keynes's theory of liquidity preference, the evidence of its practical application has not been brought to bear on its validity. Such evidence is compelling. Liquidity-preference theory predicts that deliberate action on the part of the monetary authorities will reduce (or increase) the long-term rate of interest. Classical, loanable-funds and "Keynesian" theories of interest either have very little to say on this ability or are underpinned by a natural rate of interest impervious to policy manipulation. Figure 7.5 shows that both real and nominal rates declined almost continuously throughout the period when Keynes advocated a reduction and when his monetary policy advice dominated the views of others (shaded areas on figure).

The main exception was between 1936 and 1939. This reversal of progress occurred while Neville Chamberlain was Prime Minister (from May 1937 to May 1940) and Keynes was very ill. Following his recovery, in his 1938 annual statement as Chairman of the National Mutual, he explained the movement as a consequence of purchases of gold by the Exchange Equalisation Account. With the shadow of totalitarianism looming, he pleaded with the authorities to take the appropriate action:

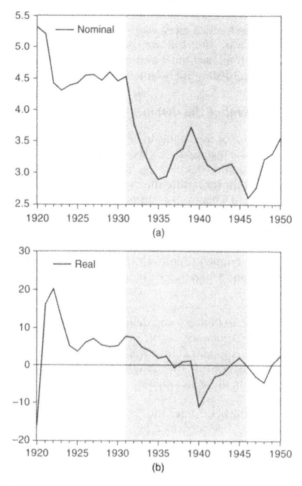

Figure 7.5   UK nominal and real long-term interest rates, 1920–50
Source: Friedman and Schwartz (1982, Table 4.9).

A great deal is at stake. We are engaged in defending the freedom of economic life in circumstances which are far from favourable. We have to show that a free system can be made to work. To favour what is known as planning and management does not mean a falling away from the moral principles of liberty which could formerly be embodied in a simpler system. On the contrary, we have learnt that freedom of economic life is more bound up than we previously knew with the deeper freedoms – freedom of person, of thought, and of faith. (*CW* XXI, p. 446)

Rates peaked in 1939, and the downward movement resumed in 1940. As discussed in Chapters 1 and 2, rates were successfully fixed at 3 per cent for the duration of the war. After the war they were pushed even lower. The year of Keynes's death marked the lowest nominal long-term rate on British government debt recorded in the twentieth century (apart from 1900).[33]

7.8 The 'resolution' of the debate

Echoing the resolution of the saving–investment debate, Keynes's theory of liquidity preference was dismissed very soon after his death. The protagonists were again Robertson and Hicks. In the June 1947 *EJ*, Hicks began to look to practical justification for raising the rate of interest (the episode will be discussed more fully in Chapter 10). His paper concluded:

> There are other instruments of economic policy which can attain the same objective as a rise in interest rates; and some of these may well be less destructive instruments. But we should not forget that in these days of scarcity time is short; and the rate of interest is the price of time. (Hicks, 1947, p. 164)

Then in December 1948 Robertson delivered a lecture at the 'Institut de Science Economique Appliquée' in Paris. Entitled 'What has Happened to the Rate of Interest?', the content involved a re-assertion of his own position with regard to the practical and theoretical importance of the rate of interest and to the appropriate theory of interest.

> In the nineteen-thirties, under the first impulse of Keynes's work, the rate of interest was elevated to a position of commanding theoretical importance. ... it became, as never before, the keystone of the whole theoretical arch. But it also became the villain of the piece, and a very powerful villain. It was the dragon guarding the cave of "liquidity preference" – of the ineradicable urge of capitalist society to run for cover and to play for safety; it became the rock against which the waves of social improvement beat in vain. Nowadays – I am still talking about high-brow opinion – things seem to have altered in two ways. The rate of interest has come to be regarded as of less importance in the causal nexus, its high *reclame* of the nineteen-thirties savouring too much, to the modern taste, of an obsolescent economics of price. And at the same time it has come to be regarded as less powerful in practice and more vulnerable to attack ...
>
> ...
>
> I think the rate of interest, in what Marshall once called its "strict sense", is the price of the use of loanable or investable funds, and is

governed like other prices by the interaction of schedules of supply and demand. (Robertson, 1966, pp. 188–9)

He also brought Hicks's argument to bear on his cause:

> [A]nd I was glad to find my greatly esteemed mentor Professor Hicks, whose previous writings on the rate of interest have sometimes troubled me, reverting to it in an article published in the *Economic Journal* for June 1947. "We should not forget," that article concludes, "that in these days of scarcity time is short; and the rate of interest is the price of time." Momentous words! Not the price of liquidity, mark you, but the price of time – just as the great nineteenth-century economists always supposed! (ibid., 1966, p. 195)

With 'momentous words' of 'high-brow opinion' replacing theoretical debate, LPT was dismissed in all but name.

7.9 Modern monetary economics

With the seamless shift towards *IS-LM*, not only the profound substance of liquidity preference, but also the richness of the monetary theory of the inter-war years, were all but forgotten. As Davidson (1978, footnote 23) has emphasised, money was 'unimportant' in these Keynesian models. The British Radcliffe Committee's *Report* (Committee on the Working of the Monetary System, 1959) may have marked a return to more sophisticated thought about money, but it inspired only scholars working on the margins of economics. 'Monetarism' was only a re-packaging of classical economics: it was a real theory masquerading as a monetary theory. The confusion and farce is plain to see; a theory that pretended to be a monetary theory ousted a theory that was not a monetary theory that claimed to represent a theory that was a monetary theory.

Modern monetary economics only emerged in substantial form with post-Keynesian economics. But while re-establishing forgotten facts about the nature and operation of money, not all aspects of the revival were consistent with the interpretation of Keynes's theory set out here.

From the means-of-exchange perspective, the critical contributions were by Kaldor. In a 1970 *Lloyds Bank Review* article[34] he rejected the empirical case for monetarism as explicable through the 'endogeneity' of money. He set out his case most fully in his book *The Scourge of Monetarism*, a collection of two items: first, his two 'Radcliffe Lectures' (originally delivered in 1981); and second, a long paper that he submitted to the Treasury and Civil Service Committee (TCSC) in July 1980. In the latter, his basic contention was as follows:

> [monetarists] assume that there is *no* important difference between the functioning of a commodity-money economy and a credit-money economy . . . (Kaldor, 1986, p. 45)

the 'money supply' in a credit-money economy is *en*dogenous, not *ex*ogenous – it varies in direct response to changes in the public 'demand' to hold cash and bank deposits and not independently of that demand. (ibid., p. 47)

The policy implication was that acting according to monetarist doctrine in a monetary economy was incorrect in exactly the same way that acting according to the gold standard was incorrect; Kaldor made the case that Keynes had made for credit rather than currency control 60 years previously. Unfortunately, despite this substantial (but not mentioned) parallel, Kaldor's wider argument was profoundly detrimental to a fuller understanding of Keynes that might have been open for debate given the criticisms of *IS-LM*. The same TCSC paper went on to ascribe a monetarist position to Keynes with regard to the supply of money:

71. Keynes himself never really questioned the assumption that the *supply of money*, however defined, is exogenously determined by the monetary authorities. At least his equations (whether those in *Treatise on Money* published in 1930, or in the *General Theory* of 1936) are not consistent with any other interpretation.

[elaborating in a footnote:] The equation $M = L_1(Y) + L_2(r)$ which appears in Keynes's *The General Theory of Employment, Interest and Money* (... p. 199), but which could more simply be written $M = L(Y, r)$, assumes M as exogenously given. (Kaldor, 1986, p. 73, by permission of Oxford University Press)

Nevertheless, at least for the post-Keynesian school, the fundamental importance of a serious monetary economics was (re-)established.[35] Of modern monetary economists, Chick and Dow have argued the position that I have attributed to Keynes, that in the *General Theory* Keynes took credit creation as 'given' (e.g. Chick, 1983, p. 184 and 2001, p. 9; and Dow, 1997). Keynes generally adopted an assumption that sufficient bank money had been created to support whatever level of economic activity had been dictated by the theory of effective demand (Chick, 2000).

Those who explicitly charge that Keynes took money as exogenous are grossly misrepresenting his whole economics. Furthermore, the extensive post-Keynesian debate between 'horizontalists' and 'verticalists' is, in my view, a side issue. It is revealed as such as soon as it recognised that the most important conclusion of Keynes's monetary theory is that interest rates, long and short, can be set by the authorities. In broader terms, in the *General Theory*, the quantity of bank money was primarily a consequence of the rate of interest, not a cause.

But an even greater matter of concern is that outside post-Keynesian economics there remains an almost universal ignorance about the monetary nature of Keynes's economics. This may be a reflection of the more general attitude of academic economics to economic history. While each of the 'grand discussions' detailed in Chapter 2 saw a clash between monetary and real theories, the triumph of real theory in policy terms appears to have justified a triumph in academic terms. Furthermore, the nature of the academic triumph was such that it dismissed the *existence* of the monetary point of view. Schumpeter (Section 2.1) may have made grand play of the real *versus* monetary debate, but the truth is that students are not presented with matters according to this fundamental division. Students are presented only with the real view of the world. Even Keynes himself appears to have been affected by this phenomenon, with Schumpeter noting that his eagerness to give Marshall priority was misplaced ('In some points the large claims made by this disciple on behalf of the originality and priority of the master must certainly be discounted', Schumpeter, 1954, p. 1083). While Keynes appreciated the contributions of other monetary theorists in the context of his Grand Discussions, he did not look back as far as the monetary contributions of John Law or even Adam Smith.

Today, the importance of monetary theory is recognised by only a minority of economists. Keynes's role in the development of monetary theory and his associated practical initiatives are recognised by even fewer economists. Until this underlying nature of his economics is fully recognised, we miss the 'very ground floor of his analytic structure' and there can be no hope of a complete understanding of his work and its policy implications.

Finally, any fuller appreciation of the theory of liquidity preference has been lost alongside the loss of monetary theory. Outside post-Keynesian economics, this loss is almost total. Even in historical retrospectives, liquidity preference is ill-served. In the edition of *The Oxford Review of Economic Policy* addressing 'Real interest rates', Joseph Stiglitz put together such a retrospective as background to his own theory of interest. He tackled Keynes's contribution as follows:

> The deficiencies in the money demand model, which has been the centre of attention at least since Keynes (see Keynes, 1936), are increasingly being recognised. In that model, the demand for money depends on the level of (money) national income and the interest rate, which represents the opportunity cost of holding money ...
>
> In the 1930s, there was a *strong* competing theory, the loanable funds theory, advocated, for example, by Robertson (1936). In that model, the interest rate is determined as the intersection of a downward-sloping demand for funds and an upward-sloping supply curve of funds. (Stiglitz, 1999, p. 60, my emphasis)

His reference to Keynes's theory is oblique, not even mentioning liquidity preference and its foundation in uncertainty; far greater emphasis is accorded to loanable funds. Among contemporary mainstream economists, only Charles Goodhart has debated the issues in any detail. Overall, Goodhart

(1989) seems to prefer the Kaldor/Kalecki variant where the long-term rate is influenced by expectations of the short-term rate. In addition, he preserves the Robertsonian position on the specific issue of LPT/LFT:

> Keynes exaggerated the importance of the 'liquidity preference' effect, relative to the longer-term 'loanable funds' theory of interest, in order to differentiate his approach from the Classical. This led to an invalid concentration upon a small set of financial interest rates as providing the sole means of short-term equilibration of the demand and supply of money and, similarly, the sole transmission channel for monetary policy. (Goodhart, 1989, pp. 214–15)

> Keynes was, however, so keen to make a break with the previous Classical analysis that he pushed his new Liquidity Preference theory, and his accompanying analysis of the process by which the demand and supply of money could be equilibrated, further than was justifiable. (ibid., p. 224).

Like Robertson, Goodhart goes on to reject Keynes's analysis for failing to treat aspects of active demand in a comprehensive manner. He misleads too. Keynes did not derive the theory of liquidity preference for the trivial reason of 'breaking with' or 'differentiating from' with the classical theory; he rejected the classical theory of interest as incorrect. The theory of liquidity preference was the central monetary component of his revised theory, a component with the most profound practical implications.[36]

The post-Keynesian approach to liquidity preference differs widely. Those who diminish the importance of liquidity preference do so in one or both of two ways: through an erroneous portrayal of LPT itself and/or diminishing the role of liquidity preference and the rate of interest in any associated wider theory of economic activity. Kaldor did both. Extracts in Section 7.6 indicated that he has adopted both the expectational term structure and portfolio approaches to LPT. Furthermore, Kaldor also rejected a role for liquidity preference in the wider sense. He argued that 'effective demand for commodities in the aggregate is not determined by monetary factors but by autonomous demand . . .'(Kaldor, 1986, p. 20) and then explicitly rejected any role for liquidity preference:

> 'Liquidity preference' turns out to have been a bit of a red herring – not the 'crucial factor' which, in the view of the great economists of Keynes's generation, such as Dennis Robertson or Jacob Viner, and, of a later generation, Harry Johnson or James Tobin, alone enabled Keynes to argue that an economy can be in equilibrium at less than full employment. It has nothing to do with that at all. (p. 26)

Paul Davidson adopts a different – but still unsatisfactory – post-Keynesian stance. On the one hand, he emphasises the importance of the theory of liquidity preference in Keynes's broad scheme (he calls it 'the revolutionary aspect of Keynes's analysis', Davidson, 2000, p. 6). On the other hand, despite his wider and extensive emphasis on 'uncertainty', his original version of LPT paid little attention to the uncertainty of the values of financial assets into which wealth is placed and tend to a 'Keynesian' version with the addition of his version of the finance motive. To him, liquidity preference existed more because of uncertainty about real considerations than monetary considerations:

> It is only in a world of uncertainty and disappointment that money comes into its own as a necessary mechanism for deferring decisions; money has its niche only when we feel queasy about undertaking any actions which will commit our claims on resources on to a path which can only be altered, if future *events* require this, at very high costs (if at all). (Davidson, 1972, p. 104, my emphasis)

At the same time, Davidson's perspective skewed post-Keynesian debate towards credit rather than wealth considerations.[37] However, despite discounting financial uncertainty in liquidity preference, Davidson does afford the rate of interest a fuller role in the determination of demand. And he finds fault with the approach of the Kaleckian post-Keynesians: 'From Keynes's liquidity preference financial market analysis perspective, therefore, the short shrift Kalecki gives the role of financial markets and the rate of interest in affecting investment is a deficiency in Kalecki's effective demand analysis' (Davidson, 2000, p. 8).

Of the post-Keynesians, Bibow and, again, Chick and Dow have perhaps done the most to keep Keynes's theory of liquidity preference alive (e.g. Chick 1983, Dow 1997, Chick and Dow 2002, Bibow 2000 and 2001). First, they have restored the role of uncertainty and expectations of the rate of interest. Second, they have afforded the theory of liquidity preference a substantial role in the wider depiction of macroeconomic activity as a key component of the theory of effective demand.[38]

Others have given emphasis to the rate of interest as the critical variable in the determination of the level of activity at which a free market operates, without such great emphasis on the detail of LPT itself. From a policy perspective, John Smithin's contributions are discussed in Section 10.8. From a theoretical perspective, an alternative approach meriting emphasis is that of the rate of interest as a 'conventional' phenomenon. Rogers (1989) and Ciocca and Nardozzi (1996) recognise the fundamental role of the rate of interest in determining the level of activity at which a free-market economy operates in both the long run and the short. The determinants of the interest rates are then institutional considerations and the expectations of those in financial markets, even to the extent that the rate of interest might be regarded as exogenous. Rogers does not go as far as advocating direct action to reduce the rate of interest, though he recognises that counter-cyclical fiscal policy will not be sufficient to offset the drag on activity from a high rate of interest. He gives emphasis instead to the socialisation of investment. Ciocca and Nardozzi (1996) do stress the feasibility of collective international action aimed at reducing rates of interest, though they acknowledge that they do not offer concrete proposals for doing so.

The present analysis differs only in pursuing the liquidity preference and conventions theories to their logical practical conclusions in the way that Keynes did. The restoration of LPT has not, so far, led to recognition that, under conditions of uncertainty, expectations can be manipulated and interest brought under control. Conventions can be overcome with deliberate policy action in the specific areas of debt-management, monetary policy and international financial policy.

Notes

1. 'In my terminology *liquidity preference* relates to the *total* demand for money for all purposes and not merely to the demand for inactive balances. Quite often one needs to distinguish the demand for active balances and the demand for inactive balances. At one time, indeed, I did try to use separate terms and drafted for about a year on these lines. But I found that in making general statements this involved an enormous amount of verbiage; and in the end I defined liquidity preference as above for general exposition, making the further distinction between inactive and active demand when required' (*CW* XIV, p. 223, italics in original).
2. Bibow appears to hint rather heavily though (e.g. Bibow, 2000, p. 823).
3. There are questions too concerning whether liquidity preference can be represented in graphical form, given the existence of uncertainty. In my view, the portrayal brings out important properties without violating common sense, which must surely be the aim of theory.
4. Though the amounts of money involved may change according to the degree of conviction.
5. 'At the extremes of high and low rates of interest, opinions coalesce; there comes to be substantial agreement that rates cannot rise any further, or fall any further. This is enough to give the speculative demand function its concave shape' (Chick, 1983, p. 206).
6. While Chick (1991) has emphasised that with developed financial markets expected events can be dealt with by maturity matching, under the simplifying assumptions of a choice only between a long bond and money (as used for the discussion of the speculative motive), even expected expenditure leads to a money demand.
7. While cash is the most liquid asset, in practice, holdings of wealth in cash are likely to be of trivial size and analytical importance (although matters are different in the separate case of a bank run).
8. Complications arising from the use of deposit accounts for savings purposes and short-term assets for speculative purposes are analysed by Chick and Dow (2002).
9. This leaves aside the complex issues tackled by Chick and Dow (2002) related to the setting of money market rates involving OMOs that exchange deposits for bills.

10. Keynes introduced the finance motive during the 'alternative theories' dialogue: 'There has, therefore, to be a technique to bridge the gap between the time when the decision to invest is taken and the time when the correlative investment and saving actually occur. . . . To avoid confusion with Professor Ohlin's sense of the word, let us call this advance provision of cash the 'finance' required by the current decisions to invest' (*CW* XIV, p. 208).
11. And this is despite a long discussion on 'The Essential Properties of Interest and Money' in Chapter 17.
12. NB the extracts therefore include fragments of sentences.
13. Moggridge points out that (c) was added later.
14. Sir Richard Hopkins, the permanent secretary to HM Treasury between 1940 and 1945.
15. This terminology might be a little confusing given liquidity preference is an attribute of the wealth-holder; 'long borrowing preference' might be more accurate from the perspective of the borrower.
16. Treasury bills were not only limited in supply but from time to time were purchased by the authorities in exchange for longer-term issues (a so-called 'funding operation').
17. Attention should be drawn to the differing meanings of 'tap issue' as used by Keynes and later by R. S. Sayers, the UK banking historian. In the 1967 edition of his *Modern Banking*, Sayers (p. 55) means by 'tap issue' a mechanism whereby the authorities issued Treasury bills to Government departments that have funds in hand, and to certain overseas monetary authorities: 'the rates of discount at which the bills are issued through the tap is unknown and is irrelevant to the discount market'. With the widespread acceptance of Sayers's terminology, it seems that the original notion of the tap – which is of course very different and much more important – has been lost.
18. An example issue notice stated 'subscriptions will be received on Tuesday, 25th June, 1940, and thereafter until further notice . . . ' (*The Economist*, 29 June 1940, p. 1119).
19. As with all Keynes's debt-management proposals, the tap issue is little discussed. However, Susan Howson (1988, p. 252), one of the few authors who has focused on the subject, also appears to accept that the method was a success. She notes with respect to wartime finance: 'The problem of ensuring the financing of the war at 3 per cent was then *solved* by a change in technique' (my emphasis).
20. This is misleading; TDRs were an integral part of the plan for post-war monetary policy.
21. The instrument *was* revolutionary.
22. Today, the post-Keynesian position is also associated with capital control. However, the argument is not put in the context of domestic interest rate policy. A good example is Paul Davidson's case for capital control published in *The Guardian*: '(1) to prevent a lack of global effective demand due to nations oversaving liquid foreign reserves (2) to induce the surplus nation to contribute to resolving the import–export imbalance, since the surplus nation has the economic wherewithal and is in the better economic position and (3) to encourage debtor nations to work their way out of debt rather than await handouts or bailouts, or to default on their international obligations' (1 December 2003).
23. Other parts of the review were more useful – e.g. 'It has however, weak places. It is easy to slip into regarding the liquidity preference curve – the curve connecting

interest with the demand for money – as a stable curve, so that we can concentrate our attention entirely upon this particular relation. But that is evidently not so, as Mr. Keynes shows clearly' (Hicks, 1936, p. 247).

24. '. . . which resulted in Keynes being sent a draft copy of Hicks' later paper "Mr Keynes and the Classics" . . . which Hicks had presented to a meeting of the Econometric Society at Oxford' (*CW* XIV, p. 74).

25. Loanable funds theorists preferred to refer to the inactive aspect of liquidity preference as the 'propensity to hoard', with hoarding an important component of their theory (see Section 3.3.2).

26. The dialogue also suggests that the LFT that Robertson advocated was not well established in the literature; Keynes asked 'Where is it to be found? Can you give me the references?' (*CW* XIV, p. 92).

27. Hicks's Preface aligns the book with the LSE perspective on economics: 'The ideas on which this book is based were conceived at the London School of Economics during the years 1930–5. They were not by any means entirely my own ideas; they came into being by a sort of social process which went on among the people who were working there, at that time, under the leadership of Professor Robbins. Those whom I remember particularly as having contributed were Mr R. G. D. Allen, Mr Kaldor, Mr Lerner, Professor Hayek, Dr Rosenstein-Rodan, and Dr Edelberg' (Hicks, 1939a, p. i).

28. This letter is not included in *CW*.

29. She also notes other attempts at integration: 'The efforts of Tsiang (1966), Leijonhufvud (1981) and Asimakopulos (1983) are only those to spring most immediately to mind' (Chick, 1991, p. 314). Bibow (e.g. 2001) has also tackled this issue very thoroughly.

30. Published in the Polish journal *Ekonomista* and later translated by Targetti and Kinda-Hass in 1982.

31. He also noted that 'further reflection has not caused me to change my views in any important degree' (ibid.). Thirlwall's biography of Kaldor (1987, p. 75, n. 46) states: 'The paper was relatively neglected, perhaps because it coincided with the publication of Hicks' *Value and Capital*. On re-reading the paper in 1986, Hicks wrote to Kaldor: "I think that your paper was the culmination of the Keynesian revolution in *theory*. You ought to have had more honour for it"'.

32. See Chick (1983, pp. 213–18) on Tobin; Chick (1991) on Hicks; and Chick and Tily (2004) on the Keynesian models chronologically.

33. Source: Homer (1963, pp. 409–10).

34. The article was the text of a public lecture given at University College London, on 12 March 1970.

35. Aspects of Kaldor's more detrimental arguments were taken up by Basil Moore, in particular the notion that Keynes took money as exogenous: 'After reading these passages in the *Treatise*, where the endogeneity of credit money is so clearly recognised, it is difficult to understand how Keynes only six years later could have assumed the money stock to be exogenously determined by the monetary authorities' (Moore, 1988, p. 195). A footnote continued on the same theme: 'Or how he could have approved of Hicks's IS-LM formulation of the *General Theory*'. While saying the change in position is 'difficult to understand', Moore does not go on to look for any explanation. Given Moore's own theoretical argument is based on the paramount importance of credit, some sort of explanation for Keynes's alleged stupidity is surely a necessary element of a serious study. (Moore's fuller argument in Jarsulic's (1984) *Money and Macro Policy* is virtually identical to

that used by Kaldor – compare Moore (1984, pp. 3–4) with Kaldor's second 1981 Radcliffe lecture (reproduced in Kaldor, 1986, pp. 20–2).)

36. Paul Krugman's (2006) essay, written as an introduction to a new edition of the *General Theory*, gives a good deal of emphasis to the importance of monetary factors to economic activity. However, he portrays policymakers as impotent victims of the monetary environment within which they find themselves. Keynes's point was that this need not be the case; policymakers could choose to be masters of that environment.

37. Bibow (2001, p. 612 n. 1) has also charged Davidson with pursuing the Robertson/Hicks line on equivalence: 'Among Keynesian reconcilers, Davidson (1965, p. 60; 1978) truly stands out in asserting that the LP-LF debate is merely a "semantic confusion"'. The article that Bibow refers to also sees Davidson referring to the debate as a 'barren controversy' (Davidson, 1965, p. 59).

38. They have also addressed the compatibility between the theories of liquidity preference and of endogenous money: Dow (1997), Chick (2001), Chick and Dow (2002) and Bibow (2000).

8
The Monetary Theory of Real Activity

8.1 Introduction

Keynes's theory of real activity provides an explanation for both the level of activity and the economic cycle. The theory is a monetary theory from three perspectives. First, the most important determinant of the level of activity is the monetary rate of interest. Second, the level of activity determined by the rate of interest and expectations is facilitated by bank money. Third, an unsustainable level of activity is reflected in an accumulation of debt and asset price inflations, and is ultimately restrained by the prospect and then reality of financial collapse. As has been noted in earlier chapters, this latter argument (in Sections 8.4 and 8.5) goes beyond Keynes's argument in the *General Theory*.

The main emphasis of my discussion of Keynes's theory of real activity concerns the issues that arise from the secular monetary policy perspective. The emphasis is, therefore, on the role of investment demand and the associated sustainability issues that in turn arise from a view of activity that goes beyond the short period. As discussed in Chapter 5, with Marshall and Keynes, these considerations will be referred to as long-period considerations.

The chapter begins with a brief overview of the theory of aggregate demand and supply, but one that looks to align that theory with the broader aim of the discussion. The same section also addresses and dismisses the 'Keynesian' theories of aggregate demand and the economic cycle. However this discussion is not protracted, because, in contrast to the dialogue addressed in the two previous chapters, there was very little debate between the 'Keynesians' and Keynes concerning the relative merits of each theory. Keynes's theories here were largely unchallenged in his lifetime; the *IS-LM* and 'Keynesian cross' perspectives on demand and the accelerator theory of the cycle were simply substituted for Keynes's theory after his death.

The bulk of the discussion concerns the economic cycle as an interaction between changes in investment demand, money and interest. On the one hand, the rate of interest sets a limit to the amount of investment that can be profitably undertaken. On the other hand, money and 'animal spirits' mean that there need be no constraint on activity from day to day. But beyond this short period the rate of interest constraint is ultimately binding and operates through a transmission mechanism based on debt. This last point goes beyond anything explored in the *General Theory*. The upswing of an economic cycle is accompanied by steady growth of debt, which eventually and inevitably ends in financial and real contraction. The argument builds to the conclusion that the obvious policy for high activity, that is low interest rates, is also the relevant policy to prevent – or at least greatly diminish – the extremes of the economic cycle.

8.2 The theory of aggregate demand

As is well known, aggregate demand is built up from theories of investment and consumption demand. From the point of view of the discussion here, investment demand has the pivotal role. Keynes argued that the amount of investment carried out by firms depends on the MEC schedule and the rate of interest that the same firms face in capital markets. The MEC schedule reflects entrepreneurs' expectation of the returns on undertaking capital expenditure, defined in Chapter 11 of the *General Theory* as follows: 'more precisely, I define the marginal efficiency of capital as being equal to that rate of discount which would make the present value of the series of annuities given by the returns expected from the capital-asset during its life just equal to its supply price' (*CW* VII, p. 135). At the start of any period, firms assess their likely returns due to various amounts of capital expenditure and will implement investment according to the interaction between this assessment (their MEC schedule) and the rate of interest. The relevant rate of interest is the benchmark rate set in the market for long-term government debt adjusted for the perceived riskiness of the corporate sector at any specific point in time ('the' rate of interest). Aggregating across all firms in the economy leads to a macroeconomic MEC schedule that links each rate of interest to a unique level of investment. The theory defines an equilibrium in the sense that the MEC is a demand schedule for investment that is set against an endogenous supply of funds at 'the' rate of interest. It is a simple but not trivial fact, following from not only the *General Theory* but also the classical theory that a lower rate of interest leads to a higher level of investment.[1]

The economic cycle and associated sustainability issues follow from the role of expectations. As with market expectations of the future rate of interest, the yield on investment is uncertain, for it depends on estimates of future demand that cannot be known: 'The considerations upon which expectations of prospective yields are based are partly existing facts which we can assume to be known more or less for certain, and partly future events which can only be forecasted with more or less confidence' (*CW* VII, p. 147). The aggregate MEC schedule, as with the liquidity preference schedule, is hence dependent on a state of expectation about the *uncertain* future. As with the theory of liquidity preference, the next critical point was that the MEC schedule would shift following a change in the state of expectation. Keynes's notion of 'animal spirits' then reflected the further insight that firms' estimates of the yields of investment will periodically be subject to either excessive optimism or excessive pessimism.

There are, therefore, two potential causes of an increase in investment demand: a cut in the rate of interest (Figure 8.1a), or a change in expectations towards greater optimism of the yield on future investment represented by a shift in the MEC (Figure 8.1b).[2,3]

In Figure 8.1a, investment increases to I_1 following a cut in the long-term rate of interest to r_1. In Figure 8.1b, investment increases to exactly the same extent following a change in expectations represented by a shift in the mec_0 to mec_1. As will be developed in the next section, the distinction between the two mechanisms underpins not only Keynes's theory of the economic cycle, but also his solution to the Economic Problem more generally.

Before turning to a fuller description of these processes, the remaining two stages in the theory of aggregate demand must be outlined. Keynes's theory of consumer demand is based on a simple 'law':

> The fundamental psychological law, upon which we are entitled to depend with great confidence both *a priori* from our knowledge of human nature and from the detailed facts of experience, is that men are disposed, as a rule and on the average, to increase their consumption as their income increases, but not by as much as the increase in their income. (*CW* VII, p. 96)

The response of consumption to changes in income is reflected by the MPC, usually denoted by c. Expressing the law of consumption algebraically and in

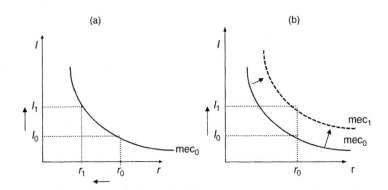

Figure 8.1   Increases to investment in theory

aggregate terms shows how, over any period, changes in aggregate consumption (C) depend on the MPC and changes to aggregate income (Y):

$$\Delta C/\Delta Y = c, \text{ where } 0 < c < 1 \qquad (8.1)$$

Second, Keynes's theory of aggregate demand and the *multiplier* follow through combining the consumption theory with a national accounts identity (for a closed economy with no government and then expressed in terms of changes across some arbitrary period):

$$Y = C + I \qquad (8.2)$$

$$\Rightarrow \Delta Y = \Delta C + \Delta I \qquad (8.3)$$

and substituting for ΔC from (8.1)

$$\Rightarrow \Delta Y = c\Delta Y + \Delta I \qquad (8.4)$$

we get the familiar multiplier

$$\Rightarrow \Delta Y = \Delta I/(1 - c) \qquad (8.5)$$

As with most relations in Keynes's economics, this multiplier is a monetary relationship. It maps directly from demand to expenditure, and shows the effect of a change in investment expenditure on income.[4] The investment and consumption theories are combined, with the investment multiplier a function of the MPC. Furthermore, the relation does not rely on an explicit functional form for any of the variables. The theory of aggregate demand is expressed in terms of changes from an arbitrary, or current, position; as addressed below, this is also the most logical way to interpret supply effects.

At this point, the assumption of a given money supply should be re-examined. Keynes generally assumed that the supply of bank money would respond to changes in aggregate demand as defined above. He did consider relaxing the assumption (as noted in Section 7.6): a demand for bank money that was not accommodated would feed back to raise the rate of interest and hence reduce investment demand. Nevertheless, assuming an accommodative supply of bank money is surely consistent with not only reality but also common sense; how otherwise would economic activity develop if the rate of interest was constantly under upward pressure?

The central question for aggregate supply is then: what proportion of a *change* in aggregate demand induces changes in quantities (volumes of products and numbers of employees) and what goes to prices (and possibly also to wages)? The answer, as touched on in Section 6.7, is simply a matter of supply and demand. Firms change price and output, and hence employment, according to the conditions of supply and to their anticipations of (to them) uncertain demand. Keynes's analysis assumed these key macroeconomic variables were determined in a short period where the supply of capital stock was given. In general, of course, a change in demand would lead to an increase in output and employment, but also in price. This also depends on the notion of 'unemployment equilibrium'. According to the *General Theory*, with insufficient aggregate demand, macroeconomic variables would be such that employment was not 'full', in the sense that at the prevailing level of wages the supply of labour would be greater than the demand for labour. Any such employment outcome is reasonably regarded as an 'equilibrium' if the supply of goods was equal to the demand for goods (in nominal terms). If that is the case there are no necessary incentives for firms to change production, prices, employment or wages.[5]

Keynes also emphasised an additional notion of 'effective' demand, probably because he wanted to stress that demand was *effective* in creating supply.[6] More specifically, he defined effective demand as the point where firms' assessment of demand met their aggregate supply (*CW* VII, p. 25). It is also of note that aggregate demand itself is 'effective', in the sense that the multiplier equation defines the change in nominal expenditure and income that actually occurs, and that can be decomposed into changes in output and price (and margins) and wages and profits.[7]

At this point the essential concepts of Keynes's theory of aggregate demand and supply have been established. Matters can be developed by contrasting the properties of Keynes's theory with those associated with the 'Keynesian' theory:

(i) The discussion here has focused on movements in income governed by changes to the rate of interest, MEC or MPC. While government demand can be incorporated into the discussion in a simple manner,[8] the baseline theory was sufficient to address the policy issues with which Keynes was primarily concerned.

(ii) Hicks (1937) was the first to set out the 'Keynesian' theory with investment as a *function* of the rate of interest: $I_x = C(i)$'. This formulation suppresses the MEC, and hence, as with liquidity preference, the role of uncertainty and expectation. As addressed in Chapter 3, Keynes objected that the 'generalised' version of the model did not take expectations into account:

At one time I tried the equations, as you have done, with I [income] in all of them. The objection to this is that it over-emphasises current income. In the case of the inducement to invest, expected income for the period of the investment is the relevant variable.

This I have attempted to take account of in the definition of the marginal efficiency of capital. (*CW* XIV, p. 80)

Hicks acknowledged Keynes's point:

> Of course I agree that it is expected income that logically matters; but the influence of current events on expectations (admittedly a loose and unreliable connection) seems to me potentially so important, that I feel much happier if it is put in and marked unreliable, than if it is merely talked about, and not impressed on the reader's mind by being put into the formula, which he will take down in his notes. (*CW* XIV, p. 82)

But *IS-LM* implicitly rejected any role for expectation.

(iii) Although Keynes discussed a consumption function in great detail in the *General Theory*, he did not suggest integrating Equation (8.1) to obtain the form $C = cY + b$, with c and b constants, which has been a hallmark of the 'Keynesian' interpretation.[9] This linear relation appears to have first emerged in lagged form (e.g. $C_t = cY_{t-1}$) in the course of the development of process analysis (see Section 6.7). Samuelson (1939) then used the technique to explore the relationship between the multiplier and the 'acceleration principle' (see viii below). Samuelson also estimated the first full linear consumption function as: '$C = 27.5 + .54Y$' in an annex to Hansen's *Fiscal Policy and the Business Cycle* (Hansen, 1941, pp. 253–6).

(iv) Moreover, Equation (8.5) relies neither on any specific functional form for the consumption function nor on a stable MPC. The value and potential stability of the MPC and consumption function may be useful for other purposes – in particular when assessing the impact of 'public works' – but its stability is irrelevant in the context of this theoretical proposition. Furthermore, regarding the MPC as a constant has allowed a wider diminution of Keynes's theory of consumer demand. The *General Theory* explicitly argues that other factors such as taxation, confidence, the discount rate or even the long-term rate of interest might influence consumer demand (*CW* VII, pp. 91–5). While the MPC may exhibit reasonable stability over some 'medium term', it is not necessarily a stable variable and certainly not a constant.

(v) More generally, there is the argument that the model of activity in the *General Theory* can usefully be treated as a theory based on change. Keynes's theory does not appear to require the explicit treatment of a consumption *function*, but can, without loss of generality, be encapsulated in terms of changes from the existing position. The model permits change of expectation, the money supply, the rate of interest, the MEC or MPC; these changes then lead to changes in output and/or price.

(vi) As in (v), Keynes's *General Theory* does not assume fixed prices. In the 'Foreword' to Amadeo (1989, p. ix), Chick discusses the 'assertion that in the *General Theory* prices are fixed':

> How this ... notion could be believed is a mystery: in the *General Theory* there are constant reminders that expansion will entail an increase in prices in the case Keynes took as typical, diminishing returns – not to mention the demonstration in Chapter 21 of just what stringent conditions must be met for expansion to be consistent with price stability.

(vii) The theory is not based on loanable funds. The rate of interest is a determinant of income and investment, not a determinate. While feedback from a change in investment to the rate of interest is possible (and explicitly addressed), it is of lesser interest than the causality in the other direction.

(viii) The 'Keynesian' 'investment function' is completely inconsistent with Keynes's theory of the economic cycle. To state the obvious, a fixed investment schedule that ignores uncertainty and expectation cannot underpin an economic cycle theory that depends on shifts to the MEC. Instead, after Keynes's death, the 'Keynesians' adopted an alternative theory of the business cycle based on the 'acceleration principle'; this approach is best explained with a textbook description:

> An expected increase in output which generates a demand for additional capital stock leads to an increase in investment. The increase in investment causes output to rise by an amount equal to the increase in investment *times* the income multiplier. The increase in income causes investment to rise further, and so the multiplier accelerator process continues. (Levačić and Rebmann, 1976, pp. 250–1)

This theory had been long established in the literature as Haberler's (1937) LoN work demonstrates:

> The following authors have developed the acceleration principle – AFTALION, BICKERDIKE, BOUNIATIAN, CARVER, and MARCO FANNO. In recent years, it has been expounded most fully by J. M. CLARK, SIMON KUZNETS, and A. C. PIGOU. HARROD, MITCHELL, ROBERTSON, and SPIETHOFF have incorporated it into their account of the cycle as a contributory factor. (Haberler, 1937, p. 82)

Footnotes to the names in his text show the contributions were published between 1903 (Carver in the *QJE*) and 1936 (Harrod in his *The Trade Cycle*).

After publication of the *General Theory*, Kaldor (1940) in the United Kingdom, and Samuelson (1939) in the United States incorporated the principle into their own analyses of activity.

The theory had nothing to do with Keynes. While *CW* record no relevant comments, the Kaldor papers contain a dialogue between Kaldor and Keynes. Kaldor submitted his 'A Model of the Trade Cycle' (1940) to Keynes as the editor of the *EJ*. Keynes published the paper, but their correspondence shows that he did not sign up to Kaldor's accelerator-related approach:

> My personal feeling about the article is that it is dangerous to assume that the credit cycle is wholly determined by the multiplier and acceleration principles, and that I is a function only of S [overstruck with a pencilled 'X']. I still prefer, when one is dealing with the general problem, to have regard to the relation between the marginal efficiency of capital and the rate of interest rather than to the acceleration principle taken in isolation. The acceleration principle is, of course, a very important determinant of the marginal efficiency of capital. But even if we regard the rate of interest as constant, which is in itself a considerable abstraction, it remains unsafe to omit other possible influences on the m e of c. (Keynes to Kaldor, 27 May 1939, Kaldor papers, file 3/30/118)

Following the last of these observations, the discussion now turns to Keynes's actual theory of the economic cycle.

8.3 The economic cycle in Keynes's economics: introduction

Keynes was from an academic tradition that recognised the economic cycle as a credit cycle. His early work discussed the widespread appeal of credit cycle theories proposed by Fisher (e.g. *CW* XIII, pp. 2–3) and Hawtrey (e.g. *CW* XI, p. 363). Keynes's contribution was to show that economic cycles were only *facilitated* by freely available credit; they were *caused* by dear credit. Based on the analysis of his *Treatise*, in June 1931 Keynes was emphatic about the cause of the Great Depression at the Harris Foundation lectures in the United States. The first of these was entitled 'The Originating Causes of World-Unemployment':

> We are today in the middle of the greatest economic catastrophe – the greatest catastrophe due almost entirely to economic causes – of the modern world. . . . I see no reason to be in the slightest degree doubtful about the initiating causes of the slump . . .
>
> The leading characteristic *was an extraordinary willingness to borrow money for the purposes of new real investment at very high rates of interest –* rates of interest which were extravagantly high on pre-war standards,

rates of interest which have never in the history of the world been earned, I should say, over a period of years over the average of enterprise as a whole. This was a phenomenon which was apparent not, indeed, over the whole world but over a very large part of it. (*CW* XIII, pp. 343–5, my emphasis)

Peculiarly, in the light of its timing, the *General Theory* does not give prominence to his analysis of the economic cycle. The material comes as the first chapter of Book VI, 'Short Notes Suggested by The General Theory'. The title, 'Notes on the Trade Cycle', reflects Keynes's stated intention:

To develop this thesis would occupy a book rather than a chapter, and would require a close examination of facts. But the following short notes will be sufficient to indicate the line of investigation which our preceding theory suggests. (*CW* VII, p. 313)

In taking this approach, Keynes did not fully integrate the cycle theory into his theory as a whole. There are two critical dimensions: real (Section 8.4) and monetary (Section 8.5).

The real dimension concerns the trajectory of investment during the economic cycle, and the associated forces dictating that trajectory. In the short period, investment demand may be dominated by animal spirits. But there are underlying forces related to the potential yield of investment at each rate of interest that define whether any investment demand will be sustainable in a timeframe that looks beyond the short period. The discussion shows that to boost short-period demand without taking into account these considerations can lead to instability.

From the monetary perspective, the analysis defines a credit cycle insofar as an endogenous supply of credit or bank money meets the changing requirements of aggregate demand. More importantly, though, the real processes are reflected in monetary processes that are crucial to the transmission mechanism. The discussion in Section 8.5 develops Keynes's recognition of the role of dear money and argues that the underlying monetary processes are the growth of corporate debt set against a captial market inflation (CMI). The collapse of this monetary inflation then leads to real collapse.

8.4 Real characterisation: the MEC and 'long-period' equilibrium

Keynes's discussion of the business cycle in the *General Theory* places primary emphasis on movements in investment caused by the 'animal spirits' of businessmen, portrayed theoretically as shifts to the MEC schedule:

But I suggest that the essential character of the trade cycle and, especially, the regularity of time-sequence and of duration which justifies us in calling it a *cycle*, is mainly due to the way in which the marginal efficiency of capital fluctuates. The trade cycle is best regarded, I think, as being occasioned by a cyclical change in the marginal efficiency of capital, though complicated and often aggravated by associated changes in other significant short-period variables of the economic system. (*CW* VII, p. 313)

I suggest that a more typical, and often the predominant, explanation of the crisis is, not primarily a rise in the rate of interest, but a sudden collapse in the marginal efficiency of capital. (ibid., p. 315)

These passages, however, have no role for the rate of interest; this is introduced shortly afterwards. Without due emphasis, Keynes argued *that for each rate of interest there is an amount of investment that is in some sense 'correct'.* This proposition is made most explicitly in the following elaboration of the business cycle process:

it is an essential characteristic of the boom that investments which will in fact yield, say, 2 per cent in conditions of full employment are made in the expectation of a yield of, say, 6 per cent, and are valued accordingly. When the disillusion comes, this expectation is replaced by a contrary 'error of pessimism', with the result that the investments, which would in fact yield 2 per cent in conditions of full employment, are expected to yield less than nothing; ... the boom which is destined to end in a slump is caused, therefore, by the combination of a rate of interest, which in *a correct state of expectation* would be too high for full employment, with a misguided state of expectation which, so long as it lasts, prevents this rate of interest from being in fact deterrent. A boom is a situation in which over-optimism triumphs over a rate of interest which, in a cooler light, would be seen to be excessive. (*CW* VII, pp. 321–2, my emphasis)

Here Keynes compared 'excessive' expectations of the yield of investment with this 'correct state of expectation' as a baseline. In terms of the MEC, Keynes essentially argued that there is a 'correct' MEC schedule against which other schedules, assessed in uncertain circumstance and influenced by various degrees of optimism, can be compared. This position constitutes a critical additional dimension to his theory that has been almost entirely overlooked. Furthermore, the dynamic of this economic cycle process goes beyond the short period that is the primary focus of the *General Theory*. The short-period analysis saw Keynes examine employment outcomes following a change in demand with *given* capital stock (as in Section 8.2). His study of the economic cycle is essentially a 'long-period' analysis, and examines the eventual employment outcomes as a consequence of *changing* the capital stock. The two periods are analytically distinct. The short period is concerned with the production decision between output and price. The long period is concerned with investment outcomes, setting expected against realised revenues and affecting employment through a longer-term impact on firms' financial position.

In the short period, positions arising from changing investment demand, and hence aggregate demand, correspond to Keynes's notion of 'shifting equilibrium':[10] 'we might make our line of division between the theory of stationary equilibrium and the theory of shifting equilibrium – meaning by the latter the theory of a system in which changing views about the future are capable of influencing the present situation' (*CW* VII, p. 293). The dynamic of the shifting equilibrium is defined by the outward shifts in the MEC that cause investment, income and employment to increase. This expansion phase can continue for a prolonged period of time, with the MEC possibly subject to a series of outward shifts. Eventually, however, in a manner which is the subject of the next section, the MEC will shift to the left. This leads to the contraction in investment that defines the 'recession' or 'depression' phase of the economic cycle.

This shifting equilibrium, or more helpfully shifting-demand equilibrium, should then be compared with an underlying position based on the 'correct' MEC. This underlying position might reasonably be regarded as special kind of long-period equilibrium. To use such terminology requires the setting aside of any connotations from classical economics. In particular, this use of long-period equilibrium does not refer to a position where labour market forces assert or work themselves out, as in the classical labour market theory, or to the equi-profit equilibrium of the surplus approach, or one in which capital has converged to some balanced growth path, as in neo-classical growth theory. The long-period equilibrium of relevance here is one based on underlying yields of investment or rates of profit. The equilibrium exerts its influence whenever investment yields turn out to be over-optimistic. In this way there *is* a 'real constraint' to the economy described in the *General Theory*: in any given situation there is an underlying limit to the amount of investment that can be profitably implemented. Such a situation accords strongly with an intuitive notion of macroeconomic equilibrium.

It is argued here that Keynes's theory of the economic cycle is a theory of shifting-demand equilibrium set against a long-period equilibrium. But the long-period equilibrium is not unique. The critical determinant of this long-period equilibrium is the long-term rate of interest. For each long-term rate of interest there is an associated long-period equilibrium level of investment and hence employment. (The MPC is also a determinant of the long-period equilibrium, and one that can also be influenced by the authorities, but considerations of space mean that this factor cannot be developed here.) Lastly, this approach does not mean the classical real factors are irrelevant:

We take as given the existing skill and quantity of available labour, the existing quality and quantity of available equipment, the existing technique, the degree of competition, the tastes and habits of the consumer, the disutility of different intensities of labour and of the activities of supervision and organisation, as well as the social structure including the forces, other than our variables set forth below, which determine the distribution of national income. This does not mean that we assume these factors to be constant; but merely that, in this place and context, we are not considering or taking into account the effects and consequences of changes in them. (*CW* VII, p. 245)

Real factors are simply of less interest and importance to explain the historical performance of national economies. Similarly, the fundamental conclusion of Keynes's economics is that policy should concentrate on the monetary factors rather than these real factors.

Keynes's notion of unemployment equilibrium can be more fully understood in the light of this interpretation of long-period considerations. On one hand, the notion of a 'correct' MEC schedule/long-period equilibrium means that for each rate of interest there is a unique appropriate level of investment, leading to a unique appropriate level of employment. The rate of interest is then seen to be absolutely central to the employment equilibrium of a free-market economy. The classical theory is turned on its head, with macroeconomic equilibrium determined by the rate of interest, not the rate of interest determined by the macroeconomic equilibrium. This long-period equilibrium is a *multiple* equilibrium in the sense that it depends on what long-term rate of interest is set or prevails. The economic cycle process then comes about through the fact that in a monetary economy there is nothing to guarantee that the economy will operate according to such a long-period equilibrium. The normal state of a free-market economy will be that agents' expectations of the future are either excessively optimistic or pessimistic.[11] An economy will often operate in a 'boom' where the amount of investment is excessive according to the long-period equilibrium defined by the rate of interest.

The earlier Figure 8.1 can be used to summarise the process, with the rate of interest, r_0, regarded as defining an equilibrium volume of investment, I_0, measured on mec_0, in this context defined as the 'correct' MEC schedule. The expansion phase of the business cycle is then illustrated by the shift to mec_1, the schedule reflecting firms' excessively optimistic assessments of the yields on investment, leading to investment underpinning effective demand of I_1.

Before moving to a fuller exploration of the monetary dimension to the economic cycle, the other theoretically possible 'states' of a free-market economy need to be set out. While the most common state is likely to be investment demand not equal to the long-period equilibrium, demand held at the level of the long-period equilibrium is a theoretical and perhaps practical possibility. Such a state can be consistent with short-period unemployment equilibrium (as, for example, in *CW* VII, Chapter 17); to borrow Joan Robinson's terminology, this might be referred to as 'tranquillity'.[12] The second is a special case, when tranquillity corresponds to full employment; this might be referred to as 'bliss'. The complex coincidence of factors required for this outcome is the state of affairs automatically assumed by classical economists, but is only one case, the 'Special Case', of Keynes's *General Theory*.

Keynes's theory of the economic cycle arises from the fact that the normal condition of a free-market economy is neither bliss nor tranquillity. On one hand, failed policy and economic theory continue to ensure that the rate of interest is too high (and the distribution of taxation such that the MPC is too low); on the other hand, the animal spirits of producers and entrepreneurs similarly ensure that the dominant feature of free-market economies are the waves of optimism and pessimism that define the economic cycle.

8.5   Monetary characterisation: revenue, capital market and debt inflations

Implicit in the notion of economic cycle theory is that the operation of an economy can 'deny' a long-period equilibrium for a very prolonged period, but cannot do so indefinitely. A theoretical analysis, therefore, requires identification of a transmission mechanism through which equilibrium is restored. This section develops Keynes's model of the economic cycle and argues that the long-period equilibrium exerts its pressure through the consequences of an excessive build-up of debt and its counterpart, captial market inflation (CMI). This mechanism provides a justification for the shift from expansion to recession that was discussed by Keynes only in terms of a shifting MEC.

In order to see how this process operates, the perspective is changed from the 'real' perspective of demand and long-period equilibrium, to a monetary or financial perspective. More specifically, the examination turns from the expectations that dominate when investment is put into place, to 'outturn' as revenue streams come in. This perspective reveals that additional factors are at work in the determination of company behaviour that go beyond investment and production decisions. Revenue flows will either validate or invalidate original expectations. In the case of tranquillity, with expectations correct, revenues validate expectations. Otherwise, revenues will not validate expectations. The latter situation can be further subdivided according to whether revenues are above or below expectations. The situation of most interest, of course, is when revenues fall below expectations in an excessive expansion.[13]

Strictly, what might be called 'validation by revenue' processes can only be judged over the full duration of an investment. The outturn of the stream of revenues for any marginal investment will then either have met or failed to have met the cost of the finance for putting that investment into place. In practice, however, it is unlikely that businesses can wait until the end of the investment repayment process to appreciate that revenues will not meet costs. Firms' cash flow calculations for the duration of an investment will have assumed a certain profile of returns over time. The extent to which excessive investment is revealed at an early stage will depend on this profile. At the extreme, if all returns are expected in the final period then firms will not know until this period. For most projects it might be reasonable to assume that returns are likely to be linear (with perhaps a positive gradient) across the investment. In these cases, the excessive nature of the investment will be revealed from fairly early on, and firms may encounter cash flow problems according to a similar timing. In the aggregate, it is likely that these types of projects will dominate. To reflect this, 'outturn' will not be used in the strict sense of the stream of revenues over the whole life of the investment, but more loosely to reflect a position where an investment has been put into place and is generating revenue. Jumping ahead, it may be that in some cases banks are willing to re-finance loans for as long as they believe that a company's shortfall in revenues is due to incorrectly profiled revenues rather than a miscalculation of total revenues. In the limit, this would mean that re-financing would take place until very late in the life of any investment.

To examine the consequence of failing revenues, the perspective is changed for a second time: from 'outturn' to repaying finance. Tranquillity, the stable situation where firms' investments yield according to expectation, is dealt with simply: under such circumstances the aggregate of loans taken out to finance the investment can be repaid exactly. Such a state of affairs is not cyclical; employment will be stable at the rate defined by the long-period equilibrium. It is the finance perspective on an excess expansion that explains the economic cycle. Here, failure of revenues to match expectations provides a theoretical justification for the transition from expansion to contraction.

As argued, the expansion phase of the economic cycle occurs as the 'animal spirits' of business people (and the financial community) lead to excessive expectations of the yield of future investment. Reflected theoretically by a rightward shift in the MEC, the consequence is greatly increased investment. If the expansion follows a period of subdued activity with capacity idle (as is likely), the increased utilisation of this capacity is also likely to lead to rapid acceleration in profits. There will also be effects in the financial markets that may be critical to the development of the cycle. In particular, CMI[14] will be a consequence of any credit-fuelled excessive expansion. The identity between saving and investment means that all new investment financed by credit will create an equal amount of saving. By definition, in an excessive expansion, the pace of credit creation and, therefore, saving creation will be at least at the pace of investment. These newly created savings will seek the high returns apparently offered by financial investments. As a consequence, prices will be pushed up on various financial instruments, most obviously equities, but equally corporate bonds. The likely consequence is that the prices of financial instruments will grow at the pace of investment during the expansion. Indeed, as assets must equal liabilities, a theoretical aggregate measure of capital market inflation should grow at exactly this pace.[15]

In turn, CMI will widely (but erroneously) be interpreted as indicating investors factoring in the excessive growth in economic activity as permanent. Capital market inflation will, thus, serve further to affirm the validity and sustainability of the state of affairs to investors and policymakers alike and no doubt will encourage even greater optimism. As euphoria about the situation spreads, additional increases in optimism may lead the MEC to shift even further to the right. This period of accelerating investment will continue until there is either some reining-in of expectations or until firms' revenues begin to display evidence of the excessive expectations. At this point, firms will begin to have difficulty meeting the scheduled repayments on loans or debt instruments. Keynes's theory as depicted here is categorical about the aggregate amount of investment that will eventually face such problems. Referring back to Figure 8.1 (with mec_0 again defined as the correct schedule), investment projects represented by the difference at the rate of interest, r_0, between aggregate investment demand and the long-period equilibrium, I_1-I_0, will, by definition, be such that revenues fail to meet expectations. Essentially the volume of investment, I_1-I_0, is excessive and is, from this perspective, 'bad' investment. In this way, the excessive expansion is unsustainable from the moment that investment demand exceeds the long-period equilibrium level, though this may take sometime to be recognised.

If it is assumed that firms have no idle resources, then, as revenues fail to meet expectations, they will be faced with two choices: cost savings or additional borrowing. A number of cost-saving options will exist, most obviously cutting back future investment plans, seeking alternative sources of raw materials, raising prices or reducing quality. More painfully, firms could cut jobs. However, for many firms, the easiest option will be further borrowing – effectively distress borrowing – to finance the inevitable shortfall between expectations and actual revenue.[16] This type of borrowing, which will henceforth be called *debt financing*, should be seen as distinct from borrowing to finance investment in the first place. In a monetary economy the process of debt financing can continue for a very long time. As a consequence of both the debt financing and the high borrowing to finance the excessive investment in the first place, an economy in an excessive expansion phase will be underpinned by a steadily increasing level of corporate debt – a *debt inflation*.

The sources of debt financing will vary but the generic types are the generation of new credit and portfolio reallocation. New credit creation may be further subdivided between that which goes directly to companies and that which goes indirectly to companies through other financial institutions. An example of the latter will be banks granting loans to various 'funds', which then purchase newly issued corporate debt instruments. In the former case, when new credit goes directly from a bank to a firm, the operation is 'merely' a balance sheet operation. Existing bank assets are paradoxically 'protected' by increased extension of debt-financing loans, for the failure of a client company is not in the bank's interest. Continuing support of troubled companies, no matter how apparently irrational or counter-intuitive, is behaviour that is endemic in the banking system. In addition, credit creation for debt financing will also contribute to CMI in exactly the way discussed earlier.

Debt financing will keep workers in jobs which would not exist if the economy was operating according to the long-period equilibrium. Other money will come to companies through a reallocation of existing stocks of wealth, with households (or financial corporations on their behalf) shifting from safer investments (including money) to equity and corporate bonds, and from other operations such as debt–equity exchanges and rights issues. At the same time, other developments in the course of an excessive expansion will also work towards generating increased demand for corporate borrowing instruments. For example, excessive expansion combined with 'sound' budgetary principles is likely to mean that the government will move into surplus. As a consequence it will issue fewer securities; and investors whose portfolios demand a certain proportion of long-term debt instruments will be directed towards the corporate sector just as firms' demand for debt financing is accelerating.

Particularly important considerations follow from wider profit opportunities created for financial institutions. These organisations will make substantial earnings through their role in arranging various issues such as initial public offerings, corporate bonds and debt–equity exchanges, as well as through their role in merger and acquisition activity which will also be an important feature of the credit cycle. Later in the excessive expansion, debt-restructuring packages and innovative financial instruments will be offered in exchange for higher interest payments. It is the good fortune for many financial institutions that commission will be earned whether or not any of these transactions make any sense from the points of view of the parties brought together or of the economy as a whole.

A particularly important aspect of this type of finance will be hedge fund operations, where high risk will be taken for very high reward. From 2000 there has also been widespread use of credit-default swaps, whereby financial organisations are able to sell on the risk of credit default.[17] Essentially, any such debt financing operations transfer the liabilities of the corporate sector into assets of other sectors – in particular the banking, financial and household sectors. Ultimately, because the source of the debt is debt financing, the assets created are assets that reflect bad debts and are worth-less. Because the predicament has been caused by excessive expectations, debt financing merely serves to put off the inevitable consequence of a level of investment greater than that permitted by the long-period equilibrium. Whether firms are taking out bank loans or issuing corporate debt, eventu-ally they will not be able to meet the interest payments and they will begin to default. The debt is by definition debt that firms will not – not ever – be able to repay out of current investment projects.[18]

On the face of it, however, the expansion will appear sustainable. Firms, optimistic for the restoration of financial health in the future, will find that their debt financing is taken up and that banks are willing to issue debt-financing loans. Fundamental to this depiction of the economic cycle is that an excessive expansion can last for a long time – experience suggests for as many as 20 years – but cannot be sustained indefinitely.[19]

The boom can be prolonged for precisely as long as demand exists to take up corporate debt financing. The practical limitation to this process is, there-fore, investors' belief that new debt issued is sustainable, that is, that firms' future revenues will ensure that they are able to meet their obligations on that debt. Sooner or later investors will realise that the additional debts they are being asked to take up, and those that they already hold, are *bad* debts. At this point there will be an erosion or a collapse of financial confidence. Evidence suggests that towards the end of a boom, the long-term interest rate on corporate debt will increase, and spreads between corporate debt and government debt will widen, reflecting an increased perception of *risk* on investors' part. The precise transmission is unclear. In financial markets there will be two key events. Capital markets will begin to deflate, that is stock exchanges and bond markets will crash (the evidence of present experience suggests that they will neither peak at the same time nor deflate at the same pace). There will be a credit crunch to the corporate sector – it may even be that this event triggers the capital market deflation (CMD), particularly if banks have a crucial role in debt financing. Keynes considered that these events happened with some force:

> It is of the nature of organised investment markets, under the influence of purchasers largely ignorant of what they are buying and of speculators who are more concerned with forecasting the next shift of market senti-ment than with a reasonable estimate of the future yield of capital-assets, that, when disillusion falls upon an over-optimistic and over-bought market, it should fall with sudden and even catastrophic force. (*CW* VII, pp. 315–16)

The 'real' events will happen in parallel. From the point at which firms can no longer re-finance debt, they will have to seek the only alternative ways to meet their costs: investment cuts (probably first, with implications for

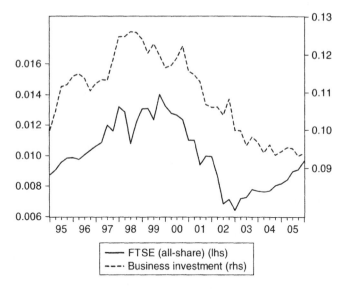

Figure 8.2 UK business investment and equity prices as a share of GDP
Source: Office for National Statistics.

employment in the investment goods industries) and then direct employment cuts. The effect of CMD on firms' balance sheets may also be important here. A sharp deterioration in the balance sheets is, in itself, likely to force cutbacks in investment. It may be that this is the primary transmission mechanism of the failing confidence, but this can only be a matter for conjecture. Nevertheless, it is clear that the UK and US investment booms of the late 1990s saw investment collapse in line with the stock market (Figure 8.2 shows UK figures).

In terms of Keynes's theoretical analysis, there will be two key phenomena. As these financial developments occur, the MEC will be shifting towards a less optimistic position. Firms will know that their revenues from investments made during the expansion phase are failing to meet the expectations that led them to borrow in the first place. They will re-adjust the MEC to a more realistic position. At the same time the failure of confidence in financial markets will cause liquidity preference and risk premia to increase, leading to a sharp rise in the rate of interest. The combination of these effects will cause sharply reduced effective investment demand and hence output and employment.

Lastly, there is the role of prices outside the capital market. While the classical theory affords inflation the key role in explaining the transition from boom to bust, it is argued here that the most important phenomenon is likely to be a price deflation that is endogenous to the cyclical processes outlined above. Once contractionary forces have begun to bite, any cutbacks in employment, costs, wages, raw materials and investment will all lead to reduced aggregate demand and hence excess supply. Through the laws of supply and demand, this will cause downward pressure on prices. As capacity becomes seriously excessive, prices may start to fall. At this point, the 'debt-deflation' considerations advanced by Fisher (1933) become relevant.[20] In particular, the real rate of interest will begin to rise, and the debt burden will increase relative to the costs of the other factors of production.[21]

In sum, the financial perspective characterises the economic cycle in two phases: an expansion that is accompanied by the company sector in steadily increasing indebtedness, and a contraction or recession that is the bursting of this debt inflation. The 'force' that brings an economy operating outside its long-run equilibrium back to (or rather back through) that equilibrium is debt. The degree of indebtedness is then a measure of the excess of the expansion, and will equally prevent the automatic recovery in the way predicted by classical economics.

8.6 Cheap money as the solution to the economic cycle

The cause of the economic cycle is a rate of interest that is too high for a level of investment consistent with full employment, compounded by a monetary system that finances excessive investment for a prolonged period. Older terminology might be usefully resurrected: the economic cycle is caused by money which is *easy* – that is, readily available – but *dear*. For Keynes, cheap money was the solution to the economic cycle:

> [T]he remedy for the boom is not a higher rate of interest but a lower rate of interest! For that may enable the so-called boom to last. The right remedy for the trade cycle is not to be found in abolishing booms and thus keeping us permanently in a semi-slump; but in abolishing slumps and thus keeping us permanently in a quasi-boom. (*CW* VII, p. 322)

The cheap-money solution to the economic cycle achieves a high level of investment by changing the long-period equilibrium of an economy rather than through the excessive expansion process that must be temporary. Keynes's substantial and far-reaching conclusion is that the normal state of a free-market economy can be a level of activity that is almost universally regarded as transitory and unsustainable. The description is again exactly illustrated in Figure 8.1, with Keynes arguing that the higher level of investment (the 'so-called boom'), I_1, should be achieved with a reduction in the rate of interest from r_0 to r_1 (the cheap-money solution) rather than a shift in expectations from mec_0 to mec_1. Keynes's theory of the economic cycle argues that high aggregate demand under dear money will only be temporary and in the long term may be catastrophic. Under cheap money, if the economy were in a state of tranquillity, the higher level of demand and hence activity could be permanent. Furthermore, with notions of 'natural rates' redundant in a multiple-equilibrium system, there is no *a priori* reason to reject the proposition that a volume of investment consistent with full employment might be achieved.

However, while a cheap-money policy allows an economy to operate according to a higher long-period employment equilibrium, it does not immediately follow that such an equilibrium must be more stable than the equilibrium in the dear-money case. From a theoretical perspective, in a cheap-money economy it is not possible to rule out substantial shifts in the MEC leading again to debt inflations and financial collapse. Keynes did not address this issue in the *General Theory*. It might be plausible to argue that such conditions are more unlikely in the cheap-money than the dear-money case. In particular, excessive expectations might be less likely in an economy already operating to high performance and one where expectations were not distorted through routine policy manipulation of the short-term interest rate. Similarly, the consequences of excessive expectations might not be so severe in a cheap-money economy because the cost of any associated debt would be less. However, the role of uncertainty and expectation in the economic process mean that no watertight conclusions can be drawn. What is certain, though, is that dear money does not prevent easy money, and dear-money policy will be likely to provoke excessive expansion followed by recession. Rejecting cheap money on the grounds that it may make money easy neglects this point that dear money does not prevent easy money and, at the very worst, amounts '. . . to refus[ing] to be cured because that will make it possible to become sick again' (Lerner, 1964, p. 222).

A further challenge to cheap-money policy is the likelihood of inflation. Classical analysis sees an inflationary threat from a level of employment higher than the equilibrium or natural rate. But, as Keynes explained, equilibrium employment depends on the interest rate. With the economy understood as this multiple-equilibrium system, the concern is simply whether capacity/supply constraints will lead to inflation. Furthermore, even if inflation occurs, Keynes's theory demands a change in perspective in its interpretation. In a multiple-equilibrium system it may be that cheap money does increase the possibility of inflation, but this increase normally can be set against increased output and employment. The economics profession's obsession with inflation is based on a theory underpinned by a unique equilibrium determined by given real factors. Moreover, in his *General Theory*, Keynes did not neglect the possibility of what he referred to as 'true inflation' when full employment was reached (*CW* VII, pp. 118–19). And in practice, as seen in the last chapter, a number of his monetary initiatives sought to keep a degree of control over the supply of money in a climate of low interest rates.

Lastly, there is Keynes's claim that the classical economics was equivalent to a 'special case' of the *General Theory*. The general case of Keynes's theory is that a free-market economy can be in equilibrium at any level of employment. The special case is an economy operating with the rate of interest (and MPC) set such that full employment or economic bliss is achieved. For this state of affairs to be equivalent to the case depicted in the classical theory, one is compelled to argue that in the absence of shocks the position will be stable and hence excessive expectations do not arise. An economy operating in the special case experiences the perfect operation claimed by the classical theory. Nor does perfection have a role for inflation, except that caused by diminishing returns. Keynes's theory explains how the perfect operation envisaged by the classical theory depends on the rate of interest, MEC and MPC; it is a possible state of affairs but its achievement is far from automatic.

Notes

1. Although, shortly after the publication of the *General Theory*, Hubert Henderson sought to show otherwise through his new 'Oxford Economics Research Group' and new journal, *Oxford Economic Papers*. Henderson's (1938) own agenda was supported by empirical work by Meade and P. W. S. Andrews (1939). Chick (1983, p. 130) explains the difficulty of empirical verification. It is also worth noting that the research environment was not ideal: discussions with representatives from large companies that took place over dinner at college.
2. In drawing such diagrams it seems more appropriate to put investment on the y-axis as it is the dependent variable.
3. It is attractive to reflect this optimism about the future as an optimism of profitability. However, this is not entirely satisfactory because the source of profits is broader than the revenue arising from future investment. For example, if there is a shift from excessive pessimism to excessive optimism, profits will initially grow as idle capacity is engaged rather than due to revenues from new investment. While it is clearly likely that growth in profits will encourage optimism, this is not the only possible determinate of a shift to the MEC.
4. At the NDE, Keynes claimed that the value of the multiplier was between two and three (*CW* XXVII, p. 392). In the General Theory, he proposed that the multilplier for the vs was '... less than 3 and probably fairly stable in the neighbourhood of 2.5'(*CW* VII, p. 128)
5. Chick (1983, p. 21) has defined 'equilibrium' as a point of rest and a point where, for output, but not for labour, supply equals demand and entrepreneurs' expectations of demand are met.
6. Others, for example Hobson (1902, p. 29), had previously used the terminology; but I have not attempted to trace its origins.
7. If firms assess demand correctly, as Keynes assumed in Chapter 3 of the *General Theory* (see Chick, 1983, p. 64), the intersection of the aggregate demand schedule and the aggregate supply schedule is equivalent to Keynes's point of effective demand. He relaxes the assumption of correct expectation in subsequent chapters.
8. $\Delta Y = (\Delta I + \Delta G)/(1 - c)$.
9. Furthermore, a differential equation cannot be integrated in this way.
10. This terminology is used on the second page of Chapter 21, 'The Theory of Prices'. Kregel (1976) has also adopted the terminology.

11. Such 'animal spirits' are neither rational nor irrational. Rationality in the face of an uncertain future remains to be defined.

12. Chick (1998, p. 16) observes 'A similar characterisation of long-period equilibrium is expressed by Robinson (1965), though she preferred to call it "tranquillity": "We may speak of an economy in a state of *tranquillity* when it develops in a smooth regular manner without internal contradictions or external shocks, so that expectations based upon past experience are very confidently held, and are in fact constantly fulfilled and therefore renewed as time goes by." '

13. Revenues do not fall short for every firm in the economy. Individual firms will both over-estimate and under-estimate profits; the correct MEC schedule is an aggregate concept and it is only expectations in aggregate that need be regarded as correct or otherwise.

14. Toporowski (1999) coined this phrase.

15. Such measures do not completely exist; CMI, if not completely ignored by policymakers, tends to be neglected. In reality, CMI simply reflects easy money for listed corporations.

16. Such borrowing will be easier for large companies. These developments will therefore contribute to a concentration of activity in larger firms: that is, to the monopolisation of activity.

17. See, for example, the *Financial Times* 25/9/01 supplement on derivatives; an article on regulation reports the then Bank of England Deputy Governor David Clementi warning that 'these instruments might equally be used to concentrate risk as to disperse it'.

18. The processes discussed here are closely related to those that Hyman Minsky outlined in his 'financial instability hypothesis'. Minsky analyses an excessive investment expansion based on optimism and proposes a sustainability criterion based on revenues such that 'the profit flows must be sufficient to validate debts' (Minsky, 1985, p. 37). He sets out three financial 'postures' on the part of firms as 'hedge', 'speculative' and 'Ponzi' finance. The latter is most closely related to the discussion here. '3. *'Ponzi' finance*. The cash flows from assets in the near term fall short of cash payment commitments and the net income portion of the receipts falls short of the interest portion of the payments. A Ponzi finance unit must increase its outstanding debt in order to meet its financial obligations' (Minsky, 1985, p. 43). The economy described in the main text is one where Ponzi finance becomes endemic. However, the transmission mechanism in Minsky's model differs; he sees real collapse brought about by the effects of rises in the rate of interest to tackle an inevitable inflation.

19. The evidence of experience suggests that policymakers will help to prolong the situation by socialising debt or by bailing out defaulting companies and failing financial organisations, as well as by indulging in extensive public works programmes.

20. Fisher's central argument was as follows: 'I venture the opinion ... that, in the great booms and depressions, ... [the] two dominant factors, ... [are] *over-indebtedness* to start with and *deflation* following soon after; ...' (Fisher, 1933, pp. 340–1). His paper examined a chain of ten events as the debt build-up process was reversed (ibid., p. 343). Ultimately, however, he saw matters based on real not monetary cause. 'The over-indebtedness hitherto presupposed must have had its starters. It may be started by many causes, of which the most common appears to be *new opportunities to invest at a big prospective profit*, as compared with

ordinary profits and interest, such as through new inventions, new industries, development of new resources, opening of new lands or new markets' (Fisher, 1933, p. 348). (He did not set his position against Keynes's emerging views, even though the timing of his paper was such that he would surely have been aware of the Harris Foundation lectures.)

21. This interpretation does not rule out a role for inflation. A particular circumstance in which inflation is likely is when credit extension to households is faster than the growth in production. Under these circumstances (those of concern to Minsky: see footnote 18 above), prices may rise and 'corrective' interest-rate policy will lead to recession as firms' interest payments on their debt become unbearable. The transmission mechanism, however, is still debt.

Part III

Macroeconomics After Keynes

9
Keynes's Response to 'Keynesian' Economics

9.1 Introduction

If I have correctly interpreted the primary emphasis of Keynes's policy initiatives and the basic approach of his theoretical argument, then there can be no question that 'Keynesian' economics bears only the slightest similarity to Keynes's economics. Moreover, the reality is that the identification of a 17-page paper (Hicks, 1937) with the *General Theory* is justified in a manner so trivial as to be beyond belief. Most economists have accepted a short sentence from Keynes, 'I found it very interesting and really have next to nothing to say by way of criticism' (31 March 1937, *CW* XIV, p. 79), as sufficient grounds to ignore his work in its entirety.

The two theories that are equivalent are the neo-classical and 'Keynesian' theories. Keynes's *actual* view of the 'Keynesian' theory should, therefore, be understood through his response to the neo-classical theory. Aspects of his response, in particular in the case of the distinction between liquidity preference and loanable funds, have been discussed in Part II.

But even though Keynes saw neo-classical economics as a distinct agenda, he was not faced with a complete and/or coherent theory long established in the literature, a fact of which he complained more than once. Instead, he was confronted with disparate contributions that departed from classical foundations that were emerging in parallel to his own theory. He could not address the thing as a whole, because it was unclear what that whole was and what that whole would amount to in terms of policy.

On the one hand, the views he expressed in the course of the period from the publication of the *Treatise* to after the *General Theory* can be brought together and amount to a substantial and robust critique of the neo-classical and hence 'Keynesian' approach. These views can be organised under a number of headings and are discussed below broadly according to these categories:

- first, observations on policy statements;
- second, the more developed views set out against the League of Nations (LoN), loanable funds and Pigou's variants of the neo-classical agenda;
- third, views expressed by others on Keynes's behalf; and
- finally, his full comments on Hicks's *IS-LM* paper.

On the other hand, it must be emphasised that Keynes failed to see the extent and seriousness of the threat posed both by this rival theory and equally by the lukewarm approach taken by the authorities to his own practical initiatives.

> The great trouble with Keynes was that he was an idealist. He thought that when people could understand his theory, could understand how the capitalistic system actually works, they would behave in a reasonable manner and operate the system in such a way as to produce favourable results, to produce a high and stable level of employment . . .
>
> . . .
>
> During this period [the twenty years after the war] the understanding which Keynes had supplied of how a market economy operates was smothered . . .
>
> . . .
>
> . . . Keynes was very innocent, he thought that an intelligent theory would prevail over a stupid one. But of course in real life the influence on policy does not come from an intelligent understanding of the economy but from the play of vested interests and from the desire to defend capitalism against the currents of radical thought which have been emerging during this period.
>
> (Joan Robinson opening the discussion at R. F. Kahn's Matiolli lectures, Kahn, 1984, pp. 203–4)

In this way, Joan Robinson saw the 'smothering' of Keynes's theory as motivated by vested interest. The last section of this chapter speculates about whether Keynes himself finally came to fear some betrayal of his work, and traces his last comments on these matters.

9.2   Keynes and neo-classical policy and theory

As examined in Section 4.2, the fullest and most widely endorsed statement of neo-classical policy was by the Next Five Years Group (NFYG). While Keynes had supported tariffs[1] and put his name to Pigou's letter, he refused Salter's request to include his name among the signatories:

> My own belief today is that neither the real remedy nor the power of persuading people to adopt it will come except from a more fundamental diagnosis of the underlying situation and a wide-spread understanding

of this diagnosis and conviction of its correctness. Now, a fundamental diagnosis is just what this document, perhaps quite wisely, entirely avoids; and where one catches a glimpse, by inference, of what the underlying theory of the authors probably is, I find myself much more conscious of differences of opinion than in the matter of the practical proposals. (*CW* XXI, p. 355)

While this refusal provides evidence that Keynes was not wholly in accord with the economic nationalist agenda, it remains light-handed, particularly given the NFYG's advocacy of a modified gold standard and wider rejection of monetary initiatives.

Keynes only occasionally set his own solutions against those pursuing neo-classical (as opposed, of course, to classical) policies. But these rare moments are highly significant.

Just after publication of *A Tract on Monetary Reform*,[2] he set out his position in a speech to the Liberal Club (on 11 December 1923) that has substantial relevance as a general statement of his lifetime policy perspective:

> To begin with a few words about what should be the attitude of Liberalism towards social policy.
> We are traditionally the party of *laissez-faire*. But just as the economists led the party into this policy, so I hope they may lead them out again.
> It is not true that individuals acting separately in their own economic interest always produce the best results.
> It is obvious that an individualist society left to itself does not work well or even tolerably.
> Here I agree with Labour.
> I differ from them not in the desirability of state action in the common interest, but as to the forms which such interference should take. Their proposals are out of date and contrary to human nature.
> But it is not safe or right just to leave things alone.
> It is our duty to think out wise controls and workable interferences.
> Now there is no part of our economic system which works so badly as our monetary and credit arrangements; none where the results of bad working are so disastrous socially; and none where it is easier to propose a scientific solution. (*CW* XIX, Vol. I, pp. 158–9)

Here Keynes is seen to favour state action to address monetary arrangements above other forms of state action.

Richard Kent (2004) has highlighted critical aspects of Keynes's 1931 lectures at the Harris Memorial Foundation symposium on unemployment at the University of Chicago (these do not appear in the *CW*). In these lectures, Keynes gave some emphasis to the necessity of a reduction of long-term interest rates. Kent cites a transcription of Keynes's comments (made at a round-table discussion of his third lecture) that contrasted the relationship between public works and monetary policies:

> I am in favour of an admixture of public works, but my feeling is that unless you socialise the country to a degree that is unlikely, you will get to the end of the public works program, if not in one year, in two years, and therefore if you are not prepared to reduce the rate of interest and bring back private enterprise, when you get to the end of the public works program you have shot your bolt, and you are no better off. I should use the public works program to fill in the interegnum [*sic*] while I was getting interest down. The public works program would in itself increase business profits, and therefore relieve people from that exceptional unwillingness to borrow.
>
> I should be afraid of that as a sole remedy. I should be afraid it would work itself out, come to an end, and then we should be back where we were unless we decided on a very definite further action. (Norman Wait Harris Memorial Foundation 1931, as cited in Kent, 2004, p. 205)

Much later, in December 1933, he re-examined this relationship in a response to a critique by Professor Edward C. Simmons in the *American Economic Review* (*AER*):

> Anyone who is well acquainted with my writings will, however, be aware that I am not one of those who believe that the business cycle can be controlled solely by manipulation of the short-term rate of interest, that I am indeed a strong critic of this view, and that I have paid much attention to alternative and supplementary methods of controlling the rate of interest. Since, however, myths once started are persistent, it may be unwise of me to allow this representation of my argument to pass uncorrected.
>
> My proposals for the control of the business cycle are based on the control of *investment*. I have explained in detail that the most effective ways of controlling investment vary according to circumstances; and I have been foremost to point out that circumstances can arise, and have arisen recently, when neither control of the short-term rate of interest nor even control of the long-term rate will be effective, with the result that direct stimulation of investment by government is the necessary means. (Keynes, 1933, p. 675)[3]

The most substantial discussion of the differing policy perspectives was in Keynes's article in *The Listener* summarising the contributions to a radio debate (referred to in Section 5.1). His approach was first to draw a distinction between those who saw the economic system as self-adjusting (at least in the long run: Henderson, Brand and Robbins) and those who did not ('Dr Dalton', 'Mr Hobson', 'Mr Orage'[4] and 'Mrs Wootton'). He then examined the views of the latter group concerning the fundamental cause of the failure of the system to self-adjust; of these, Barbara Wootton's view appeared the most neo-classical: 'Mrs Wootton,... calls for planning, although she only half-rejects the theory of self-adjustment, having not reached, one feels, a synthesis satisfactory to herself between her intellectual theory and her spiritual home' (*CW* XIII, p. 487). Keynes described his own practical perspective as follows:

> Now the school which believes in self-adjustment is, in fact, assuming that the rate of interest adjusts itself more or less automatically, so as to encourage just the right amount of production of capital goods to keep our incomes at the maximum level which our energies and our organisation and our knowledge of how to produce efficiently are capable of providing. This is, however, pure assumption. There is no theoretical reason for believing it to be true. ... Those standing on my side of the gulf, whom I have ventured to describe as half-right and half-wrong, have perceived this; and they conclude that the only remedy is for us to change the distribution of wealth and modify our habits in such a way as to increase our propensity to spend our incomes on current consumption. I agree with them in thinking that this would be a remedy. But I disagree with them when they go further and argue that this is the only remedy. For there is an alternative, namely, to increase the output of capital goods by reducing the rate of interest and in other ways. (*CW* XIII, p. 490)

His comments on some neo-classical theoretical initiatives were equally unequivocal. On the LoN work, Boianovsky and Trautwein (2004, p. 6) discuss his objections to Haberler's work:

> *Keynes* reacted negatively to the whole project. In a letter of 30 August 1934 [5] he wrote [to] Haberler that "I cannot think that you have gone the right way to work. The method of taking various propositions in isolation is to bring authors into the same pigeon-hole who are really leagues apart and have very little in common". (ibid.)

Haberler's reply to Keynes alluded to the support that the work commanded across the economics profession: 'the comments which I have received on my memorandum from many of the writers concerned express on the whole considerable sympathy with my attempt at reconciliation' (ibid.). In his response, Keynes re-iterated his point:

> My essential point is that the method you have adopted forces you to a high degree of superficiality ... I cannot believe that the solution can be

reached by bringing together . . . excerpts from the views of a large number of writers, each differing from the other more or less in fundamentals. The answer must lie somewhere deeper down, yet your methods tempts you to skating rather than digging. (ibid.)

But a substantial number of those who would take leading roles in post-Second World War economics appeared content. Boianovsky and Trautwein (2004, p. 9) record the following economists participating in a discussion in Geneva in March 1936 (i.e. one month after the publication of the *General Theory*) of Haberler's work:

- Dennis Robertson (Cambridge)
- Otto Anderson (Economic Research Institute, Sofia)
- John Maurice Clark (Columbia University)
- Leon Dupriez (Catholic University of Leuven)
- Alvin Hansen (Department of State, Washington DC)
- Oskar Morgenstern (Austrian Business Cycle Institute)
- Bertil Ohlin (Stockholm School of Economics)
- Charles Rist (University of Paris)
- Lionel Robbins (London School of Economics)
- Wilhelm Röpke (University of Istanbul)
- Jan Tinbergen (Dutch Institute of Economics).

A memorandum by a Rockefeller Foundation employee (John Van Sickle) reported: 'a number of those in attendance told me privately that they had come with considerable scepticism as to the usefulness of such a conference. At the end there was not a single one who did not feel that the meeting had been definitely worthwhile' (ibid., p. 14). Equally, *Prosperity and Depression* was reviewed in the main economic journals 'with largely positive reactions to its synthetic approach' (ibid., p. 15). In this way the leaders of the post-war profession and Keynes are revealed as taking the opposite views. (Keynes got Kahn to respond; this is discussed below.)

Keynes's most vigorous criticism of the neo-classical approach was aimed at what would become known as the loanable funds theory of interest. He even anticipated these debates in the *General Theory* itself: '. . . the attempt to build a bridge [between the theory of interest and the theory of money] on the part of the neo-classical school . . . has led to the worst muddles of all' (*CW* VII, p. 183).

After publication, the critique continued as the alternative theories debate (discussed in Chapter 7). Keynes categorically rejected as 'fundamental heresy' any notion that the loanable funds and liquidity preference theories were one and the same. Furthermore, as will be discussed in the next section, he regarded his contributions as relevant to Hicks, because he saw that Hicks adhered to loanable funds. The same critique can, therefore, be applied to *IS-LM*, given its loanable funds properties.

Pigou's (1937) work is the third area of the neo-classical theory on which there is a record of Keynes's views. As discussed in Chapter 4, Keynes was horrified by the publication of what Pigou referred to as an article in atonement for his failure to produce a Presidential Address to the Royal Economic Society. He prepared a short critique (published in the December 1937 *EJ*) addressing logical inconsistencies in the argument, rather than the method of the argument itself. The same journal contained Kaldor's critique which incorporated *IS-LM*, and that Pigou was prepared to accept. Keynes made no public statement on Kaldor's work. Nevertheless, his private correspondence with Pigou strongly suggests that he was not satisfied with the approach that Kaldor advocated. First, on 20 October 1937, he wrote, 'It is also difficult for me to leave the matter to Kaldor, because, at any rate in the first version of his article, there is, from my point of view, a very important mistake ... ' (*CW* XIV, p. 257). Keynes does not, however, explain the nature of this mistake. Second, on 3 January 1938, he wrote,

> Kaldor is mainly a re-statement of my *General Theory* with reference to your special assumptions. These special assumptions make it possible, of course, to reduce it to a simpler form without losing anything. On the other hand, it is really the general case one has to consider, and that it seems to me would be very difficult to treat along these lines. (*CW* XIV, p. 267)

As Young (1987, p. 111) has noted, Kahn appears to have been most alive to the consequences of events: 'I have not seen Kaldor's article but I am sure that publication of it will darken counsel. After all we could all of us write replies to Pigou if you wanted them and I do not see why Kaldor should be thus favoured' (Kahn to Keynes, 22 October 1937, *CW* XIV, p. 260). Robertson, on the other hand, was content: 'I'm glad that Kaldor's thing is to appear, as I found it enlightening' (KP file GTE/2/4/125, 28 November 1937).[6]

Pigou's (1941) *Employment and Equilibrium – A Theoretical Discussion* would build on his own work. Kaldor's rather favourable review was published in the *EJ* (see Section 4.7).

The third strand of views that indicate Keynes's opposition to the neo-classical theory are the items published by his close collaborators in Cambridge. After the publication of the *General Theory* there are three main incidents that indicate how Keynes used (or intended to use) these colleagues as mouthpieces for his own views. First, towards the end of the prolonged dialogue about Pigou and Kaldor's work, Keynes wrote to Kahn as follows: 'My present intention is not to say any more myself, but to leave to you any further stage in the controversy' (25 October 1937, *CW*

XIV, p. 262). While Keynes discussed Pigou's draft response with Kahn, the two appear to have been content to let it stand alone. The second incident was Kahn's review of Haberler's work and was much more substantial. Skidelsky (2000, p. 7) suggests that Kahn's assault was motivated by Keynes: ' "Why is there such obstinacy and wilfulness in error?" he [Keynes] asked about Gottfried Haberler's *Prosperity and Depression*, which he got Kahn to savage in the *Economic Journal*, . . . '.[7] Kahn's review (1937), Haberler's rejoinder (1938) and Kahn's (1938) brief reply were bitter and acrimonious. In retrospect, perhaps this was inevitable. In this debate there is a glimpse of the high stakes not seen in Keynes's more constructive but perhaps too mild contributions. The third incident was Lerner's response to Myra Curtis that was discussed in Chapter 6. Again the Keynes papers contain a letter that indicates Keynes's role:

> At my instigation Lerner has prepared a reply to Miss Curtis which strikes me as exceedingly good. He does not devote anything like all his space to her, but tries to classify and deal with all the various reasons people have found for rejecting the conclusion S = I. (Keynes to Kahn, 7 October 1937, Kahn Papers, File 13/57)[8]

9.3 Keynes's 'approval' of *IS-LM*

All of these direct and indirect comments indicate a fundamental opposition to the neo-classical work. So given this opposition, why did Keynes approve Hicks's *IS-LM* paper?[9] The universal acceptance of this approval rests on the single sentence from the private letter to Hicks that was cited at the start of this chapter. Throughout his life, Hicks maintained that this justification was sufficient:

> I think I may conclude from this letter (as I have always done) that Keynes accepted the *ISLM* diagram as a fair statement of his position – of the nucleus, that is, of his position. That, in any case, was what it was meant to be – a means of demonstrating the nature of the difference between Keynes and his predecessors – not a statement of what I believed myself. (Hicks, 1977, p. 146)

It is fundamental to the argument in this book that this interpretation of Keynes's comments is incorrect, not justified, has misled to a staggering extent, and, as Kahn put it, tragic: 'The result has been that the elementary teaching of 'Keynesian' economics has been the victim of *IS-LM* and related diagrams and algebra. It is tragic that Keynes made no public protest when they began to appear' (Kahn, 1984, p. 160).

A number of points must be made, four within the specific context of Hicks's paper, and then taking Hicks's paper as part of the wider opposition to the *General Theory*. First, in the most trivial and simplistic sense, neither Keynes's short statement or the whole of his letter to Hicks hardly constitute a wholehearted endorsement of *IS-LM*. Second, by no stretch of the imagination can this brief comment be regarded as an endorsement of the 'necessary propositions' (Section 4.8); chronologically it can have *no relevance* to the fourth necessary proposition that involves the grafting of the classical model onto the *IS-LM* framework. Third, it also seems to have been overlooked that Keynes's comments relate to a draft of Hicks's paper that has not survived (*CW* XIV, p. 77), and it is simply not known to what extent the draft may have differed from the version published. Fourth, without the 'benefit' of hindsight – even from the published paper – it is arguably impossible to understand exactly what Hicks was trying to get at and exactly what Keynes was endorsing. Hicks's first objective appears to have been to construct a neo-classical theory of money wages; but then when he begins to make comparisons it is not clear what models are being compared. When he brings in Keynes's theory it is not clear whether he is bringing it in order to develop the classical model or to develop the Keynes theory in its own right. Even his claim to generality is ambiguous. Overall it is not at all obvious how Keynes would have interpreted Hicks's argument and what therefore he was 'not criticising'.

More substantially, though, for me, it is almost certain that Keynes came to see Hicks's work as merely a variant on the wider Robertson/Haberler neo-classical agenda. We see this first in two points of theoretical substance that Keynes proceeded to address both in the same letter to Hicks and in the course of the more general controversy about the *General Theory*. These points were, of course, loanable funds and uncertainty/expectation. In his original private letter he drew attention to these points only as 'notes', but nonetheless, they were substantial criticisms. In the case of loanable funds, as examined in Chapter 7, there can be no doubt that Hicks and his *IS-LM* paper were one of the targets for Keynes's attack. Keynes had spotted that *IS-LM* had loanable funds implications and he stressed with as great a force as possible that he rejected the notion that liquidity preference and loanable funds were alternative statements of the same theory. As discussed in Section 8.2, Keynes tackled Hicks for ignoring the role of expectations in assessing the yield of investment.

While Keynes's critique was unambiguous, it was private and light-handed. However, he made strong and unambiguous public comments on precisely the same issue. In February 1937, Keynes published a paper in the *QJE* that was ostensibly a response to four critiques published in the previous issue. But as Young has suggested (1987, pp. 18–20; see below), this paper might be interpreted as a general response to all of his critics. I would go further and argue – in a manner that is complementary to the post-Keynesian position – that Keynes regarded this paper as a step towards his commitment to Townshend to produce a more general statement of his theory. Entitled

'The General Theory of Employment', Keynes also observed that setting the response at a very general level had the positive side effect of avoiding controversy:

> There are other criticisms also which I should be ready to debate. But though I might be able to justify my own language, I am anxious not to be led, through doing so in too much detail, to overlook the substantial points which may, nevertheless, underlie the reactions which my treatment has produced in the minds of my critics. I am more attached to the comparatively simple fundamental ideas which underlie my theory than to the particular forms in which I have embodied them, and I have no desire that the latter should be crystallised at the present stage of the debate. If the simple basic ideas can become familiar and acceptable, time and experience and the collaboration of a number of minds will discover the best way of expressing them. I would, therefore, prefer to occupy such further space as the editor of this Journal can allow me in trying to re-express some of these ideas, than in detailed controversy which might prove barren. (*CW* XIV, p. 111)

The first issue he chose to emphasise was the nature of expectation in the face of uncertain knowledge of the future. After four pages, he brought the discussion to bear on two substantive mechanisms: first, how uncertainty affected holdings of money and the rate of interest:

> [O]ur desire to hold money as a store of wealth is a barometer of the degree of our distrust of our own calculations and conventions concerning the future. Even though this feeling about money is itself conventional or instinctive, it operates, so to speak, at a deeper level of our motivation. It takes charge at the moments when the higher, more precarious conventions have weakened. The possession of actual money lulls our disquietude; . . . (*CW* XIV, p. 116)

second, the impact of uncertainty on investment:

> It is not surprising that the volume of investment, thus determined, should fluctuate widely from time to time. For it depends on two sets of judgements about the future, neither of which rests on an adequate or secure foundation – on the propensity to hoard and on opinions of the future yield of capital assets. (*CW* XIV, p. 118)

After the discussion of investment he makes a statement that is exactly applicable to Hicks:

> This completes the first chapter of the argument, namely, the liability of the scale of investment to fluctuate for reasons quite distinct (*a*) from

those which determine the propensity to *save* out of a given income and
(*b*) from those physical conditions of technical capacity to aid production
which have usually been supposed hitherto to be the chief influence
governing the marginal efficiency of capital.

If, on the other hand, our knowledge of the future was calculable and
not subject to sudden changes, it might be justifiable to assume that the
liquidity-preference curve was both stable and very inelastic. (*CW* XIV,
pp. 118–19)

Furthermore, in autumn 1936, shortly after producing the *QJE* paper, he
lectured in Stockholm. The lecture led to another paper, 'The Theory of
the Rate of Interest'. As Young also observes, again there was emphasis on
uncertainty:

> For the rate of interest and the marginal efficiency of capital are particu-
> larly concerned with the *indefinite* character of actual expectations; they
> sum up the effect on men's market decisions of all sorts of vague doubts
> and fluctuating states of confidence and courage. They belong, that is
> to say, to a stage of our theory where we are no longer assuming a
> definite and calculable future. The orthodox theory, on the other hand, is
> concerned with a simplified world where there is always full employment,
> and where doubt and fluctuations of confidence are ruled out, . . . (*CW*
> XIV, pp. 106–7)

Young discusses the relevance of the *QJE* critique as follows:

> It is therefore highly probable that Keynes took the opportunity offered
> by the 1937 *QJE* paper to address not only his critics and the specific
> *QJE* reviews but the IS-LM approach as presented by Harrod, Hicks and
> Meade respectively. . . . [H]e is pointing out the main shortcoming of
> the IS-LM approach which does not, and cannot, take uncertainty into
> account, . . . (Young, 1987, p. 19)

He goes on to cite his own interview with George Shackle as support for this
position:

> When asked if the core of the *QJE* paper was the emphasis on uncer-
> tainty, Shackle replied 'I certainly think so.' Finally, when questioned
> as to whether he agreed with the contention that Keynes's basic and
> implicit response to IS-LM is the *QJE* article, he replied 'that is my view
> exactly'. (ibid.)

Skidelsky has also put forward this argument independently of Young (at
least he does not attribute it to Young):

Ostensibly his answer to criticisms by Taussig, Leontief, Viner and Robertson, it may also be seen as a warning to his mathematical interpreters – a warning completely ignored. It is significant that this restatement of the 'essence' of the *General Theory* is concerned particularly with the effects of uncertainty on investment demand and the rate of interest... (Skidelsky, 1992, p. 616)

The relation of this argument to Hicks's 'little apparatus' might seem to be this. Keynes is saying that his own theory is what the classical theory would have had to be had it taken uncertainty seriously. Hicks's 'generalised' *General Theory* was, in other words, redundant, unless it was attached to 'Mr. Keynes's special theory'. (ibid., p. 618)

On the other hand, Moggridge rejects this position:

Since Warren Young's *Interpreting Mr. Keynes: The IS-LM Enigma*, it has come into the literature that the *Quarterly Journal of Economics* paper 'was intended as a counterweight to the IS-LM approach as endorsed by Meade, Harrod and Hicks', as Peter Clarke (1988, 302) puts it, citing Young (1987, 9–10, 178). There are two problems with this line of argument. One is chronological. The *Quarterly Journal* paper appeared in February 1937. It was thus written before the end of 1936. Keynes did not 'catch up' on his reading and 'go through' Hicks's seminal paper, 'Mr. Keynes and the Classics', until late March 1937, although, of course, he may have browsed in it after Hicks sent it to him the previous October (*JMK*, [*CW*] XIV, 77, 19). The second is the praise Keynes bestowed on the three papers, going so far with Harrod to suggest that 'I should like to read your paper instead' of his own in Stockholm (*JMK*, [*CW*] XIV, 84). Given this praise, it would seem most unlikely, given his normal behaviour, that Keynes would, as Young suggests, turn and attack these views, especially without explicit attribution. (Moggridge, 1992, p. 595)

But the timing of the article *was* exactly right. The Oxford conference was in September 1936 and this is when Keynes received drafts of the papers (it is unclear if he saw Meade's) and this timing is thus entirely consistent with the provocation for and writing of the *QJE* paper at the end of 1936 (and therefore he *is* likely to have 'browsed in it'). Furthermore, while he waited until March 1937 to respond to Hicks, he actually responded to Harrod on 30 August 1936. Most important though, in the context of the broader post-Keynesian depiction of the *General Theory*, a critique from the perspective of uncertainty is *exactly the right critique of 'Keynesian' economics*.

One can only speculate why, as Moggridge observes, Keynes did not tackle his 'Keynesian' critics more vigorously. Two reasons come to mind. The first is emphasised in the *QJE* article itself – 'the desire to avoid controversy'.

Keynes was clearly stung by the charge that the *General Theory* was excessively critical of classical theory. Those who were developing the 'Keynesian' theory appeared to be engaging in a dialogue with him and he must have been eager not to discourage these younger academics, given his total failure with his older colleagues. The approach adopted in the *QJE*, namely to explain why his model is different without setting out explicitly the views he is criticising, is exactly consistent with a less antagonistic stance. It would explain too why Keynes did not identify who he was aiming the article at. The second reason is his ill health. This was hinted at in the course of the controversy with Pigou: 'So far as my health goes, it is for me certainly much better that I should get my short note off my chest – without any obligation to return myself to the charge' (*CW* XIV, p. 257).

9.4 Keynes's private perspective

Keynes's published theoretical contributions were constructive and positive, barring the odd rebuke (as, for example, in his (1933) *AER* response to Simmons). However, private correspondence reveals a degree of exasperation with others' approach to theory. Equally, Keynes's contributions to the public policy debate were unfailingly enthusiastic and optimistic. Only at the very end of his life did he allow a note of pessimism to sound.

Prior to the publication of the *General Theory*, Robertson's approach to the galley proofs was so negative and unhelpful that Keynes terminated the dialogue. Keynes's comments on doing so were highly perceptive in the light of what was to come:

> This brings me to the main impression with which your criticisms leave me. I feel that you must, as said above, either differ from me much more or less. You make no frontal attack on any of my main points. Yet there is not really a single point of importance where I have succeeded in making you change your mind. I am baffled by your practice of reading into everything I write something not very incompatible with what you already believe. (*CW* XIII, p. 520)

Similarly, his private response to Robertson's published comments in the *QJE* illustrated his recognition and rejection of the position Robertson was taking:

> I see that you are saying that it all makes no difference, that Marshall related it all to a Royal Commission in an affirmative sigh, that it has been well known to Pigou for years past and is to be found in a footnote to *Industrial Fluctuations*, that Neisser's bunk comes to the same thing, and the like; . . . You are like a man searching for a formula by which he can agree without changing his mind. (Keynes to Robertson, 13 December 1936, *CW* XIV, p. 94)

Keynes's most candid comments were contained in correspondence with Kahn:

on Pigou (1937) in August 1937:
> It seems to me the work of a sick man, which no one would print who was in his right mind, . . . (*CW* XIV, p. 238);

on Pigou and Robertson in October 1937:
> Many thanks for sending me a copy of the Prof's new book [*Socialism versus Capitalism*]. As in the case of Dennis, when it comes to practice, there is really extremely little between us. Why do they insist on maintaining theories from which their own practical conclusions cannot possibly follow? It is a sort of Society for the Preservation of Ancient Monuments. (*CW* XIV, p. 259)

On Meade, on 26 January 1938:
> Have you read Meade's funny little book [Meade, 1938], about which I have written the enclosed [not found]. . . . All the younger generation except you seem to have a passion for producing the half-baked. And you, on the other hand, are hard-boiled! Why not produce while the white is set and the yolk still fluid.[10]

On Robertson's final contributions to the alternative theories debate, on 23 April 1938:
> Thank you very much indeed for your notes on my rejoinder to Dennis. I agree with you that I ought not really to have accepted Dennis's, and that the whole controversy is most objectionable. But there is no impartial court to which I can appeal in these cases.[11]

On Tinbergen's LoN work in August 1938:
> I do not know if it is obvious that I think it all hocus – worse than Haberler [*Prosperity and Depression*]. But everyone else is greatly impressed, it seems, by such a mess of unintelligible figurings. (*CW* XIV, p. 289)

In terms of theory, his final published statement on the neo-classical approach was a review of Haberler. In 1939, Keynes provided an anonymous review of the second edition (1939) of *Prosperity and Depression* for the *EJ*. While he picked out the critical point, the tone of the review as well as the manner of its publication perhaps indicates that Keynes did not see the full extent of the threat posed by his rivals' initiatives:

> Generally speaking, Prof. Haberler accepts the broad line of Mr Keynes's theory as valid, but finds nothing significantly new in it except the insistence on the relationship between hoarding and the rate of interest. 'Apart from this' he concludes (p. 237), "we have not yet discovered any essential differences between Mr Keynes's theory and that of the other recognised authorities . . . as represented by, say Prof. Pigou's *Industrial Fluctuations*, Prof. Robertson's writings or the synthesis attempted in Part II of the first edition of this book . . .". (*CW* XXIX, p. 275)

But war was already looming. And it is difficult to imagine how Keynes viewed the state of the debate at that time. What would surely have been most important to him would have been the success in terms of the implementation of his policies. In the years just before the war, currency management and cheap money had begun to prevail across the world, perhaps with the exception of the totalitarian economies. During the war, the British government would permit the full development of his debt-management and monetary policies. But towards the end of the war, both at national and at international level, there was a gradual retreat from those policies and a move more into line with 'Keynesian'/neo-classical/economic nationalist thinking. In terms of national policy, the British Employment White Paper (*EWP*) was lukewarm towards cheap money. In terms of international policy, the Bretton Woods negotiations moved away from the Clearing Union towards a modified gold standard. The extent to which Keynes regarded these developments as a distinct trend in policy is unclear. He was used to having to fight an intransigent Treasury/Bank for implementation of any policy, which he had tradition-ally seen as a result of caution and conservatism rather than anything more sinister.

Keynes's (mainly private) comments on these post-war policy delibera-tions reveal a different perspective as well as some disagreement. In May 1943, on receiving Meade's preliminary work for the *Employment White Paper*, Keynes was perceptive: 'I think you lay too much stress on cure and too little on prevention' (*CW* XXVII, p. 326). But when the paper was published, comments in his briefing for the Chancellor indicate that he did not appreciate the underlying rejection of monetary reform, though they do reveal a degree of bafflement:

> *Criticism.* Reference to interest rates in Paragraph 59 has been subject to criticism in some quarters of the Press. It is said that whilst we are pro-mised a continuance of the cheap money policy for the time being, we are threatened with a reversal of it at some later date.
> *Answer.* I have never myself been able to make much sense of that paragraph... (*CW* XXVII, p. 375)

It is equally notable that briefing was deemed necessary to counter a public perception that authorities intended to terminate cheap-money policy after the war.[12]

The *Report* of the NDE indicates that it was set up in part to make amends for shortcomings of the *EWP* with regard to monetary policy: 'We were asked to define more closely an appropriate Treasury policy in regard to cheap money with particular reference to statements in the White Paper on Employment Policy' (Report, para. 2). Included was a fairly categorical response on the part of the monetary reformers to the 'Keynesian' agenda set out in the *White Paper*:

We have been led to form a series of views not completely consistent with the brief references to the matter in the Employment White Paper. Rather we say that the White Paper ought to mean that, subject to uncertainties as to the extent to which and the conditions in which moderate fluctuations should be admitted, (which uncertainties need not be brought too much into the open), the object of Government should be to maintain low interest rates, long and short, for as far ahead as can reasonably be the subject of discussion – certainly far beyond the transitional period. (NDE Report, para. 25)

The actual debate at the Enquiry (recorded in the minutes) brought the different views into sharper relief. On the one hand, most Enquiry members purported to agree with the theory and policy that Keynes had articulated:

Prof. Robbins... confirmed that the doctrinal analysis was one with which he (in common with most other professional economists at the present time) agreed. (PRO File T230/94, p. 220)

Mr Meade concluded by saying that he entirely agreed with the practical suggestions put forward by Lord Keynes. (ibid., p. 121)

On the other hand, Keynes again found himself having to defend the secular nature of cheap-money policy:

Mr. Meade, while agreeing with Lord Keynes in his general analysis, preferred to lay more emphasis on the importance of keeping interest rates down when we are entering a period of possible stagnation, with a view to lowering the cost of socially desirable public and semi-public investment. (PRO file T160/1408, p. 119)

But he [Prof. Robbins] felt that there should be a certain flexibility. .... During the transitional period, if the physical controls were to crumble, there might be a case for a slight upward movement of rates; ... [and] expressed some uncertainty about his proposals regarding short term rates... It might well happen that, if the leading nations were for political reasons to put the Trade Unions in a strong position, this would lead to a rise in wage-rates and in the general level of prices, resulting in an upward pressure on interest rates. (PRO File T230/94, p. 220)

The *Report* was in line with Keynes's views. And with the post-war general election victory of the Labour Government, the policy was brought into practical effect. Keynes's final statement on the matter indicates exasperation with the manner in which policy was being conducted: 'If we offer a further funding loan now, whom do we expect to subscribe? Where do we expect the money to come from? And why do we want it?' (1 April 1946, PRO T

273/428).[13] As Howson (1993, p. 152) has argued, Keynes would not have supported the manner in which policy was conducted after his death.

From the international perspective, Keynes was a vigorous advocate of the Bretton Woods proposals almost to the end. His House of Lords speech is widely regarded as carrying the day for them in Britain (alongside the loan proposals). Later pronouncements might, however, indicate a slight change in perspective. In a February 1946 speech to the Political Economy Club in Cambridge, he continued to defend the arguments of his House of Lords speech. But Keynes again chose to emphasise economic liberalism, and was conscious of 'totalitarians in our midst':

> Assuming that the policy of deliberate economic isolationism should be rejected, have we nevertheless agreed to return to a version of 19th century *laissez faire* which is bound to break down?
> I consider this a grossly ignorant misunderstanding of what has happened. The classical doctrine
> Supplemented by exchange variations and overall import control. This seems to me the modern version of economic liberalism. My H of L speech. To that charge I would plead guilty. I can easily see that it is not acceptable to the totalitarians in our midst, but it seems to me soundly consonant with our national attitudes, instincts, principles of self-interest. A Totalitarian economy must be a large one. The British Empire for obvious reasons not a suitable unit for totalitarian experiments.
> Here is a genuine attempt at agreed rules and principles of action. My complaint would be that they do not go far enough in the liberal direction . . . But they go a long way. The opposite of the law of the jungle. (Moggridge, 1992, p. 824)[14]

These views on classical mechanisms were echoed in his posthumously published *EJ* article (see Section 5.3). I can only surmise that he chose to assert this perspective in such a robust manner on each of these occasions because he feared that economic policy and theory were becoming dominated by those who preferred non-market solutions to the Economic Problem – solutions that were later disguised as 'Keynesian' economics by the Economic Nationalists (the 'totalitarians in our midst'?).

Then, in March 1946, he began to look more pessimistically on the postwar arrangements under the International Monetary Fund, to which he had contributed so much. Keynes closed his speech at the inaugural meeting of the governors of the Fund and Bank as follows:

> I hope that Mr Kelchner has not made any mistake and that there is no malicious fairly, no Carabosse, whom he has overlooked and forgotten to ask to the party. For if so the curses which that bad fairy will pronounce will, I feel sure, run as follows:– 'You two brats shall grow up politicians;

your every thought and act shall have an *arrière-pensée*; everything you determine shall not be for its own sake or on its own merits but because of something else.'

If this should happen, then the best that could befall – and that is how it might turn out – would be for the children to fall into an eternal slumber, never to waken or be heard of again in the courts and markets of Mankind. (*CW* XXVI, pp. 216–17)

Keynes's final words to the world were contained in *Two Memoirs* 'published by his Executors in order to carry out an express desire in his will that these papers, and these alone of his unpublished writings, should be printed' (Keynes, 1949, p. 8), as the introduction by his close friend David Garnett explained. As far as I am aware, nobody has speculated why he made this instruction or why he chose these specific works. The second of these, 'My Early Beliefs', contained a fairly categorical rejection of the philosophy of his life that has been so richly celebrated by his biographers:

We claimed the right to judge every individual case on its merits, and the wisdom, experience and self-control to do so successfully....

... What matters a great deal more is the fact that it was flimsily based, as I now think, on an *a priori* view of what human nature is like, both other people's and our own, which was disastrously mistaken....

... We were among the last of the Utopians, or meliorists as they are sometimes called, who believe in a continuing moral progress by virtue of which the human race already consists of reliable, rational, decent people, influenced by truth and objective standards, who can be safely released from the outward restraints of convention and traditional standards and inflexible rules of conduct, and left, from now onwards, to their own sensible devices, pure motives and reliable intuitions of the good.... it was because self-interest was *rational* that the egoistic and alturistic systems were supposed to work out in practice to the same conclusions.

In short, we repudiated all versions of the doctrine of original sin, of there being insane and irrational springs of wickedness in most men. We were not aware that civilisation was a thin and precarious crust erected by the personality and the will of a very few, and only maintained by rules and conventions skilfully put across and guilefully preserved. We had no respect for traditional wisdom or the restraints of custom. We lacked reverence, as [D. H.] Lawrence observed and as Ludwig [Wittgenstein] with justice also used to say – for everything and everyone. It did not occur to us to respect the extraordinary accomplishment of our predecessors in the ordering of life (as it now seems to me to have been) or the elaborate framework which they had devised to protect this order.... As cause and consequence of our general state of mind we completely misunderstood human nature including our own.... I behave as if there really existed some authority or standard to which I can successfully appeal if I shout loud enough – perhaps it is some hereditary vestige of a belief in the efficacy of prayer. (*CW* X, pp. 446–8)

He closed the essay, '[b]ut that is why I say that there may have been just a grain of truth when Lawrence said in 1914 that we were "done for" '.

In his biography of Keynes, Harrod contrasted an outlook fostered by Oxford philosophers who chose to emphasise the concept of 'duty', with that which the Cambridge intellectuals derived from G. E. Moore.

> In Oxford – no doubt owing partly to the special attention paid to Aristotle's *Ethics* – great reliance was placed on what may be called traditional morality, embodying the intuitions of wise men through the ages. In Cambridge the doctrine of intuition was interpreted – anyhow by those disciples who were to be for many years the intimate intellectual companions of Keynes – as giving fairly complete licence to judge all things anew.
>
> . . .
>
> ... In one's general view of things, when going out into the world to face the practical problems of life, it makes an enormous difference to one's point of view whether one holds that one must judge one's own actions according to whether or not they tend to promote some ultimate good which one may have in mind, or supposes oneself limited on every hand by a number of hard and fast duties, intuitively recognised as such. (Harrod, 1972 [1951], pp. 89–90)

Perhaps Keynes had finally seen the importance and relevance of his own words, written originally in 1938, and the power of 'traditional wisdom or the restraints of custom'.

E. A. G. Robinson, who reviewed the work for the *EJ*, said of the first essay 'Dr. Melchior: a Defeated Enemy': 'It is a tragedy of great events and little men. As one reads it again and again, I believe that one's abiding impression are the first and the last – Melchior the man, and the tragedy of little men' (Robinson, 1949, p. 556).

Notes

1. But only as second best. See *CW* XXI, pp. 204–10 for a clear statement of his position.
2. Much of the material was re-working of articles that had been published in 'Reconstruction Supplements' of the *Manchester Guardian Commercial*, mainly in April 1922.
3. Not included in the *CW*.

4. Alfred Richard Orage (1873–1934); an economist who advocated 'social credit' schemes.
5. Not included in *CW*.
6. The letter is excerpted in *CW* XXIX, p. 164; but this passage is omitted.
7. Skidelsky does not provide a reference for this quotation, which I have not been able to find elsewhere.
8. An extract from this letter to Kahn is included in *CW* XIV, p. 259; this passage is not included in the extract.
9. It is interesting that emphasis has centred on Hicks's paper, particularly given that Keynes's enthusiasm for Harrod's was far more wholehearted: 'I like your paper . . . more than I can say. I have found it very instructive and illuminating, and I really have no criticisms. I think that you have re-oriented the argument beautifully' (*CW* XIV, p. 84). Though, again, the comments were on a draft and Keynes emphasised that Harrod '[did not] mention *effective demand*' (ibid., p. 85).
10. Kahn papers, file 13/57.
11. Kahn papers, file 13/57.
12. A further remark of interest was included at the end of one of Keynes's internal HM Treasury minutes concerning debt-management policy: 'After reading these, and also some other recent papers, I am left with the feeling that the bureaucracy have to beware of drifting into [a] position in which they are equally opposed both to socialism and private enterprise – to the former because it brings in politics, and to the latter because it depends on speculation and money making. It is much sounder, *I* think, to believe in both than to thwart both' (30 January 1945, *CW* XXII, pp. 430–1).
13. Not included in *CW*.
14. Not included in *CW*; but available in the Keynes Papers, file PS/7/509, dated 2 February 1946. Sir Ian Lloyd's account of the talk has just been published in the *Cambridge Journal of Economics* (Lloyd, 2006)

10
The 'Keynesian' Counter-Revolution and After

10.1 Introduction

Keynes's response to the neo-classical initiatives was of no interest to those that promoted and developed the post-war consensus that would be known as 'Keynesian' economics.

The 'Keynesian' counter-revolution saw Keynes's policies and theory replaced with the 'Keynesian' approach, the monetary roots of the theory erased, and Keynes re-invented as the intellectual support for the 'Keynesian' agenda. Chapter 4 examined how the 'Keynesian' theoretical arguments were aired, developed and endorsed between the wars. 'Keynesian' economists lavished praise on each other's work in articles and reviews; and the LoN endorsed their approach to economics (Haberler, 1937). In terms of policy, Chapter 4 traced early contributions and argued that the agenda was formalised as the *EWP* in Britain and the Employment Act in the United States.

These statements set the backdrop for government intervention in economic activity, with the professed goal of full employment. But the means would become 'Keynesian' – with emphasis on fiscal policy and monetary policy set aside as ineffective (although in reality monetary conditions were more conducive to growth; see Chapter 11).

Academically, the 'Keynesian' agenda was promoted through the textbooks. From a theoretical perspective, economics would be divided into two distinct domains. Microeconomics would become dominated by the welfare initiative asserted by Hicks (1939a) and Samuelson (1947). Macroeconomics would be dominated by *IS-LM* and its extension by Modigliani (1944). Debate, in both policy and theoretical arenas, would concern the extent to which markets should be allowed to operate freely. The 'Keynesian' theory and practice was set against a right and a left:

- on the right, classical arguments that were first re-asserted, with panache and vigour, in Hayek's *The Road to Serfdom* (1944) re-emerged; and
- on the left, a more extended 'Keynesian' position was defined by Beveridge's *Full Employment in a Free Society* (1944).

In this way 'Keynesian' economics was opposed to the market; whereas Keynes's position was that monetary reform arrangements would facilitate a more optimal operation of the market. With the new debate invented, the difficult debate with Keynes's theory and policy was entirely avoided. Moreover, participants were able – as many did – to claim an importance to the debate without taking a firm or even unambiguous stance themselves.

Policy and theoretical positions had an institutional character. Prior to the *General Theory*, opposition to Keynes was centred at the LSE. Hayek was brought from Austria to bolster the attack. After the *General Theory*, the 'Keynesian' position emerged from Oxford. Henderson moved from his Treasury post to All Souls in Oxford. Beveridge, Hicks and Kaldor all left LSE to end up and be 'converted' to the 'Keynesian' cause in Oxford. London School of Economics itself remained the bastion of the classical cause. Cambridge was, and remained, the only true home of Keynes's economics (though strong opposition resided there as well). After the war Keynes's bitterest rivals took the leading economics posts. Robertson became Professor of Political Economy at Cambridge, Henderson at Oxford and Robbins at LSE.

The discussion in this chapter traces the critical contributions that served to promote this theoretical and policy agenda. First, the core textbooks of teaching after the Second World War are examined. Second, a series of statements in articles in the *EJ* published very shortly after the end of the Second World War are detailed. Contributing to this series were the new leaders of economics in Britain: Robertson, Robbins and Henderson. The series addressed several perspectives at the same time. First, the authors sought to undermine the cheap-money policy of the British Labour Government. The British historian Ben Pimlott has observed in connection with this work:

> In weighing the criticisms which began to spread from the academic community just as Labour's extraordinary programme of reform reached its peak...we should consider how far the ideal society sought by the elected Government and the vision of Dalton's most expert critics coincided, and whether indeed they were compatible. (Pimlott, 1995, p. 475)

Second, the 'Keynesian' policy perspective was promoted. Third, in line with the new debate, this promotion of the 'Keynesian' perspective was opposed to a revival of the classical position on both theory and policy. Fourth, the authors sought to enfeeble the 'economist' as a commentator on practical policy.

Those of Keynes's colleagues who were genuine followers maintained a low-key protest against the development of 'Keynesian' economics. Only occasionally was the full truth of what was occurring to Keynes's message uttered, but the sum of these contributions undoubtedly rejects the 'Keynesian' agenda in its entirety. These contributions are examined.

Finally, the discussion turns to the new generation of economists who continue to oppose the 'Keynesian' interpretation from the margins of the profession.

Facilitating and perpetuating this transition was, and perhaps up to a point *is*, an academic environment of a special character: first, a journal system that permits the selection of papers according to less than complete intellectual rigour; second, the endorsement of certain books through 'friendly' reviews in key journals; third, the creation of a 'taught consensus' that refers only to one strand of literature and ignores any opposition that might exist; and fourth, rewarding the pursuit of the agenda so established through promotions, prestigious posts and awards – none greater or more ostentatious than the so-called 'Nobel Prize' for economics.[1]

10.2 The taught consensus

Critical to the 'Keynesian' counter-revolution was the development and promotion of a 'taught consensus'. Through textbooks, for over half a century, economists would be indoctrinated to an acceptable economics set within acceptable parameters of debate. Any dissent was extinguished by omission or trivialisation.

The debate was first divided into two. First, the validity of the use of public works expenditure as a stabilisation tool was the research project underpinning 'macroeconomics'. Second, the restoration of utility and welfare was the research programme underpinning 'microeconomics'. This compartmentalisation was opposed to the main thrust of Keynes's economics, where the paradoxical interactions between individual behaviour and aggregate activity were central elements of the theoretical story.

On both sides of the Atlantic, textbooks were provided by leading 'Keynesians', put together before, during and after the war. The teaching of microeconomics was based on Hicks's *Value and Capital* (1939a) and Samuelson's graduate level *Foundations of Economic Analysis* (1947). The teaching of macroeconomics was defined by Samuelson's *Economics: An Introductory Analysis* (1948).[2] No British macro text gained a similar status until Lipsey's *An Introduction to Positive Economics* (1963), but Cairncross's *Introduction to Economics* (1944) covered very similar ground and preceded Samuelson by four years.

Crudely put, the macroeconomic texts were obviously more important to the immediate future of 'Keynesian' economics, but the microeconomic texts were more important to the future of economics in the longer term. Both Samuelson and Cairncross covered very similar ground. Starting from Robbins's definition of economics as the problem of the allocation of scarce resources, both covered a great deal of elementary microeconomics. The discussion of macroeconomics 'proper' came at the end of both books. A 'Keynesian' theory was set out, centred on the relation between saving, investment and income (the approach was discussed in more detail in Chapter 8 as the 'output-adjustment approach'). The key points can be simply stated:

- saving and investment decisions are independent, and hence might not 'match';
- investment is lumpy;
- saving is determined by the MPC; and
- saving and investment are brought together (or into equilibrium) by changes in income/output.

Samuelson introduced the 'Keynesian cross' to solve the consequent linear relations, with liquidity preference diminished through its not being a necessary component of the basic structure. Both books go on to undermine the role of the rate of interest, and attribute only limited control to the state, for example:

> The State has comparatively little *direct* control over long-term rates of interest. . . . But in the main, the State is forced to influence long-term rates *indirectly* by Bank Rate policy. Now Bank Rate policy, as we have seen, generally affects only short-term rates of interest, and even a very large change in short-term rates will be ineffective in producing a comparable change in long-term rates. . . . (Cairncross, 1944, p. 410)

Samuelson goes further to add that even if rates are lowered, 'A number of questionnaire studies of businessmen's behaviour suggest that the level of the interest rate is not an important factor in their investment decisions' (Samuelson, 1948, p. 353). Lastly both books look to fiscal policy, but even then the approach is lukewarm; and both claim only limited power for economics as a force for substantial social change.[3]

At the same time, economics branched out into the new directions that continue to define the subject today. Hicks's *The Social Framework* (1942b) set the study of economics in the framework of the 'National Accounts' (which had seen developments under Keynes's impetus in the 1930s, and were refined substantially during the war). Even more significantly, the post-war era saw the full emergence of econometrics. Arguably, the LoN were the driving force behind this development. Jan Tinbergen's *Statistical Testing of Business-Cycle Theories* (1938) was the result of the second phase of the LoN economic work; he tested the theories that Haberler had outlined in *Prosperity and Depression*. The work established the techniques of building and estimating models of macroeconomies. In the preface handsome thanks were offered to Robertson: 'who has ungrudgingly put his time at the disposal of the League for the purpose of consultation with Professor Tinbergen on the economic issues involved' (Tinbergen, 1938, p. 10). Lastly, monetary economics became a separate discipline at LSE,[4] served in part by Sayers's *Modern Banking*. First published in 1938 (with a steady series of revisions to 1967), the work is detailed and technical. Despite its publication just after the *General Theory*, it avoids any mention of Keynes or of any controversy associated with the gold standard and the monetary crises of the 1930s. The book is set in an abstract scholarly context with no history, precedent or context. There is no mention of Keynes's detailed and groundbreaking work on money in the *Treatise*, or on the developments in the *General Theory*. Occasionally, the author betrays his prejudice: 'At the other extreme have been monetary cranks who sometimes, and especially at times of trade depression, gain the public ear by imputing to the operations of bankers most of the ills of our economic society' (Sayers, 1967, p. 197).

10.3 The post-war *Economic Journal*

For a brief period after the war, monetary reform continued to be the official policy of Government. The first-ever majority Labour Government in British history began to pursue the cheap-money policy that was set out in the *Report* of the NDE. Keynes stayed on as advisor to the Treasury, on Dalton's request, and began to advise on the conduct of cheap money. But almost directly after Keynes's death, Dalton found his policy in difficulty. 'The forces against me, in the City and elsewhere, were very powerful and determined, ... I felt I could not count on a good chance of victory. I was not well armed. So I retreated' (Dalton, 1954, p. 239).

Academic economists began a public attack on the cheap-money policy. In June 1947, Hicks raised the spectre of inflation and looked to arguments for the re-assertion of interest-rate policy as a stabilisation tool (see Section 7.8). Henderson followed up with an alarmist piece in the next issue of the *EJ*. In 'Cheap Money and the Budget', he argued that the pressure of aggregate demand could not 'be allowed to persist indefinitely without disaster' (Henderson, 1947, p. 265). He sought to undermine both the feasibility and the purpose of Dalton's cheap-money policies:

> A few months ago there was a disposition among financial experts to lay much if not most of the blame for this over-strong aggregate demand upon the cheap money policy of the Chancellor of the Exchequer. . . . Well, my personal opinion is that the cheap money policy has only been a very minor factor in the inflationary complex, so unimportant relatively to other factors as to be scarcely worth considering; and yet I am convinced that Mr. Dalton has carried this policy much too far. I do not believe that it will be possible to keep interest rates down over the next few years at anywhere near the low level of a few months ago; and I fear that it will prove that in trying to establish a long-term rate of $2^1/2\%$,

or even less, Mr. Dalton may have missed the opportunity of turning a large part of what is now either floating or comparatively short-term debt into really long-dated securities on a 3% basis.

I see no good reason to suppose that the strength of demand in the general economic system would be materially reduced by somewhat tighter conditions in the money market, or by somewhat higher interest rates, whether short or long. I do not believe that a single industrialist or trader would be deterred thereby from a single act of real investment, whether this be the purchase of additional stocks of materials or the renewal or extension of his plant. (ibid., pp. 265–6)

Alongside his attacking the monetary initiatives, Henderson bolstered the case for public works, endorsing home, school and hospital building (Henderson, 1947, p. 268). In the next issue, Robertson endorsed the notion of planning through addressing:

...a widespread and growing conviction that its [the post-war economy's] completion requires something called a National Plan – that for the purpose of effecting it our country must become or remain something which, by contrast with our pre-war arrangements, can fairly be described as a Planned Economy. (Robertson, 1947, p. 422)

He chose to put matters in the context of the debate that post-war economics permitted:

... the question of how far we want to modify the distribution of income which the free play of economic forces would bring about.... how far the satisfaction of wants should be organised *communally* instead of being left to the operation of the market. (ibid., p. 434)

In the following year, Robertson gave his 'What has happened to the rate of interest?' lecture (Section 7.8). Then in 1949 he sought to offer a clearer steer for the agenda of academic economics. This steer was offered in part as a response to Hawtrey's (1946)'The Need for Faith' which had looked to enfeeble his science:

It is a paradox that, as Economic Science has progressed, it seems to have become less authoritative. The authority which economists possessed in public affairs a century ago is neither claimed by them nor conceded by the public. They waver in their advocacy, and retire or compromise apologetically when challenged

...

I am by no means proposing to commend unyielding faith of that kind to economists. They should undoubtedly be ready at all times to revise their opinions and theories in the light, not only of fresh experience and fresh facts, but of fresh reasoning and criticism. (Hawtrey, 1946, p. 351)

Robertson (1949) first re-iterated the role for economics in assessing the validity of public works. Second, he made a case for the return of utility and welfare:

As I understand it, the concept of measurable utility, after going through a rough patch, has now been pretty firmly re-established on its throne....

. . .

... [W]hat I am trying to suggest is that the concept of economic welfare is solid and substantial enough to give the economist plenty to think about, ... (Robertson, 1949, pp. 506–7)

Robertson closed the paper echoing Hawtrey's view, as well as the view emerging in textbooks, on the economist's role in public affairs:

But in the last resort I want him, too, to be rather humble – humbler than some of his great predecessors were disposed to be – content to bow to the judgement of the prophets or even the men of affairs if he is convinced that his case has been properly understood and fairly weighted. (ibid., p. 509)

It is scarcely plausible that 'great predecessor' referred to anyone but Keynes. The economists stood aside as the 'men of affairs' dismantled the instruments of monetary reform that he had spent 35 years fighting for.[5]

10.4   The 'discovery' of classical economics

But matters did not stand still for long. The 'Keynesians' themselves completed their betrayal by re-building the classical theory. The 'historic' contributions of Solow, Samuelson and Modigliani began the reversion to a macroeconomics based on classical microeconomic behaviour.

Modigliani started things off, in his own words:

Between 1952 and 1954, Richard Brumberg and I wrote . . . 'Utility Analysis and the Consumption Function: An Interpretation of Cross-Section Data' (1954) . . . Our purpose was to show that the well-established empirical regularities could be accounted for in terms of rational, utility-maximizing, consumers allocating optimally their resources to consumption over their life . . . (Modigliani, 1984, p. 299)

In doing so, he dismissed the already bastardised 'Keynesian' theory of consumption and substituted time-preference, that is, the rate of saving determined by the interest rate.

Then Solow's 'A Contribution to the Theory of Economic Growth' (1956) set out the 'model of long-run growth' that is the foundation of modern macroeconomics and is known to all students as the Solow growth model. More specifically, he restored the saving constraint and its priority over investment.

Samuelson's 'An Exact Consumption-Loan Model of Interest with or without the Social Contrivance of Money' (1958) restored a real theory of interest. The paper claimed a 'complete general equilibrium solution to the determination of the time shape of interest rates' (Samuelson, 1958, p. 467) based on intergenerational transfers, and paved the way 'for a rigorous attack on a simple model involving money as a store of value and medium of exchange' (ibid.).

Diamond (1965) then brought the intergenerational and growth models together. The introduction of a government sector allowed increased public expenditure to cause interest rates to rise, given the newly restored saving constraint; this reinvention of what used to be known as the 'Treasury view' became newly labelled as 'crowding out' (following Poole, 1970).

In the same year, Cass (1965) fully resurrected the Ramsey model; and so brought together Solow's production perspective and Modigliani's approach to consumption through inter-temporal utility maximisation. Ramsey's paper, written in 1928, contained the essence of all of the elements of the revival of classical economics so richly rewarded by Nobel Prizes.

In parallel, Samuelson and Solow set in motion the textbook story of the demise of their own 'Keynesian' counter-revolution. Their 'The Problem of Achieving and Maintaining a Stable Price Level: Analytical Aspects of Anti-Inflation Policy' (1960), condensed 'Keynesianism' into the 'Phillips curve'.[6] The profession stood by and watched all of Keynes's genius transformed into a simple mechanical relationship that related inflation to the level of unemployment. Policy was directed to exploit the claimed 'trade-off'. When the relationship broke down in the period of 'stagflation', as common sense and Keynes (in Chapter 21 of the *General Theory*) tell us that it would, 'Keynesian' economics was dismissed. The reality of the dismissal of 'Keynesianism' was, of course, far more complex; but for present generations of economists, only the textbook version is important:

> The Phillips curve seemed the answer to the problem of choosing macroeconomic policy in the 1960s, when Keynesian economics was at its most fashionable.... By selecting fiscal and monetary policy, the government could determine the level of aggregate demand and the extent of involuntary unemployment.... Something happened to the Phillips curve. (Begg *et al.*, 1991, pp. 506–7)

With the Phillips curve 'revealed' to be vertical, the stage was set for the modern position that has a short run based on *IS-LM* 'Keynesianism' and the long run taken from Ramsey. While Friedman is credited with the classical counter-revolution, the 'Keynesians' provided not only the target but also the long run to which Friedman appealed. This had already been conceded in their macroeconomic growth theory, newly given microeconomic foundations. Over a quarter of a century later, the 'contributions' listed in this section continue to constitute the foundation for modern macroeconomic teaching.

10.5 The counter-counter-revolutionaries

The 'Keynesian' counter-revolution was consistently and robustly opposed from the moment it began, despite the textbook portrayal of a harmonious evolution of consensus. The centre of opposition was Cambridge. That those who were widely recognised as Keynes's closest colleagues opposed 'Keynesianism' is in itself a further and substantial statement against the validity of the 'Keynesian' interpretation that has been too easily ignored.[7] Others in both Britain and the United States added their voices. We should not forget either that those opposing 'Keynesianism' were economists of the highest calibre.

Considerations of space preclude a detailed discussion of this 'resistance', but the following paragraphs offer illustrative examples of the nature of the opposition. In my view the most consistent and truest critic was Richard Kahn, who had, of course, previously been Keynes's closest theoretical confidant. However, of all the critics, Kahn's critique was the lowest key: ' . . . rarely did he come out in the battlefront' (Pasinetti, 1987, p. 2).

Kahn's first reaction to the counter-revolution was a commentary on planning. In 'Professor Meade on Planning' (1949) he drew attention to the equivocal stance of those who seemed to be advocating such initiatives: 'The appearance of yet another book about planning inevitably provokes the question whether its authoritative and distinguished author is "for" or "against"' (Kahn, 1949, p. 1).

But his most important comments were on monetary theory. His 1954 'Some Notes on Liquidity Preference' defended and developed Keynes's theory of interest. The article was aimed primarily at rejecting Hicks's *Value and Capital* perspective on the rate of interest, a perspective he attributed to 'Keynesian' economists:

"To say that the rate of interest on perfectly safe securities is determined by nothing else but uncertainty of future interest rates seems to leave interest hanging by its own bootstraps." In this famous passage Professor Hicks expressed his dislike of bootstraps. He sought to find a line of escape, based on explaining long-term rates of interest "in terms of speculation on the future course of the short rate," rather than of the long-term rate itself. The same line of escape has been explored by Mr. Kalecki, Mr. Kaldor, and others. (Kahn, 1954, p. 229).

He re-iterated Keynes's own comment – regarding this 'modern approach to the theory of the rate of interest which is alternative to Keynes' as 'heresy' (ibid., p. 255).

He made equally important statements concerning interest rate policy. In two articles, 'The case for cheap money', in the *Financial Times* (3 and 4 June 1954) he put forward the case for monetary policy action to increase investment:

> Monetary policy is surely the answer – in the shape of cheap money and credit expansion . . . Do not present problems call for lower long-term rates of interest and for an expansionist rather than a restrictionist application of the machinery of bank credit? . . . The trouble, it appears to me, is that the seat of power has been moved back to the Bank of England. . . . It would be a terrible thing if we were to drift back to the situation of some of the inter-war period with the Bank of England subjecting the economy to a monetary stranglehold in order to avoid an excessive capital outflow.

In his October 1958 evidence to the Radcliffe Committee, in response to questioning from Sayers, he again turned to cheap money:

> If you are thinking of the difficulty of making money very cheap again in the light of the abandonment of the $2\frac{1}{2}$ per cent. regime, without asking me to express a view as to whether either then or now it would be desirable, I would say that, if it was thought desirable, it could be done; once the market realises that the authorities are serious they will dash in and help the authorities. . . . But if they really wanted $2\frac{1}{2}$ per cent., not tomorrow, but as something to aim at in the near future, I certainly believe that they could get it, provided that they did not mind how much the quantity of money went up in the process. (Cmnd. 837, 1960, para. 10993)

Twenty years later (1977), in *Lloyds Bank Review*, Kahn challenged an article by Mr Walter Eltis entitled 'The Failure of the Keynesian Conventional Wisdom':

> [H]e is not really attacking a defect in *The General Theory*. In effect, he is attacking 'vulgar Keynesians', who think of Keynes almost exclusively as the author of 'Can Lloyd George Do It?' (published in 1929), in which, jointly with Hubert Henderson, he advocated public works as a means of reducing unemployment.
>
> . . .
>
> . . . Keynes, in his *General Theory*, writes very little about public expenditure as a means of increasing employment. His main concern was that private investment should be adequately stimulated by low rates of interest. (Kahn, 1978, p. 2)

In the same year, Kahn was offered the opportunity to present a series of lectures as 'an exercise in the development of thought, culminating in the completion of Keynes' *General Theory*' (Kahn, 1984, p. xvii). These Mattioli Lectures – published in 1984 as *The Making of the General Theory* – addressed Keynes's work in a detailed, albeit rather oblique, way. At the broadest theoretical and practical levels, his comments on *IS-LM* and 'Keynesian' policy are perhaps most fundamental. In a section entitled 'Misconceptions about the *General Theory*', he addressed the inadequacy of the 'Keynesian' portrayal of Keynes's policy and theory:

> 1) The book [*General Theory*] contains almost no references to international trade and the problem of reconciling an acceptable balance of payments with a high level of activity. And yet in Keynes' more practical writings this problem was uppermost in his mind. Very often it took the form of regarding excessive overseas lending as part of the cause of the country's troubles, both because, if in excess of the current account balance of payments, it resulted in a loss of monetary reserves, and because, to avoid this, the necessary rise in rates of interest had a discouraging effect on domestic investment and so caused unemployment.
>
> Keynes did develop this theme in 'Notes on Mercantilism', his penultimate chapter on a number of historical topics. At the very end of the book he wrote that 'if nations can learn to provide themselves with full employment by their domestic policy [...] there need be no important economic forces calculated to set the interest of one country against that of its neighbours', each country's exports benefiting from the other countries' high level of activity.
>
> The world has still to accept this simple lesson taught by Keynes.
>
> 2) Only in one passage did Keynes advocate the policy with which his name still is so closely associated – largely as a result of *Can Lloyd George Do It?* – 'loan expenditure' by public authorities as a means of sustaining employment if other means fail . . .
>
> . . .
>
> . . . The behaviour of the economy is an immensely complicated subject. The diagrams and bits of algebra in the text-books up to the present day have often led to the difficulties being submerged, and incidentally to Keynes being discredited.
>
> For example, both in his exposition of the liquidity preference theory of the rate of interest and in his exposition of the inducement to invest, Keynes made use of schedules – simple relationships between two parameters, one of the rate of interest in both cases – which could be represented by a curve or by a piece if algebra of the type $y = f(x)$. And yet Keynes' insistence on the overwhelming importance of expectations,

highly subject to risk and uncertainty, was one of his biggest contributions. This completely undermines the prevalent idea – for which Keynes' attempt at simplification is responsible – that such schedules can be regarded as stable relationships handed down from heaven. (Kahn, 1984, pp. 158–9)

But the most prominent and outspoken Cambridge critic was Joan Robinson. Her 'Rate of Interest' (1951) preceded Kahn and developed Keynes's position, asserting the more general proposition that the main influences on the rate of interest were social, legal and institutional factors (see quotation at the start of Chapter 1). She went on to dismiss the term-structure theory attributed to Robertson, Kaldor, Kalecki and Hicks: 'The view that the long rate can be determined solely from expectations about the short rate is untenable' (Robinson, 1951, p. 102).

Robinson used a 1962 review of a book by Harry Johnson to deliver a message to the economics profession (cited by Harcourt, 1987): 'These remarks are directed to the whole school of latter-day neo-classicals, who flourish after twenty-five years with honour and respect . . . ' (Robinson, 1962, p. 692). The piece criticised 'Keynesian' theory for having no sense of time or institutional dimension and offered this quite blunt assessment: 'But the bastard-Keynesian model is not only silly. It is seriously defective in logic' (ibid., p. 691). Her most famous attack, and the only one actually acknowledged by the mainstream, was on the classical growth models. She persistently reminded the profession that these models 'throw away the *General Theory*' by 'mak[ing] savings govern investment' (Robinson, 1961, p. 360).

But Robinson never pursued the interest rate critique with any vigour and was content to align herself with Kalecki's basically 'Keynesian' position in terms of policy. Her 1972 Ely Lecture to the American Economic Association contained the following categorical (and somewhat disheartening) statement: 'The supply of finance has an influence on these plans – cheap money makes investment easier. In my opinion, Keynes rather exaggerated the influence of the rate of interest . . . ' (Robinson, 1972, p. 4).[8]

The other Robinson, Austin, was less forthcoming. But in a lecture following the publication of the first volumes of the *CW* (which he had contributed to editing), he gave his personal view of the contemporary understanding of Keynes. He concluded as follows:

Were there greater objectives than those he set himself? To create a world monetary and financial system that could achieve adjustment without disaster to one of the parties to the adjustment; to create a world economy in which all countries all the time might be better able to use to the full their manpower and their resources. Almost all that he did, almost all that he wrote throughout his life, was devoted to those two ends. If in the process of reappraisal Keynes does not emerge as a truly great man, something, let me repeat, will have gone sadly wrong with the criteria of greatness. (E. A. G. Robinson, 1972, p. 546)

Harrod appears to have been the only Oxford scholar to be reasonably faithful to Keynes's policy line. His 1951 biography of Keynes (commissioned by Keynes's executors) remains a fine achievement. The monetary dimension was prominent and straightforward:

Most important of his contributions during this year [1930] was his article in the September issue of the *Svenska Handelsbanken Index* on the future of the rate of interest. He had become convinced that the time was ripe for a large and permanent reduction throughout the world. This was to be the basis of all his future thinking on economic policy; . . . (Harrod, 1972, p. 469)

Equally, he gave front place to the importance of cheap money in his own fairly frequent policy interventions. In 1963, in a retrospective article and his book, *The British Economy*, he deplored the widespread disregard of the theory of liquidity preference and advocated a return to a 3 per cent long-term rate of interest (Harrod, 1963a and 1963b). In a January 1964 article in *Encounter* magazine, he forcefully re-asserted the policy dimension (cited by Leijonhufvud, 1968, pp. 14–15):

Keynes always attached the utmost importance to low interest rates; he never ceased to preach them. . . . They [members of the Establishment] are being completely anti-Keynesian in regard to the matter that he held to be of the *greatest importance of all*. (Leijonhufvud's insertion and emphasis)

He was vigilant to the end, finding it necessary to emphasise that Keynes well understood the nature of the money supply in a credit economy despite the Monetarist *versus* 'Keynesian' debate suggesting otherwise (Harrod, 1970).

In the United States, Keynes was defended by a number of scholars. Leon Keyserling chaired the Council of Economic Advisers under President Truman. He was replaced when Eisenhower took office, but began to publish a steady stream of monographs against the Eisenhower administration's economic policy and mainstream economics. He devoted particular attention to the damage wrought by rising interest rates, and regarded the 1951 Federal Reserve Accord as one of the United States's greatest policy mistakes.[9] In a 1972 discussion on the 'Keynesian Revolution' he offered the following categorical message to the economics profession:

The noisy quarrel between the fiscal and monetary enthusiasts seems to me largely a misplacement of emphasis. The real travesty is that the prevalent monetary policy has fed the fat and starved the lean, restrained the essential and had little effect on the overexuberant, and since 1952 transferred more than $400 billion in the wrong direction by all economic and social criteria . . .

. . .

The time is long overdue for the American Economic Association to start to help overcome the dismal poverty of American economics, for which it and its cherished literature are so largely responsible, and to commence promoting the real purposes of the Employment Act of 1946. Let's get on the track.

I am aware that I may have offended some of your sensibilities, but I hope that I may have also appealed to your saving common sense. (Keyserling *et al.*, 1972, pp. 138–9)

Sidney Weintraub was equally alive to developments in monetary policy in the 1950s, especially with regard to the inappropriate and unjust actions of monetary policymakers: 'Economic stabilization would suffer a sharp setback if the view took root that the central banking mechanism was designed to protect bondholders from changes in capital values rather than reserved for broader conceptions of economic policy' (Weintraub, 1955, p. 296). He maintained a fairly prolific output of articles, books and book reviews that identified him as a bold defender of Keynes's intellectual tradition and opponent of the omnipresent 'Keynesian' view.

Much of his own research was concerned with developing a fuller treatment of inflation consistent with the *General Theory*. Like Harrod, as a response to the monetarist assault, he drew attention to Keynes's monetary economics: 'Undoubtedly the late Sir Dennis Robertson, and Keynes himself, would have approved the modern monetarist inscription that "money matters." Both might be astonished to learn that any economist thought otherwise' (Weintraub, 1971, p. 37).

Lastly, Abba Lerner had moved from Britain to the United States. In the late 1940s and early 1950s, he opposed the raising of the rate of interest as a solution to inflation (which he saw as caused by military expenditure) and emphasised Keynes's general position that inflation was determined by supply and demand (Lerner, 1951). But perhaps his most notable contribution was his response to Samuelson's (1958) part in the restoration of classical theory. He rejected the approach in a robust and rigorous attack that is equally relevant today. He could not argue with the rigour of Samuelson's mathematical analysis, but challenged the relevance of the mathematical technique and its relevance to economic thought:

Meanwhile, in the philosophical speculations the imagination is set free from any responsibility for rigorousness of thought, since it can shrug its shoulders and point to the mathematics, which displays all the rigour that one could ask for. (Lerner, 1959a, p. 518)

I owe an apology to Professor Samuelson. In his article he answers a different question from the one I thought he was answering, and his answer is the correct one for his question. But he is answering the wrong question – wrong, that is, if one is to expect it to be fruitful for economics. (Lerner, 1959b, p. 523)

10.6 The 'Keynesian' retraction

In the 1970s and 1980s, some of the British 'Keynesians' effectively conceded the validity of their critics' arguments. In the introduction to his 1977 *Economic Perspectives*, Hicks made the following – astonishing – retraction:

What in Keynes corresponds to my *week* is his *short period*. Like my week, it has a past and a future. Its past is embodied in its given initial capital; its future is represented by given expectations, which are wrapped up in his Marginal Efficiency of Capital schedule. ... It was this formal model of Keynes which I myself summarised in the ISLM diagram. There is indeed much more in the *General Theory* of Kenyes [sic] than this formal model, and very much more in some of Keynes's other writings, which can quite properly be used to elucidate his work. (Hicks, 1977, p. viii)

He thus redefined *IS-LM* – rightly according to the argument here – as depicting matters in a given state of expectation. He did not, however, go as far as pointing out that the potential for a state of expectation to change was one of the fundamental contributions and causal mechanisms of the *General Theory*. Ten years later both Meade and Kaldor conceded the same point in interviews with Warren Young:

I saw it [*IS-LM*] as a general consistent structure; a determined system given expectations. And of course Maynard Keynes was very insistent that expectations were very variable. But given expectations, I saw it as a coherent system of simultaneous determination in a macro situation... (Meade interview, Young, 1987, p. 15)

What is wrong with the IS-LM diagram is that it regards investment as a single valued function of these two variables, income and interest, whereas this is only true if the structure of expectations is given ... But this is something which can vary and is very capricious in its variations ... (Kaldor interview, ibid., pp. 112–14)

In the winter 1980–81 number of *The Journal of Post Keynesian Economics*, Hicks published 'ISLM: an Explanation'. He finally and grudgingly conceded the contrast between Keynes's and the 'Keynesian' treatment of the rate of interest (albeit in a footnote to the final sentence of the article):

> It is well known that in later developments of Keynesian theory, the long-term rate of interest (which does figure, excessively, in Keynes' own presentation and is presumably represented by the *r* of the diagram) has been taken down a peg from the position it appeared to occupy in Keynes. (Hicks, 1980–81, p. 153)

But such confessions were set against the advent of monetarism. The 'Keynesians' had permitted Keynes to be discarded; it was hardly a large gesture to concede, only then, the invalidity of their own construct.

10.7 The emergence of post-Keynesianism

As has been seen throughout the theoretical discussion in Part II, from the 1960s a new strand of economics had been emerging as post-Keynesian economics. This approach sought to overthrow 'Keynesianism' and to return to an economics based on the *General Theory* itself. Post-Keynesian scholars gave increased emphasis to monetary policy and the nature of money. Uncertainty was restored as a key component of the wider analytical framework. These innovations were of great significance and, as already seen, have enabled the recovery and elaboration of much of Keynes's true perspective. Here, however, I want to discuss how elements of the analysis were, or later became, regressive in terms of Keynes's original theory. From a policy perspective, although interest rate policy was emphasised, this was mainly in the context of active demand management rather than as the secular necessity portrayed here. From a theoretical perspective, many post-Keynesians rejected the theory of liquidity preference. In doing so they denied the central component of Keynes's theory as well as losing the route to interest rate manipulation through debt-management policy. Lastly, while emphasising the importance of 'endogenous money' to their own theory, some post-Keynesians (in particular Kaldor and Moore) attributed a very primitive understanding of the nature of money as a means of exchange to the author of the *General Theory*.

In terms of historical development, the move away from *IS-LM* and the quest for a more substantial monetary theory might be regarded as beginning in 1965, two years after Harrod's forthright re-assertion of the importance of the rate of interest. Two contributions were of particular interest: Davidson's (1965) 'Keynes's Finance Motive', which attempted to incorporate Keynes's neglected finance motive into the *IS-LM* framework; and Clower's (1965) 'The Keynesian Counter-Revolution: A Theoretical Appraisal' that challenged the 'applicability to macroeconomics of the neo-Walrasian system of counting equations and unknowns' (Chick, 1992, p. 55).

Leijonhufvud's *On Keynesian Economics and the Economics of Keynes* (1968) developed Clower's position and gave prominence to the notion that 'Keynesian' and Keynes's economics were different. On matters of policy, he cited Harrod on interest rates. The book captured and held the attention of the profession in a manner denied to the longer-standing Cambridge opposition.[10] The spotlight then returned to Davidson, whose *Money and the Real World* (1972) would constitute a manifesto for post-Keynesian economics that for many remains unchallenged. Again the work was not set in the context of the long-standing opposition to the 'Keynesian' construct detailed above, but stressed Leijonhuvfud's precedence.[11]

The new line of thought also led to a revised historical interpretation of Keynes's policy interest. Howson and Moggridge (1974), explicitly motivated by Leijonhufvud's and Davidson's books, introduced the world to a new Keynes. In line with the post-Keynesian perspective, this Keynes regarded monetary policy as a powerful instrument to be used when the situation required.

Additional impetus came in 1978 from the founding of *The Journal of Post Keynesian Economics*. Kaldor re-emerged, aided and abetted by Basil Moore (see Chapter 7, n. 35), as the leading proponent of 'endogenous money' and opponent of monetarism (Kaldor, 1986; Moore, 1979). As discussed in the previous section, a number of other 'Keynesian' economists also distanced themselves from *IS-LM* and lined up with the uncertainty/monetary post-Keynesian perspective.

But, as Chick (1992, p. 57)[12] argued, 'Clower's analysis is neoclassical in structure and thus unable to illuminate the nature of the Keynesian Revolution'. Similarly, Weintraub (1982, p. 422) observed that Leijonhufvud's 'creative fame [was] less in setting Keynes's theory right than in scuttling the mischievous Keynesian versions'. Furthermore, Howson and Moggridge have hardly been evangelical. Their new Keynes does not obviously emerge from Moggridge's (1992) biography. While Howson has gone on to a number of detailed studies of monetary policy in the first half of the twentieth century, she has not advocated the policy position she implicitly attributes to Keynes. Lastly, Davidson's and Kaldor's post-Keynesianism has led to a policy consensus that is little different – if more plausibly justified – than that of the mainstream. Demand management by both monetary and fiscal means is seemingly accepted by the great majority of the economics profession. And there is no shortage of triumphalism about this happy outcome. If the fuller analysis in this thesis is correct, the need to manage demand only scratches the surface of Keynes's economics and misses the considerations related to the long-term rate of interest that I regard – and I think Keynes regarded – as having the most important bearing on prosperity and sustainability.

10.8   Keynes's economics re-emerges

Nevertheless, post-Keynesian economics has an underlying validity in its treatment of money and uncertainty entirely absent from the *IS-LM* version. And from this starting point, other post-Keynesian economists have pursued their own, often quite individual, lines of thought to restore much of the genuine Keynes.

The present author considers that the work here belongs to the post-Keynesian tradition that perhaps originated with Minsky and has been pursued and developed by Jörg Bibow, Victoria Chick and Sheila Dow. These scholars adhere to a theory of economic activity that encompasses both liquidity preference and endogenous money (in the manner examined in Chapter 7). The most substantial difference between their work and the work here concerns the policies I have attributed to Keynes and, following from this, a development of their depiction of liquidity-preference theory in line with these policies. The importance of using debt-management and monetary policy to achieve permanently low rates of interest across the spectrum as a means to allow economic activity to thrive has not been fully restored. From a methodological perspective this follows a shortcoming in this post-Keynesian restoration of expectations. The treatment and analysis of uncertainty has not led to a recognition that expectations can be manipulated. The manipulation of expectation offers policymakers the ability to harness uncertainty and through this, economic activity itself. Taking this small step, much of Keynes's policy perspective can be restored.

Finally, there are those who are perhaps not wholly consistent with the Chick/Dow/Bibow theoretical tradition but who have emphasised the monetary dimension of Keynes's policies. John Smithin has perhaps put matters most clearly.[13]

This view [that Keynes's policy was not just a 'counter-cyclical fine-tuning strategy'] is also consistent with the idea that Keynesian policy should be particularly identified with 'cheap money' or low interest rates. More specifically, though Keynes and many of the early Keynesian writers did not make much distinction between real and nominal interest rates, Smithin and Wolf (1993: 373) have argued that in contemporary conditions 'Keynesian' policies should generally be associated with attempts to bring about low real rates of interest on financial instruments. Although this point may not be stressed in the standard textbooks it can none the less be argued that this is the interpretation which is most consistent with Keynes's own writing. It is supported, for example, by Kaldor (1986: xxi) and at the other end of the professional spectrum by Meltzer (1988), in a book length study. (Smithin, 1996, p. 57)

His references to Kaldor and Meltzer lead to the following:

> The appearance of Keynes's *General Theory* in 1936 gave the [UK] cheap money policy [in the first half of the 1930s] its theoretical underpinning. The policy of low interest rates was maintained throughout the war the Government borrowed enormous sums, at very low interest rates, not only on short-term but also in medium and long-term paper, without the slightest difficulty. (Kaldor, 1986, p. xxi, by permission of Oxford University Press)

> He [Keynes] favoured policies to reduce interest rates to the level at which investment would absorb saving at full employment. That rate, he believed, would bring interest rates to zero in a generation. This is the correct interpretation, I believe, of Keynes's statements favouring lower interest rates. (Meltzer, 1988, p. 280)

In Harcourt's and Riach's *A 'Second Edition' of The General Theory*, Skidelsky, writing as if he were Keynes, offers this evaluation:

> Nothing I wrote has been subject to more misinterpretation than the sentence: 'I conceive... that a somewhat comprehensive socialisation of investment will prove the only means of securing an approximation to full employment.' This was widely understood as a call for the State to take over the accumulation function from the private sector by methods which included the nationalization of industry. It was supported by the alleged interest-inelasticity of investment – a doctrine I was also supposed to uphold, despite the *fact* that *all* my theoretical writings, including *The General Theory*, were directed to the problem of securing a reduction in the rate of interest. (Skidelsky, 1997, pp. 432–3, my emphasis)

In the second volume of his biography of Keynes, after the passage that opens the first chapter of this book, Skidelsky adds: 'For today, in truth, there is little left of Keynes's vision, only some crumbling bones of scholasticism, disinterred for first-year macroeconomics students' (Skidelsky, 1992, p. 502).

Notes

1. On the fourth point, the converse was/is the marginalisation and belittling of those not pursuing the consensus path, a process well documented by Lee (2004).
2. Victoria Chick tells me that later Ackley (1961) was important; and that Minsky used to refer to a Keynes 'entombed in Ackley'.
3. 'Incompatible' textbooks were sidelined. Lorie Tarshis's (1947) *The Elements of Economics* encountered great opposition at Stanford. 'The National Economic Council published an essay saying that *The Elements of Economics* "plays upon fear, shame, pity, greed, idealism, hope.... This is not an

economics text at all; it is a pagan-religious and political tract"'. (Source: Stanford University News Release on Tarshis's death in October 1993: *http://www.stanford.edu/dept/news/pr/93/931011Arc3112.html*; thanks to Geoff Harcourt for drawing my attention to this.)

4. In part this had its roots in the need at the LSE to break economics up into separate departments to accommodate the professorial qualifications of several of its members. The tradition at the time was to have only one Professor *per* department. Members of Economics Analytical and Descriptive (Robbins's Department) regularly ridiculed the theory of money until the rise of monetarism, and asserted that 'money did not matter' in 'Keynesian' economics.

5. In the United States, journal articles developed the same themes as in Britain: see 'Full Employment in a Free Society', a review article of Beveridge (1944) by Arthur Smithies (1945); 'Is a Rise in Interest Rates Desirable or Inevitable?' by Lawrence H. Seltzer (1945); 'The Future of "Keynesian" Economics' by David McCord Wright (1945); and 'The Changing Significance of the Interest Rate' by Henry C. Wallich (1946). The penultimate page of the latter included a footnote: 'In the long run, I have no doubt but that economic forces rather than policy are determining for the level of interest rates.'

6. Thus, traducing Phillips as well as Keynes. See Desai (1975) and Corry (2002).

7. Two who did not contribute to the opposition but were firmly on Keynes's side were Townshend and Shove. Gerald Shove died in 1947, the year after Keynes. Hugh Townshend appears to have given up making contributions to economics in 1940.

8. I have not followed the work of Kalecki in this section because he also aimed away from monetary conclusions. Jan Toporowski tells me that this was because he did not believe that capitalism could be 'fixed' by monetary means.

9. Cited by Brazelton (1997), to whom I am grateful for drawing to my attention the importance of Keyserling's work.

10. For example, Solow's (1984) retreat from the 'Keynesian' position gave Leijonhufvud a role but gave no mention to Kahn despite the publication of *The Making of the General Theory* in the same year.

11. He gave generous tribute to his 'mentor' Weintraub; but Weintraub's role as predecessor to the post-Keynesian view was confined to footnotes, whereas Leijonhufvud was central to the main text on the opening page.

12. Originally published in June 1978 in the *Australian Economics Papers* as 'The nature of the Keynesian revolution: a re-assessment'.

13. See also papers by Moore, and Lavoie and Seccareccia, in Hamouda and Smithin (1988). From a history-of-thought perspective, Blaug's (1990) interview with Reddaway and Booth's (1989) discussion both emphasise the importance of interest-rate policy.

11
The *General Theory* and the 'Facts of Experience'

11.1 The *General Theory* and practical policy

Neglecting Keynes's warnings on the opening page of the *General Theory* proper, Modigliani, Samuelson and Solow fostered a return to the classical theory:

> I have called this book the *General Theory of Employment, Interest and Money*, placing the emphasis on the prefix *general*. The object of such a title is to contrast the character of my arguments and conclusions with those of the *classical* theory of the subject, upon which I was brought up and which dominates the economic thought, both practical and theoretical, of the governing and academic classes of this generation, as it has for a hundred years past. I shall argue that the postulates of the classical theory are applicable to a special case only and not to the general case, the situation which it assumes being a limiting point of the possible positions of equilibrium. Moreover, the characteristics of the special case assumed by the classical theory happen not to be those of the economic society in which we actually live, with the result that its teaching is misleading and disastrous if we attempt to apply it to the facts of experience. (*CW* VII, p. 3)

Nevertheless, despite this critically positioned warning, Keynes's discussion was never explicit about the specific nature of, and reason for, this disaster that the application of the classical theory could cause. Perhaps the fullest statement came in Chapter 23:

> Under the influence of this faulty theory the City of London gradually devised the most dangerous technique for the maintenance of equilibrium which can possibly be imagined, namely, the technique of bank rate coupled with a rigid parity of the foreign exchanges. For this meant that the objective of maintaining a domestic rate of interest consistent with full employment was wholly ruled out. (*CW* VII, p. 339)

But this quotation illustrates what I regard as a significant problem: a blurred distinction between the short-term and long-term rates of interest. The discussion in this chapter sets out an interpretation of economic events based in part on clarifying the roles of the two rates of interest. It is argued that Keynes did not make this sufficiently explicit, though this may have followed from his desire only to touch on business-cycle processes. While the *General Theory* was, of course, fundamentally motivated by the events of the 1920s and early 1930s, in particular the prolonged high unemployment in Britain and then the Great Depression, Keynes did not explain these events in the light of his theory. The long-term interest rate was identified as the cause of the Economic Problem, but the specific processes at work beyond this general cause were not detailed. In addition to this, the confusion must have been compounded by his earlier work giving greater prominence to the role of the discount rate under the gold standard.

In this chapter certain economic events are explained as a consequence of the interaction between policies on short- and long-term interest rates. The analysis is conducted at a general level; events are regarded as having a significant international dimension, though, with aspects of country-by-country performance of interest through certain periods. This follows from the long-term rate of interest being an international phenomenon. Domestic policy might vary significantly from country to country at any point in time, but all countries remain subject to the same underlying forces determined by the long-term rate of interest. Most obviously a country or group of countries recording outstanding growth relative to others will only do so for a temporary – though quite possibly very prolonged – period.

Before this discussion, Section 11.2 characterises the movements of the long-term rate of interest over the course of the twentieth century. According to my interpretation of the *General Theory*, these movements amount to a fundamental condition for the extent of economic activity that can prevail in market economies.

In the historical discussion, special emphasis is given to events following financial liberalisation in the 1970s–80s. Reports by the Bank for International Settlements (BIS) and the International Labour Organisation (ILO) are used to illustrate the financial, economic and social instability that has dominated the last quarter of a century. Finally, the role of modern domestic monetary and international financial policies in exacerbating this situation is assessed.

11.2   The long-term rate of interest

As has been discussed in Chapter 7, the long-term rate of interest was high throughout the 1920s. Under deliberate policy, it fell during the 1930s and remained low until the end of the war. Then, in Britain specifically, under the newly elected Labour Government, the rate was reduced perhaps to its lowest-ever level in 1946. These movements hold true in both nominal and inflation-adjusted terms. Until 1980, inflation-adjusted long-term rates of interest remained relatively low. But from 1980 onwards, rates rose very rapidly and remained at a high level for the rest of the twentieth century. In the twenty-first century interest rates have fallen, but this does not follow the direct and deliberate actions of policymakers; indeed present (2006) low rates are regarded as a temporary aberration.

These movements are not extensively debated by mainstream economists. One can only surmise that this is a consequence of the dominance of the classical paradigm. The rate of interest is now regarded as primarily a consequence of activity, the exact opposite of Keynes's perspective. The long-term rate of interest has, therefore, been only of marginal and occasional interest to the profession. However, policymakers have not been blind to developments. In the early days of the modern dear-money era, the IMF assessed the movement of interest rates in the first half of the 1980s.

Perhaps the most striking and puzzling feature of monetary conditions in the major industrial countries over the past several years has been the persistence of high real interest rates, on both short-term and long-term financial instruments. These high real rates, which have no historical precedent outside periods of price decline during depressions, have persisted, despite lower inflation and the continued existence of a significant margin of economic slack. The phenomenon is quite widespread. Although real interest rates have differed across the major industrial countries, on the whole there has been less divergence of these rates, especially during 1982–84, than in previous periods.

. . .

These measures imply that real interest rates in the major industrial countries during the 1980s have been significantly higher than those that prevailed in the 1950s and early 1960s and even further above those of the 1970s. Real interest rates increased sharply during the period from 1980 to 1982 and then remained at relatively high levels in 1983 and 1984. . . . The average real short-term interest rate in the major industrial countries in 1980–84 was 5.5 per cent per annum and the average real long-term interest rate was 5.8 per cent [Figures shown here in Table 11.1]. In contrast, average real long-term interest rates for the major industrial countries during the period 1952–65 ranged from roughly 1.5 to slightly over 3 per cent per annum. The contrast is even sharper with the experiences of the late 1970s. During 1976–79, for example, the average real long-term interest rate in the major industrial countries was 0.9 per cent per annum. (IMF, 1985, pp. 123–4)

Table 11.1   Major industrial countries: Real long-term interest rates on government debt

	1977	1978	1979	1980	1981	1982	1983	1984
Canada	0.4	0.7	0.3	0.7	4.2	7.0	7.5	8.4
United States	0.9	−0.2	−0.3	2.0	6.8	8.7	8.0	9.0
Japan	3.7	3.7	1.4	4.3	6.0	6.9	6.8	6.1
France	1.6	−0.7	−2.6	0.8	2.4	6.2	5.0	5.9
Germany, Fed. Rep. of	2.7	2.0	1.0	2.9	5.0	5.8	4.9	5.4
Italy	1.6	0.2	−5.0	−3.6	−0.7	5.9	4.6	4.4
United Kingdom	2.2	1.7	−1.1	−0.1	5.5	7.3	6.1	5.8
Average, above countries	1.7	0.8	−0.3	1.9	5.4	7.5	6.8	7.4
Average, four major European countries	2.1	0.9	−1.3	0.7	3.5	6.3	5.2	5.5

Source: IMF (1985).

At the end of the twentieth century, an edition of the *Oxford Review of Economic Policy* on 'real interest rates' provided a useful overview of subsequent developments. The summary by Allsopp and Glyn (1999, pp. 3–4) assessed the figures reproduced here in Table 11.2 as follows:

> There is a widespread impression that real interest rates have been very high since 1980 in comparison with post-Second-World-War experience. The data in [Table 11.2] confirm that this is indeed the case. Short-term real interest rates, averaging nearly 4 per cent, have been much higher and a little more stable than between 1950 and 1980. The general picture is confirmed by data on long rates as well.

Most of Allsopp and Glyn's work is based on short rates, though they confirm the relation for long rates. Moreover, they do not consider explicitly the rate paid by firms for capital expenditure, except by association. They do,

Table 11.2   Real interest rates since 1950 (average of US, UK, Germany and France)

	Mean real short rate (%)	Standard deviation of real rate (%)	Inflation rate (% p.a.)	GDP growth (% p.a.)	Profit rate (%)
1951–68	0.7	2.6	3.2	4.5	15.0
1969–79	0.3	2.3	7.6	3.3	9.3
1980–97	3.8	1.9	3.0	2.1	9.3

Source: Allsopp and Glyn (1999).

however, emphasise the international nature of the phenomenon under discussion:

> So it would be wrong to think of 'the world interest rate' as much more than summarizing average experience. However, country experience has *not* been so diverse as to make such an average a misleading abstraction. (Allsopp and Glyn, 1999, p. 2)

More recently the UK Pensions Commission have produced a detailed analysis of long-term rates of interest on both government bonds and equity, hence establishing the costs of capital for government and business alike. The Commission shows time series of returns on UK gilts, fixed-rate US Treasuries and UK and US equities held for various periods over time. Table 11.3 here shows their figures for returns over 5 years. Their analysis emphasises the distinction between the returns over the whole period and the significantly higher returns after 1977.

In order to define more clearly the long-term rate of interest prevailing throughout the period between the end of the First World War and the present, I have constructed two annual time series. Figures 11.1a and 11.1b show inflation-adjusted long-term interest rates on UK government debt and US corporate bonds.

These time series, taken together with results described above, support a characterisation of interest rates as follows:

- dear money during the 1920s;
- cheapening money through the 1930s and into the Second World War;
- an era of relatively cheap money between the end of the Second World War and the 1970s;
- a period of negative real interest rates in Britain in the 1970s;
- an era of dear money from the start of the 1980s; and
- a brief period of cheaper money at the end of the twentieth and start of the twenty-first century.

Table 11.3 Mean annualised real rates of return over 5-year period

	US 1925–2003 UK 1899–2003 (%)	1977–2003 (%)
UK Gilts	1.4	7.0
US Treasuries	2.2	6.8
UK equities	5.7	10.4
US equities	7.1	10.0

Source: Pensions Commission (2004, pp. 55–63).

296

(a) UK long-term government bonds

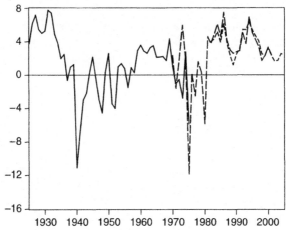

Source: Freidman and Schwartz (1982); Bank of England, Monetary and Financial Statistics; Office for National Statistics for deflator.

(b) US corporate bonds

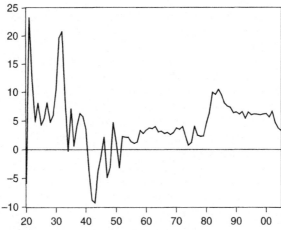

Source: Interest on Moody's BAA corporate bond from Federal Reserve website; GDP deflator from Freidman (1982) and OECD Main Economic Indicators database.

Figure 11.1 UK and US real long-term interest rates, twentieth century

11.3 An interpretation of economic events from the First World War

Prior to the *Treatise*, Keynes's pre-occupation was the manner in which the gold standard precluded a discount-rate policy appropriate to domestic requirements. Keynes only arrived at the fundamental importance of the long rate towards the end of drafting the *Treatise*, with the material consequentially positioned at the end of the work. But after the *Treatise*, as seen in Section 3.8, Keynes began a concerted and sustained effort to emphasise the long-term rate of interest. His statements at the Harris Foundation Lectures, the Macmillan Committee, in newspapers and in academic discourse were unequivocal.

In terms of interpreting economic events, in the *General Theory*, Keynes made the fundamental shift of emphasis from short- to long-term rates of interest. The theory concluded that the underlying equilibrium of a free-market economy, and hence the level of employment that prevailed, was determined by the long-term rate of interest. Equally importantly, the trade cycle was caused by a high rate of interest. But Keynes did not review the role of the short rate in the light of this change of emphasis, either in terms of policy requirements or in terms of its role in determining economic outcomes when ill-used. As outlined in Chapters 3 and 7, Keynes finally specified the policy role at the NDE. In terms of economic outcomes, Keynes never detailed the role of the short rate. But it is likely that this role is relatively simple. The costs of some company borrowing might depend directly on the short-term rate. But the most important transmission mechanism will be through effects on 'animal spirits'. Under low short-term interest rates entrepreneurs may feel optimistic about the future, expect high demand for future production, and therefore will extend capacity. In terms of Keynes's theory, persistently low short-term interest rates can *shift* the MEC to the right through changing expectations. The history that is set out in the rest of this section implies that this role is not trivial.

The characterisation of long-term rates of interest in the previous section permits a fuller re-evaluation of economic dynamics through the twentieth century. But to aid interpretation this must be complemented by an understanding of the effects of the discount-rate policies of the monetary authorities on expectations.

11.3.1 The end of the First World War through to the start of the Great Depression (1920–31)

Between the 1920s and the start of the 1930s, the US economy experienced a very rapid expansion of economic growth followed by the collapse in activity and employment that is known as the Great Depression. Most other countries saw similar, albeit less extreme, cyclical phenomena. The repercussions were felt across the world and led to the economic reforms with which this work is ultimately concerned.

The *General Theory* substantiated and formalised the conclusion Keynes first aired at the Harris Foundation Lectures: that the underlying cause of the worldwide Great Depression was the high long-term rate of interest that prevailed across the world throughout the 1920s (see Section 8.3).

The backdrop to the expansion of the US economy in the 1920s was the 'transformation of the US from debtor to the world's leading creditor nation' (Fearon, 1987, p. 15) that had occurred during the First World War. In addition to this, the United States had remained on the gold standard throughout the war. In terms of specific monetary policies, Fearon argues that in the post-war years:

> [t]he Fed, and Strong [the Chairman of the Fed] in particular, were anxious to ensure that those European countries which had abandoned the gold standard during, or shortly after, the war should return to it. In order to encourage them to do so, credit was extended to foreign central banks and US interest rates were kept low to reduce inward gold movements. (Fearon, 1987, p. 76)

The apparently sound financial conditions permitted these low discount rates to prevail without any weakening of the currency. The environment fostered high 'animal spirits' and a great expansion of investment, facilitated by freely available credit; Fearon (ibid.) characterises the period as 'the era of easy money between 1924 and 1928'. But long-term interest rates remained high (see Figure 11.1). According to the interpretation of Keynes's theory set out in Chapter 8, high long-term interest rates coupled with excessive shifts of the MEC are the conditions for extreme movements in the business cycle. As Keynes argued as early as 1931 (see Section 8.3), the private investment projects that followed from the 'extraordinary' willingness to borrow failed to yield returns to cover rates of interest that were 'extravagantly high'. Eventually the US economy collapsed in the wake of the unprecedented volume of private debt that Fisher's 'The Debt Deflation Theory of Great Depressions' (1933) indicated.[1]

In France the monetary authorities pursued a similarly easy credit policy over the second half of the 1920s. This was supported by a return to gold at only a fifth of the pre-war parity. Germany adopted a new currency, the Reichsmark, in 1924; this was followed by rapid reductions in discount rates over the next 2 years. Both economies experienced very rapid growth until just before the end of the decade, when, as in America, activity went into reverse.

In all of these economies the gold standard facilitated rather than prevented these excessive expansions. In Britain, however, the gold standard inhibited expansion. The preparation for, and return to, gold at an over-valued rate for sterling led to high short-term rates damping 'animal spirits' and the level of activity for the whole of the 1920s.

11.3.2 Depression and recovery: managed currencies and falling rates (1932–45)

Recovery for all countries was critically dependent on the initiatives of monetary reform that Keynes advocated. Unemployment data from the United Kingdom and United States, in Figure 11.2, show improvements beginning in 1933 and 1934, respectively. These followed the abandonment of the gold standard, in Britain in 1931 and in the United States in 1933, and the implementation of currency management and cheap-money policy.

(a) Britain

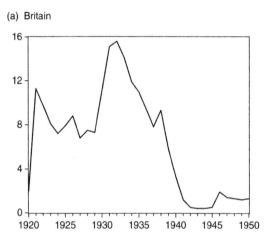

Source: Feinstein (1972).

(b) US

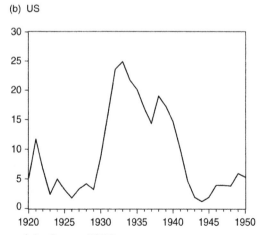

Source: US Bureau of the Census (1976).

Figure 11.2 Britain and US unemployment, 1920–50. (a) Britain. (b) US

After a brief setback in 1938, progress resumed, in part driven by preparation for war. Then, in Britain, deliberately setting the long-term interest rate at 3 per cent facilitated the successful management of the Second World War, with national resources utilised to a surely unprecedented extent.

11.3.3   Bretton Woods and post-war cheap money (1945–70)

In the light of wartime experience, at the 1945 NDE Keynes set out a detailed proposal for British monetary policy in the post-war era, just as he had tried to do for the world at Bretton Woods. While the policies were never genuinely adhered to, immediate post-war economic policy did preserve relatively low real interest rates around the world, as the figures in Section 11.2 show. Kahn has referred to the period as a 'Bastard Golden Age': 'The possibility of a Bastard Golden Age turns on the absence of any *progressive* tendency towards the easing of the state of finance, and, more particularly, towards a lowering of rates of interest and of yields on ordinary shares' (Kahn, 1972, p. 201; my emphasis). I interpret this as meaning that while interest rates were low, there was no deliberate policy aimed at further reductions into the future.

The relatively cheap money that did prevail should, according to this interpretation of the *General Theory*, be regarded as the primary cause of the improved performance – the high investment, low unemployment and abatement of the economic cycle – of the world economy during this period. Allsopp and Glyn (1999, p. 3) observe: 'the most remarkable feature . . . is

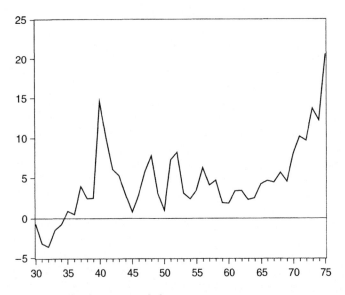

Figure 11.3   UK GDP deflator, annual change
Source: Friedman (1982).

that during the "golden age" of the 1950s and 1960s, short-term real interest rates averaging less than 1 per cent coincided with extremely high real profits rates, which were in turn associated with exceptional rates of growth of capital stock and output'. In turn, the Bastard Golden Age should be regarded as providing a degree of affirmation for Keynes's diagnosis of the Economic Problem. Moreover, for a large part of the era, inflation was relatively low (Figure 11.3).

11.3.4 Very easy and very cheap money (1970–79)

At the start of the 1970s, the monetary reforms of the post-depression/post-war world began to be dismantled. Bretton Woods was abandoned and credit was liberalised just as the British authorities permitted a phenomenal boost to demand from both monetary and fiscal policy (see Kynaston, 2001, pp. 429–81). As Smithin (1996, p. 22) has observed, '... real rates of return on financial instruments in many jurisdictions were allowed to fall very low, and actually became negative at times' (Figure 11.2 shows interest rates on British government bonds doing so). Excess demand and inflation and then, as liberal discount rate policies were reversed, deterioration in real activity were inevitable consequences. As Susan Strange (e.g. 1986) in particular has emphasised, this monetary backdrop to the adverse events of the 1970s has been all but ignored by policymakers and mainstream economists alike. The conventional supply-side interpretation, based on the actions of unions and oil producers, neglects wholly the demand side of the story.

11.3.5 The modern dear-money era (1981 to the present)

The rejection of 'Keynesian' economics by policymakers and the academic economics profession alike coincided with the return of dear money under the aegis of full financial liberalisation. Modern classical theory has been powerless to explain these dear rates. Having examined almost all possibilities, the IMF concluded:

> The preceding discussion does not suggest any very clear-cut answer to the question of why real interest rates have remained so high after the initial impact of the introduction of monetary restraint had worn off. . . .
>
> . . .
>
> Two factors, however, suggest that it would perhaps be unwise to assume that nominal interest rates adjusted for current inflation will decline all the way back to the average levels of the 1960s and 1970s. First, the gradual acceleration of inflation over the earlier period may have resulted in expected inflation being systematically below actual inflation, and thus in some downward bias in estimated real rates. Second, the possibility cannot be dismissed that new production techniques have increased the

productivity of capital in a way that would justify higher real interest rates for an extended period. (IMF, 1985, p. 129)

The *Oxford Review* sees them as natural: '[w]e find that high real rates since 1980 seem to be a return to a long-run norm ... ' (Chadha and Dimsdale, 1999, p. 17). In contrast, this interpretation of the *General Theory* leads to the conclusion that dear money had its origins in the change of international and national monetary regimes. The liberalisation of the 1970s was extended to the removal of all capital and exchange controls. Dear money was pursued to fight inflation. Smithin (1996, p. 23) identifies three 'symbolic harbingers of the political revolution that was to come during the crucial year of 1979':

> One such was the much-publicised change in the operating procedures of the US Fed, after the appointment of a new chair, Paul Volker, who was very much the candidate of the financial markets .... There ensued a three-year effort to bring inflation down via monetary tightness and high real rates of interest.
>
> Also in 1979, the most famous adherent of monetarism among politicians, Margaret Thatcher, was elected to her first term as British Prime Minister, and in the next year her government begun a similarly draconian disinflation policy, the so-called 'medium term financial strategy' (MTFS).
>
> Finally, perhaps less-remarked at the time than the first two events, but of equal significance in hindsight, the year 1979 also saw the inauguration of the European Monetary System (EMS), and the associated exchange rate mechanism (ERM) ... In the future, this would ensure that pan-European monetary policy would be determined essentially by the German Bundesbank, which, because of previous history, was an institution traditionally committed to the type of hardline anti-inflationary policy which became very much the order of the day in the 1980s and 1990s. (Smithin, 1996, p. 23)

He concludes ' ... the new regime clearly did succeed in restoring the value of financial capital and in raising the real rate of return earned on that capital' (Smithin, 1996, p. 24). As indicated by the quotes just above from Chadha and Dimsdale and the IMF, during the dear money era, high real rates became a matter of convention.

The 'real' effects have been exactly as the *General Theory* predicts. The world economy has operated at a significantly lower utilisation of resources than in the bastard golden age. The ILO (2005) estimated that total global unemployment in 2005 was 191.8 million (up by 34.5 million since 1995), and emphasised that almost half the unemployed are young people. The press release accompanying the publication of the 2005 ILO report summed up the findings as follows:

"This year's report shows once again that economic growth alone isn't adequately addressing global employment needs. This is holding back poverty reduction in many countries," said ILO Director-General Juan Somavia. "We are facing a global jobs crisis of mammoth proportions, and a deficit in decent work that isn't going to go away by itself. We need new policies and practices to address these issues."

The financial and cyclical effects have been equally pronounced. While the first half of the liberalisation period saw inflation continuing to pose a threat, it is now recognised by some that the conditions of financial instability and potential deflation are becoming endemic.

Davis (1999) studied the main episodes of financial market instability from 1933 (Table 11.4). First, apart from the Great Depression, all of these episodes occurred in or after 1970. Second, Davis's detailed analysis shows that the most common phenomenon accompanying these crises was debt accumulation.[2] If Davis updated his paper, he would have to add most of the other South American and many African economies. Many of these crises were, of course, associated with real collapse of a violent nature.

Moreover, throughout the modern dear money era, certain countries have been held up as 'model' economies. The eventual failure of the German and Japanese economies reflected the inevitable consequence of dear-but-easy monetary expansions. Stagnation, deflationary conditions and high-unemployment equilibria have prevailed ever since. The Southeast Asian 'Tiger' economies were the next prominent failures. The US and, to some extent, the UK economies have been held up as models in recent years. But, again, these countries saw excessive expansions of investment that peaked at the turn of the century with the stock market in the third quarter of

Table 11.4   Selected episodes of financial instability (1933–98)

1933	USA Great Depression	1990	Swedish CP crisis
1970	USA Penn Central1	1990	Norwegian banking crisis
1973	UK secondary banks	1991	Finnish banking crisis
1974	Germany Herstatt	1991	Swedish banking crisis
1982	LDC debt crisis	1992	Japanese banking crisis
1984	USA Continental Illinois	1992	ECU bond market collapse
1985	Canada regional banks	1993	UK exit from ERM
1986	FRN market collapse	1994	Bond market reversal
mid-80s	USA Thrift crisis	1994	Mexican crisis
1987	Stock market crash	1997	Asian crisis
1989	USA junk bond market	1998	Russia and LTCM
1989	Australian banking problems		

Source: Davis (1998).

2001. From this point onwards, finance was not so readily available and investment went into reverse.

However, policymakers have been unwilling to let the debt burden unwind and have implemented possibly the most substantial relaxation of monetary and fiscal policy on record. Consumer and government demand have taken over as the engines of economic growth. The BIS characterise the associated role of house-price inflation in the context of a wider portrayal of financial instability since the 1970s:

> Yet the single most remarkable feature in the financial area has been the recurrence of credit, asset price and investment booms and busts. A first cycle began in the industrial countries in the 1970s, affecting both equities and real estate. A second cycle started in the mid-1980s, ending in a property bust a few years later. While the Nordic countries, Germany and Japan were most affected, each made vulnerable by other domestic problems, many other countries were also caught up by the exuberance. Moreover, it seems increasingly evident that we are today well into the boom phase of a third such cycle, dating from the economic upturn of the mid-1990s. Equity prices were affected first but, after their sharp decline in early 2001, the upward momentum of demand was transferred to the housing market. Indeed, it is not an exaggeration to say that, over the last year or so, the house price phenomenon has achieved global sweep. Most industrial countries are showing symptoms of overheating in the housing market. So too are many emerging market economies, including China and Korea. (BIS, 2005, p. 6)

The BIS emphasise too the extent of the relaxation of fiscal policy:

> Despite a modest tightening of fiscal policies in 2004, the budget deficits of the major industrial countries remained well above historical averages . . . The widening of deficits was particularly pronounced in Germany, the United Kingdom and the United States, where fiscal positions have deteriorated by 5–7% of GDP since 2000. (ibid., p. 29)

> Fiscal policy has also been eased recently in many countries, recalling the joint impact of the Vietnam War and the Great Society programmes of that earlier era. (ibid., p. 140)

In the meantime private business investment has remained subdued:

> Increased risk aversion shown by corporate management after the equity market collapse appears to have restrained fixed capital formation. Firms had focused primarily on the restructuring of balance sheets, visible in the efforts to reduce debt ratios and in 'cash hoarding'. . . .

The focus on the reduction of leverage probably reflected concerns about continuing vulnerability to changes in financial market conditions. (ibid., p. 26)

Fortunately, corporations have been quite successful in reducing their debt burden in recent years and have both high profits and high liquidity. Yet it must also be said that the recent rebound in investment remains far less robust than that seen in earlier cycles. (ibid., p. 143)

More generally the BIS infer a specific and strong relation between corporate indebtedness and investment activity:

Moreover, headwinds seem sometimes to have arisen also from over-stretched corporate and household balance sheets and the overhang of unprofitable capital investment. The decade-long decline in corporate investment in Germany and Japan, the continuing weakness of post-crisis investment in most countries in Asia (excluding China), and the recent sluggishness of consumption in Korea and the Netherlands may all be illustrations of this phenomenon. (ibid., p. 6)

And while China is now the 'model economy', the BIS see potential causes for concern:

From this historical perspective, the continuation last year of the longer-term trend towards increased household debt in many industrial countries, particularly those characterised by relatively rapid economic growth, is worth watching. The same might be said for the balance sheets of the production sector in China, assuming that the basic data are reliable enough to support such examination. (ibid., p. 6)

The measures adopted since the stock market decline have not addressed the underlying problem of the debt burden; indeed they have simply served to make it worse. As President Roosevelt said in his inaugural address on 4 March 1933, 'Faced by a failure of credit they have proposed only the lending of more money'. The analyses in Appendix 11.1 show US and UK debt remaining at historic highs. Counterparts to these liabilities are the CMIs in the bond markets, the phenomenal expansion of hedge funds and house prices. The BIS look to the potential consequence of high debt:

The build-up of debt levels over time, both domestically and internationally, can eventually also lead to economic problems with attendant and often substantial costs....

...

...Any or all of these numbers might well revert to the mean, with associated implications for global economic growth. Such an unwinding might be gradual, and possibly benign, but it could also be rapid and disruptive. In large part, what happens will be determined by real–financial interactions that we should not pretend to fully understand. (ibid., p. 142)

The interpretation of the *General Theory* in this book has offered a theory of these 'real–financial' interactions that suggests that any unwinding will be rapid and disruptive.

11.3.6 Interest rates at the start of the twenty-first century

In many developed economies real interest rates, particularly those on government debt, declined at the end of the twentieth century and into the twenty-first century. These reductions appear to be related to responses to the crises starting with the Southeast Asia collapse through to the stock exchange collapse and subsequent investment falls in the United States in 2001. Central banks around the world reduced discount rates; assets perceived as safer became more desirable, leading to increases in price and reductions in interest rates.

However, the reductions in government interest rates have not been matched with correspondingly large reductions on rates paid by businesses (see Figure 11.1). In addition to this, large accumulations of debt and lower business confidence have inhibited a fuller recovery in business investment. Moreover, lower interest rates are regarded mainly as an aberration rather than an ongoing condition for future activity. Indeed policymakers and commentators alike are fostering expectations of higher not lower rates into the future.

11.4 Macro policy and inflation targeting in the dear-money era

The preceding interpretation abstracts from the thriving debate on macro-economic, and specifically monetary, policy throughout the dear-money era. Under the influence of economists, policymakers have chosen to set monetary policy by targeting certain financial and macroeconomic aggregates:

- money supply;
- exchange rate; and
- inflation.

According to the interpretation set out in this chapter, the primary impact of these policies have been through their implications for the short-term rate of interest and the associated (as well as wider) conditions of animal spirits. To take the UK experience as example: first the restrictive policies during the early days of monetarism greatly inhibited demand for goods, put pressure on firms' balance sheets and led to recession. As policy was relaxed in the 1980s, excessive demand for goods relative to supply caused an inflationary expansion. The consequent high short rates brought down inflation by raising interest payments on corporate debt to unsustainable levels, eventually forcing firms into bankruptcy and their workers into unemployment. Membership of the Exchange Rate Mechanism (ERM) exacerbated the situation, and the consequent prolonged deficiency of demand put an end to any inflationary pressure.

At this point the modern era of inflation targeting began. From the perspective of Keynes's theory, such policies amount to an attempt at demand management through the short-term rate of interest against a backdrop of dear money. While achieving low price inflation has been unanimously celebrated, policy has not been so successful in preventing a great expansion in money and the associated capital market, property and debt inflations that were discussed in the previous section.

The evidence of experience is that pursuing and achieving low rates of inflation does not prevent the easy money that leads to these debt and capital market inflations: 'Clearly, the achievement of price stability has not been sufficient to ensure the avoidance of financial instability' (BIS, 2003, p. 149).

According to the classical theory, achieving low inflation is a guarantee of stability, and the existence of easy money, debt and capital market inflations are incidental. But according to the interpretation of Keynes presented in Chapter 8, matters are reversed. Build-ups of debt and capital market inflations reflect a great threat to the prosperity of a free-market economy. The scale of indebtedness might be regarded as an indication of the unsustainability of the celebrated real performance that is judged only according to GDP growth and ILO employment figures.

11.5   The role of international financial architecture

Domestic easy money has also been facilitated through the post-Bretton-Woods international financial architecture. Inflationary pressures have been restrained in part through excess domestic demand relative to domestic supply being met by cheap imports. In the United Kingdom the consequent balance-of-trade deficit has been of unprecedented scale in terms of cumulative effect. Each year, too, the US trade deficit registers a new unprecedented high; conversely, other countries (most notably China) have huge surpluses. Prior to liberalisation, international financial arrangements at least aimed to limit the degree to which such imbalances (for Keynes, on both the surplus and the deficit side) might be permitted. As the BIS have said,

> In a sense, it is odd that domestic financial imbalances are not higher on policymakers' list of priorities since international imbalances have been a source of concern for centuries. Indeed, earlier versions of the international monetary system were all designed to prevent such imbalances

from getting dangerously out of hand. For example, the gold standard incorporated a process (not always smooth) of automatic adjustment of trade imbalances. Against the backdrop of the so-called "impossible trinity", countries retained a fixed exchange rate and free capital flows but had to give up monetary independence in the interests of systemic discipline. Under the Bretton Woods system, they kept fixed exchange rates and independent monetary policies but gave up free capital flows. The IMF essentially played the role of referee, disciplining in particular countries running large external deficits. Subsequently, after increasingly free capital flows brought an end to the Bretton Woods system, floating exchange rates were assumed to be the mechanism through which trade imbalances would be reduced before they attained disorderly proportions. (ibid., p. 150)

But floating exchange rates have not operated in the manner expected. For wealthy economies the existing international financial architecture has amounted to *laissez-faire*. For a very prolonged period few pressures have been exerted on the currencies of such economics whatever the extent of domestic demand relative to domestic supply. In effect the international architecture has complemented domestic easy-money policies.

Finally, the BIS concede that liberalisation and associated developments may be at the root of financial imbalances:

> Somewhat paradoxically, it might be argued that the new challenges faced by central banks today result in part from the confluence of three unquestionably welcome developments: the globalisation of the real economy; liberalised financial markets; and the newly established anti-inflation credentials. In this view, globalisation provides the underlying disinflationary force, financial liberalisation the weaker financial constraints on self-reinforcing credit-asset price processes, and the anti-inflation credibility the anchoring of expectations that can help to delay the translation of excess demand pressures into higher inflation (see the Conclusion of this Report). (ibid., p. 76)

It should not be surprising that the dismantling of the post-war financial architecture has led to a situation that bears a good degree of similarity to the environment of the 1930s. The primary motivation for the implementation of that architecture was prevention of a recurrence of the disasters of the 1930s.

Moreover, after 20 years of the so-called 'liberalisation' or 'globalisation', states have not shrunk to any significant extent; indeed growth and employment have become increasingly dependent on state-sponsored activities. In the meantime, as in the 1930s, some countries are seeking to gain short-term advantage by protectionist trade policy, domestic subsidies and what amount to aggressive devaluations in exchange rates. The doctrines of Economic Nationalism, now re-branded as Economic Patriotism, have returned.

Appendix 11.1

UK and US debt

In his 'The Debt Deflation Theory of Great Depressions', Fisher (1933) produced an estimate of the level of debt in the US economy at the start of the Great Depression. The present level of UK and US debt can be calculated using national accounts balance sheets and flow of funds accounts. UK figures are based on summing 'total debt liabilities' for the private non-financial corporations, central and local government, and household sectors (*UK Economic Accounts* tables A57, A62, A63 and A64, with ONS database codes, NIJT, NJIZ, NNPP, NLBB-NLBU; readily available and consistent data only extends back to 1987). US figures are based on summing 'debt outstanding' for the federal government, households, businesses and state and local government (*Flow of Funds Accounts of the United States*, with figures taken from table D3). Figures are then presented as a share of Gross Domestic Product at current prices.

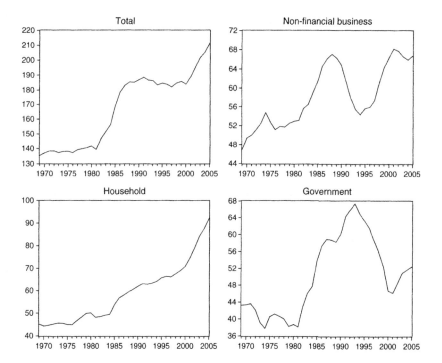

Figure A11.1   US debt as a share of GDP (%)
Source: see text.

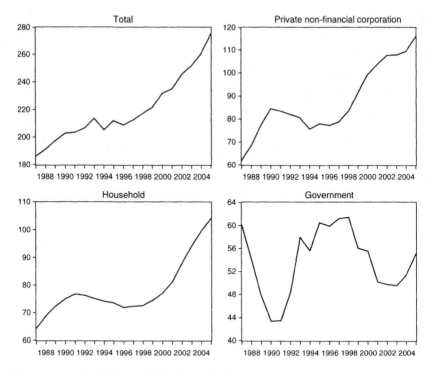

Figure A11.2   UK debt as a share of GDP (%)
Source: see text.

In 2005, total US and UK debt were 211 per cent and 275 per cent of GDP, respectively. Fisher's estimate of US internal debt at £200 billion in 1929 corresponds to 193 per cent of the present estimate of 1929 GDP.

Figure A11.1 shows the very substantial increase in the level of indebtedness in the US economy in the period since financial liberalisation. Over the past decade, the growth in US debt has had a very distinct sectoral pattern. In the 'new economy' era of the late 1990s, business debt first grew very sharply but was curtailed as the stock exchange contracted. At this point there was an even sharper acceleration in the accumulation of debt by the household sector, as well as a return to increasing indebtedness of the government sector.

Figure A11.2 (over a shorter time span) shows UK corporate debt accumulation also accelerated sharply over the new economy period, but has not been arrested. The household sector has accumulated debt rapidly, particularly since 2000. The government sector's debt liabilities began to increase again from 2003.

Notes

1. Fisher cited 'internal debt' figures at about 200 per cent of GDP. Appendix 11.1 sets these estimates against the debt accumulated over the past 30 years.
2. The UK exit from the Exchange Rate Mechanism was the only exception, when difficulties arose from fixing an inappropriate exchange rate rather than the consequences of an economic cycle.

12
Conclusion

1

For roughly the past quarter of a century the majority of the world economy has operated under a policy consensus that has been advocated by politicians (of left and right), supra-national authorities, economic commentators and academic economists alike. Workers should be 'flexible' so that they tolerate relatively low wages, spells of unemployment and general uncertainty. Governments should be fiscally responsible and restrict their borrowing. Above all, the setting of monetary policy should be independent from government and aimed at low inflation (though policy aimed at this goal has operated by variously targeting the money supply, exchange rates and consumer price inflation). From a global perspective, finance capital or wealth should be 'free' so that it can be invested in whatever country its owners choose; and exchange rates should be set by markets, not managed by financial authorities.

Yet from the perspective of what Keynes called the 'facts of experience' it is not plainly apparent that, viewed across the world as a whole, these policies have been successful. The same 25 years of policy consensus has been characterised by great economic and social instability. As seen, the ILO have spoken of a 'global jobs crisis of mammoth proportions'; the BIS have referred to the 'remarkable . . . recurrence of credit, asset price and investment booms and busts'. Moreover, as the United Nations lament,

> At the start of the twenty-first century we live in a divided world. The size of the divide poses a fundamental challenge to the global human community. Part of that challenge is ethical and moral. As Nelson Mandela put it in 2005: "Massive poverty and obscene inequality are such terrible scourges of our times – times in which the world boasts breathtaking advances in science, technology, industry and wealth accumulation – that they have to rank alongside slavery and apartheid as social ills." (UN, 2005, p. 4)

While it used to be regarded as reasonable to assume that a progressive society might be one where the lot of the poor gradually improved, over the

312

past 25 years there has been a transfer of wealth from poor to rich on a scale unprecedented in history.

The justification for this consensus is classical economics. This is the economics that is taught to students, accepted by policymakers, politicians, civil servants, financiers, commentators, industry, most academics and even some unions; collectively those who accept and advocate these doctrines make up the 'mainstream'. According to this economics, market outcomes are optimal and the consensus straightforwardly follows. While economists are often portrayed as holding many inconsistent and opposing views, few do not support the basic policy consensus. Indeed, the economic theory that dominates permits only slight divergence from that consensus and the extent of any debate is really very small when it comes to practical implementation. The main area of debate has been the extent of government expenditure that should be permitted. The policy consensus over the past 25 years has generally tended towards the side of restricting government expenditure and especially government borrowing. However, it should be noted that those who have most vigorously advocated market values have not been able to diminish the size of the state.

When it comes to facing the problems of the world, the classical economics has very little to offer. Where shortcomings in 'outcome' are acknowledged, these are regarded as caused by inappropriate applications of the theory, not by defects in the theory itself. Within the mainstream economics profession there is effectively no alternative to the present consensus.

The argument of this work could be restated as a claim that a substantial rival to this consensus does exist. In general terms this rival might be characterised as monetary economics. In this work, the emphasis has been most especially on the monetary economics of J. M. Keynes.

In a manner that is of grave concern, this rival is not recognised by the main-stream economics profession. Keynes's major theoretical contributions have been to a great extent accommodated within a variant of the classical frame-work. The name of Keynes is primarily associated with the fiscal policies of the post-war era that are perceived as failed and reckless because of the economic turmoil of the 1970s. It was concluded, therefore, that the associated theoretical doctrine was wrong and the work of Keynes of little interest.

Mainstream economics neglects entirely not only Keynes but also the substantial body of work that is post-Keynesian economics. These 'heterodox' economists have consistently argued that the mainstream interpretation of Keynes's theory has been incorrect, and they have similarly questioned what passes for Keynes's policy conclusions. In the mainstream, all the invention, insight and radicalism of Keynes's work have been lost. Moreover, the argument here is that the extent of the radicalism and implication of Keynes's economics has not been fully captured even by the post-Keynesians, particularly in respect of policy. For, in truth, Keynes turned economic theory and policy upside down.

The fundamental claim of this interpretation and application of Keynes's theory is that the condition of the world economy today is a consequence of the neglect of this theory. Keynes offered a theory that challenged all aspects of the classical theory. The condition of the world is not an inevitable or necessary state of affairs. But the scale of the solution that Keynes's theory prescribes is immense in both political and economic terms. For Keynes was concerned above all with international and domestic monetary reform.

2

The vast majority of Keynes's contributions to economic theory were concerned with monetary economics. This interest followed from practical pre-occupation with international exchange systems, the foremost policy issue of the day. The target of his work was the international gold standard. In his first books, Keynes sought to expose the standard as a 'barbarous relic' of a monetary environment that no longer existed (if, indeed, it ever did).

Keynes understood that economies were based on what he would later label bank money. Banking systems could create credit and hence money because agents were increasingly willing to accept promissory notes on deposits in banks in lieu of payment. In such monetary economies, activity is not constrained by an imaginary mass of saving; money can and quite often will be created to whatever extent demanded by agents. These notions were the foundation of all of Keynes's analysis. They were understood by most economists practising when Keynes began his work. Keynes's contribution was to recognise the far-reaching implications of bank money and to develop the theory of the workings of a bank-money economy. He was fully aware of the far-reaching nature of the project. In 1931, in his 'reply' to Hayek's review of the *Treatise*, he quoted, with approval, this passage from *Prices and Production*:

> [I]t means also that the task of monetary theory is a much wider one than is commonly assumed; that its task is nothing less than to cover a second time the whole field which is treated by pure theory under the assumption of Barter,... (*CW* XIII, p. 254)

The classical economics is a theory of a real-exchange economy that failed and continues to fail to recognise the importance of monetary conditions except to determine prices. Even though most would purport to see this distinction, few take its implications seriously. For at least 300 years the British economy has been based on bank money.

Keynes's analysis ultimately revealed that the distinction between these two approaches is profound; it leads to the most far-reaching practical conclusions. The first of these conclusions was that forcing bank-money systems to operate under a gold standard led to perverse and sometimes disastrous policy action. Using discount-rate policy to support gold standard exchange rates would, perhaps frequently, be inappropriate to domestic economic conditions.

Matters came to a head after the end of the First World War when the financial architecture of the world took centre stage. Most countries had abandoned strict gold standard principles during the course of the war. Keynes's *Tract on Monetary Reform* was an appeal to policymakers, in particular those at the Bank of England, not to return to gold. Keyne's opposition was to the system itself, not to the specific exchange parities at which the system operated in practice.

But he did not just oppose; he provided an alternative. Countries should *manage* their currencies through their central banks buying and selling currency across a pre-announced range of exchange rates. Exchange rate and interest rate policies would, therefore, be separated. Initially, Keynes advocated the use of the discount rate in a counter-inflationary role, through the control of credit.

Needless to say, Keynes failed to prevent the return to gold. He retreated to write his *Treatise on Money*, his first attempt at a full theory of a bank-money economy. As he did so, he began his shift of emphasis from the short-term rate of interest to the long-term rate as *the* critical monetary factor. And he began to explore techniques to bring that rate under control.

Finally, the hardships in Britain of the 1920s and then the cataclysm of the worldwide Great Depression appeared to affirm Keynes's analysis. In the 1930s, under his advice and supervision, a monetary environment in accord with Keynes's theoretical insights was gradually developed. With the implementation of the EEA, Britain became the first country in the world to put in place *de jure* exchange/currency management policies. Domestic monetary policy was simply aimed at cheap money on both short- and long-term borrowing. The most emphatic act in Britain was the conversion of the 5 per cent war debt to $3\frac{1}{2}$ per cent. To support this operation, capital controls were implemented. The discount rate was reduced to 2 per cent and abandoned as an instrument of active policy management; this would remain the policy until November 1951. These monetary reforms permitted the British economy to begin to recover from the Great Depression.

Monetary reform gained its mightiest champion in President Franklin Delano Roosevelt. With his rejection of the 'old fetishes of so-called international bankers' at the 1933 World Economic Conference, the world was confronted with the desire for a new monetary order in the most emphatic manner possible. Over the 1930s, country by country, the rest of the world followed Britain's lead. Only the totalitarian economies stood apart.

Keynes published his *General Theory of Employment, Interest and Money* as this process was well underway. As the title of the book suggests, the rate of interest was brought to centre stage. The work stood all the conclusions of classical theory on their head. Say's Law was reversed: demand created supply; supply did not create demand. Investment created saving; increased saving was not necessary for increased investment. Insufficient demand will result in underutilised resources and is the primary cause of unemployment.

Activity and employment can, therefore, be created by direct intervention to foster demand. High real wages are the consequence of high activity not an inhibitor to high activity.

For Keynes, the best approach to increase employment was to encourage private investment through a cheap-money policy. Here was where his theory departed most substantially from the classical conclusions when applied to policy. Under classical doctrine, the rate of interest is a passive variable responding to human industriousness and thrift and not amenable to policy action (at least in the long run). Under Keynes's liquidity preference theory, interest rates were revealed to be a variable under the control of the monetary authorities. In the *General Theory*, a cut in the rate of interest will lead to higher investment and, as a consequence, higher saving. In the classical theory, if a cut in the rate of interest were possible, it would lead to lower saving and hence lower investment.

In political terms, the 1930s saw control of monetary conditions wrested from financial interests and given to representatives of democratically elected, mainly left-of-centre, governments. Central banks were nationalised, currencies were managed and cheap money implemented on a global scale. To paraphrase the British Labour Party, finance became, for a brief period, the intelligent servant not the stupid master of the world economy.

The Second World War interrupted the progress of monetary reform. But the war was fought according to mainly socialist principles. Finance and industry were not permitted to profiteer from the conflict to the same extent as in the First World War. In terms of practical policy, British debt-management policies were developed; and, for the first time in history, the long-term rate of interest was deliberately and successfully set at a specific rate: 3 per cent. The discount rate remained redundant as an instrument of active policy management. The systems then developed would underpin Keynes's practical recommendations for post-war monetary policy. At the NDE, he detailed comprehensive practical measures that would enable the continuation and development of the cheap-money policy after the war. Initially, Keynes favoured long-term rates of 3 per cent, medium-term rates from $1\frac{1}{2}$ to 2 per cent and short-term rates below 1 per cent. From an international perspective, Roosevelt encouraged Keynes to produce a blueprint for an international currency system that would foster post-war economic activity and prevent the disasters of the great depression from ever recurring in the future. As a result, Keynes produced his plan for an International Clearing Union that at Bretton Woods was adopted as the official position of the British Government.

3

But the world would emerge from the war with a different 'Keynesian' theory and policy practice. Post-war policy saw the monetary reforms quickly diluted. The eventual Bretton Woods Agreement was neither currency management nor Keynes's proposal. In practice the supply of liquidity was restricted in a manner not wholly different to the gold standard. Keynes's debt-management principles were gradually abandoned. Then, in 1951, with a lead provided by the US Federal Reserve Accord, interest rates around the world began to rise and discount rates were reactivated as an instrument of macroeconomic policy.

Such actions were only of slight interest to the post-war economics profession. With Keynes's death in 1946, policy and theoretical emphasis turned to fiscal policy. Both had roots in the 1930s, in the policy debate concerning the response to the Great Depression.

Contrary to the conventional wisdom of a hard-fought conversion to 'Keynesianism' after the war, in the face of depression many opinion-formers and policymakers accepted the failure of *laissez-faire* and advocated deeply anti-market measures as a solution. These measures emerged over the course of the 1930s. The first action was a bankers' 'Resolution' that recommended the enforcement of tariffs on imports. Over the next years there was widespread advocacy of public works. This was extended to arguments for some centralised planning of economic activity. Harold Macmillan, later to be the Prime Minister of a British Conservative Government and a leading advocate of and figurehead for this approach, referred to the agenda as 'economic nationalism'.

Those who presented these arguments did so as the only possible alternative to *laissez-faire*. Monetary reform was dismissed out of hand, but there was no effort to explain why.

Post-war economic policy in Britain owed more to economic nationalist arguments than to monetary reform. While Keynes had remained dominant in the Treasury, advising on the conduct of wartime domestic and international monetary policies, the famous Employment White Paper (*EWP*) emerged from the Cabinet Office, fostered by Keynes's most bitter opponents, Lionel Robbins and Hubert Henderson. Keynes was barely involved; and the deliberations of the NDE later showed fundamental differences in approach on matters of monetary policy. In a sleight of hand of great significance, the economic nationalist policies became known as 'Keynesian' policies.

The same was true of the 'Keynesian' theory that was based on J. R. Hicks's *IS-LM*. In reality, 'Keynesian' economics was a different and rival theory that originated with Ralph Hawtrey and Dennis Robertson. *IS-LM* was an algebraic representation of their theoretical arguments. Hicks re-invented Keynes's economics as a macroeconomic simultaneous equation model underpinned by a variant of the classical saving–investment theory that Keynes had sought to dismiss.

'Keynesian' theory offered an analytical framework which was then primarily used to interpret the effects of fiscal policy. Keynes's agenda of

monetary reform was betrayed. In the 'Keynesians" denial of the importance of monetary policy, the main point of Keynes's theory and its practical
application was dismissed. While the importance of fiscal policy cannot be
denied, history has repeatedly shown that public spending and borrowing is
not controversial or resisted when economic downturn is threatened. History
has repeatedly shown that monetary reform is terribly controversial and
bitterly resisted.

Keynes's interest in fiscal policy was secondary. He endorsed its relevance
in recession; but his primary concern was preventing recession through
appropriate monetary policies. 'Keynesian' economics, on the other hand,
was 'depression economics', concerned only with the former course of
action. In a depression, monetary policy is powerless and therefore of no
interest. The 'Keynesian' conclusion that monetary policy is powerless in
recession and Keynes's conclusion that monetary policy could prevent recession may not be contradictory, but as guides to practical macroeconomic
policy they are wholly different conclusions.

While the economics profession rejected the *General Theory* immediately
and decisively, it happily embraced what Robertson and Hicks presented as
their 'revision' or 'modification' of the classical economics. As with policy,
contrary to popular history, acceptance of the 'Keynesian' model was immediate. Hicks's work was favourably cited in Britain and the United States
from the moment it was published.

4

But despite both the practical and theoretical developments, post-war
economic policy did permit the preservation of relatively low real interest
rates. With capital control still in place, the low rates could prevail across
the world.

The post-war era was an era of prosperity that has become known as
the golden age. This prosperity was primarily underpinned by strong and
sustained growth in private investment. According to this interpretation of
the *General Theory*, the golden age affirmed Keynes's analysis. The 1930s and
1940s had shown that interest rates could be brought under control; the
golden age showed that these low rates would lead to high investment, high
activity and high employment.

But the golden age would not last forever. From a theoretical perspective,
'Keynesian' economics contained, and its practitioners built on, the seeds
of its own destruction. Modigliani gave us the sticky-wage interpretation that further diminished Keynes's theory, and in a later contribution
he substituted a theory based on time preference for Keynes's theory of
consumption. This 'innovation', along with Hicks's investment demand
function based solely on the rate of interest, brings us back to the classical
theory of the rate of interest. Liquidity preference was declared redundant.

Solow re-introduced a saving constraint to investment. Finally, the most destructive step of all was Samuelson and Solow's incorporation of the Phillips curve into the 'Keynesian' theory in a manner that traduced not only Phillips but also Keynes's careful work in the *General Theory*, Chapter 21, substituting for its subtlety an immutable relationship between inflation and unemployment. The 1970s combination of high inflation and stagnating economic activity was at odds with this relationship, and therefore 'Keynesianism', and by association Keynes were rejected. Monetarism was merely waiting in the wings for this to happen.

The period from the 1970s to 1980s then saw a political, social and economic revolution that continues today. While the theoretical debate had concerned fiscal policy, early actions amounted to a monetary counter-revolution. The institutional reforms that had facilitated cheap money, already compromised, were reversed. Finance was 'liberalised'. With Bretton Woods abandoned and capital controls removed, interest rates rose to previously unprecedented levels and remained at a high level from that point until the end of the 1990s. The age of the macroeconomic consensus had arrived. Despite differences in practical approach, monetarism and all subsequent monetary policies were underpinned by the same basic theory, the theory of which Keynes had warned ' . . . its teaching is misleading and disastrous if we attempt to apply it to the facts of experience' (*CW* VII, p. 3). The dear money which Keynes had warned should be avoided 'as we would hell-fire' was re-applied.

The economic and social ills of the past 25 years have at root cause this dear money. They have led to conditions of low but volatile aggregate demand, high unemployment and inactivity, and severe financial and social instability. So far the most severe hardships have been concentrated on the 'developing' world. The developed economies have sustained a seemingly politically acceptable level of activity and employment, but these remain underpinned by a debt inflation of unprecedented scale. While the debt inflation has not unwound, the retreat of private enterprise is indicated by low levels of business investment, and activity is supported instead by consumer demand backed by house price inflations as well as high government expenditure.

5

For the 30 years from the end of the Second World War, 'Keynesian' economics dominated economic discourse. Post-war policies were attributed to 'Keynesian' economics, and the compromised monetary reforms that remained in place were ignored. The debate with Keynes's theory was avoided by re-inventing it.

Thus was Keynes's theory lost. This loss has left modern economics powerless to explain the events of the past 25 years. That monetary considerations may be a fundamental determinant of the extent of economic activity over such a long period of time is not contemplated by an economics that rules out such causality by assumption. Even monetarists only permit money an impact on activity in the short run. Furthermore, this assumption of long-run monetary neutrality has been applied retrospectively. The gold standard might be identified as having a role in the Great Depression, but only insofar as there were errors of implementation and day-to-day management. Most economic discourse does not even acknowledge the existence of currency management as a distinct and substantial period of international financial policy. And fundamentally, in terms of our understanding of the world, the delineation of economic policy and history into the two periods: from the end of the Second World War to the end of Bretton Woods, and from the end of Bretton Woods to the present is simply not relevant to the mainstream.

At the very best, if monetary conditions are acknowledged as having some causal role in the prosperity of the golden age, they appear to be regarded as a matter of luck. The introduction that was prepared by Paul Krugman for a new edition of the *General Theory*[1] exemplifies this point of view:

> Keynes made it clear that his skepticism about the effectiveness of monetary policy was a contingent proposition, not a statement of a general principle. In the past, he believed, things had been otherwise. "There is evidence that for a period of almost one hundred and fifty years the long-run typical rate of interest in the leading financial centres was about 5 percent, and the gilt-edged rate between 3 and 3 $1/2$ percent; and that these rates were modest enough to encourage a rate of investment consistent with an average of employment which was not intolerably low." [307–308] In that environment, he believed, "a tolerable level of unemployment could be attained on the average of one or two or three decades merely by assuring an adequate supply of money in terms of wage-units." [309] In other words, monetary policy had worked in the past – but not now.
>
> Now it's true that Keynes believed, wrongly, that the conditions of the 1930s would persist indefinitely – indeed, that the marginal efficiency of capital was falling to the point that the euthanasia of rentiers was in view. . . .
>
> . . .
>
> The strongest criticism one can make of *The General Theory* is that Keynes mistook an episode for a trend. He wrote in a decade when even a near-zero interest rate wasn't low enough to restore full employment, and brilliantly explained the implications of that fact – in particular, the trap in which the Bank of England and the Federal Reserve found themselves, unable to create employment no matter how much they tried to increase the money supply. He knew that matters had not always been thus. But

he believed, wrongly, that the monetary environment of the 1930s would be the norm from then on. (Krugman, 2006)

But such errors as Krugman's are hardly surprising. Keynes's message was distorted from the moment it was first published. Most modern economists seem to have no idea what Keynes really said.

Most economists remain aloof from the Economic Problem of the world, content with the low inflation that is the sole aim of a monetary policy consensus that is scarcely challenged. Almost by definition any failures of the world economy are to be attributed to failures of business and worker efficiency; they cannot be failures of economic policy and the financial environment within which economies are forced to operate.

Only post-Keynesian economists consider it worth re-visiting and re-building Keynes's arguments. They have long rejected the adequacy of *IS-LM* as a theoretical depiction of Keynes's economics. They have identified the central theoretical inconsistencies between the 'Keynesian' model and the actual model of the *General Theory* as the inadequate treatments of money and uncertainty. They recognise that the consensus of today neglects Keynes's economic reasoning.

In his time, Keynes could not be ignored. He had been born into the life of a Cambridge don. Under Alfred Marshall, Cambridge was already established as a centre of excellence in a small economics profession. Keynes's advancement in the Civil Service was remarkable. And with the *Economic Consequences of the Peace* he became a public figure of some repute. Despite his growing unorthodoxy, his views on any issue were seemingly eagerly sought by government, the public and publishers alike. But the economics profession today is mighty and huge, and not open to challenge from unorthodox views. Those who have sought to oppose the mainstream depiction of Keynes have been marginalised. Post-Keynesian work is sidelined into its own journals and does not feature at mainstream conferences. Furthermore, and critically, a practising economist does not need even to be aware of post-Keynesian views, let alone to be able to respond to them. The mainstream assumes that post-Keynesians are misguided and post-Keynesianism has no relevance to modern economic discourse.

Yet the name Keynes retains a certain cachet. Policymakers and economists appeal to his name and work whenever possible, no matter how implausible the association. In the textbooks, Keynes has been re-invented as 'New-Keynesian' economics. But the following quotation from a leading and prominent practitioner exemplifies the utter disregard about the extent to which the interpretation actually accords with that of Keynes: 'If New Keynesian economics is not a true representation of Keynes's views, then so much the worse for Keynes' (Mankiw, 1992, p. 560). Though hardly admirable, such arrogance is pre-requisite for mainstream 'Keynesians' because even a cursory reading of the *General Theory* leads to conflicts with mainstream interpretations. Indeed to study Keynes in depth appears to have meant disqualification from contributing to the mainstream interpretation of Keynes.

That is not to say that Keynes is straightforward. In particular, there are a number of tacit assumptions on both theoretical and practical context that are not obvious to the reader today.

As discussed earlier in this conclusion, the *General Theory* was Keynes's analysis of the far-reaching implications of bank money. Yet in the *General Theory*, beyond a brief reference in the Preface, Keynes does not spell out his assumptions about the supply of credit. This has allowed many to conclude that the *General Theory* is not even a monetary theory, an interpretation that could not be more wrong. Second, it has been argued here that Keynes's discovery of the saving–investment identity was the critical step to the *General Theory* from the *Treatise*. Yet in the *General Theory* itself, the identity is discussed in a piecemeal manner and the theoretical treatment is very basic and not complete. Up to publication its importance seems to have been more fully recognised by his contemporaries. Only afterwards did Keynes begin to emphasise its importance. Third, in this book, the importance of 'bills' to the theory of liquidity preference has been developed. From this perspective, liquidity preference shows that the authorities can set the rate of interest on long-term debt if they are willing to issue as much short-term debt as the public wishes to hold. In the *General Theory* itself, the application of liquidity preference to bills is mentioned only in a footnote, and the associated practical policy mentioned only briefly and in quite an oblique manner. Fourth, the interpretation of Keynes's theory of activity is hampered by his not clarifying sufficiently the distinction between short- and longer-period considerations. In this book, an equilibrium-based framework within which both the *General Theory* and its predecessors can be interpreted has been outlined. Interest rates affect both the long-period equilibrium of the system and short-period cyclical tendencies. Finally, Keynes's theory has been extended to offer a fuller explanation of the business cycle. Debt and capital market inflations are identified as the critical transmission mechanisms through which excessive expansions eventually come to contract.

The historical analysis provided here shows Keynes's theory and policy to be a coherent whole, ultimately pre-occupied by monetary goals. Keynes rescued the rate of interest from the real analysis of classical economics and vested interests. Properly understood, Keynes's economics advises that governments should take a degree of control over the monetary system in order to aim interest rate policy at cheap money. His international policies permitted nations a good degree of autonomy over their own monetary conditions. His domestic policies constituted practical mechanisms to achieve low interest rates at the same time as preserving a degree of control over the extension of credit. His development of monetary, debt-management and international financial policies were not side issues, but the core practical mechanisms that followed from his theoretical reasoning.

But notwithstanding difficulties of interpretation of Keynes, the mainstream is dismissive of monetary economics and of history taken in its widest sense. The grand discussions of monetary history and the views and theories that emerged in those periods are not regarded as of any significance. In spite of an acknowledgement that monetary factors may have dominant effects in the short run, and a monetary-policy framework that accords a fantastic power and precision to movements in the discount rate, economists remain content to assume long-run monetary neutrality. Surely the burden of proof *should* be on those who appeal to this highly contrived long-run situation, rather than those who seek to understand the economy through the implications of the very real and undeniable effects of the monetary factor. But this is not the world of economics today; the dominance of the classical theoretical paradigm is such that to oppose it to be seen as opposing reason itself.

6

The central propositions of this book are that

1. the monetary authorities have the capacity to control the rate of interest;
2. a low rate of interest results in, and is necessary for, prosperity and stability.

These have been supported through an appeal to Keynes's economic theory and practice.

The importance of the rate of interest to prosperity has been sporadically understood throughout history. In Britain, Josiah Child and John Law recognised the necessity of low interest rates at the end of the seventeenth century. This understanding followed from earlier practical advances, first in fifteenth-century Italy and then in seventeenth-century Netherlands. The ebb and flow of prosperity is critically dependent on policy action; prosperity coincides with cheap money and high interest rates bring recession or stagnation. Adam Smith's work is in part a testament to the monetary advances in England and Scotland over the eighteenth century. And he was by no means ignorant of the critical importance of the monetary factor.

Later, Karl Marx emphasised the importance of monetary conditions. But he saw too the relevance of such considerations to the conflict between classes. The development of banking interests was a great threat to finance capital, the class that made its income from lending inherited wealth at usurious rates of interest.

The industrial capital that prospered under lower interest rates had opposing interests to finance capital. Furthermore, in monetary matters, the interests of industrial capital coincided with the interests of labour. Lower interest rates fostered high activity and therefore high employment as well as high profits.

The grand discussions that Keynes identified and celebrated pitted industrial against financial interests. Ricardo's classical economics emerged in the first of these conflicts. Keynes saw the victory of financial interests as a victory of classical reasoning. 'Ricardo conquered England as completely as the Holy Inquisition conquered Spain' (*CW* VII, p. 32). He did not see the debate, as Marx may have, through class considerations. Continuing to celebrate the power of reason, Keynes argued in the closing pages of the *General Theory* that 'the power of vested interests is vastly exaggerated compared with the gradual encroachment of ideas' (*CW* VII, p. 383). Yet the fourth grand discussion was interpreted by the British Labour Party as socialist political forces bringing finance to heel. Between 1945 and 1950, the social and economic progress under the first majority Labour government in British history gave a glimpse of what monetary reform might achieve.

'Keynesianism' deeply undermined this agenda. Ultimately it is possible that 'Keynesianism' was a compromise in the wake of the plainly apparent failure of *laissez-faire* and a policy agenda of monetary reform that was unacceptable.

It is notable that the 'Keynesian' version of Keynes is more congenial to finance capital. With the election of the Conservative Government in 1951, a great part of Keynes's agenda was already lost. As a City historian says 'On the night of the 25th [October 1951] and the day after, the *F[inancial] T[imes]* sponsored a large election results board near the Royal Exchange, and crowds of City workers thronged the street to cheer Churchill home. The six-year nightmare was over' (Kynaston, 2001, p. 46).

Eventually the compromise was swept aside and power restored to financial interests. Ricardo's classical economics had again conquered. From a class perspective the rich rewards to finance capital have been gained at the expense of labour and industry.

7

Keynes's theory – never refuted by genuinely impartial analysis – offers the ability to understand and fully and justly address the mechanisms at work in the global economy. The solution to what surely is undeniably a breakdown in prosperity is large-scale reform of national and international financial policies. Such an approach may seem implausible given the immense scale and power of finance; but finance has only grown to such an extent because the *choice* was taken to re-position the world economy as servant to these interests. Finally, while the rewards to finance capital have been staggering, the theory here suggests that the economic forces set in motion by financial liberalisation will eventually turn on their master. I find myself hoping for that event, for there seems to be no possibility of any fuller awakening to the world's Economic Problem without it.

Note

1. The introduction has not been published, but it is available on the internet: http://www.pkarchive.org/

Bibliography

Ackley, Gardner (1961) *Macroeconomic Theory*, New York: Macmillan.

Allsopp, Christopher and Andrew Glyn (1999) 'The Assessment: Real Interest Rates', *Oxford Review of Economic Policy*, 15 (2), Summer, 1–16.

Amadeo, Edward J. (1989) *Keynes's Principle of Effective Demand*, Aldershot: Edward Elgar.

Asimakopulos, A. (1983) 'Kalecki and Keynes on Finance, Investment and Saving', *Cambridge Journal of Economics*, 7, September, 221–33.

Backhouse, Roger E. (1999) *Keynes. Contemporary Responses to the General Theory*, South Bend, Indiana: St Augustine's Press.

Balogh, Thomas (1976), 'Keynes and the International Monetary Fund', in A. P. Thirlwall, Ed., *Keynes and International Monetary Relations*, London and Basingstoke: Macmillan.

Bank for International Settlements (2003) *73rd Annual Report*, June, http://www.bis.org/publ/annualreport.htm.

Bank for International Settlements (2005) *75th Annual Report*, June, http://www.bis.org/publ/annualreport.htm.

Bank of England (2002) 'The Bank of England's Operations in the Sterling Money Markets', *Quarterly Bulletin*, September, 42 (2), 153–61.

Begg, David, Stanley Fischer and Rudiger Dornbusch (1991) *Economics*, Third Edition, London: McGraw-Hill.

Beveridge, William H. (1944) *Full Employment in a Free Society*, London: George Allen and Unwin.

Bibow, J. (1990) 'On Keynesian Theories of Liquidity Preference', *Manchester School*, 66 (2), 238–73.

——. (2000) 'The Loanable Funds Fallacy in Retrospect', *History of Political Economy*, 32 (4), 789–831.

——. (2001) 'The Loanable Funds Fallacy: Exercises in the Analysis of Disequilibrium', *Cambridge Journal of Economics*, 25 (5), 591–616.

Blaug, Mark (1990) *John Maynard Keynes: Life, Ideas, Legacy*, London and Basingstoke: Macmillan in association with the Institute of Economic Affairs.

Boianovsky, M. and Trautwein, H. (2004) 'Haberler, the League of Nations, and the Search for Consensus in Business Cycle Theory in the 1930s', UKHET Conference, Kingston University, September, 1–3.

Booth, Alan (1989) *British Economic Policy, 1931–49: Was there a Keynesian Revolution?* London: Harvester Wheatsheaf.

Boyle, Andrew (1967) *Montagu Norman*, London: Cassell.

Brazelton, W. Robert (1997) 'Retrospectives: The Economics of Leon Hirsch Keyserling', *The Journal of Economic Perspectives*, 11 (4), Fall, 189–97.

Cairncross, A. (1944) *Introduction to Economics*, London: Butterworth and Co. Ltd.

Caldenty, Esteban Pérez (2000) 'Chicago, Keynes and Fiscal Policy', Centre for Full Employment and Price Stability at the university of Missouri-Kansas city, Seminar Paper No. 7, October.

Cannan, Edwin (1924) 'Limitation of Currency or Limitation of Credit?', *Economic Journal*, 34 (133), March, 52–64.

Carabelli, Anna M. (1988) *On Keynes's Method*, Basingstoke and London: Macmillan.

Carver, T. N. (1903) 'A Suggestion for a Theory of Industrial Depressions', *Quarterly Journal of Economics*, 17 (3), May, 497–500.

Cass, David (1965) 'Optimum Growth in an Aggregative Model of Capital Accumulation', *Review of Economic Studies*, 32 (3), July, 233–40.

Chadha, Jagjit S. and Nicholas H. Dimsdale (1999) 'A Long View of Real Rates', *Oxford Review of Economic Policy*, 15 (2), Summer, 17–45.

Chick, Victoria (1983) *Macroeconomics After Keynes*, The MIT Press Cambridge, Massachusetts.

——. (1987) 'Townshend, Hugh', in John Eatwell, Murray Milgate and Peter Newman (Eds), *The New Palgrave: A Dictionary of Economic Theory and Doctrine*, London: Macmillan.

——. (1991) 'Hicks and Keynes on Liquidity Preference: A Methodological Approach', *Review of Political Economy*, 3 (3), 309–19.

——. (1992) *On Money, Method and Keynes: Selected Essays*, Philip Arestis and Sheila C. Dow, Eds, London: Macmillan; New York: St Martin's Press.

——. (1997) 'The Multiplier and Finance', in G. C. Harcourt and P. A. Riach, Eds, *A 'Second Edition' of* The General Theory, Vol. I, London and New York: Routledge.

——. (1998) 'Two Further Essays on Equilibrium', *UCL Discussion Paper*, No. 98-13.

——. (2000) 'Money and Effective Demand', in John Smithin, Ed., *What is Money?* London and New York: Routledge.

——. (2001) 'Varieties of Post-Keynesian Monetary Theory: Conflicts and (Some) Resolutions', paper for the Association for Heterodox Economics Conference, July 2001.

Chick, Victoria and Sheila C. Dow (1988) 'A Post-Keynesian Perspective on the Relationship Between Banking and Regional Development', in Philip Arestis, Ed., *Post-Keynesian Monetary Economics*, Aldershot: Edward Elgar, 219–50.

——. (2002) 'Monetary Policy with Endogenous Money and Liquidity Preference: a non-Dualistic Treatment', *Journal of Post Keynesian Economics*, 24 (4), Summer, 587–607.

Chick, Victoria and Geoff Tily (2004) 'Transfiguration and Death: Keynes's Monetary Theory', paper for the Association for Heterodox Economics Conference, July.

Child, Sir Josiah (1668) *Brief Observations Concerning Trade and the Interest of Money*, London.

Ciocca, Pierluigi and Giangiacomo Nardozzi (1996) *The High Price of Money: An Interpretation of World Interest Rates*, Oxford University Press.

Clapham, Sir John (1944) *The Bank of England: A History*; Vol. I, *1694–1797*, Cambridge University Press.

Clarke, Peter (1988) *The Keynesian Revolution in the Making 1924–1936*, Oxford: Clarendon Press.

Clower, R. W. (1965) 'The Keynesian Counter-Revolution: A Theoretical Appraisal', in F. H. Hahn and F. Brechling, Eds, *The Theory of Interest Rates*, London: Macmillan, 103–25.

Cmd. 3897 (1931) *Macmillan Committee Report on Industry and Finance*, London: His Majesty's Stationery Office.

——. 6437 (1943) *Proposal for an International Clearing Union*, London: His Majesty's Stationery Office.

——. 6527 (1944) *Employment Policy*, London: His Majesty's Stationery Office.

Cmnd. 827 (1959) 'Radcliffe Report': Committee on the Working of the Monetary System, *Report*, London: Her Majesty's Stationery Office.

——. 837 (1960) 'Radcliffe Report': Committee on the Working of the Monetary System, *Minutes of Evidence*, London: Her Majesty's Stationery Office.

Corry, B. A. (2002) 'Some Myths About Phillip's Curve', in P. Arestis, M. J. Desai and S. C. Dow, Eds, *Money, Macroeconomics and Keynes: Essays in Honour of Victoria Chick*, Vol. I, London: Routledge, 163–72.

Crick, W. F. (1927) 'The Genesis of Bank Deposits', *Economica*, 20, June, 191–202.

Curtis, M. (1937) 'Is Money Saving Equal to Investment?', *Quarterly Journal of Economics*, 51 (4), August, 604–25.

———. (1939) 'Saving and Savings', *Quarterly Journal of Economics*, 53 (4), 623–6.

Dalton, Hugh (1935) *Practical Socialism for Britain*, London: George Routledge & Sons, Ltd.

———. (1954 [1922]) *Principles of Public Finance*, London: Routledge.

Davidson, Paul (1965) 'Keynes's Finance Motive', *Oxford Economic Papers*, 17 (1), March, 47–65.

Davidson, Paul (1972) 'Money and the Real World', *Economic Journal*, 82 (325), March, 101–15.

———. (1978) 'Why Money Matters: Lessons from a Half-Century of Monetary Theory', *Journal of Post Keynesian Economics*, 1 (1), Fall, 46–70.

———. (1978 [1972]), *Money and the Real World*, Second Edition, Macmillan: London.

———. (2000) 'There are Major Differences between Kalecki's Theory of Employment and Keynes's General Theory of Employment Interest and Money', *Journal of Post Keynesian Economics*, 23 (1), Fall, 3–25.

Davis, Eric (1980) 'The Correspondence Between R. G. Hawtrey and J. M. Keynes on the *Treatise*: the Genesis of Output Adjustment Models', *Canadian Journal of Economics*, 716–24.

Davis, E. Philip (1999) 'Financial Data Needs for Macroprudential Surveillance – What are the Key Indicators of Risks to Domestic Financial Stability?', paper for *Workshop on Financial Market Data for International Financial Stability*, Centre for Central Banking Studies, Bank of England, January 11–15.

Desai, M. J. (1975) 'The Phillips Curve: A Revisionist Interpretation', *Economica*, 42, 1–19.

Diamond, Peter A. (1965) 'National Debt in a Neoclassical Growth Model', *American Economic Review*, 55 (5), December, 1126–50.

Dimand, Robert W. (1988) *Origins of the Keynesian Revolution: the development of Keynes's theory of output and employment*, Aldershot: Edward Elgar.

———. (1999) 'The Beveridge Retort: Beveridge's response to the Keynesian challenge', in L. L. Pasinetti and B. Schefold (Eds), *The Impact of Keynes on Economics in the 20th Century*, Cheltenham: Edward Elgar, 221–39.

Dow, S. C. (1997) 'Endogenous Money', in G. C. Harcourt and P. A. Riach (Eds), *A 'Second Edition' of The General Theory*, Vol. 2, London: Routledge.

Eltis, W. (1977) 'The Failure of the Keynesian Conventional Wisdom', *Lloyds Bank Review*, October.

Fearon, Peter (1987) *War, Prosperity and Depression: The U.S. Economy, 1917–45*, Oxford: Philip Allan.

Feinstein, C. H. (1972) *National Income, Expenditure & Output of the UK 1855–1965*, Cambridge: Cambridge University Press.

Fisher, Irving (1911) *The Purchasing Power of Money*, New York: Macmillan.

———. (1933) 'The Debt Deflation Theory of Great Depressions, *Econometrica*, 1 (4), October, 337–57.

Fletcher, Gordon (2000) *Understanding Dennis Robertson: The Man and his Work*, Cheltenham: Edward Elgar.

Fletcher, Gordon (2004) 'Money and the Management of the Short Period: Dennis Robertson's ". . . odd little book"', European Society for the History of Thought, Eighth Annual Conference, February.

Friedman, Milton and Anna J. Schwartz (1982) *Monetary Trends in the United States and United Kingdom: Their Relation to Income, Prices, and Interest Rates, 1867–1975,* Chicago and London: University of Chicago Press.

Galbraith, James K. (1996) 'Keynes, Einstein and Scientific Revolution', in Philip Arestis, (Ed.), *Essays in Honour of Paul Davidson,* Vol. I, *Keynes, Money and the Open Economy,* Cheltenham: Elgar, 14–21.

Galbraith, John K. (1975) *Money: Whence it Came, Where it Went,* Pelican.

Gleeson, Janet (1999) *Millionaire; The Philanderer, Gambler, and Duelist Who invented Modern Finance,* New York: Simon and Schuster.

Goodhart, Charles A. E. (1989) *Money, Information and Uncertainty,* Second Edition (First Edition 1975), London: Macmillan.

Haberler, Gottfried von (1937) *Prosperity and Depression: A Theoretical Analysis of Cyclical Movements* (Second Edition 1939), Geneva: League of Nations, London: Allen & Unwin.

——. (1938) 'Some Comments on Mr Kahn's Review of *Prosperity and Depression*', *Economic Journal,* 48 (190), June, 322–33.

Hamouda, O. F. and J. N. Smithin (Eds) (1988) *Keynes and Public Policy After Fifty Years.* Vol. II: *Theories and Method,* Aldershot: Edward Elgar.

Hansen, A. H. (1938) *Full Recovery or Stagnation?* London: Adam and Charles Black.

——. (1941) *Fiscal Policy and Business Cycles,* London: George Allen & Unwin Ltd.

——. (1953) *A Guide to Keynes,* London: Adam and Charles Black.

Harcourt, Geoff (1987) 'Bastard Keynesianism', in John Eatwell, Murray Milgate and Peter Newman (Eds), *The New Palgrave: A Dictionary of Economic Theory and Doctrine,* London: Macmillan.

Harris, Seymour E. (Ed.) (1943) *Postwar Economic Problems,* New York: McGraw Hill.

——. (1948) *The New Economics: Keynes' Influence on Theory and Public Policy,* New York: Knopf.

Harrod, Roy (1934) 'The Expansion of Credit in an Advancing Community', *Economica,* 1 (3) (new series), August, 287–99.

——. (1936) *The Trade Cycle: An Essay,* Oxford: Clarendon Press.

——. (1937) 'Mr. Keynes and Traditional Theory', *Econometrica,* 5 (1), January, 74–86.

——. (1939) 'Review of *Value and Capital*', *Economic Journal,* 49 (194), June, 294–300.

——. (1963a) 'Retrospect on Keynes', in Robert Lekachman, Ed., *Keynes' General Theory: Reports of Three Decades,* London: Macmillan.

——. (1963b) *The British Economy,* New York and London: McGraw-Hill.

——. (1964) 'Are We Really All Keynesians Now?', *Encounter,* January, pp. 46–50.

——. (1970) 'Reassessment of Keynes's Views on Money', *The Journal of Political Economy,* 78 (4/1), July–August, 617–25.

——. (1972 [1951]) *The Life of John Maynard Keynes,* Harmondsworth: Pelican.

——. (2003) The Collected Interwar Papers and Correspondence of Roy Harrod, electronic version, Ed. Daniele Besomi. *http://economia.unipv.it/harrod/edition/editionstuff/contentsfr.htm?rfh.htm~target.*

Hawtrey, R. G. (1913) *Good and Bad Trade: An Inquiry into the Causes of Trade Fluctuation,* London: Constable and Co. Ltd.

——. (1919) *Currency and Credit,* London: Longmans, Green and Co.

——. (1932) *The Art of Central Banking,* London: Longmans.

——. (1937) *Capital and Employment,* London: Longmans.

——. (1938) *A Century of Bank Rate,* London: Longmans.

——. (1946) 'The Need for Faith', *Economic Journal,* 56 (223), September, 351–65.

Hayek, F. A. (1931) *Prices and Production,* London: Routledge.

Henderson, H. D. (1938) 'The Significance of the Rate of Interest', *Oxford Economic Papers*, 1, October, 1–13.
——. (1947) 'Cheap Money and the Budget', *Economic Journal*, 57 (227), September, 265–71.
Hicks, J. R. (1932) *The Theory of Wages*, London: Macmillan.
——. (1935) 'A Suggestion for Simplifying the Theory of Money', *Economica*, 2 (6), February, 1–19.
——. (1936) 'Mr. Keynes' Theory of Employment', *Economic Journal*, 46 (182), June, 238–53.
——. (1937) 'Mr. Keynes and the "Classics": A Suggested Interpretation', *Econometrica*, 5, April, 147–59.
——. (1939a) *Value and Capital*, Oxford: Clarendon Press.
——. (1939b) 'Mr. Hawtrey on Bank Rate and the Long-term Rate of Interest', *The Manchester School*, 10 (1), 21–37.
——. (1942a) 'The Monetary Theory of D. H. Robertson', *Economica*, 9 (33), February, 53–7.
——. (1942b) *The Social Framework: An introduction to Economics*, Oxford: Clarendon Press.
——. (1947) 'World Recovery After War – A Theoretical Analysis', *Economic Journal*, 57 (226), June, 151–64.
——. (1965) *Capital and Growth*, Oxford: Clarendon Press.
——. (1977) *Economic Perspectives; Further Essays on Money and Growth*, Oxford: Clarendon Press.
——. (1980–81) 'IS-LM: An Explanation', *Journal of Post Keynesian Economics*, 3 (2), Winter, 139–54.
——. (1982) 'Methods of Dynamic Analysis', *Collected Essays on Economic Theory* Vol. 2, *Money, Interest and Wages*, Oxford: Blackwell, 217–35.
Hilferding, Rudolf (1981 [1910]) *Finance Capital: A Study of the Latest Phase of Capitalist Development* London, Boston and Henley: Routledge & Kegan Paul.
Hirai, Toshiaki (2005) 'How, and for How Long, Did Keynes Maintain the *Treatise* Theory?', Paper for the 2005 conference of the European Society of the History of Economic Thought.
Hobson, J. A. (1902) *Imperialism: A Study*, London: George Allen & Unwin Ltd.
Hobson, J. F. and A. F. Mummery (1889) *The Physiology of Industry*, London: Murray.
Homer, Sidney (1963) *A History of Interest Rates*, New Brunswick, New Jersey: Rutgers University Press.
Howson, S. K. (1988) 'Cheap Money and debt-management in Britain 1932–51', in P. L. Cottrell and D. E. Moggridge (Eds), *Money and Power: Essays in Honour of L. S. Pressnell*, London: Macmillan.
——. (1993) *British Monetary Policy 1945–51*, Oxford: Clarendon Press.
——. (2000) 'James Meade', *Economic Journal*, 110 (461), February, F122–F145.
Howson, S. K. and D. E. Moggridge (1974) 'Keynes on Monetary Policy, 1910–1946', *Oxford Economic Papers*, 26, 226–47.
Hume, D. (1955 [1752]) *Writings on Economics*, Eugene Rotwein, Ed., London: Nelson and Sons Ltd.
International Labour Organisation (2003) *Global Employment Trends 2003*, Geneva: ILO.
——. (2005) *Global Employment Trends 2005*, Geneva: ILO.
International Monetary Fund (1985) *World Economic Outlook*, April 1985, Washington DC: IMF.

Kahn, Richard F. (1931) 'The Relation of Home Investment to Unemployment', *Economic Journal*, 41 (163), June, 173–98.

——. (1937) 'The League of Nations Enquiry into the Trade Cycle' [Review of Haberler, 1937], *Economic Journal*, 47 (188), December, 670–9.

——. (1938) 'A Rejoinder', *Economic Journal*, 48 (190), June, 333–6.

——. (1949) 'Professor Meade on Planning', *Economic Journal*, 59 (233), March, 1–16.

——. (1954) 'Some Notes on Liquidity Preference', *Manchester School of Economic and Social Sciences*, 22, September, 229–57.

——. (1972) *Selected Essays on Employment and Growth*, Cambridge University Press.

——. (1977) 'Mr Eltis and the Keynesians', *Lloyds Bank Review*, 124, April, pp. 1–13.

——. (1984) *The Making of The General Theory*, Cambridge University Press.

Kaldor, Nicholas (1937) 'Prof. Pigou on Money Wages in Relation to Unemployment', *Economic Journal*, 47 (188), December, 745–53.

——. (1939) 'Speculation and Economic Stability', *Review of Economic Studies*, 7, October, 1–27.

——. (1940) 'A Model of the Trade Cycle', *Economic Journal*, 50 (197), March, 78–92.

——.t(1941) Review of *Employment and Equilibrium – A Theoretical Discussion*, A. C. Pigou, *Economic Journal*, 51 (204), December, 458–73.

——. (1960) *Essays on Economic Stability and Growth*, London: Gerald Duckworth & Co.

——. (1970) 'The New Monetarism', *Lloyd's Bank Review*, July, 1–18.

——. (1986) *The Scourge of Monetarism*, Second Edition (First Edition 1982), Oxford University Press.

Kalecki, Michał (1937) 'A Theory of the Business Cycle', *Review of Economic Studies*, 4 (2), February, 77–97.

—— (1940) 'The Short-Term Rate and the Long-Term Rate', *Oxford Economic Papers*, 4, September, 15–22.

Kent, Richard J. (2004) 'Keynes's Lectures at the New School for Social Research', *History of Political Economy*, 36 (1), 195–206.

——. (2005) 'A 1929 Estimate of the Multiplier', paper for the June 2005 Conference of the European Society for the History of Economic Thought, Stirling University.

Keynes, J. M. (1933) Communications: 'Mr. Keynes's Control Scheme', *American Economic Review*, 23 (4), December, 675.

——. (1949) *Two Memoirs*, London: Rupert Hart-Davis. Reprinted in *CW* X, pp. 387–429.

—— (1971–1989) *The Collected Writings of John Maynard Keynes*, 30 Volumes, General editors Donald E. Moggridge and Elizabeth S. Johnson, London: Macmillan and New York: Cambridge University Press for the Royal Economic Society. Cited in the text as *CW* [Vol. no.].

Keyserling, Leon H., Robert R. Nathan, Lauchlin B. Currie (1972) 'Discussion', *The American Economic Review*, 62 (1/2), 134–41.

Kregel, J. A. (1976) 'Economic Methodology in the Face of Uncertainty: The Modelling Methods of Keynes and the Post-Keynesians', *Economic Journal*, 86 (342), June, 209–25.

Krugman, Paul (2006) Introduction to *The General Theory of Employment, Interest and Money*, www.pkarchive.org/economy/GeneralTheory/KeynesIntro.html.

Kynaston, David (1999) *The City of London*, Vol. III, *Illusions of Gold 1914–1945*, London: Chatto and Windus.

——. (2001) *The City of London*, Vol. IV, *A Club No More, 1945–2000*, London: Chatto and Windus.

Laidler, D. (2001) 'From Bimetallism to Monetarism: The Shifting Political Affiliation of the Quantity Theory', lecture delivered at the 2001 Conference of the European Society for the History of Economic Thought.

Laidler, David and Roger Sandilands (2002) 'An Early Harvard Memorandum on Anti-Depression Policies', *History of Political Economy*, 34 (3), pp. 515–52.

Lange, Oscar (1938) 'The Rate of Interest and the Optimum Propensity to Consume', *Economica*, 5 (17), February, 12–32.

——. (1939) 'Saving and Investment: Saving in Process Analysis', *Quarterly Journal of Economics*, 53 (4), August, 620–2.

Law, John (1705) *Money and Trade Considered with a Proposal for Supplying the Nation with Money*, Edinburgh: Andrew Anderson.

——. (1994) *Essay on a Land Bank* (dated 1703–1704), Ed. Antoin E. Murphy, Dublin: Aeon Publishing.

Lee, Frederic S. (2004) 'To Be a Heterodox Economist: The Contested Landscape of American Economics, 1960s and 1970s', *The Journal of Economic Issues*, 38 (3), September, 747–63.

Leijonhufvud, A. (1968) *On Keynesian Economics and the Economics of Keynes*, New York; London: Oxford University Press.

——. (1981) *Information and Coordination: Essays in Macroeconomic Theory*, Oxford: Oxford University Press.

——. (1987) 'IS-LM Analysis', in John Eatwell, Murray Milgate and Peter Newman (Eds), *The New Palgrave: A Dictionary of Economic Theory and Doctrine*, London: Macmillan.

Lerner, A. (1936) 'Mr. Keynes' "General Theory of Employment, Interest and Money" ', *International Labour Review*, 34 (4), October, 435–54.

——. (1938a) 'Saving Equals Investment', *Quarterly Journal of Economics*, 52 (2), February, 297–309.

——. (1938b) 'Alternative Formulations of the Theory of Interest', *Economic Journal*, 48 (190), June, 211–30.

Lerner, A. (1951) 'Fighting Inflation', *The Review of Economics and Statistics*, 33 (3), August, 194–6.

——. (1959a) 'Consumption-Loan Interest and Money', *The Journal of Political Economy*, 67 (5), October, 512–18.

——. (1959b) 'Rejoinder', *The Journal of Political Economy*, 67 (5), October, 523–5.

——. (1964) 'The General Theory', in Robert Lekachman, *Keynes' General Theory*, New York: St Martin's Press.

Levačić, Rosalind and Alexander Rebmann (1976) *Macroeconomics: An Introduction to Keynesian-Neoclassical Controversies*, Basingstoke and London: Macmillan.

'Liberty and Democratic Leadership' (1935) *The Next Five Years: An Essay in Political Agreement*, London: Macmillan and Co., Ltd.

Lipsey, Richard G. (1963) *An Introduction to Positive Economics*, London: Weidenfeld and Nicolson.

Lloyd, Ian (2006) 'Summary of an Address by Lord Keynes to the Political Economy Club, Trinity College, Cambridge on the 2nd February 1946', *Cambridge Journal of Economics*, 30 (1), 2–6.

Lutz, F. A. (1939) 'Final Comment', *Quarterly Journal of Economics*, 53 (4), August, 627–31.

Macaulay, Thomas Babington (1907) *The History of England from the Accession of James II*, Vol. III (First editions of five volumes were published between 1848 and 1861), London: J. M. Dent and Co.

Macleod, Henry D. (1879) *The Theory and Practice of Banking: with the Elementary Principles of Currency, Prices, Credit and Exchanges*, 2 Vols, Third Edition (First Edition 1855–56), London: Longmans, Green, Reader, and Dyer.

MacGorain, Seamus (2005) 'Stabilising short-term interest rates', *Bank of England Quarterly Bulletin*, Winter, 45 (4), 462–70.

Macmillan, Harold (1933) *Reconstruction: A Plea for a National Policy*, London: Macmillan.

Mankiw, N. Gregory (1992a) 'The Reincarnation of Keynesian Economics', *European Economic Review*, 36 (2–3), April, 559–65.

——. (1992b) *Macroeconomics*, New York: Worth.

Marshall, Alfred (1920 [1890]) *Principles of Economics* (Eighth Edition), London: Macmillan.

——. (1926) *Official Papers*, Ed., J. M. Keynes, London: Macmillan for the Royal Economic Society.

Marx, Karl and Friedrich Engels (1967 [1872]) *The Communist Manifesto*, Harmondsworth: Penguin Books.

Marx, Karl (1909 [1894]) *Capital: A Critique of Political Economy;* Vol. III: *The Process of Capitalist Production as a Whole*, Chicago: Charles H. Kerr and Company.

McKenna, Reginald (1928) *Post-War Banking Policy: A Series of Addresses*, London: William Heinemann Ltd.

Meade, J. E. (1937) 'A Simplified Model of Mr. Keynes' System', *The Review of Economic Studies*, 4 (2), February, 98–107.

——. (1938) *Consumers' Credits and Unemployment*, London: Oxford University Press.

——. (1948) *Planning and the Price Mechanism*, London: George Allen and Unwin.

——. (1993) 'The Relation of Mr Meade's Relation to Kahn's Multiplier', *Economic Journal*, 103 (418), May, 664–5.

Meade, J. E. and P. W. S. Andrews (1938) 'Summary of Replies to Questions on Effects of Interest Rates', *Oxford Economic Papers*, 1, October, 14–31.

Meltzer, A. H. (1988) *Keynes's Monetary Theory: A Different Interpretation*, Cambridge University Press.

Millikan, Max (1938) 'The Liquidity-Preference Theory of Interest', *American Economic Review*, 28 (2), June, 247–60.

Minsky, Hyman P. (1985) 'The Financial Instability Hypothesis, A Restatement', in Philip Arestis (Ed.), *Essays in Post Keynesian Economics*, Aldershot: Edward Elgar.

Modigliani, Franco (1944) 'Liquidity Preference and the Theory of Interest and Money', *Econometrica*, 12 (1), January, 45–88.

—— (1984) 'Life Cycle, Individual Thrift, and the Wealth of Nations', *The American Economic Review*, 76 (3), June, 297–313.

Modigliani, Franco and Richard Brumberg (1954) 'Utility Analysis and the Consumption Function: An Interpretation of Cross-Section Data', in K. Kurihara (Ed.), *Post-Keynesian Economics*, New Brunswick: Rutgers University Press.

Moggridge, D. E. (1976) *Keynes*, Harmondsworth: Penguin Books.

——. (1992) *John Maynard Keynes: An Economist's Biography*, London and New York: Routledge.

Moggridge, D. E. and S. K. Howson (1974) 'Keynes on Monetary Policy, 1910–1946', *Oxford Economic Papers*, 26 (2), July, 226–47.

Moore, Basil J. (1979) 'The Endogenous Money Stock', *Journal of Post Keynesian Economics*, 2 (1), Fall, 49–70.

——. (1984) 'Wages, Bank Lending and the Endogeneity of Credit Supply', in Marc Jarsulic (Ed.), *Money and Macro Policy*, Boston: Kluwer-Nijhoff.

——. (1988) *Horizontalists and Verticalists: The Macroeconomics of Credit Money*, Cambridge University Press.

Next Five Years Group (1935) *The Next Five Years: An Essay in Political Agreement*, London: Macmillan.

Norman Wait Harris Memorial Foundation (1931) *Reports of Round Tables: Unemployment as a World-Problem*, Chicago.

Pasinetti, L. L. (1987) 'Kahn, Richard Ferdinand', in John Eatwell, Murray Milgate and Peter Newman (Eds), *The New Palgrave: A Dictionary of Economic Theory and Doctrine*, London: Macmillan.

——. (1994) 'Richard Kahn, 10 August 1905–6 June 1989', *Cambridge Journal of Economics*, 18, 3–6.

Pensions Commission (2004) *Pensions: Challenges and Choices; the First Report of the Pensions Commission; Appendices*, London: The Stationery Office.

Pimlott, Ben (1995 [1985]) *Hugh Dalton*, London: HarperCollins.

Pigou, A. C. (1937) 'Real and Money Wages in Relation to Unemployment', *Economic Journal*, 47 (187), September, 405–22.

Poole, W. (1970) 'Optimal choice of monetary policy instruments in a simple stochastic model', *Quarterly Journal of Economics*, 84 (2), May, 197–216.

——. (1938) 'Money Wages in Relation to Unemployment', *Economic Journal*, 48 (189), March, 134–8.

——. (1941) *Employment and Equilibrium – A Theoretical Discussion*, London: Macmillan.

——. (1950) *Keynes's General Theory: A Retrospective View*, London: Macmillan.

Radcliffe Report – see Cmnd. 827.

Ramsey, Frank (1928) 'A Mathematical Theory of Saving', *Economic Journal*, 38 (152), December, 543–59.

Robbins, Lionel C. (1932) *An Essay on the Nature and Significance of Economic Science*, London: Macmillan.

——. (1937) 'How to Mitigate the Next Slump', *Lloyds Bank Monthly Review*, New Series 8 (87), 234–44.

Robertson, Dennis H. (1915) *A Study of Industrial Fluctuation*, London: P. S. King.

——. (1922) *Money*, London: P. S. King.

——. (1926) *Banking Policy and the Price Level: An Essay in the Theory of the Trade Cycle*, London: P. S. King.

——. (1931) 'Mr. Keynes' Theory of Money', *Economic Journal*, 41 (163), September, 393–411.

——. (1933) 'Saving and Hoarding', *Economic Journal*, 43 (171), September, 399–413.

——. (1934a) 'Mr. Harrod and the Expansion of Credit', *Economica*, 1 (4), November, 473–5.

——. (1934b) 'Industrial Fluctuation and the Natural Rate of Interest', *Economic Journal*, 44 (176), 650–6.

——. (1936) 'Some Notes on Mr. Keynes' General Theory of Employment', *Quarterly Journal of Economics*, 51 (1), November, 168–91.

——. (1937a) 'Alternative Theories of the Rate of Interest: Three Rejoinders', *Economic Journal*, 47 (187), September, 423–43.

——. (1937b) 'The Trade Cycle – An Academic View', *Lloyds Bank Monthly Review*, New Series 8 (89), September, 506–20.

——. (1938a) 'Mr. Keynes and "Finance" ', *Economic Journal*, 48 (190), June, 314–18.

——. (1938b) 'Mr. Keynes and "Finance" ', *Economic Journal*, 48 (191), September, 555–6.

——. (1938c) 'A Survey of Modern Monetary Controversy', *Manchester School*, 9 (1), 1–19.

——. (1940) *Essays in Monetary Theory*, London and New York: Staples Press.

——. (1947) 'The Economic Outlook', *Economic Journal*, 57 (228), 421–37.

——. (1949) 'On Sticking to One's Last', *Economic Journal*, 59 (236), 505–9.

——. (1966) *Essays in Money and Interest*, London: Collins.

Robinson, E. A. G. (1947) 'John Maynard Keynes, 1883–1949, *Economic Journal*, 57 (225), March, 1–68.
——. (1949) Review of J. M. Keynes (1949) *Two Memoirs*, *Economic Journal*, 59 (236), December, 556–9.
——. (1972) 'John Maynard Keynes: Economist, Author, Statesman', *Economic Journal*, 82 (326), June, 531–46.
Robinson, J. (1933) 'A Parable on Savings and Investment', *Economica*, 39, February, 75–84
——. (1951) 'The Rate of Interest', *Econometrica*, 19 (2), April, 92–111.
——. (1961) 'Equilibrium Growth Models: A Review Article', *The American Economic Review*, 51 (3), June, 360–9.
——. (1962) Review of *Money, Trade and Economic Growth*, by H. G. Johnson, *Economic Journal*, 72 (287), September, 690–2.
——. (1965) *The Accumulation of Capital* (Second Edition), London: Macmillan.
——. (1972) 'The Second Crisis of Economic Theory', *The American Economic Review*, 62 (1/2), June, 1–10.
Rogers, Colin (1989) *Money, Interest and Capital*, Cambridge University Press.
Romer, D. (1996) *Advanced Macroeconomics*, New York: McGraw-Hill.
Rymes, Thomas (1989), *Keynes's Lectures, 1932–35 Notes of a Representative Student*, Macmillan in association with the Royal Economic Society.
Samuelson, P. A. (1939) 'Interactions between the Multiplier Analysis and the Principle of Acceleration', *Review of Economics and Statistics*, 21 (1), February, 75–8.
Samuelson, P. A. (1941) 'Professor Pigou's Employment and Equilibrium', *American Economic Review*, 31 (3), September, 545–52.
Samuelson, P. A. (1947) *Foundations of Economic Analysis*, Cambridge, Mass.: Harvard University Press.
Samuelson, P. A. (1948) *Economics: An Introductory Analysis*, (reprint of first edition published in 1997), New York: McGraw-Hill.
Samuelson, P. A. (1958) 'An Exact Consumption-Loan Model of Interest with or without the Social Contrivance of Money', *The Journal of Political Economy*, 66 (6), December, 467–82.
Samuelson, P. A. and R. M. Solow (1960) 'The Problem of Achieving and Maintaining a Stable Price Level: Analytical Aspects of Anti-Inflation Policy', *American Economic Review*, 50 (2), May, 177–94.
Sayers, R. S. (1956) *Financial Policy: 1939-1945*, London: Her Majesty's Stationary Office and Longmans, Green and Co.
Sayers, R. S. (1967) *Modern Banking*, seventh edition, Oxford University Press.
Sayers, R. S. (1976) *The Bank of England, 1891-1944*, Cambridge University Press.
Schumpeter, J. A. (1954) *A History of Economic Analysis*, New York: Oxford University Press.
Seltzer, Lawrence H. (1945) 'Is a Rise in Interest Rates Desirable or Inevitable?', *American Economic Review*, 35 (5), December, 831–50.
Skidelsky, Robert (1992) *John Maynard Keynes*, Vol. II: *The Economist as Saviour 1920-1937*, London and Basingstoke: Macmillan.
Skidelsky, Robert (1997) 'Keynes's "Concluding Notes"', in G. C. Harcourt and P. A. Riach, Eds., *A 'Second Edition' of The General Theory*, London, Routledge.
Skidelsky, Robert (2000) *John Maynard Keynes*, Vol. III: *Fighting for Britain 1937-1946*, London and Basingstoke: Macmillan.
Smith, Adam (1812 [1776]) *An Inquiry into the Nature and Causes of the Wealth of Nations*, London: Ward, Lock and Co.

Smithies, Arthur (1945) 'Full Employment in a Free Society', *American Economic Review*, 35 (3), June, 355–67.

Smithin, J. N. and B. M. Wolf (1993) 'What would be a "Keynesian" approach to currency and exchange rate issues?', *Review of Political Economy*, Vol. 5, 365–83.

Smithin, J. N. (1996) *Macroeconomic Policy and the Future of Capitalism*, Cheltenham, Edward Elgar.

Solow, Robert (1956) 'A Contribution to the Theory of Economic Growth', *Quarterly Journal of Economics*, 70 (1), February, 65–94.

Solow, R. M. (1984) 'Mr Hicks and the Classics', *Oxford Economic Papers*, New Series, 36, Supplement: Economic Theory and Hicksian Themes, November, 13–25.

Somerville, H. (1931) 'Interest and Usury in a New Light', *Economic Journal*, Vol. 41, No. 164, December, 646–9.

Stiglitz, Joseph E. (1999) 'Interest Rates, Risk, and Imperfect Markets: Puzzles and Policies', *Oxford Review of Economic Policy*, 15 (2), Summer, 59–76.

Strange, Susan (1986), *Casino Capitalism*, Oxford: Basil Blackwell Ltd.

Targetti, F. and B. Kinda-Hass (1999) 'Kalecki's Review of Keynes' General Theory', in Malcolm C. Sawyer, Ed., *The Legacy of Michał Kalecki*, Vol. I, Cheltenham: Elgar.

Tavlas, G. S. (1997) 'Chicago, Harvard, and the Doctrinal Foundations of Monetary Economics', *Journal of Political Economy*, 105 (1) 153–77.

Thirlwall, Anthony P. (1987) *Grand Masters in Economics: Nicholas Kaldor*, Brighton: Wheatsheaf Books.

Tinbergen, J. (1938) *Statistical Testing of Business-Cycle Theories*, Vol. I: *A Method and its Application to Investment Activity*; Vol. II: *Business Cycles in the United States of America, 1919–1932*, Geneva: League of Nations.

Tobin, James (1958) 'Liquidity Preference as Behaviour Towards Risk', *Review of Economic Studies*, 25 (2), February, 65–86.

Togati, T. D. (1998) *Keynes and the Neoclassical Synthesis: Einsteinian Versus Newtonian Macroeconomics*, London and New York: Routledge.

Toporowski, Jan (1999) *The End of Finance: Capital Market Inflation, Financial Derivatives, and Pension Fund Capitalism*, New York: Routledge.

Townshend, Hugh (1937) Review of *Capital and Employment* by R. G. Hawtrey, *Economic Journal*, 47 (186), June, 321–6.

Tsiang, S. C. (1956) 'Liquidity Preference and Loanable Funds Theories, Multiplier and Velocity Analysis: A Synthesis', *American Economic Review*, 46 (4), September, 539–64.

United Nations (2005) *Human Development Report*, New York: United Nations Development Program.

U.S. Bureau of the Census (1976) *The Statistical History of the United States: From Colonial Times to the Present*, New York: Basic Books Inc.

Wallich, Henry C. (1946) 'The Changing Significance of the Interest Rate', *American Economic Review*, 36 (5), December, 761–87.

Weintraub, Sidney (1955) ' "Monetary Policy": A Comment', *The Review of Economics and Statistics*, 37(3), August, 292–96.

Weintraub, S. (1971) 'Keynes and the Monetarists', *The Canadian Journal of Economics*, 4 (1), February, 37–49.

Weintraub, S. (1982) Review of *Information and Coordination: Essays in Macroeconomic Theory* by A. Leijonhufvud, *The Journal of Money, Credit and Banking*, 14 (3), August, 420–24.

Wright, David McCord (1945) 'The Future of Keynesian Economics', *American Economic Review*, 35 (3), June, 284–307.

Young, Warren (1987) *Interpreting Mr Keynes: The IS-LM Enigma*, Oxford: Polity Press.

Index

Printed in Great Britain
by Amazon

47253114R00205